The Trollopes

The Chronicle of a Writing Family

By Lucy Poate Stebbins
and Richard Poate Stebbins

LONDON: SECKER & WARBURG

1946

MARTIN SECKER & WARBURG LTD.
7 John Street, London, W.C.1

First published 1946

TO JACQUES BARZUN

Preface

THE phenomenal popularity of Anthony Trollope's novels, the inexplicable absence of any full-scale biography of their author, and the prevalence of singular misconceptions concerning his remarkable family will probably be held sufficient justification for the writing of this book. We take pleasure in acknowledging our indebtedness to the trustees of the Boston Public Library for permission to quote from original letters and reproduce photographs in the Kate Field Collection; to the trustees of the Boston Athenaeum for permission to reproduce the photograph of Anthony Trollope which appears as frontispiece; to Baylor University Press, Constable and Company, Macmillan and Company, Oxford University Press, and Yale University Press for permission to quote briefly from works bearing their imprint; and to the numerous individuals and institutions whose generous assistance was indispensable to the successful completion of our work.

Some of the quotations in the text have been slightly condensed in the interest of readability. Contemporaneous rumors concerning the private conduct of Theodosia Trollope and Ellen Lawless Ternan, although impossible to ignore, had in our judgment no basis in fact. Statements concerning Anthony Trollope's relations with American publishers, on the other hand, rest on evidence which would appear to be irrefutable.

LUCY POATE STEBBINS
RICHARD POATE STEBBINS

Cambridge
May, 1945

Contents

List of Illustrations

CHAPTER I

Keppel Street

1780-1816

MORE leisure and larger freedom were allowed to Frances
Milton, younger daughter of the vicar of Heckfield and Mattingley,
than convention usually granted a girl of the upper middle class in
the last decades of the eighteenth century. Her elder sister Mary, more
domestically inclined, kept to the parsonage and assisted their cool,
capable stepmother; and, when Frances began her wanderings,
Henry, four years younger, was too nearly a baby to be her comrade.

The winding road over Heckfield Heath was safe ground for the
lonely little girl; the forest of oak and birch, hawthorn and pointed
holly, standing deep in beds of fern, was nowhere dense enough to
bewilder her. Growing a seasoned explorer, she could venture to
Mattingley Green, where her father held occasional services in the
small, half-timbered chapel, or cautiously skirt the bleak plain where
Bramshill House stood frowning.

Her happiest haunt lay to the east of Heckfield parsonage, under
a great oak on Bramshill. There, quite alone, she looked abroad on
England and thought as she pleased, until she heard the village clock
strike the urgent hour which sent her flying home. From Bramshill
she could see all that she knew of the round world: the little churches,
the white cottages with long and narrow garden plots, the deep-
rutted lanes, the stiles, boys at cricket, cattle browsing—here lay a
child's universe, secure and orderly and very fair.

In the spring, the thatch roofs were crowned with roses and the
orchards piled with bloom. Then the young folk built their May
Houses, long alleys of green boughs which they decorated lavishly
with pendent bouquets of lilacs and tulips, stock, and the peonies
which everyone called "pionies." Partnered with boys in their Sunday clothes, girls in straw bonnets and white dresses danced in the

May, while the gingerbread man sold out his tray to the children, and the country lads, who had defiantly come in their smock frocks, stood dolefully at a distance to watch the frolic which they had not smartened themselves to join.

Nor could Frances Milton, being a little lady, make one of the village revelers. Except as a very small and undiscriminating young person, she would not have wished to do so, for she possessed a strong sense of propriety and felt the beneficent limitations of class. Yet she loved dancing and was little and light, with pretty feet and ankles; and the balls to which she was asked and taken were sadly infrequent. Fortunately for her, she was seldom in need of direct entertainment, being, even as a child, amused by what she saw others enjoying. Thus, day after day, she found existence pleasant, although the time was not long in coming when, as a young lady, she began to ask herself if a lifelong aggregate of just such days could be desirable.

Frances Milton's birthplace was not at Heckfield, but at Stapleton near Bristol, where she was born on the tenth of March, 1780. Her mother, a Gresley, came of a family superior to her husband's, but she did not survive her children's births long enough to impress upon them this difference in gentility. William Milton's father, the grandfather of Frances, lived to be ninety-nine. He had been in trade, a saddler of Bristol, but could write "Gentleman" after his name and had sent his clever son to Winchester and to New College. In due time, New College granted young William Milton the Hampshire parish of Heckfield, which lay in its gift. Oxford had turned him out a classicist, but his aptitude for mathematics and invention was only in abeyance. He originated a scheme, which was considered although not adopted, for the improvement of Bristol Harbor.

At Heckfield he devoted his talents to the improvement of stage-coaches, and spent the abundant leisure from his pastoral duties in constructing models and publishing pamphlets, illustrated by drawings of vehicles which could not be capsized. His foibles were never injurious, except as they depleted the family purse; but he was abstemious in the matter of wines, and the education of his two girls cost nothing. His teeth were set on edge by the scraping of knife against china, and consulting his comfort, he ordered a set of plates each with a depression in the center, which he filled with silver. Thus he continually tried to improve what was already satisfactory to everyone else, a habit to which he gave his own humorous name of "au-mieux-ing." The character etched by such innocent oddities was charmingly lovable; he was immaculate in appearance, courteous, witty, and a companionable father.

Mary and Frances Milton learned from their stepmother, who controlled the family expenditures, how a house should be managed and how both plain and fancy needlework should be done; but they had leisure to read, and allowances of money from which books could be purchased to add to those in the vicar's library. *Castle Rackrent* came out when Frances was twenty-one, and won her enthusiastic approval; but she had grown up with Fanny Burney's *Evelina*, while *Udolpho*, read when she was entering her teens, had prepared her to receive the scenery of sea and mountain with enthusiasm. She read poetry, plays, and novels; her taste was for European literature of the great centuries; she enjoyed Molière and Racine, and, having taught herself to read Italian, memorized passages of Dante and daily studied Tasso. Although history and philosophy were not in her curriculum, she was in a fair way to become a bluestocking.

Her sister and Mrs. Milton took their pleasure in housekeeping, her father pottered among the models in the carriage-house, and Frances had no girl friends. She liked people, but at Heckfield there was a dearth of social events. Mrs. Mitford, whom she met at a dinner party in Reading, wrote her young daughter, Mary Russell Mitford, that Frances Milton was livelier and a better talker than her sister Mary; perhaps she was the more inclined to this favoritism because Frances had good-naturedly spent the evening playing cards with her elders. But a life with such meager social opportunities was not what Frances desired.

Neighboring families were beginning to regard her as an old maid, this Frances Milton, first of the "little brown girls," slender and small, not quite pretty, with her long straight nose and the breadth between slanting brows, dressing herself with a nice daintiness which hinted at the incipient spinster. Her mouth was always on the brink of a smile, and the bright eyes had an amused, observant expression; but her drolleries made people suspicious and uncomfortable. What if the clever Miss Frances Milton were treasuring their small inanities for parsonage consumption? She was very witty, and had no idea how much more pain can be inflicted by the arrow than by the mace.

She had reason for sober thought as to her future. In the middle of the first decade of the new century, the year of Trafalgar, she was twenty-five. As long as her father lived, she could count upon a home and a yearly allowance of fifty pounds, an ample provision for clothes, gifts, books, and even occasional travel. When the vicar died, she would have nothing but the interest of £1,300, on which she would be reduced to living in the house of someone else as a poor relation, or by herself in painfully straitened fashion. She had a cousin in Exeter who managed on almost nothing, but Fanny Bent's happiness did not depend on luxuries; her independence was almost belligerent; and as she was very plain, she could not expect to marry. Frances Milton, socially ambitious, would have liked to make "a good match," have an establishment, entertain, and travel.

Henry Milton, her younger brother, did not go to New College. Wartime expansion was creating new opportunities in the civil service, and in 1803, at the age of nineteen, the only son of the vicar of Heckfield went up to London as one of fourteen clerks in a new department of the War Office. He went to work at a salary of £90 a year, with easy hours from eleven to four, extra pay for overtime, and the expectancy of a steady rise of income and a pension. He was as charming and sincere as his father, but his hobbies were less outlandish, perhaps because of the paternal example set in Heckfield, perhaps because he was essentially urban. He had friends in London and was in a position to broaden his acquaintance and cultivate his talents. Taking a house at Number 27 Keppel Street, Russell Square, he invited his sisters to make their home with him. This was an opportunity for Frances, whose ambitions transcended the narrow circle of a Hampshire parish. Although there had never been active unpleasantness between the girls and their stepmother, the arrangement was felt to benefit all three. The vicar would miss his daughters, but the distance was not great and the arrangement was temporary, as Henry might marry young.

Bloomsbury had not only metropolitan advantages, but provided country pleasures; a short walk brought one to open fields in the direction of Hampstead Heath and the quiet ponds of Highgate. Behind the substantial Keppel Street houses were brick-walled gardens. The Miltons had experience in rose culture, and Henry wished to attempt rare varieties. Although he was so much younger than his sisters, they admired him, and his opportunities had fitted him to direct their taste. He knew a great deal about paintings, while they had seen only the portraits hanging in the country-houses which they visited infrequently. Life was not too serious at 27 Keppel Street. The girls met their brother's friends, went to theatre and opera; charades, amateur acting, impromptu dances expressed the joy of life with which Frances and Henry were highly dowered. They were alike in gifts and temperament; but he possessed a greater sense of the obligation of doing a thing as well as it could be done—a refinement on his father's "au-mieux-ing."

In the summer of 1808, Henry introduced to his sisters a young barrister, Thomas Anthony Trollope, who had been at Winchester and New College ten years earlier. This promising, serious young man, who bore the name of a distinguished family, was also the child of a country parsonage. He had been born thirty-four years earlier, on May 23, 1774, at Cottered in Hertfordshire, where his father had been vicar. The recent death of the old man had broken up the Hertfordshire home and turned the son's thoughts to the establishment of a new branch of the Trollope family.

In the early autumn Thomas Anthony Trollope began to pay marked attention to Frances Milton, forgetting his umbrella in order to call for it, writing her notes in a majestically jocular vein, lending her books, sending her his pedantic translation of the Latin verses of a contemporary. His criticism of the "New School" of Wordsworth and Coleridge was caustic; he referred to their poems as "paltry things." She agreed with him that elegance, perfection of form, and restraint were higher qualities than the expression of unchecked emotions.

She had a little time to decide what answer she should make when he asked the question to which all his course had tended.

He seemed to possess every advantage, even to being six years her senior. His father had been the youngest of the four sons of Sir Thomas Trollope, and had given his only boy both the baronet's name and his own, Anthony. The prospect of his coming to the title was negligible, but there were high expectations of worldly position from another quarter. His mother, who had died while Thomas Anthony was at school, was one of the eleven children of Adolphus Meetkerke, Esq., owner of the substantial Hertfordshire estate of Julians. The Meetkerkes had been English since Elizabeth's reign, when an eminent Dutch grammarian had served in England as ambassador of the United Netherlands. His diplomatic duties over, he had settled in Hertfordshire, and there the family had continued in undiminished wealth down to the nineteenth century. Among them had been men of learning—Thomas Anthony's great-great-great-grandfather had been Hebrew professor at Oxford and a prebendary of Winchester—but the present proprietor of Julians was a loutish, opinionated squire, much inferior to his sister and the clergyman she had married. As Squire Meetkerke had no children, it was understood that his sister's son, Thomas Anthony Trollope, should be his heir, and the child had grown up expecting to be master of Julians.

Thomas Anthony was the holder of a fellowship from New College which would probably have to be resigned on his marriage, but even without that, and setting aside his bright expectancy of Julians, the prospects of such an able and erudite lawyer appeared thoroughly good.

She was far too sensible to consider his family name an argument against marriage. Probably it was derived from some place name like "Trolls-hope" (Elf-dale) in Northumbria; possibly from *trois loups* with which the founder of the family was said to have contended. Its more familiar and homelier connotation was not difficult to overlook.

Personally, in spite of a prominent upper jaw and a harassed expression, he was a big, distinguished-looking man. The Trollope and Meetkerke families were superior to hers, his expectations were noble, he loved her. If he seemed ill at ease, if, in his striving for accuracy of expression, his features assumed the look of a man stretched on the rack, for all she knew these might be marks of love. She was inexperienced; but, even had she known many suitors, she could not have interpreted his nervous distress at a misapprehension, and his determination to argue until every hair was split triumphantly, as signs not of love but of ill-health and psychological maladjustment.

On November 1, 1808, she received his letter asking her in marriage. It was long. In involved language he reminded her that she had once remarked that proposals should be made in writing. She could not remember; perhaps in her satirical way she had been thinking privately that a designing woman could hold a man more easily if his offer were set down plainly over his own autograph. Distressed by his allusion, Frances regretted that Mr. Trollope had not asked his question when they were together, and thus allowed her to see the quality of the love she hoped he bore her. Only that reminder of her foolish wish and a statement of his financial position conveyed his meaning; the rest of the letter meandered beyond the bounds of sense.

"Let me avoid compliments, which were always my detestation," he had said—"fit tools only for knaves, and to be employed against fools." Such was not a lover's language. Neither was it altogether complimentary that he should have addressed her directly instead of through Henry or her father—as if he had told himself, she is twenty-eight and circumlocution is unnecessary. From the style in which her brother was living, Mr. Trollope might believe that all three of the young Miltons possessed snug fortunes, and this too troubled her.

He had given her three weeks for consideration, but she replied at once; his letter had been left with her on Monday evening, and Tuesday morning brought him his answer. Proper beginning and ending it had none; with hasty and almost naïve candor she explained that she was not an heiress; independently of her father, she had £1,300; from him, she received a dress allowance of £50 a year. It was not pleasant to smirch her first love affair with sordid details. She closed her brief letter with a reproachful: "I have not, nor can I express myself quite as I wish. There is something of cold formality in what I have written, which is very foreign to what I feel,—but I know not how to mend it. *Fanny Milton.*" His answer was warmly reassuring. It was signed "Yours most truly and devotedly" and contained no reference to dowry. They had both been so expeditious that, although he had proposed no earlier than the previous evening, this third note begged her to receive him that day at half past three.

Thus they became engaged. A month passed, and she went down to

Heckfield to make ready her trousseau. No sooner had she reached the parsonage, after the long drive from Reading in an uncomfortable cart devised by her inventive parent, than she asked her stepmother, who held the purse strings, what she could bring her husband. She wrote Thomas Anthony that she feared he would be disappointed; she had been mistaken even on the £1,300, which had dwindled to £1,200 with another £100 for clothes. That she was thus painfully anxious not to misrepresent her eligibility suggested not only pride, but doubts about the attitude of a man who was parsimonious in small matters. However, her lack of fortune did not perturb him; he loved her, and although frugal with pence, did not trouble much over pounds.

The vicar did his duty as a parent and went up to London to interview his daughter's suitor. Thomas Anthony suggested that if he approved his daughter's choice, her husband would appreciate the continuance of her allowance. After some cogitation the vicar agreed, adding with affecting simplicity that she was also to have an eighth share of his "patent coach." Imitating Frances in raillery, Thomas Anthony wrote to ask her if she would undertake an eighth of its expenses. But his jokes were ponderous, and occasionally his letters gave glimpses of a man easily irate and cantankerous. Old Dr. Nott, the Winchester prebendary who had supervised the reconstruction of the cathedral, came up to London to inspect the suitor of his favorite Frances and bring him a piece of legal business. Unfortunately tithes concerned not barristers but the lower order of solicitors, and notwithstanding Dr. Nott's courtly manners and his reputation as a fine Italian scholar, Thomas Anthony considered himself affronted and wrote to Frances, "There never was a man, I believe, so little conversant with the common circumstances of life."

But if he often showed himself ungracious or obtuse, there was still much to gratify her in their engagement. In their letters the lovers discussed poetry and she sent him a sonnet of her own written in Italian. He urged her to come up to London to a party; the tiny violin sketched on the invitations signified dancing, and the "old dowagers" were not to be there. When he reminded her of those two stanzas in "The Cotter's Saturday Night" which commence, "Oh happy love," she realized that he was capable of romantic passion. His family, too, welcomed her; his sister Diana, herself not long married, was eager for her friendship, and the baronet and his lady gave much thought to the choice of the wedding present.

Yet, early in May, 1809, after the wedding day had been fixed for the 23rd—it would be his thirty-fifth birthday—it seemed as though she could not marry him; he was too serious and she was by nature too carefree; how could she be a fit companion for this grave, austere man? She wrote that she was fearful lest a year hence he would not love her so well, and broke off her letter to walk once more in the spring sunshine flooding Heckfield Heath.

But they were married, and settled in Bloomsbury among his professional friends, a few doors from her brother. Henry had offered them his own house, but Frances thought it too cramped for the style she intended for the Trollopes. Given her first opportunity of spending as she pleased, she envisaged a large and hospitable way of life. Thomas Anthony already owned at 16 Keppel Street a more impressive dwelling than her brother's, and they determined to occupy it. Servants were engaged, a footman fitted with the Trollope livery, draperies hung in stiff folds from the high windows, curtains at the beds. The dining room was on the first floor, two spacious drawing rooms upon the second. Elegant pieces of furniture, following the suave flowing lines of the period, were drawn against the walls as if in dignified retreat, to leave clear the ample floor space. The handsome cut-glass chandeliers were lighted only for parties; for ordinary use Thomas Anthony's taste for frugality was gratified by tallow candles burning in heavy silver candlesticks.

The first child of Thomas Anthony and Frances Trollope was born eleven months after the marriage, on April 29, 1810, and was named Thomas Adolphus for his father and his great-uncle Meetkerke, whose eventual heir his parents expected him to be. The christening was postponed until December 19; the mother spent the summer with her baby at Heckfield parsonage while the father was on circuit with the assize court; both parents were in the country for the Long Vacation which barristers were accustomed to take from August to November. During the early separation from her husband, Frances wrote that the vicar was "perfectly delighted" with little Tom. Every day after the early dinner he devised some new means of exhibiting his grandson's extraordinary precocity; the baby was gratifyingly responsive, and Frances admitted that she was forced to assume an expression of great severity lest pride be read upon her countenance.

In the following year a second healthy son was born to the Trollopes and christened November 11, 1811, at St. George's, Bloomsbury, with the name Henry, for his mother's brother. In 1812, Arthur William was added to the family. The little sons were very welcome, for Frances was perfectly well, the children did not interfere with her hospitality and visits, and, if Thomas Anthony seemed to be losing more clients than he took on, the war with France offered a comfortable reason to suppose that such fluctuations of fortune were but temporary. In 1813, the first daughter was born to the family at Keppel Street, but this time the baptism could not be delayed; she received the name of Emily and died before the day was done. The little boys knew nothing of their lost sister, nor was mention ever made of her except in the family Bible, where the father summed up her life in one short line.

The fourth son and fifth child, Anthony, was born on April 24, 1815, the year of Waterloo. Like his three brothers he was a fine, fair little Saxon.

At night the nursery was now well filled, but by day Tom and Henry were already beginning to desert it for rambles about the purlieus of Bloomsbury, exercising the same independence their mother had shown in her childish wanderings over Heckfield Heath. They were hearty and healthy, fed upon minced mutton, porridge and milk. Nurse Farmer was an "Anabaptist," and the mischievous youngsters made up a rhyme which delighted them and plagued her. With a shout on the final syllable of each line, they would declaim,

> "Old Farmer is an Anabap*tist!*
> When she is gone, she will not be *missed!*"

Old Dr. Nott, who had come up to town and inspected Frances's lover, now came to see her children. He had been tutor to the Princess Charlotte and understood the ways of youth. The little Trollopes, summoned to the drawing room, stared solemnly at his voluminous white stock, his knee breeches and gaiters, while they waited to be told to recite their catechism. Were they good children? he asked briskly. Tom was spokesman: No; they were not good children; but they could not be blamed for that; it was because Nurse Farmer was an Anabaptist.

The father and mother were forced at last to admit that, as a barrister, Thomas Anthony was doing less well than many who were his inferiors in enterprise and ability. Clients deserted and new ones were warned away. It was actually a question of personality: he was overbearing in manner, hectored the very men who employed him, and permitted himself to laugh at their stupidity. Where Frances was witty, he was brutally sarcastic. In society he was tolerated for her sake, and intelligent people respected his integrity and learning. But he made himself thoroughly disagreeable, insulting not only his friends but his clients, and, more perilously, his uncle Meetkerke, owner of Julians. As business fell away, his headaches became more frequent. He dosed himself lavishly with calomel and, prostrated by pain and by the harrowing effects of the drug, would retire to his bed until the attack passed, leaving him weak and depressed. At such times, he asked only to be left alone.

Frances, pitying him yet scarcely able to comprehend his misery, had much to divert her. Friends and relatives were not sorry to see her without Thomas Anthony; with her brother she shared not only family feeling but growing intellectual interests. The publisher Longman had commissioned Henry to go to Paris in 1815, the year little Anthony was born, to see the art collection of Napoleon before it was broken up after Waterloo. In 1816 he had published an opinionated little book of criticism under the title, *Letters on the Fine Arts, Written from Paris during the Year 1815,* the first of many volumes by the children and grandchildren of old Mr. Milton.

Many guests came to the Trollope house, among them foreigners with radical views. Frances, though reared in a conservative environment, considered herself a "liberal," and it is probable that her husband really was one. He did not try to curb either her opinions or her expenditures, but was frugal in trifles, as if he believed that extreme care in saving wood and lights, in having the boys' clothes patched instead of replaced, would rectify the major situation. Frances had the optimism of a vivacious, healthy woman; true, their means were temporarily straitened, but Uncle Adolphus would soon die and leave them all his property.

The parents were united in their paramount interest, which was the welfare of their boys. Frances taught Tom to read at such an early age that Henry, a year younger, could not be invited to share the lessons, and a neighbor's little girl was asked in to be his companion. The reading lessons were a game, in which Mrs. Trollope tossed tiny bone letters on the floor, the children scrambled to make words, and the quicker won a prize. She was of a generous nature, never wishing to absorb her children, but Tom, as the eldest, secured proprietary rights in her. He liked to get her by herself where her attention could not be distracted from him. While she dressed for a party, he would stand on a chair close to the mirror and watch her toilette. Once he remarked judicially, "Now you have made yourself as fine as poso [possible], and you look worse than you did when you began!"

At Christmas, the little boys went to the pantomime, and once, when Mrs. Siddons played Lady Macbeth, the whole family, except Anthony, who was much too small, took their lunch and stood in the queue at the theatre from two until six, less to save Thomas Anthony's shillings than to impress on the children the epochal nature of the occasion.

Frances was unconcerned when the boys wet their feet or were reported missing, but possessed a special sense which warned her, now and then, of actual danger. Once, as she walked in a field with Tom galloping on before, she cried out, "Tom! Stop!" The little boy, trained to obey, came to her like a puppy. He had just escaped falling into an old well, of which she had never heard; nor had she seen anything amiss, but had known in one anguished moment that her child was threatened. It was one of those odd incidents from which arose her later interest in the occult.

She was no musician, but could sing a little, airs from Mozart, and old English ballads. A nursery favorite was a song about "a captain bold of Halifax," and a Miss Bayly whom he had seduced. Frances was a woman of refinement and breeding, but Georgian ladies were not mealymouthed, nor was she unique in believing that what children did not understand could not harm them. Tom and little Anthony may not have understood the song but both of them remembered it.

Farmer was always busy with those mere infants, Arthur and Anthony, so that, when the mother's absence coincided with a paternal headache, Tom and Henry were perfectly free. Hand in hand, little boys of four and five, they wandered where they listed, staying away sometimes until after eight in the evening in order to see the mail coaches start from the Post Office and the White Horse Cellar in Piccadilly. They could distinguish the "Telegraph," the "High-Flyer," and the "Magnet"; on the King's birthday they saw the fine new red coats of the guards and the flowering wreaths upon the heads of the horses. Sometimes they would roam eastward to the docks, to watch the ships with boards at their masts bearing the painted names of the far harbors whither they would soon be sailing. Down in Saffron Hill the handkerchief thieves held a market to dispose of their stolen goods; every size and color of kerchief fluttered from lines stretched between smoke-darkened windows. The little Trollopes never had a penny for purchase money, nor were their grubby possessions worth filching from their jacket pockets. When they went home, they confided strange adventures to an interested mother.

But the routine of a day when father was himself was inflexible. Tom must be up before seven, ready to recite his Latin at the breakfast table. To save a fire, an economy in which the father took peculiar satisfaction, breakfast was carried up to the back drawing room. While he waited its appearance, Tom would be on his knees before the sofa, his head clutched in his chubby hands, the grammar open on the cushion, as he strove frantically to master the assignment. Then down would come father and mother, and up would come the footman with the silver urn, and Tom must say his lesson right, or have his hair pulled. Before five in the afternoon, he would be posted with Henry at Lincoln's Inn ready to walk home with long-legged father, not for pure affection but to recite those Latin verses which had been meted out by the too generous paternal hand.

Thus far they had been taught at home, but by 1816 the question of immediate formal schooling had to be considered. Family precedent on both sides of the house made it appear obligatory to send them first to Winchester and then to New College. But the boys must wait their turn for Winchester, as vacancies for scholarships occurred. In the interval their education could no longer proceed on haphazard lines. Fortunately, so it seemed, the famous old school at near-by Harrow accepted town boys without payment of tuition, and a recent decision of the courts, as Mr. Trollope was aware, had confirmed this practice. Family friends, the Merivales of Bloomsbury, intended to send their three boys to Harrow. Mrs. Merivale was nearly related to the Drurys, who were the masters of Harrow; and the Merivales themselves, although nonconformists, were highly intellectual: their bookish boys acted out plays from Roman history on the Bloomsbury pavement. What was suitable for the Merivales should fit the Trollopes.

Thomas Anthony, pleased at saving on tuition, unwisely agreed with Frances to expend a far greater sum in establishing himself as a resident of Harrow. He was even willing to retain his town house as well as his indispensable chambers in Lincoln's Inn, to which he would drive himself daily. In Harrow he would farm in the desultory fashion becoming an English country gentleman; there he would be free of his agonizing headaches, while his sons spent the period between nursery and Winchester in imbibing knowledge without pecuniary obligation.

CHAPTER II

The Trollopes of Julians

1817-1827

THOMAS ANTHONY's mind interested itself in details. Free though he was from any conceited wish to impress his family by a parade of learning, when he drew from his astounding memory all sorts of curious items—the fragments of recondite studies—he seemed a man who knew everything. His vision thus was limited, the broader aspect beyond its scope; but his wife's imagination was not so circumscribed, nor had the sobering effect of scholarship curtailed her flights. Those brilliant, impractical Trollopean ideas popularly supposed to have originated with her husband were much more probably the fruit of her unbridled temperament. He may have realized that it was useless to check an exuberance which, if repressed at one point, would break out at another. More probably, in his admiration for his wife, he trusted to a discretion which she, among her many merits, did not possess.

Left to himself, Thomas Anthony would, in all likelihood, have bought a small farm near Harrow—such as Harrow Weald which he later inhabited—made the dwelling livable, and employed a working bailiff and his wife. Under Frances's influence, he leased several hundred acres from Lord Northwick at a high rental, and built, on another's land, a country house, with well laid-out gardens and grounds. Later the family maintained that the terms of the lease had been misrepresented to them; but the father's uncertainty on this, as on other legal matters connected with his wife's marriage settlements, evidenced a lack of lucid thinking even in his own profession.

The house at Harrow was built in 1816, the Trollopes remaining in Keppel Street until after the birth of a sixth child, Cecelia. Early in the following summer, they removed to their new estate of "Julians." There was something peculiarly defiant in calling the pretentious new house by the name of the Hertfordshire manor which they expected to inherit. Thomas Anthony was on bad terms with his Uncle Meetkerke, but as yet remained his heir; the old squire may well have felt that the new "Julians" was intended to flout him—to show that his nephew was independent of his bounty. The death of the old man's wife, occurring just at the time of the removal from Keppel Street, prepared the way for reprisals. Fourteen months later, Uncle Adolphus married a stout young woman, and a nurseryful of children soon followed. Julians was lost to the Trollopes; yet, as it fell out, this defeat of Thomas Anthony was purely psychological, for Uncle Meetkerke not only outwitted but outlived his quondam heir. The real and permanent loser of the Hertfordshire property was the small boy, Thomas Adolphus Trollope.

The boundary of the Harrow farm lay at the foot of the hill which is topped by Harrow's famous spire and school, so that the boys had but a half-mile to climb, after leaving their own land. Harrow church, almost hidden by the close boughs of elm trees, stood on a terrace which afforded a view of the rough High Street, edged with picturesque Tudor houses, and the battlemented parish church with weathered tombstones standing askew in the yard.

The great school which had brought the Trollopes to Harrow had been for many generations the resort of privileged English youth. Originally founded solely for the purpose of educating the boys of the parish, its charitable function had fallen into almost complete desuetude. Recently certain Harrow residents had sought to limit the number of patrician "boarders," alleging that their own sons were mistreated and scorned, and that even when tolerated by their social superiors, they learned from them vicious and extravagant habits. Few of the Harrow farmers and tradesmen cared, however, to submit their sons to snobbery and bullying, and the strictly classical curriculum was considered another and more serious drawback.

But if Thomas Anthony reflected on the invidious social position of the parish boys, he was untroubled by it, supposing that a gentleman's sons were gentlemen, whether or not they paid tuition. As for the classical curriculum, in his opinion Harrow could have no better recommendation; the future of his sons depended on their thorough grounding in Latin and Greek. The light-hearted mother, knowing little of public schools, believed that the position she intended to occupy in the society of Harrow would ensure proper acquaintance and consideration for her sons.

When little Tom and Henry started up the hill to Harrow School in the fall term of 1818, both boys were sturdy and independent, far better able to cope with a difficult situation than the average English child of seven or eight. But the school proved a place of torment. The "boarders" called them "charity boys"—and there were three hundred of these gilded youths to oppose ten lads of the parish. Even among the little band of outcasts, Tom and Henry were friendless; the children of petty tradesmen and small farmers held aloof from the sons of the gentleman who had built Julians.

The bright young Trollopes learned something of English manners, but scarcely anything else. Class teaching was adapted to the slowest intelligence in the form, which, regardless of individual progress, was promoted in a body at the end of the term. Any instruction of real cultural value or suited to personal needs was reserved for private tutoring, of which Tom and Henry received only the fag ends. After hiding like sparrows in the monstrous shadow of the Reverend Mark Drury during a form recitation, the little boys might hop out for a crumb of learning between classes, but were given no systematic tutoring.

The Drurys, who controlled Harrow, were subject to a glandular affliction which resulted in gross obesity. Mark Drury, the under master, seldom left his great chair. His nephew Henry, he who had been Byron's tutor and friend, although energetic enough once he was up, found it exceedingly difficult to coax his huge body from his bed. Daily the "boarders" posted a sentry to report, "Going up!" or "Not going up!" If the Reverend Henry Drury intended to climb Harrow Hill that morning, it behooved them to arise; if he yielded to sloth, they could luxuriate a little longer. The boys were proud of "Old Harry," and boasted that he could compose Latin verses faster than the other masters could write English. "Old Harry" was always nibbling; as he strode up and down the long classroom, watched by ninety pairs of anxious eyes, he would punctuate a sonorous phrase with a periodic bite of pear.

All of the seven masters of Harrow were clergymen, but if from such a personnel the parents expected an odor of sanctity, or even decent piety, they were deceived. The cat-and-dog fights promoted by Harrow schoolboys were but a reflection of the bellicose propensities of their High Church masters. Toward dissenters they evinced an ugly intolerance, which was even more strongly marked in their dealings with Evangelicals, whom they regarded as castaways from their own persuasion. They were on quarrelsome terms with the local vicar, a good man but a Low Churchman, author of a religious work entitled *The Velvet Cushion*, to which he owed his jeering nickname of "Velvet" Cunningham.

Tom and Henry sustained the hard-flung snowballs and stones of the winter term, but in the spring of 1819 fell ill as the result of their unofficial inspection of open drains. There was then a new baby at Julians, a second Emily (the only child born to the family at Harrow), and owing to the confusion at home, the London physician was not summoned to attend the little boys. The local man had administered calomel in such quantities that the sick children were very near death, when a friend of Frances brought in a competent doctor who stopped the drug and ordered port wine. Tom was soon as hardy as ever, but Henry's recovery may have been less complete. To their great joy neither was forced to finish the term at Harrow, and that autumn, in the Long Vacation, Tom went with his father and mother on a tour of half a dozen counties in the southwest of England.

Mary Milton, a spinster in her early forties, had recently been married to Commander Charles Clyde, an old Bristol man and a retired naval officer, who had seen much service in the wars with France. The couple had settled at Ottery St. Mary. Affection between the sisters was more formal than the full sympathy between Frances and her brother, and the Commander was neither a well man nor one markedly hospitable, but there were visits made and visits paid with proper observance. Cousin Fanny Bent, down Devon way, was another and more congenial attraction.

The great tour was made in a gig, Tom sitting on a box between his parents' knees while the Trollopes' man rode behind on the spare horse. The little boy was wildly excited over the prospect. His favorite books were *Robinson Crusoe* and *The Mysteries of Udolpho;* this journey promised to combine adventures of both types. If at Harrow "boarders" were his overlords, at Julians Tom had developed self-confidence as the overlord of the nursery. Henry was necessary as a companion, nor could he by any means be kept under, but he and Arthur were not allowed to forget the older brother's superiority. But now, Tom had scarcely settled himself on his box, after the last complacent wave at his wretched stay-at-home brothers, when to his dismay he observed a Virgil in his father's hand and heard the paternal voice bidding him construe. He squirmed with pain. Was it for such a fate that he had strutted about the nursery? Was it for this he had risen before dawn to repack? The mother was too well-bred to interfere at the moment, but in private she persuaded Thomas Anthony to reserve the lessons for interruptions of the journey.

The incident was not without an undertone of pathos. The father was smarting from the shock of knowing himself supplanted as his uncle's heir. Henceforth the future of his sons seemed to depend entirely on his exertions. If they could not secure an education, they would be nobodies. He was persuaded that not a moment should be wasted. The mother too was ambitious, and hoped to see her boys in Parliament, but trusted more to social connections than to education.

A few days later Tom gave the father a glimpse of what it would mean to lose his oldest son. In Gloucester Cathedral, one of the seven bell-ringers being absent, Tom dashed to seize the dangling rope. Upward swung the mighty bell, and up went Tom, clear to the height of the nave. There were, of course, cries to Hold On, but they were not needed. Not Harrow school, nor his stern father, nor the height of mountain top and belfry tower could ever intimidate or utterly subdue that stout spirit.

From this first remembered journey of much-traveled Thomas Adolphus Trollope, the boy returned to Harrow with Henry, and after a second unhappy winter term, was taken to Winchester to be enrolled in the school where Trollopes educated their sons.

His father was at this time forty-six years old, an age when most
men suffer a second disillusionment. He had his special griefs: he had
been balked of the original Julians, was troubled because he lived
beyond his present means and had no larger expectations, harassed
by the necessity of providing for many children. Nevertheless this
taking of his oldest son to Winchester was in the nature of a festival.
He trusted that this boy of his was heir, although not to the Hertfordshire property, to his father's scrupulous scholarship and to his mother's wit. He was bringing him up to Winchester as in ancient times
Samuel had been brought to the temple.

With his usual economy, Thomas Anthony planned to make the
sixty-mile journey in one day, but it was equally characteristic of the
man to reject the direct route in order to show his boy the scenery of
the bishop's park. They jumped down from the gig and wandered a
little way along the forest glades. Ten-year-old Tom was proud when
his father told him that the diocese stretched all the way to London,
for William of Wykeham had once been Lord Bishop, and tomorrow
he, young Tom Trollope, would be made one of William of Wykeham's boys. Reverent but complacent, he felt himself, by proxy, the
owner of the park.

Arrived in Winchester, father and son put up at the "Fleur de Lys,"
a wretched inn which met all Thomas Anthony's requirements, as it was
very cheap and very venerable, close to the college, and familiar, since
he had often stayed there. Even as a young and unencumbered man,
with fine prospects, Thomas Anthony had not been extravagant; prod-
igality had commenced with his marriage and was the flowering of his
wife's ambitions.

The next day Tom, with other little candidates, climbed the winding
stone stairs to the election chamber, where they underwent an examination conducted in traditional form by six bewigged and gowned
gentlemen:

"Well, boy, can you sing?"

"Yes, sir."

"Let us hear you."

Then the neophyte, without pretense of tune, piped up, "All people that on earth do dwell"—and with this formality became a member of William of Wykeham's College of Winchester.

Tom's residence did not begin until the autumn, nor was he long alone at Winchester. In the following spring, 1821, Henry became again his fellow student. Henry was a misfit, but Tom was of the stuff which enables English boys to be happy at a public school unless conditions are peculiarly adverse. At Harrow he had been called a "charity boy" because he was granted free tuition; at Winchester, which provided him not only with free tuition but with his living, no such invidious distinction was made. Rather, it was understood that the greater ability of the scholarship boys outweighed any advantage derived from wealth.

Tom's temperament was one to delight in the historical sense which pervaded the school. The ancient stone buildings, the dormitory with its coffinlike beds blackened by age, the games played after ritualistic patterns, traditional supplies of beer and mutton, Latin and salutations, punishments ceremonious rather than harsh, foot journeys of "Speedyman" from Oxford to announce a vacancy at New College; these and countless other quaint observances deepened his sense of the living past. As at Harrow, the religious instruction was perfunctory, and its effect marred by enmity toward dissenters and Low Churchmen; but Tom's need for an object of devotion was met by Winchester itself, for which he felt an ardent attachment.

Arthur, the third son of the Trollopes, entered Harrow in 1823 as a day pupil with his little brother Anthony, but never went to Winchester. Like a gentle wraith, he drifted in and out of his turbulent family. Scarcely had he begun his schooling, when he was removed and sent to his grandparents at Heckfield. There the frail boy was both friend and pupil of the old vicar, who made Arthur feel that he needed his arm on his "short fine-weather walks," and to please the child wrote letters to the brothers at Winchester. Arthur had the Milton aptitude for mathematics; the old gentleman prophesied that through life Euclid would be his staff and lamp. Support and light were not long needed; the journey was soon made. He died in July, 1824, at Heckfield parsonage. That same month the old man followed him.

The mother, who had not complained at the death of the first little Emily, bore the greater loss with fortitude. She was one of those who sink under the weight of anguish, seeming for a brief time unable either to live or die; afterward life goes on almost unchanged. Such women have many interests; there are always others dependent upon them. She had a husband and five children to comfort, for the older boys were at home from school, and even the little girls knew that something appalling had happened. Grandfather Milton's death added its own sadness, for he had been greatly loved. Mirth and confidence in life were expected from the mother, and though at first she simulated them, they were so natural to her that soon they were genuine once more.

Socially, Frances Trollope was accomplishing what she had intended. The best society of Harrow was open to her. The masters, who flogged the Trollope sons and allowed the "boarders" to bully them, were on excellent terms with the parents. The large drawing room at Julians made a practicable theatre; family and friends presented French plays under the tutelage of a protégé of the hostess, Auguste Hervieu. Visitors from London enlarged the circle. George Hayter, painting his celebrated "Trial of Lord William Russell," came to sketch Thomas Anthony for one of his lawyers, and the mother wrote proudly to young Tom, "I shall like to see your father's head there."

Both she and her husband had been writing. With deadly seriousness he had brought forth a diminutive work entitled *A Treatise on the Mortgages of Ships as Affected by the Registry Acts*. Frances, in heedless fashion, had composed a satirical poem on the arguments of Harrow vestrymen over the memorial to little Allegra, Byron's illegitimate daughter. The subject suited the Georgian taste, the audacious wit of the author delighted the Harrow masters, and even "Velvet" Cunningham, the vicar, who suffered worst from her shafts, took no umbrage.

She had become intimate with Mary Russell Mitford, a childhood friend whose mother had long ago admired vivacious Frances Milton. Miss Mitford, in the middle thirties, short, with swollen neck glands and inflamed finger joints, was living precariously with her family in a laborer's cottage at Three Mile Cross, where she gardened and wrote

poems, plays, librettos, and sketches of country life, struggling daunt-
lessly to support her gambling father by her pen.

Such women need influential friends; to Miss Mitford's limited understanding of the situation, Frances was a wealthy, cultured patroness, who might live in the country but had the highly convenient use
of a house in town; she knew the great Macready well enough to speak
of him as "dear William"; she might—but did not—know him well
enough to persuade him to stage Miss Mitford's tragedies.

Living nearby at Pinner were other family friends, Sir Francis
Milman and his wife, who had long ago been a parishioner of Frances
Milton's father. Lady Milman had spent many years in London with
her suave, handsome, incompetent husband, who was physician first
to George III and later to Queen Charlotte. Now at Harrow and Pinner the pleasant relations between the two families deepened to intimacy.

The Milman sons and daughter, somewhat younger than Frances,
were congenial, and "Old Lady Milman" was as kind as she was autocratic. The youngest son, Henry Hart Milman, was already known as a
brilliant dramatic poet and had recently married a lady of such extraordinary beauty that Tom Trollope never modified his opinion,
formed at fourteen years of age, that she was the perfection of woman-
hood.

Many of the Trollopes' friends needed their assistance. The young
Frenchman, Auguste Hervieu, son of a colonel who had died in the
retreat from Moscow, was supporting himself by giving lessons in
drawing. Obligingly eager to sketch everyone at Julians, he became
an inmate of the house, while Frances exerted herself to find him
pupils and patrons.

Another guest was Guglielmo Pepe, the Italian revolutionary, who
had been introduced to the Trollopes by their old friend Sir Thomas
Dyer. Keppel Street and Julians furnished handsome General Pepe
refuge and congenial society. Through his efforts, Frances first saw
her own literary work published; he requested her to translate an ode
which Alfieri had written in honor of Lafayette, and caused her verses
to be printed in several London newspapers. The poet Campbell
praised her translation, and Lafayette, himself already an acquaint-

ance, wrote his thanks to the Italian general, together with compliments to *l'excellente Madame Trollope* and her husband.

The impression which Mrs. Trollope made on her distinguished circle varied with the individual. When she dined at the Merivales to meet Ugo Foscolo, the famous Italian man of letters, she was, he thought uncomfortably, "in her deepest blue stockings"; while on another occasion, Kean attributed to her, "Siddonian glances." She was most charming when entertaining a group of Harrow schoolboys at her own fireside. Proud as she was of her own children, she was always delighted with the merits of other women's sons: little Herman Merivale was, she said, "by far the most wonderful child I ever saw."

Frequent journeys lent a cosmopolitan air to the cultured life of the elder Trollopes. Almost every summer they toured the south of England, and several times they ventured as far as Paris, where they met old friends and made new ones. More than once they were royally entertained by Lafayette at his princely château of La Grange. Mrs. Trollope took a wifely pride in watching the condescension of her stately husband as he danced with the pretty girls from the château at a village fête patronized by the aristocrats. On one of their Parisian visits Mr. Washington Irving and Mr. James Fenimore Cooper made their acquaintance. Impervious to Mrs. Trollope's charm, Irving dismissed her in his journal as "a tall [*sic*], thin, talking woman."

When at home the father was economizing where he could, attending to his dwindled practice, and studying Italian to please his clever wife. She wrote Tom that "Papa" would go beyond them, if they were not careful. While the boys were in school, the father tried to supervise the education of his daughters, and with gloomy tactlessness ruined the success of Emily's birthday party by publicly setting her a problem in fractions. Meanwhile the mother continued to lead the old extravagant, busy, purposeless life—dining out, entertaining, running up to London, running down to Devon, writing letters, reading French and Italian, but paying far too little attention to her youngest son.

The middle child of a large family is usually lonely. Tom and Henry bullied little Anthony, and his sisters were as yet too young to be satisfactory playmates. When the children of nursery age were summoned to meet guests in the drawing room, the petting was all for

Cecelia and Emily. Anthony was an overgrown, awkward, near-sighted
little boy, who was always deplorably dirty. He felt that he was not
much liked. His mother had jokes with Tom and Henry, but he did not
know what they were laughing at. He thought it must be at him. His
nurse was faithful but ignorant. The ethical teaching of such women,
especially if they were sectarians, was characterized by allusions to
boys and girls whom nobody could love, and gloomy prognostications
as to the future of wicked children who would find themselves even
worse off after they were hanged. Tom and Henry were stout-hearted
and indifferent; they were much with their mother, and at an early
age freed themselves from Anabaptist domination; but Cecelia's painful overconscientiousness and Anthony's dislike, ostensibly of Evangelical teachings, but at bottom of nearly all organized religion, argue
an intimidated childhood.

In the spring of 1823 he entered Harrow school with Arthur and
submitted to a repetition of the indignities which had been heaped on
Tom and Henry. He was the less able to bear it because he was also an
outcast at home. Arthur was soon sent to Heckfield, and eight-year-old
Anthony had no one to sympathize with him through the hooting and
bullying of the "boarders." He had neither Tom's natural calm contentment nor Henry's fierce spirit. He appeared sullen, perhaps stupid.
If his mother observed his unhappiness, she probably thought he had
inherited his father's disposition.

After three degrading terms as "lag," or last boy, at Harrow, he
was removed and sent to Sunbury on the Thames, where one of the
Drurys kept a private school. In his hopelessness, the child supposed
his parents were ashamed to have him at home, but his brother's recent
death furnished a better reason, and the mother probably believed her
youngest son would benefit by the atmosphere of a small school. Besides, the family was often away from Julians and, when the absence
was prolonged, Frances scarcely liked to leave Anthony with the
servants, especially when she took Farmer and the little girls to stay
in Keppel Street.

Anthony, now himself a "boarder," made the humiliating discovery
that his people were delinquent in paying their bills. Such a disgrace,
though it made a lasting impression on him, did not sever but rather

tightened the lax bonds between him and his family. A more terrible
calamity, however, excluded him from the society of his fellows.
Anthony and three other little boys were accused of perversion. Anthony, as coming from a public school, was suspected of being the
leader of the wickedness. Too guileless to know of what he was suspected or why he was being punished, he did know that he was innocent, that authority was unjust, and that the boys, the "curled darlings
of the school," who never would have chosen him to share their sins
and yet did not clear him of complicity, were dishonest. They too were
perhaps terrified and bewildered. The next term, the master, feeling
that he had erred in Anthony's case, started to speak of it; but the
purposefully blank look the boy turned on him either embarrassed
him or suggested that the matter had been forgotten; he could not
finish. Far from forgotten, the disaster reverberated throughout Anthony's life. A man's reason could subdue the resentment against society and authority; it could not uproot it. At the time there was a
subtle fascination in speculating on the nature of the unknown crime;
more injurious to the child's self-respect was his belief that, however
ghastly the sin, he would have committed it if only those boys would
have played with him.

In the spring of 1827, Anthony at length exchanged Sunbury for
Winchester, the Trollopes' own school. The mother, very anxious to
have unity and affection among her children, wrote to Tom, now seventeen and senior prefect: "I daresay you will often find him idle and
plaguing enough. But remember, dear Tom, that, in a family like ours,
everything gained by one is felt personally and individually by all.
He is a good-hearted fellow, and clings so to the idea of being Tom's
pupil, and sleeping in Tom's chamber. I well remember what I used to
suffer at the idea of what my little Tom was enduring."

Of the two problem sons of the Trollopes, Henry's case seemed at the
time more exigent than Anthony's. Gifted with the scientific mind of
the Milton family but with neither interest nor aptitude for the classics,
Henry was making a poorer record than many a dull boy with a good
memory. His father wrote his sons rasping letters, calculated to file
away the affection which had never been strong. Were the boys employing every moment? What rivals had they? How were their chances

for scholarships at New College? Tom took parental nagging for what it was worth, but Henry's haughty temper, tried already by his own failures, was stirred to fury.

In 1826 Henry was taken from school and set to work in a Paris countinghouse. His parents did not turn him off; they went with him to Paris and arranged for his board in a clergyman's family. The father was concerned at the high figure asked. The fifteen-year-old exile, free of his countinghouse stool at four in the afternoon, wandered through the streets of Paris, as in happier days he had roamed London hand in hand with Tom. That elder brother was perhaps dearer to him than anyone else. To Tom he wrote, without dreading exposure to his father's scorn, that the street boys yelled when they saw him, "See the little goddam," and that the seven-year-old heir presumptive to the French throne might wear a sword, but was not too dignified to make faces as he leaned out of his carriage window.

Meanwhile the affairs of Thomas Anthony had entered upon the visible stage of their long decline. The hay crop failed, a financial panic adversely affected his investments, the London tenants did not pay their rents. When Frances sent Tom a trifle of pocket money, she gave the credit to her husband: "I enclose half a crown from Papa,— a proof at once of poverty and kindness. Without the former it would be more, without the latter it would be nothing." She wrote him about the books they were both reading—for Tom had leisure to read—the Waverley Novels, Byron's *Cain* (which the next generation of mothers would be chary of discussing with their sons), and about a visit to the newly opened National Gallery, to which she hoped they would go together in his holidays.

In that autumn of 1826 she still refused to believe in ruin. With her husband, she enjoyed the usual English tour, went to France, picked up Henry in Paris, and took him to La Grange to visit Lafayette. Returned to Julians, she busied herself with theatricals. Molière's *Femmes Savantes*, followed by a burlesque, was staged in her large drawing room.

But it was useless to ignore the unmistakable signs of collapse. They had been living beyond their means for fully ten years, and had come to the end of them. A drastic change in their way of life could no longer be postponed; though it must, if possible, be accomplished without public disgrace. Unfortunately, Thomas Anthony, long accustomed to submit to his wife's erratic leadership, could offer no constructive solution. To get rid of the expense of Julians was an obvious step; but this by itself would be merely an acknowledgment of defeat. For herself and her sons Frances was not yet ready to renounce the ambitions she had formed. Some bolder stroke was necessary to redeem the family fortunes.

In this crisis Frances Trollope yielded to the influence of the most dangerous member of all the Trollope circle, the ardent and notorious feminist, Frances Wright. Their friendship had begun in the early 1820's as the result of a natural attraction between two intelligent women, neither of whom found anything to envy in the other. Mrs. Trollope, who was fifteen years the elder, was amused and delighted at the splendid flow of language and the grand enthusiasm of the tall, handsome girl, who in turn considered her friend as a likable parasite. Frances and Camilla Wright were heiresses who had been orphaned in early youth. Frances, who was the elder and infinitely the more determined, had taken Camilla on a two years' tour of America, from which she returned in 1821. Her *Views of Society and Manners in America* made her such friends as the historian Grote, Jeremy Bentham, and Lafayette, whom she visited at La Grange. Lafayette was already an old man with a weakened mentality; his family looked with dire suspicion on the young woman. The Wright sisters followed Lafayette on his tour of the United States in 1823, but before its completion Frances had outgrown her infatuation and was deep in the project of founding the colony of Nashoba for the gradual emancipation of slaves.

In May, 1827, she sailed for Europe, leaving Nashoba in the charge of the charming but foolish Camilla and two male colleagues. The voyage restored her health, which had been broken by malaria, and gave her time to plan what had branched into a dual project. She intended on the one hand to emancipate Negro slaves, and on the other to found a co-operative colony for whites. These settlers were to come from the cultured class, would be accommodated with small separate houses, and would contribute $200 each, yearly, to the expenses of the community. Meanwhile, in her absence, her male deputies were outraging American sympathies by the practice of free love without racial discrimination.

In September Frances Wright visited the Trollopes and, finding Henry there without occupation or prospects, suggested that he join her recruits for the colony at Nashoba. His father did not know what to do with him, nor could he treat the boy civilly. Henry was the only one of his sons who would not be silent under rebuke; and this resemblance between Thomas Anthony and the offender did not make their interviews pleasanter. The desire of most families is to expatriate the disturbing member. But Frances had left Henry to himself in Paris, and the experiment had not answered. She was loth to send a sixteen-year-old boy into so hazardous a future. Ishmael did not go alone into the wilderness, for Hagar was at his side. She too would carry her son into exile in America and save him from the enmity at home.

The most natural of mothers, Frances loved best, while the need lasted, the child whose need was greatest. But there were other reasons impelling her to go with Frances Wright. Her easy optimism could not continue to deny that her husband was ruined, nor, although healthy and strong, had she escaped the destroying restlessness of middle age. In her soul she was a wanderer; the little girl who had sat sedately under the oak at Bramshill surveying England yearned, before old age, to see the world which was not England. All her radical acquaintances spoke of America as the promised land of freedom and equality. The excited imagination which had given shape to Mrs. Radclyffe's shadowy scenes conceived a New World with turbulent rivers broad as seas, mountains whose summits cut the zenith, and amiable Redskins who would reverence her, because she was an English lady.

She spoke seriously to her husband of the necessity of retrieving his fortunes. She proposed to settle Henry in America and to look over the commercial possibilities of the Western States. A bazaar might be undertaken in a frontier city: backwoodsmen might prove to be eager purchasers of rare and artistic objects. She had heard that Cincinnati, on the Ohio, was a city of limitless opportunity. Her husband, fascinated by her daring imagination, was pained by her wish to leave him. Consolingly, she said that he could join them a year hence; added, perhaps, that the separation would draw them closer to each other.

Thomas Anthony consented. Frances would have with her the little girls and Henry. Auguste Hervieu, engaged as Nashoba's drawing master, was devoted to them. The husband sent also their trustworthy manservant, William, to take care of his wife. He himself was now entirely alone, Anthony and Tom being at Winchester. Renting Julians to the vicar, "Velvet" Cunningham, he leased a small farm at near-by Harrow Weald. There, in a shabby dwelling darkened by ancient trees, he struggled through his sick headaches, went to his fields to work inexpertly at his bailiff's side, returned to bury himself in his obscure researches—a taciturn, unhappy, and yet not unadmirable man.

CHAPTER III

Westward Ho!

1827-1831

FRANCES TROLLOPE sailed for New Orleans with Frances Wright on November 4, 1827. In their party were young Henry Trollope, his two little sisters, the artist Hervieu, and William, the Trollopes' man-servant. From behind the comfortable authority of father, brother, or husband, Frances Trollope had always, in reality, directed her own destiny and her family's. This was the first venture in which her responsibility stood forth bare of protective disguise.

The "Edward's" seven weeks' voyage, uneventful save for one day's chase and counter-chase of pirates, gave her ample time for speculation while her friend paced the deck, her ardent eyes piercing the dwindling space which separated her from Nashoba. Miss Wright was remote, spoke little, took no interest in the hardness of the bread, the saltness of the beef, the crowding-in of life. The Trollopes had brought books, and Hervieu carried the equipment of an artist; the voyage did not weary them, although they were glad when at last the pelicans rose from the mud flats below Belize and they knew that land was near.

Frances Trollope had loved the ocean, finding in its Protean forms, in the sunset, and in the vast, starred sky, a satisfaction as keen as that of little Frances Milton beneath the Bramshill oak. The world was wide, and it was well that she should see it; yet she had much to trouble her. It would be long before she could return to Tom and Anthony, long before her husband came to her. Already she missed him, and though the freedom from his saturnine temper had its sweetness, she was sensible of a prop removed and of something precarious in her position.

It was Christmas Day when the travelers reached New Orleans. The Trollopes set out to explore as soon as they could leave their boarding-house. To Frances the southern city seemed a replica of some French provincial town, save that in France one did not see little groups of savage-looking Indians, graceful quadroon girls, or black slaves. They spied a young Negro girl scouring the steps of a house, beyond a hedge laden with oranges; and Mrs. Trollope spoke to her in a low, compassionate voice. She was afraid to speak louder, lest the slave's owner punish the wretched creature, and she could not help the note of pity for one who, in a land of freedom, was not free. But the slave laughed hilariously and gave the queer English folk a handful of peppers.

They spent a week in New Orleans, seeing the sights and strolling gingerly in the verge of the forest which encroached upon the town. Then the party boarded the "Belvedere" for the voyage up the Mississippi. The steamer was luxurious, especially in the accommodations of the men, but Mrs. Trollope's domestic eye viewed with concern the condition into which the saloon carpet had been brought by what she was already learning to know as "the incessant, remorseless spitting of Americans." William, her servant, was assigned to the open deck, occupied by flat-boat men who were returning to Kentucky after the disposal of their cargo. He was horrified by their fighting, drinking, and gambling; but she, as she watched them vault to the shore at every stopping place to fetch the wood which paid their passage, observed that they were nobly made and wildly handsome.

At Memphis they left the dreary river, intending a plunge into the sinister Tennessee forest. The town was mired deep in mud, and the Trollopes and Auguste Hervieu determined to wait at the hotel for better weather. But the invincible Miss Wright set off at once for Nashoba on horseback, attended by the unfortunate William. The Trollopes took their midday meal at a long table with some fifty men, whose wives were reported to be dining off mush and milk at home.

Contrary to her optimistic expectations, Mrs. Trollope was beginning to have serious doubts about the character of American society. In New Orleans she had been disconcerted at the invidious position occupied by lovely creole girls, who, she was told, were as well educated as the whites but were legally unable to marry. The slaves and the dispossessed Indians also seemed anomalies in a country founded on the principles of freedom and equality. Here in Memphis, husbands feasted on venison and turkey at a common table, because their wives were too lazy to cook for them. Such women must indeed be insignificant. She considered their indolence no less deplorable than the obvious overwork of women of the laboring class.

After a day's delay the Trollopes and their excitable French cavalier ventured upon the wild ride of fifteen miles to Nashoba in a vehicle known as a "Dearborn." Only three white people were there to receive them, Frances Wright, her sister Camilla, and the crude adventurer whom Camilla had imprudently married. Mrs. Trollope greeted her friends and looked about her.

A Bible phrase summed up what she saw and felt—*the abomination of desolation.* There was a rude clearing, there were several two-roomed cabins with mud-plastered chimneys. Food was not wanting— if one could swallow Indian meal with rain water to wash it down. Mrs. Trollope stared at Frances Wright, the friend of Jeremy Bentham and Lafayette, and Frances Wright stared back at her. In a moment of tardy illumination each woman understood the other. Frances Wright, the idealist, might well ask herself why she had ever induced this worldly, luxury-loving woman to come to Nashoba; Mrs. Trollope might wonder what evil magic had bemused her. In that pregnant moment she realized beyond the possibility of doubt that she had come five thousand miles on a fool's errand.

Auguste Hervieu created a diversion: he said he could not find the schoolhouse. There was, Miss Wright told him, as yet no schoolhouse; like all other good, it would come to Nashoba in the fullness of time. This vague assurance could not pacify him. He was transported by his rage, wept, and, to Mrs. Trollope's laughing but rueful eyes, was as absurd as pathetic. He fled immediately back to Memphis, where he consoled himself with painting Memphians' portraits until his patroness should be ready to travel farther.

Any idea Mrs. Trollope might have had of joining the colony had perished on the instant. When the shivering Camilla Wright confessed to chills and fever, she was glad of the excuse to profess alarm for her children and declare for an immediate removal. Nevertheless, she was constrained to linger for ten days. She had invested money in the Nashoba experiment and had no ready cash. Her party could not leave until the "trustees" had authorized a loan of three hundred dollars.

This was the first disaster of the American project. There was no one to help her bear it, nor was there anyone to share the blame. She it was whom the siren's voice had beguiled. In her forlorn situation she was in a measure dependent on the advice of her visionary friends, and listened all too credulously when they proposed a new scheme for Henry's benefit.

In a milliner's shop in New Orleans the Trollopes had become acquainted with a philosophic old Scot, Mr. William Maclure, who was on his way to Mexico in search of geological specimens. At Nashoba they heard more about Mr. Maclure. Not only was he the most distinguished geologist in America; he was a philanthropist and a believer in progressive education. At the famous communistic settlement of New Harmony on the Wabash he had founded a school where promising boys could secure a first-rate education while earning their living. He had made New Harmony a scientific center, the cosmopolitan headquarters of a whole "boat load" of geologists, botanists, zoologists, and ichthyologists. Unfortunately he would not be there himself, but he had left the school in the competent hands of the Frenchwoman who shared his home. Mrs. Trollope decided to send Henry to New Harmony.

In parting with him the mother separated herself from the last male protector from among her own family; though he was only a boy of sixteen, he was tall, exceptionally well-built, intelligent, and devoted. It did not occur to her that without him her association with Hervieu, and even with her servant William, could appear irregular; nor, if she knew that at school her little boys had been ridiculed as "trollops," did she imagine her name made a subject of mockery.

Their new destination was Cincinnati, a town of 20,000 inhabitants, which had been depicted in the English press as a situation of unrivaled opportunity. They arrived on February 10 and, as soon as they had dined, the little girls and their mother set forth with a boy from the real estate office to find a house. The lad, as helpless as they, roamed the streets peering for "To Let" signs. When Mrs. Trollope remonstrated at his aimless method, he began to ring every doorbell.

She had to pay a dollar for his disservices and, weary and disheart-
ened, felt the money had been filched from her by Yankee sharpness.
She found a house for herself and went back to the hotel, where a kind
Irish maid brought tea to her rooms. As the little family clung to each
other, solacing themselves with dried beef and brown sugar candy, the
landlord stumped to their door to announce that, if the English old
woman was not sick, they must eat at the general table; what was
good enough for his "folks" was good enough for hers. Much embarrassed and a little frightened, she explained apologetically that she
was unused to American ways.

"Our manners are very good manners, and we don't wish any
changes from England," he answered brutally.

Next day she moved to the rented dwelling, too much in haste to
observe that it possessed neither pump nor cistern. After waiting in
vain for a garbage cart, she sent for her landlord to ask what she
should do with refuse. He too addressed her as "Old Woman," and
ordered her to have all rubbish thrown into the middle of the street,
where the pigs would dispose of it.

Frances Trollope soon knew for a certainty what she had already
suspected: she did not like Americans. Her instinctive repulsion
would have presented no mystery had she been in truth the prejudiced,
censorious harridan which Americans have united in calling her.
But the prejudices of this gifted, sensitive, impressionable woman were
all in favor of the United States. She had expected to find in the New
World a country where man's noblest aspirations were realized in
living act; and as her anticipations had been high, her disappointment
at the crude realities of frontier life was correspondingly bitter.

It was often said of her that she did not meet "the best people"
of Cincinnati, and it was indeed injudicious not to have secured letters
from important friends at home. But she was soon acquainted with
those few Cincinnatians whose talents made them worth her knowing,
and she was moreover too shrewd a woman to judge a people solely by
its aristocracy. Later one lady who had held aloof excused herself
with the half-hearted allegation that it was scarcely safe to recognize a
woman traveling without her huband—a protestation which would
have been painful to Frances Trollope, however much the thought of

so timid a *grande dame* would have amused her. Other matrons objected to her style of dress, which, though *soigné* upon occasion, was much plainer than Cincinnati ladies thought proper for church wear. But Mrs. Trollope had come to America not to enter provincial society, but to improve the family fortunes. At home, and in France, a far better society was regularly open to her.

Like an escaped bond servant Henry made his way from New Harmony to his mother. He was gaunt and languid, and terrified her by his fits of shivering. He had found New Harmony a very different place from what Miss Wright had pictured. Pretense of teaching had been abandoned and hard labor had been exacted from the boys. Henry had worked all day in the fields and at night had baked his own bread— painful experience for a boy brought up at Julians. When he rejoined his mother, his health was permanently broken.

This was the second phase of the disaster; she was compelled to admit that she had been as impulsive about New Harmony as about Nashoba. Henry had learned a great deal of geology, which doubtless made the family walks more profitable, but he could not earn his living by discoursing upon stones. However, there remained the project of the bazaar, which would now have to be undertaken in good earnest; her husband was coming, and on his arrival Henry would be established in business.

In May the excessive heat of the town sent her again to house-hunting, both for Henry's sake and for the purpose of receiving her husband in a dignified manner. She secured an airy dwelling in the suburbs, so new that it still smelled of wood shavings, with a wide piazza and ample grounds. There seemed to be no flowers indigenous to the locality, and vegetables were too cheap in the market to make raising many of them profitable, but potatoes and tomatoes were planted, and a cow was purchased to crop the rough lawn.

In the kitchen she had sometimes one "hired help," sometimes two. The servant girls could not understand the mistress's edict against their eating with the family, especially as the "English old woman" was unbelievably kind in other ways, sewing for them with her daughters, and nursing them when they were ill. Nor could Frances Trollope understand the neighbor who addressed Henry by his Christian name, called him "honey," and took her own arm with terrifying familiarity.

Thomas Anthony was looked for all that summer. In spite of her anxiety, his wife made some congenial friends and kept the family happy. The deep forest was impassable, but the open glades reached from the house by a short walk across the meadow furnished a cool drawing room, where they went often with books and artist's materials, glad to be so far out of town that their peculiar occupations were unnoticed.

A young Mexican from the Paris Conservatory, professor of music at the Female Academy, was a frequent visitor. He became especially devoted to Henry, who, he told the gaping Cincinnatians, was able to converse in seven languages. More lasting was the Trollopes' friendship with Hiram Powers, an artistic youth who had been working in a clock factory until the opportunity arose to model wax figures for the local museum. With Mrs. Trollope to translate Dante, and Henry as "The Invisible Lady," he contrived a full-scale representation of the Infernal Regions which long fascinated the citizens.

Thomas Anthony, intending a glad surprise, brought with him his oldest son. Tom had finished Winchester in July and gone home to Harrow Weald to wait for a vacancy at New College, Oxford. The young man had found the Harrow farm a dreary place, but it was not to make him happy that the Spartan father permitted the long journey; it was to please Tom's mother. The pair had traveled in steerage, thus salving Mr. Trollope's conscience for incurring the double expense. The voyage had been horrible; the weather rough, the ship filthy, the food insufficient. For thirty-eight days, Thomas Anthony groaned upon his narrow bunk, but Tom installed himself on deck, where he was knocked about and stumbled over, was half frozen, narrowly escaped being swept overboard in a storm, and yet enjoyed himself. From New York the Trollopes traveled westward by way of Pittsburgh, which Tom pronounced "a nightmare of squalor," and crossed the Alleghenies by stagecoach. At long last Cincinnati was attained; in late November husband and wife, brothers and sisters, the Trollope family, all but one, young Anthony, were reunited.

Frances Trollope's spirits rose, for she was again under authority and therefore, paradoxically, free to do as she pleased. The walks, the drives, the visitings were redoubled in interest and number. In her exuberance she gave a party in the Julians tradition—a little perhaps because she wished to educate the people of Cincinnati. There were a hundred guests, music of violins and cello, theatricals. In *Les Deux Amis* she impressed her hearers by the quality of her French; in *The Merry Wives of Windsor* Henry as Falstaff swept them off their feet. He had been drinking, and though he was excruciatingly funny his mother was distressed. She disliked overindulgence in liquor, and shuddered at tobacco; her notions of propriety were not the less strict because they did not accord with Cincinnati standards. After theatricals came supper, and then the young folk danced until daybreak.

Tom and his father remained in Cincinnati only until February, 1829, but Thomas Anthony promised to return in the spring of 1830. Before he left, plans were made for the bazaar, of which Henry was to be proprietor. His mother felt that she must stay until he was well established, but the duration of her exile could better be decided when her husband came again.

The Trollopes wanted to make money, but hoped at the same time to indulge their humanitarian sentiments. It seemed certain that folk so inquisitive as the Cincinnatians would welcome an opportunity to hear good music and see fine pictures; therefore the rotunda and the gallery of their bazaar were to be consecrated to art, leisure, and the pleasures of the table. In the lower story luxuries from Europe and fine work done in Cincinnati homes—a foreshadowing of the Women's Exchange—would be displayed for sale. Fifty years later such an enterprise, in the hands of shrewd promoters, would have succeeded. But the Cincinnatians of that day were, in their own words, "too smart" for the Trollopes.

Thomas Anthony promised to send ten thousand dollars' worth of goods from London. Hervieu worked on an enormous canvas for the rotunda, depicting the meeting of Lafayette with the Governor of Ohio. Architects were engaged, but their taste was uninformed, and the building which arose in Cincinnati in 1829 showed all too clearly the influence of Mrs. Trollope's puckish sense of humor. Since the bazaar was in any case an exotic, nothing seemed less unsuitable to this accomplished lady than the creation of an Arabian Nights fantasy.

Throwing convention to the winds, they created a spacious building with a Saracenic façade, a dome surmounted by a spire, and an immense display of Gothic windows. Within were gaslit lobbies, offices, saloons, galleries, and ballroom.

But at the end of August, before the building was completed, Mrs. Trollope fell seriously ill with malaria. Cincinnatians, refusing to believe in the insalubrity of their climate, said it was because the "English old woman" walked in all kinds of weather. With her collapse came the final phase of the American disaster; for the girls were mere children, and Henry was not only too young but too erratic and out of health to stem the tide of calamity.

The unfinished bazaar was sold at a sheriff's auction, to pay the workmen who had been engaged on it. The ten-thousand-dollar consignment of goods from London was disposed of in small lots to enterprising storekeepers. All personal property was taken from the Trollopes, even to the carpets and the beds; the mother and her daughters shared a borrowed pallet, and Henry and Auguste Hervieu lay on the bare boards of a neighbor's kitchen floor. The young Frenchman remained perfect in loyalty, when he might have prospered by himself.

This illness was the very nadir of Frances Trollope's life. Fifty years old, sick, penniless in a hostile society, distant beyond the help of family and friends, with two young daughters and a son dependent upon her, she had the unpleasing reflection that after wasting almost twenty thousand dollars in a speculation she had not sufficient funds to take her home. Yet, underneath her volatile spirits, concealed by constant witty talk and mimicry, there had always lain integrity, dauntless courage, and capacity for work. She turned the corner and began to convalesce.

Her joints ached, she could not walk, her eyes pained her, she felt herself a helpless old crone. Nevertheless, to save her family she had to re-create herself and to make money. For such a purpose, there was but one way open; she must pursue the course common to travelers, the writing of a book. If Hervieu furnished the drawings, an account of her American experiences might perhaps be favorably received at home.

At present she was too ill to make a start. Resolutely she closed her mind to her anxieties, soothing herself with that anodyne which, next to sleep, is the most merciful—she read. Cooper's Indians gave her bad dreams; she substituted Walter Scott and reread every novel. When her eyes hurt too much for reading, she thought of her own book.

There was ample time for other reflections. What sort of life would her children have? She had not married young, but she had borne many children, and was therefore not one of those mothers who at fifty are superfluous. There were moments when her daughters' prospects gave her poignant anxiety. "Nothing shall keep me here after my eldest girl is sixteen," she wrote to Miss Mitford, "—at least, nothing that I can possibly foresee or imagine, as I think I owe it to her to let her see young ladies' daylight in a civilized country." Nor was she easy about Tom. That placid youth had not yet received his appointment to New College and consequently was expecting to study for the bar. She feared he had no inclination for the law—"Poor fellow, he means to be a good boy and a lawyer—but his heart and soul are literary." She wrote him frequently, thinking, perhaps, that the letters would be passed on to Anthony. Perhaps, in her trouble, she forgot that Anthony was growing up. Reasonable as her attitude seemed in her own eyes, it had a most unfortunate effect upon her youngest son, who never forgave these years of neglect.

Very early in 1830 she made the noble sacrifice of sending Henry home to England. Another hot summer would, she feared, mean his death. She was not able to scrape up enough money for them all to go —could raise only a bare sufficiency for Henry's passage. At parting with him, she could not bring herself to write even to Tom into what dreadful straits they were fallen, but left it to Henry to recount the American misfortunes. It was some comfort that all the Trollopes were at last through with Cincinnati. When in early March the ice broke in the Ohio River, mother and daughters left the scene of humiliation and disaster.

Yet the two worst sufferers from the Trollope debacle were not those most immediately involved in it, but the father and the youngest son. Their positions were much alike, although a total want of sympathy and confidence prevented a sharing of their loneliness. What each of them endured, he bore alone. Thomas Anthony, who had promised to return to America in 1830, had not yet started when news of the collapse reached England. He, too, was ill, in mind and body, and now abandoned hope, neglected even the ruins of his law business, and made only futile and sporadic efforts about the farm.

Anthony, the last of his sons, was entering his adolescent years without solace of any kind. At ten he had looked forward to going to Winchester, because he loved Tom and was to be Tom's pupil and sleep in Tom's room; but when he was actually there the big brother had daily thrashed him with a big stick—so at least the little brother persuaded himself. Although they were together at Winchester only a year and a half, the amorphous shade cast by that experience darkened the man's life. Afterward Tom had gone to America, but Anthony had—of course—been left behind.

While the older boy prepared for the voyage, the younger had spent the days disconsolately in his father's chambers at Lincoln's Inn. He shuddered to remember that a pupil had killed himself in one of those gloomy rooms, where there was now nothing worth reading but an old Shakespeare. When Anthony wearied of the fine print of the plays, he wandered alone through the shady, deserted courts. Other boys would have found more books and been off on longer rambles, but Anthony was shy and sullen.

When the father went to America he neglected to pay his youngest son's term bill at Winchester. The town's tradespeople were warned by the school authorities not to extend credit to Anthony. Still more painful—for he had never been in the habit of "treating" or being "treated" at tuckshops—was his inability to give the customary gratuities to the college servants. There was a shocking publicity about his indigence; masters, servants, and fellow pupils all were privy to his want. At Winchester his personal slovenliness was less remarkable than it had been at Harrow, for all Winchester boys went dirty, their long black gowns spotted with the accumulated filth of years. Candle grease as well as spilled food sullied such raiment; there was nothing so satisfying to a prefect's soul as to send a wretched child scuttling after candlestick or snuffers. Often was Anthony summoned from his bed in the night watches to go forth in his shirt and hunt for snuffers. He hunted them in the most improbable places, hardly conscious of the stubborn will which drove him on to thwart his bullying superior by looking where he knew he would find nothing.

After three barren years at Winchester, Anthony was unceremoniously removed to the farm at Harrow Weald and once more sent to Harrow School. Sunbury and Winchester had had their special miseries, but for sheer desolation neither of them could rival Harrow. Four times each day the outcast shambled over the three miles of muddy or dusty lanes—a rough, strongly built figure, pondering the injustices of his fate. If his father had only refrained from interfering and allowed him to stay at Winchester, he believed he might have won a scholarship to New College—as Tom had failed to do. But he had gloomily to acknowledge that to get to Oxford would be of no avail, since there was no money to keep him. He was resolved not to work in the vegetable garden at the farm, and remained firm in his determination not to study Latin, although beneath his father's eye he found it necessary to seem attentive to his book. His father, though he had never beaten him, had once knocked him down with a folio Bible. His mother had deserted him. His brother Tom had been out to visit her, and to Tom she even wrote letters. To him came nothing.

From such bitter reflections on his invidious lot, he fell to telling stories to himself. At Harrow Weald, the only book he liked was Cooper's *Prairie,* but the third volume was missing. He finished the tale himself; there were many other tales, of which he was the hero. At school he was, as always, unpopular. One day he fought for a full hour with the pampered son of a London bookbinder. A master stopped the fight, his adversary was too badly mauled to stay in school, and Anthony kept glorious memories of his Homeric combat. Although he was on hostile terms with his father, he had moments of sympathy with him in which he felt vaguely that they had much in common. She, the brilliant, the gay and debonair, had abandoned them both. The opposition of these two contrasting characters, his mother and his father, afforded much to reflect upon whenever he should gain sufficient detachment. Already he felt some explanation was demanded.

Tom was seldom at Harrow; but it was Tom, the ever fortunate, who first saw Henry, home from America. Sleeping at the farm on the night of April 19, 1830, Tom answered a knocking at the outer door and found his brother sinking with fatigue after a fourteen-mile walk from London. The funds which he had received from his mother had sufficed only to pay the coach fare from Liverpool, not to carry him out to Harrow. Tom got Henry into his bed and slept in the chair beside him. The next day Thomas Anthony, with no pretense of pleasure, received Henry as the embodied proof of the failure of the great Trollope scheme. His second son, he pronounced, must proceed to Cambridge University to see what he could do for himself. Henry was forthwith enrolled at Caius College, where he remained as long as could be expected of a boy who had no money.

For the better part of two years, Tom had been awaiting a vacancy at New College, Oxford, and as he was now twenty, the chances of a timely opening were slight. The law project had been given up, but the two exhibitions with which Winchester had provided him could be applied elsewhere at Oxford. He was therefore now entered at St. Alban's Hall under Dr. Whately, the theologian. Having little interest in the fervid religious discussions in which the Oxford Movement was taking shape, Tom did very much as he pleased at the University, where he was more often seen on the river than in chapel. Nevertheless he read widely and pursued the historical and antiquarian interests which Winchester had fostered.

Hitherto Tom's education had suffered less from the arbitrary interference of his father than had Henry's and Anthony's. But in the middle of term Thomas Anthony's misplaced zeal suddenly immersed his eldest son in difficulties which nearly cost him his degree. Dr. Whately had labored manfully to purge Alban Hall of idle and dissolute characters, and with this ambition had strenuously insisted that every student respect the academic calendar. Thomas Anthony, for reasons which undoubtedly seemed good to him, obliged his son to return from vacation a day late. Whately decreed a monetary fine;

Thomas Anthony, challenging his authority, refused to pay it, very probably being without funds. Whately summoned Tom, the late-comer, threatened expulsion, and obliged him to withdraw his name from the books of the hall. Unless a place could be found immediately in another college, Tom stood in grave danger of forfeiting his stipend. None would take him in except Magdalen Hall, a recognized asylum for destitute misfits, where he pursued his self-education in his usual unruffled spirits.

It was Tom who remained most closely in touch with his mother and sisters. Frances Trollope wrote to him from America with a confidence and intimacy she never used toward her husband. But the mother did not forget her youngest son: "My poor dear Anthony will have outgrown our recollection. Tell him not to outgrow his affection for us. No day passes,—hardly an hour—without our talking of you all. I hope a letter from your father is on the way." Her morose husband was not writing to her, though she loyally assured Miss Mitford that he was an excellent correspondent. Either he was sunk too deep in gloom to rouse himself to writing, or, like Anthony, he was resentful—moved to bitterness not only by her desertion but by the failure of her many schemes.

She, wretched woman, was sitting all day at the book which was to save the family. If it should achieve a moderate success, she was sure a second book would bring clear gain. Meanwhile Emily and Cecelia were wonderfully uncomplaining, wonderfully kind to her and to each other. She had sold her trinkets to buy shoes for the elder girl. Both daughters mended their own clothes and never said the truth, that they were not worth mending. The mother tried to be cheerful and seemed so, but they knew that she suffered.

From Cincinnati they had gone up the river to Wheeling in West Virginia, and thence by stage over the Alleghenies into Maryland. Once "Western America" was left behind, they had rediscovered the appurtenances of civilization. It was the frontier life which had offended Frances Trollope's sense of decency. Henceforth she was no captious visitor. Baltimore, beautiful in white marble, won her instant praise, and her enthusiasm for Washington was boundless; the Americans, she said, should be grateful to the British for burning the old town. Almost her only complaint was that Americans were not happy people; they could be excited, but not healthily gay.

Early in May, 1830—two months after leaving Cincinnati—Mrs. Trollope was reunited with a childhood friend, a Mrs. Stone, now a widow, who lived with her children at her estate of Stonington on the Potomac. Mrs. Stone had almost no money, and Mrs. Trollope was unwilling to add to the expenses of her beautiful home. No remittances arrived from England, but the faithful Auguste Hervieu plied his art and kept them from starvation. Had the household been free from anxiety, the summer which she spent there would have been delightful. Mrs. Stone was a musician, and her tastes chimed with her friend's. Poor as she was, there was no dearth of household service; after poetic walks the airs of Mozart charmed the evening hours, while the listeners sat in the broad verandah sipping coffee or iced sangaree.

Mrs. Trollope's appreciation of American hospitality did not blind her to the darker aspects of life. She observed that Irish laborers employed on the Chesapeake and Delaware canal drank heavily, and thus suffered the more from the fever which raged along the Potomac. The life of a sick Negro slave represented *property*, and was guarded far more carefully than that of such an exile. She and Mrs. Stone took in a boy of twenty, found lying unconscious in the open country. He died that night, and the family buried him in a grove of locust trees, pitying his mother who would never know what had happened to her son.

Eventually the requirements of her book took her from Stonington to Philadelphia, where she particularly disapproved the idle boarding-house existence of middle-class wives, the arid routine of the rich, the gloomy Sabbath, and the general air of smug respectability. New York won higher praise: "We saw enough to convince us that there is society to be met with in New York which would be deemed delightful anywhere." Yet at the theatre she was dismayed to see a woman nursing her baby in the front of a box, while the men, coatless, sprawled in horrid attitudes.

No writer on America could afford to omit a chapter on Niagara, and after anxious financial discussions the trip was made by stage and canal. She rose to the occasion admirably. She had been prepared

for a sublime and awful spectacle, but the reality out-distanced her
excited imagination. The pages she devoted to it revealed an artistic
sense and a descriptive power to which America had, on the whole,
given little scope.

She had seen little of the South, and nothing of the New England
States; but after more than three years she was determined not to remain longer away from home. Her protracted residence had done little
to modify her first reluctant judgment on the mass of Americans. She
praised their scenery, their steamboats, their countryseats; but the
people she could not praise—"Jonathan was a very dull boy." Doubtless the Americans were the most enterprising folk in the world, but,
"It is not in the temper of the people either to give or to receive. The
moral sense is on every point blunter than with us. I certainly believe
the women of America to be the handsomest in the world, but
as surely do I believe that they are the least attractive"—a verdict in
which her famous sons were to concur.

The political complacency of Americans had been especially irritat-
ing: "Had I observed any single feature in their national character
that could justify their eternal boast of liberality and the love of
freedom, I might have respected them, however much my taste might
have been offended by what was peculiar in their manners and
customs. But it is impossible for any mind of common honesty not to
be revolted by the contradictions in their principles and practice. All
the freedom enjoyed in America, beyond what is enjoyed in England,
is enjoyed solely by the disorderly at the expense of the orderly."
To Mrs. Trollope, once a professed liberal, America was a horrid
example of the effects of political extremism. "I had," she wrote, "a
little leaning towards sedition when I set out, but before I had half
completed my tour I was quite cured. Were I an English legislator,
instead of sending sedition to the Tower, I would send her to make a
tour of the United States."

It was not her intention to revenge herself by a satirical book. She
could not have afforded such a personal satisfaction, since the fortune
of her whole family rested on success. *The Domestic Manners of the
Americans* was intended to furnish an impartial account of her
observations and impressions. She did not claim any knowledge of

those sections of the country which she had not visited; she was careful to distinguish between what she had seen for herself and what had been reported to her. Occasionally her sarcastic faculty surmounted her judicial, and, like most amateurs, she was prone to overgeneralize; but it was because her writing came so close to truth that it was unendurable to Americans.

In her many journeyings into odd European corners, Frances Trollope would never meet with the ill-treatment and misunderstanding accorded her in America. But she was not a woman to hold a grudge; when she had said her caustic say over her experiences, they lost their importance. As yet she lived rather in the future than in the present, and the past was easily forgotten.

During the summer of 1831 the father and the sons at Harrow Weald were constantly on the lookout for the return of the mother and the girls. On August 5, Tom went to London hoping to get news of the ship. Returning, disappointed, to that dreariest of farmhouses, he found his mother, Emily, Cecelia, the faithful Auguste, his father, bashful young Anthony—the reunited family. Desolate Harrow Weald had become a home.

CHAPTER IV

Harrow Revisited

1832-1834

The Domestic Manners of the Americans, although it was virtually finished when Frances Trollope returned to England in early August, 1831, was not published until March 19 of the next year. The seven months' interval was not due to any difficulty in finding a publisher, for America was just then a subject of enormous interest, and Frances Trollope's book was the first which promised to reveal the social life of the young country with an amusing readability, refreshing after the weighty works on the American experiment published during the preceding decade. As with so many other public and private enterprises, the fate of Mrs. Trollope's first book was entangled in the great debate over the Reform Bill of 1832.

This measure, designed to eliminate rotten boroughs and provide the great industrial centers with equitable representation in Parliament, had been the occasion of mass meetings and demonstrations in England even before Mrs. Trollope had sailed from New York. In the autumn of 1831, ugly riots had occurred all over the country. The Tory propertied classes and their adherents, in whose ranks Frances Trollope had now enrolled herself, fearing that passage of the Reform Bill would undermine their entire position in the country, betrayed their anxiety by violently denouncing every sort of liberal government, particularly the American. The Whigs, who sponsored the Bill, were, on the contrary, well-disposed toward American republicanism; thus it became still more the part of every good conservative to condemn the American experiment. Frances Trollope, sensing a commercial opportunity and enthusiastically willing to abet the opponents of Reform, strengthened the political passages in her book and wrote a scathing preface on the evils of democracy.

She submitted the manuscript to Whittaker and Treacher, publishers of her friend Miss Mitford, and they consulted Captain Basil Hall, whose book on America had given him an authoritative position in transatlantic criticism. After his generous report, it was read in several influential quarters. John Murray, the Edinburgh publisher, saw it and regretted that he had not been offered the chance to bring it out; Henry Milman, the historian, read Mrs. Trollope's second copy and approved the pages dealing with American religious practices. Most important, John Gibson Lockhart, editor of the great Tory *Quarterly Review*, went over the unpublished book with amused appreciation and set aside no less than forty pages in the spring *Quarterly* for excerpts interspersed with fervid praise.

The magazine, appearing in the same month as the book, made Frances Trollope's literary fortune. The Whig periodicals might still abuse *The Domestic Manners of the Americans*, but on the heels of the *Quarterly* could not ignore it. *Blackwood's* critic conceded that the book showed talent and was amusing; *Fraser's* found the author "singularly acute"; the *Athenaeum* had "never met with a traveller so clever and so difficult to please." The Whig *Edinburgh Review* devoted a full forty-eight pages to excoriating the writer and denouncing her work, attempting first to destroy her credibility as a witness by recounting the shabby necessities behind her emigration, angrily rebuking her opposition to the Reform Bill, and accusing her of endangering the peace between nations!

In the London literary world and in society occurred the same great cleavage as in the press; to the Tories Mrs. Trollope was a heroine—to the Whigs, an impertinent adventuress; to both, she was the sensation of the hour. In an age when gentility was vastly important, it was natural to try to dispose of her by saying she had not mingled in good society in America, while ignoring her own repeated assertion that what she wrote did not apply to good society. Harriet Martineau observed that she "had thought proper to libel and slander a whole nation." "I would not dirty my pages with her stories, even to refute them," said Miss Martineau virtuously, superbly oblivious of the impossibility of refutation.

But Frances Trollope's present necessities were too urgent for her to object to what was said about her, provided she was paid for what she had said. The fall and winter months at Harrow Weald had been a period of privation during which the family could afford neither tea nor butter for their bread. The farm, where she and the girls had never lived before, was almost unfurnished. Not one of the children had a pillow, and when Tom was at home on one of his frequent visits, he lay prostrate with migraine on an attic bed with only straw beneath him. Anthony was too old to be going to Harrow School, but there was no money to send him away. Henry, unable to remain at Cambridge without funds, was now reading for the bar—a pursuit for which he felt only disgust. He and his father quarreled violently on the omnipresent subject of money; the son insisted on calling in his mother as mediator. After such shattering scenes, she dosed herself with laudanum or went sleepless.

After years of travel, the wardrobe she had taken to America was in tatters, and the girls had outgrown as well as outworn their dresses. She had been determined to have her daughters see "young ladies' daylight" in England, and here they were—but with no prospect of a début. Worst of griefs, the decadence of her husband's powers seemed irremediable. Her prop was gone. She had friends and relatives to advise, but none behind whom she could shelter. If her book did not sell, the reunited family might again have to be broken up; they were already going hungry; beggary, death in a ditch, were fancies not too remote for her terrified imagination.

The children installed her in a little room which they called the Sacred Den. As soon as the book was accepted, an access of hope enabled her to begin a second, a hodgepodge work of fiction which at first she called *The American Exile*, later *The Refugee in America*. When she emerged from the Sacred Den to mingle with the world, she heard delightful voices promising the success of the forthcoming *Domestic Manners of the Americans*. Compliments were converted into necessities: John Murray's regret that he was not her publisher gave her confidence to buy a half pound of butter, Lockhart's report turned into a quarter pound of tea, another favorable reading replaced her tallow candle with wax.

To quiet her fretful husband, she encouraged him in a vast work of research which he had undertaken; he designed a history of all

Christian denominations, with explanation of their ceremonies and rituals. The *Encyclopædia Ecclesiastica* would be illustrated by the tireless Hervieu, who remained a member of the family. To have Thomas Anthony occupied was a blessing to the hectored children and their burdened mother. But she was a better mother than wife. Without conscious malice, she held up her husband's oddities before her children, embellishing them with her fantastic wit. The stupendous task he had undertaken as he neared sixty, without a library, handicapped by frequent attacks of migraine—and, even more, the dreariness of his research—amused Frances Trollope. Her satirical remarks behind the scholar's back led the young people to regard his project with pitying scorn. So great was her influence that he fell in their opinion to a place too mean for such a man to occupy, however broken. Yet Anthony, though sharing the belief that the *Encyclopædia Ecclesiastica* was food for laughter, and restive under his parent's interminable readings aloud from *Sir Charles Grandison*, felt dimly that his inexplicable father was not altogether absurd.

The wretched man made his effort to preserve the family. Backed by Uncle Meetkerke, now the father of many children, he applied for a post as a London magistrate. Lord Melbourne, the Home Secretary, wrote a civil letter which Thomas Anthony misconstrued as a promise. A month before his wife's book was to be published, his hopes were disappointed. Frances wrote sadly to their oldest boy, "The bubble has burst, my dearest Tom; and the magistracy can be dreamt of no more by any of us."

A few weeks later she discovered her own fame and, unabashed by it, went up to town, taking sixteen-year-old Cecelia as her secretary. Tom and Emily were dispatched to Exeter to spend the Easter vacation with Cousin Fanny Bent, Henry was already in London, and the moody Anthony was again left in Harrow Weald, more dismal because his mother had once brightened it.

The society she met was as brilliant as the Tories could boast. At a dinner given by the publisher John Murray she was splendidly entertained with the literary Lockharts, Captain Hall, and Walter Savage Landor. At Miss Berry's in Curzon Street, the Countess of Morley told her that if London recognized her identity, she could have the horses removed from her carriage and be drawn in triumph by the populace! Lady Charlotte Lindsay *implored* her to go on writing; Lady Louisa Stewart said *everyone* was talking Yankee talk; Lady Alderson gave a splendid party for her. "How strange all this seems!" she wrote wonderingly to Tom.

Her portrait, by Hervieu, was exhibited at Somerset House. A critic commented: "The painter has not flattered her good looks. He has had vinegar in his brush, too." The Trollope children were amused by what they considered a baseless innuendo. Their mother's conversation had a taste of salt; they did not think it sour. "Old Madam Vinegar" became a term of endearment.

Cecelia copied manuscripts, went to parties and to the theatre, and wrote Tom letters full of girlish exaggeration: "I liked him [Macready] about sixty thousand times better than I did Young in the same part." Henry also wrote Tom, while he squired his mother, neglected the law, and, through Captain Hall, made the acquaintance of the president of the London Geological Society. New Harmony, which had undermined Henry's health, had given him a genuine scientific interest. In the following autumn the Geological Society elected him a Fellow.

Ambitious for her children, Mrs. Trollope was doing what she could to secure them brilliant futures. Tom was twenty-two and very eager to accompany her to Germany, where she had half promised to travel with the object of writing a book, should her new novel prove a success. Tom suggested optimistically that he could pay his expenses by writing a travel book of his own, but she replied firmly that he must finish his course at Oxford.

She understood her eldest son; he was gifted, lovable, well-conducted, not exactly lazy, but unwilling to work except on what interested him. Magdalen Hall was a poor place for such a young man. There was no spirit of emulation, no one went out for honors, there was none of the discipline which prevailed in other colleges; most of the students were middle-aged men tardily taking degrees. Tom filled his hours with reading strange old books, pleased with the fancy that of all men living only he had seen the pages he perused.

He did not care for liquor, and his gravest extravagance was to hire a horse and gig and race the mail coach. The river delighted him; he was a champion walker who set himself trials of endurance; laden with a knapsack, he once covered forty-seven miles in a day's walk.

On another occasion Tom and young Anthony walked fourteen miles from Harrow Weald to Vauxhall Gardens to see the fireworks. There was dancing; Tom was shy, and feared to make a show of himself, but Anthony, throwing aside the sullen reserve he displayed at home, danced boisterously all the evening with wild young partners. The brothers had not a penny to spend on food or drink, but trudged the fourteen miles home without grumbling.

When Tom was at home he relieved his mother of family errands, doing them the more cheerfully the farther they took him. On another London excursion he spent his small surplus for a pair of singlesticks with basket handles. One was broken in a bout with Anthony, and replaced by a blackthorn cudgel. Tom admitted—to his diary—that young Anthony was generally quicker and more dextrous than himself, and made less complaint over bruises.

Under his sullen exterior, the boy Anthony was extraordinarily sensitive. Dr. Longley, the recently appointed head at Harrow, a man whom Anthony in later years professed to have reverenced and loved, rarely called on him for a recitation, probably because, like any quick-witted teacher, he disliked to hear a pupil blunder. When he did give Anthony an opportunity, his face assumed such a tragic expression at the expected stupidity of the response that the boy was overcome with shame. Yet in the weekly English themes Anthony was at no disadvantage. Prizes were not difficult to win at Harrow, but on at least one occasion Anthony's English style gained him the prize which a schoolmate and future lord had hoped to win.

No such recognition was accorded him at home. Anthony—Tony, as the family called him—was not a valued contributor to *The Magpie*, the amateur magazine which his vivacious family had invented and dedicated to "Literature, Politics, Science, and Art." Henry was the editor; Cecelia, Mrs. Grant from next door, Thomas Anthony, and Frances (signing herself as *Grub Street*) contributed articles which were pasted into a large scrapbook and read aloud. The young Trollopes were not in favor of admitting the public to these weekly readings, but their incorrigibly social mother managed to smuggle in an occasional guest.

Mrs. Trollope lived only a year at Harrow Weald. When *The Domestic Manners of the Americans* brought her £1,000, she determined to move to a better house nearer Harrow. Such women can always present unchallengeable reasons for extravagant actions: Harrow Weald was small, dismal, unwholesomely situated in a damp hollow, dank with the shade of encroaching trees, inaccessible. But her friends were uneasy at her rapid disbursements, warning her that she could not expect so much return from future writings.

The purchases were justifiable—a bed, a sofa, pillows, bolster, and half a year's rent and taxes paid in advance on the new house, which was to be called Julians Hill. Besides these cash expenditures, she undertook to pay for some £70 worth of fixtures for the new home and for the purchase of a cow. Her money was her own; the law and custom of the times gave her husband rights over it, but he did not dispute her possession. If she had placed her earnings in his hands, Lord Northwicke would have taken them as rent for the property of Julians, which the Trollopes still held. That territorial magnate, although regarded by the young Trollopes as the vampire of Harrow, was a connoisseur of Italian art, and needed the rent which Thomas Anthony could not pay him in order to maintain his country seat and his collections.

Mrs. Trollope's first novel, *The Refugee in America*, appeared in January, 1833, and was most vehemently attacked by the *Quarterly Review*, which a year before had done everything possible to make *The Domestic Manners of the Americans* a success. She was distressed to hear that her friend Captain Hall, who had reviewed the former book, was suspected of writing the critique, and with her usual impetuosity asked him if he had done so. He cleared himself and advised her good-humoredly not to let herself be troubled by hostile criticism; her earlier book had made enemies who would never be placated. But leaving revenge out of the question, he may have felt that *The Refugee* deserved all that was said of it. The dialogue was natural, the phrase telling, but she was working for money, and wished to attract a wide public: with the amateur's impulse to put in

everything possible, her fecund imagination had provided smugglers,
English aristocracy, travel, hypocritical ministers, disguise, stabbings,
village gossip, and true love, all in a melodrama which might be mistaken for farce.

Mrs. Trollope had not disliked all Americans; she had known
lovable young people, and the heroines of *The Refugee* and of *The
Widow Barnaby* were charming American girls. She could sustain
the vicious attacks which were being made upon her from across the
Atlantic, but hostile criticism from her own class and countrymen was
less easy to bear. It was again hinted that she was not at home in upper
circles and that her aristocrats were impossible. But even if she had
never before been acquainted with the fashionable world, she had seen
enough of it while writing *The Refugee* to furnish her plenty of
models. Unfortunately, she had supposed that she would be well
advised to make her lords and ladies not what they were, but what her
public believed them to be.

In the spring of 1833, after the Trollopes settled in Julians Hill,
there was an epidemic of influenza. All of them were ill. The
apothecary applied leeches so generously that Cecelia had hysterics,
Anthony fainted, and Henry, already deplorably emaciated, was almost drained of blood. Emily never fully recovered from her attack.
She was then fifteen, a pretty girl with long fair curls and wide blue
eyes. Someone, no doubt the indefatigable Hervieu, had once painted
her in her brown pinafore, seated at a little desk, blowing soap
bubbles, under the didactic motto, "Study with determined zeal."
Hervieu himself contracted influenza and, not consenting to the leech
treatment, dosed himself with various concoctions until he became
delirious and was found wandering in the fields.

Frances Trollope rose from her sickbed to finish her second novel,
The Abbess, a tale of cloister intrigue in fifteenth-century Italy. Still
another work published that same year was *The Mother's Manual*, an
exceedingly clever and good-humored satirical essay in verse, on the
means of catching husbands for young lady daughters. The book was
brought out in a *de luxe* edition with twenty charming illustrations by
the family artist. The theme was not one on which the author needed
to feel any personal bitterness, as her own girls had scarcely reached

marriageable age. No doubt, however, the husband-catching efforts of other Harrow mammas had been the subject of caustic comment in the Trollope household. Anthony was not too young to receive the first seeds of his lifelong horror of woman on the hunt for a husband.

The first of June, accompanied by Hervieu and Henry (the disappointed Tom staying at Oxford to take his degree, and Anthony being as usual abandoned without explanation), Mrs. Trollope began a tour of Belgium and the Rhine. Her reasons were, as always, excellent; she preferred writing travel books to novels, and she and Henry needed a change after illness. At Ostend, the British consul and his wife—an old friend—were expecting them and had arranged amateur theatricals, in the course of which Henry had the misfortune to incur an injury which kept him ten days in bed.

From Ostend they went on to Bruges, making the journey by canal boat, as easier for Henry, and thence to Ghent, Antwerp, and eventually to Brussels and the battlefield of Waterloo. Less than two decades had elapsed since the great battle, and vendors were still offering bullets, brass buttons, and imperial eagles salvaged from the field. Frances Trollope walked about until she was exhausted, rested in the inn where Wellington and Blücher had met, and wandered out again alone, over the desolate plain. Night had come on, and a thunderstorm was approaching. She was sensitive to electrical disturbances, and as little used to solitude as a queen. The place was tragic enough to subdue for the moment her usually irrepressible spirit.

From Namur, where Henry visited a collection of the geological specimens of Belgium, the party sailed down the Meuse on what his mother called "a little dirty packet-boat"—the noble steamboats of America remained her lifelong ideal. On the whole she was lenient in her judgments of the country; there were, she observed, the usual differences between the well-bred and the peasants, but the common people were clean, cheerful, and hard-working; if they had the fault of liking tobacco, at any rate they did not chew it as the Americans did.

At Aix-la-Chapelle, or Aachen, over the Prussian frontier, she was enchanted by the church of Charlemagne. She sat in the chair where eleven emperors had been crowned, where Josephine had seated herself under Napoleon's saturnine approval. Lending a sympathetic ear to the praises of Prussia's reactionary king, she grieved at changes in her "own dear country" since her childhood, when the lower classes had "loved their church and flag." But partisan as she was, she was a shrewd observer and admired Germany's rapid progress in arts, commerce, wealth, and education.

A week was spent at Godesberg on the Rhine while she scribbled, Hervieu sketched, and Henry tapped and chipped and filled his journal with geological notes. He wrote well, had the Trollopean flow of language and the family style, more serious and masculine than his mother's. His German was excellent and, as the others spoke the language haltingly, he was of great service. Up and down the Rhine they traveled, investigating crypts where petrified monks were on display, and penetrating dungeons into which they begged to be locked while Hervieu sketched and Madam held the candle. At Baden-Baden Mrs. Trollope went repeatedly to the gaming tables, not to play but to study the faces of the gamblers. She saw much she could not approve—English women gambled on Sunday, her countrymen were extravagant, picked flowers, snubbed strangers, growled about the food. Their vulgar pretensions contrasted badly, in her eyes, with the quiet dignity of the German nobility.

Familiar with *Der Freischütz*, she felt deeply the kindred romance of the Harz Mountains and the Brocken. When she and Henry breakfasted among the gilliflowers in the garden of a primitive inn below the mountain, she could hear the weird music of the Wolf's Glen in the wind which swept down the valley. They ascended the heights on muleback and spent the night in the guesthouse on the summit. A fearful storm was raging over Europe, and there upon the peak of the Brocken they felt the full violence of the wind. Sleep was impossible, for the noise was frightful, and as morning dawned, the fog assumed strange and sinister shapes.

The kindly inn people, concerned for the descent of the little old lady, helped her to mount her mule in the shelter of the stable, pinned her in securely so that no flutter of veil or skirt should catch the wind, and put her in charge of the guide who led her down the perilous, magnificent descent, back to the gilliflowers blowing in the garden and a feast of Westphalian ham. When she wrote up her little adventure, she finished with a prim, "Full of interest and enjoyment as this expedition proved to us, I doubt whether I can fairly recommend the ascent of the Brocken to the generality of female travellers."

On the same night, August 31, 1833, Thomas Anthony had been in peril of shipwreck in the North Sea. His wife had not been gone a week when the wretched man had suffered an obscure attack, been bled by leeches, and recovered somewhat, only to sustain a second seizure. Cecelia had written her mother, but her letter had been delayed and before its arrival others had come with news of his improvement. By the end of August, he was able to travel to the woman whose vital presence made his only joy in life. He met them at Hamburg, explaining lamely that he had come to see Cologne Cathedral in the interests of his *Encyclopædia Ecclesiastica*.

On their return to Harrow, they found that the family affairs had reached a desperate condition. The Trollopes were again penniless. The receipts of the mother's two novels had fallen far below those from *The Domestic Manners of the Americans*, and the money had already been spent. Mr. Trollope's rentals from the London property were not coming in, and therefore nothing had been paid to Lord Northwicke, who was preparing to evict his unprofitable tenants.

Under such conditions Mrs. Trollope was unable to put even the first half of her new manuscript into shape before February, 1834. She went over the family business with her brother, Henry Milton, who, probably without consulting Thomas Anthony, called in his solicitor. It was found that his sister's marriage settlements were insecure, and that her husband had given up the deeds of various pieces of property as collateral without securing receipts. Mrs. Trollope was in some respects a timid woman, and these discoveries, which ought to have been made some years earlier, frightened her horribly. Fortunately, much if not all of her dowry was salvaged and converted into an annuity, subject to her disposal or her daughters', an arrangement due not to danger from Thomas Anthony himself, but to fear that his creditors would seize the money.

The winter, under the shadow of impending collapse, was trying to all of them. Cecelia spent Christmas in Lincolnshire with the distant clergyman-cousin whom her father's sister had married—a generous relative who made loans, not to Thomas Anthony, but to Frances, and gave the children their only spending money. After the holidays Cecelia visited her mother's brother, Uncle Henry Milton, and saw something of her own brother Henry, who had found a pupil and taken a room for himself near his relations. But Henry's engagement was of short duration, and he returned to Harrow looking very ill.

At Oxford Tom was tardily concerned about his approaching final examination. His mother, who took some comfort in writing him about her problems, was now afraid to mention them lest he take them so much to heart as to fail—a motherly anxiety she might have spared herself. It did not occur to her to seek sympathy from her "little Tony."

That young man was suffering under a personal disappointment. He had pulled himself so far out of the mire of daily circumstance as to make an independent attempt to better his prospects. He had twice failed in scholarship competitions at Harrow; but hearing of a competitive examination for a sizarship at Trinity College, he had blundered through Aristotle's *Ethics* and gone to Oxford, where, quite understandably, he failed. After this lamentable check, he returned to Harrow School to brood over his blighted life. He would be nineteen in April and, although he was now a monitor and seventh boy, he had risen rather by length of years than because his worth was appreciated. He was taciturn; he appeared engrossed in dark projects. He was merely telling stories to himself in which he played the role of saturnine hero. On this imaginative plane, he could find compensation for his failures in the actual world.

In such a family, he had not been able to escape smatterings of culture, and now that he was sometimes animated by a secret longing to become an English gentleman, he made several sporadic efforts in that direction. In his infancy he had watched Auguste Hervieu sketch, he had seen Hayter when Miss Mitford brought him to Julians. His mother and Uncle Henry Milton talked about pictures, and though he did not understand their enthusiastic interest, he believed it was genuine. In those days the National Gallery was lodged in a dingy dwelling house on Pall Mall. It was dark, the walls dwarfed with enormous paintings. Thither went Anthony in secret, bent on culture, and stood and stared. Much standing and staring were necessary before he could understand what pleasure or profit his family could derive from those dim Italian canvases, but the time came when torture turned to grim satisfaction and he could tell what he liked and why he liked it; when he could admire the treatment while he disdained the subject.

Nor was he entirely ignorant of his country's literature. His lifelong partiality for Milton's "Lycidas" and Dryden's "Alexander's Feast" probably dated from this period of late boyhood. He was enthusiastic over Henry Taylor's two long plays of *Philip van Artevelde*, which were published in 1834; the revolutionary fervor of the lines provided a counterirritant to his mother's reactionary Toryism.

Separations between Anthony and his mother had been too protracted to allow intimacy. The comfortable way of life at Julians Hill pleased him; her mimicry was fascinating, he admired her quick wit, but he was envious of her dependence on Tom and Henry and took a bitter satisfaction in despising her loquacity. He felt a growing resentment on his father's account and suspected that injustice had been done to both of them. Repeatedly she deserted both his father and himself; during her last long absence his father had all but died. He did not realize the enormous pressure she sustained; he heard much talk of the importance of money, but did not fully sense that the little Trollope boom was over and the crash impending; nor did it occur to him that his father must soon flee the country or take lodging in a debtors' prison.

His mother knew all this. Another woman would have collapsed under the imminence of disaster, but Frances Trollope had saved the family once and was ready to make the attempt a second time. She had decided on Belgium as their refuge. The house of her Ostend friend was large; they might board there until a residence could be found at Bruges, the cheapest and most suitable resort for English refugees. To spare her husband humiliation and the danger of arrest, as well as to get him out of the way, she planned to send him in advance.

The scheme was not so much kept secret from Anthony as unnoticed by him amid his own preoccupations. But when he was told one April

morning to drive his father to the London docks, he realized that
dramatic events were in progress. Thomas Anthony was just up from
a sickbed, and his lined face had a yellowish pallor. The pair had
been much left to each other's company, although a mutual lack of
confidence had prevented a true sharing of their solitude. But
Anthony, the son who most resembled the father, was beginning to
understand the bitterness of the older man's existence.

He saw his father aboard the Ostend boat, and thoughtfully drove
home through the April landscape. In the neighborhood of Julians
Hill the gardener suddenly appeared from ambush, to inform him
that bailiffs were already in the house; should Anthony return the
horse and gig, both would be seized. He advised driving straight on to
the village to sell the outfit. The drama was developing, and Anthony
felt cast for a heroic part; but the family fortunes did not benefit
directly from the maneuver, for the Harrow ironmonger said that
horse and gig would do no more than cover his outstanding bill.

Anthony, however, had felt the inspiriting effects of performing a
positive action. Going home to Julians Hill, he found the work of
dispossession far advanced. He helped his sisters pass their mother's
little treasures over the garden wall to their neighbors, the Grant girls.
The bailiff's men remonstrated, but forebore to lay hands on the
young marauders.

Frances Trollope slept that night, April 18, 1834, at the Grants'.
Next day she had an interview with Lord Northwicke, arranged to buy
back the pieces of furniture on which she placed most value, and sent
her trunks aboard the Ostend boat. By this time the news of the dispossession and flight was know to everyone in Harrow, and the family
doctor felt it necessary to offer Mrs. Trollope his solemn warning.
The Belgian coast, he said, meant certain death for Henry.

Such a blow, falling on so great a catastrophe, almost deprived her
of the power of thought. Half frantic, she dispatched Anthony and
Hervieu to get the luggage off the boat before it sailed, scrawled a hurried note bidding her cousin Fanny Bent expect them, told the other
young people to stay at the Grants' until she could get back to Harrow,
and started off for Devonshire with Henry. Fanny Bent was as poor as

any self-respecting spinster, and Frances would not let her keep Henry unless she paid his board. This should be done even if her healthy children went hungry.

As soon as she returned to Harrow, she sent Cecelia and Anthony to join their ailing father at Ostend. Her brother, Henry Milton, lifted a little of her burden by undertaking to read the proof sheets of *Belgium and Western Germany*, for which Murray was waiting. Her affairs arranged temporarily, she crossed the Channel with Emily, leaving her two older sons in England. Tom was still at Oxford, and Henry ill at Dawlish. Once more the family was broken up. If they were ever to be reunited, it must, she knew, be through her unaided efforts. Nevertheless, strong bonds more tenacious than habit or even affection continued to hold them together. Absent from each other, they remained Trollopes, her children and their father's.

CHAPTER V

The Refugees on the Continent

1834-1835

No LONG stay was made at Ostend, since Henry was expected to rejoin the family, either as convalescent or as hopeless invalid, and his mother in her anxiety was unable to remain quiet. She settled her shrunken household outside the walls of Bruges in an unfurnished house known as the Château d'Hondt, and contrived, with economical purchases and the few pieces bought back after the disaster at Julians Hill, to make the place a home for Cecelia, Anthony, and Emily.

Her husband was indifferent to his surroundings, but for her the house was crowded with the invisible inmates of foreshadowed sorrow. Henry, of all her children, had been longest with her; he had shared her exile in America, and she had taken his part against his father. When the present was most powerful in her thoughts, she feared that he was dying in England without her; but when in more tranquil but not less grievous moments she thought of the future, she was almost equally distressed because, even though Henry were to recover, he was unprepared for any career.

As her nerves were too unsteady for writing, she was grateful when visitors came to the Château d'Hondt. The accomplished Mrs. Fauche and her musical daughter, Mary, brought other interesting friends. Soon, as so often in the past, Frances Trollope found herself the center of a clever and amusing group. Tom appeared late in May, with the news that he had taken fourth class honors at Oxford. In spite of cheerful negligence, he had not been able to fall below a place equivalent to a *cum laude*. His mother made no complaint at the grade, unworthy his ability though it was, and his father had long ceased to expect anything remarkable from his sons. Tom at twenty-four was splendidly healthy, and dependent on his impecunious parents; yet his habits were not expensive and, when he was in company, his conversation and good-humor might be said to pay his way. He spent three weeks with the family and one in touring the cities of Belgium and then, a London pupil having been secured for him by a friendly clergyman, departed to take up his duty as a tutor.

Henry wrote from Dawlish in July that he was much better, and very eager to rejoin his family. His mother's buoyant spirit rose at this good news, her natural optimism inclining her to disregard the doctor's solemn warning. In a cheerful letter to Tom, she suggested his crossing with Henry, in order to make the journey less tedious for the convalescent. She added that she felt equal to resuming work on her book, but Tom must bring her paper because she had used up hers on the family correspondence. She also needed six pounds of wax ends for writing at night, and a great quantity of "Windsor soap—old," because it was more economical for laundry purposes; thus oddly she blended the necessities of the author and the house mother. A touch of conscience prevented Tom's deserting his pupils, of whom he now had several, for a second holiday within a month; but he met his brother when he came up to take the Ostend boat and realized from Henry's appearance that his mother had been deluded by her hopes.

Nevertheless, when she saw her son she was persuaded that the Harrow doctor had been mistaken in his diagnosis. Henry seemed to be getting well. However, when he begged to be sent with Tom on a voyage to the West Indies, she listened hungrily to his hopes of healing from the sea and the warm climate. At once she wrote her eldest son, urging him to apply all his intelligence to the problem: Would such a voyage save Henry? Could he, Tom, go with him? How much would it cost? She hoped the book on which she was hard at work would defray the expenses.

Almost immediately, Henry abandoned that scheme for another, and suggested a Mediterranean cruise. Again the mother wrote Tom. She asked if he had seen any reviews of *Belgium and Western Germany*—not because she felt the usual interest of an author in her book's success, but because she regarded it as an instrument which might save her son. "It is dreadful to think that dear Henry's *life* may perhaps depend upon it!" The news that King Leopold of the Belgians had enjoyed the book could not make her proud, for golden opinions had for her less meaning than cash sales.

In the heat of Cincinnati summers, she had accustomed herself to rise as early as four o'clock in the morning. If it had not been for such a habit, she could not now have earned her money, as her only free hours were before breakfast. Two heavy-handed Flemish girls did the coarse work of the Château d'Hondt, but she was Henry's nurse, and his strength and stay. It was wonderful that a woman formed for society, by nature fond of ease, should after fifty years school herself to such inflexible persistence. Her severe discipline gave her what little comfort she had, for her work had power to absorb her while she was at it, and when she glanced up for a momentary lessening of the strain on eyes and hand, she could assure herself that she was actually coining money for her children. But in longer intervals of freedom, she was continually asking herself how long Henry need suffer, if after all he could not get well; and how long she, who felt old and broken, could hold out.

She could not have left England or settled the Château d'Hondt without borrowed money, but she was no sponger. Before the summer was over she had accumulated enough to pay a debt to her intimate friend, Lady Dyer, who refused to accept what she knew Mrs. Trollope needed. When Henry learned that the sum was actually at his mother's disposal, he implored her to spend it by taking him to London for medical advice. There was no English doctor in Bruges, and the young man felt a scientist's doubt of the competency of the Harrow apothecary. Mrs. Trollope could deny him nothing, and was herself so restless that any change attracted her; yet she had scruples about spending the money and wrote Tom that she hoped he would not think her very extravagant.

Cecelia was left to keep house for her father and Anthony, but Mrs. Trollope took Emily, who needed to see a doctor more perhaps than Henry. Tom had secured them dreary lodgings in Northumberland Street, and an old friend sent the well-known Dr. Harrison to the new arrivals. He paid several visits and held a consultation, but refused to accept any fee. When Tom came round to Northumberland Street after Henry's first examination, his mother told him cheerfully that she wanted a walk with him in Regent's Park, perhaps adding gaily for the benefit of Emily and Henry, who were dependent on her for all amusement, that for once she meant to take her time about returning to them. Alone with Tom, hurrying along at his side, she told him her sad story, forced even then to hide the tears of anguish lest passers-by see an old woman crying. Dr. Harrison had said that Henry would die—it was not too late to save Emily, but Henry must die.

She could not always conquer life, but she could accept defeat. From every battle something might be snatched—Henry must not know the cruel truth, and Emily should be saved. During that September fortnight she visited her brother Henry out at Fulham. He urged her to send Cecelia to him, since the Château d'Hondt must now become a kind of nursing-home—a sorrowful place, and perhaps an unhealthy one, for a sensitive young girl. Murray paid over to her the sum owing for *Belgium and Western Germany*, and thus in funds she took the Ostend boat from Tower Wharf with Emily and Henry. Tom came to see them off and found great difficulty in hiding his grief from the brother whom he would not see again.

Frances Trollope was ill with neuritis in her shoulders after her return to Bruges. Since her attacks of malaria in the United States, she had shown rheumatic tendencies. When she could use her arm, she adopted a stringent plan, under which she slept one night with a dose of laudanum, and the next night wrote three hours, bracing herself by frequent brews of green tea. Thus in writing *Tremordyn Cliff*, she averaged only an hour and a half of work out of the twenty-four— haste which allowed neither leisure to reflect on the intricacies of the plot, nor time for revision. The story, based on a woman's love of power, was fantastic and yet singularly interesting, both for the light it cast on the author and because of its vitality and the joyous culmination of the plot. It reflected the tragic situation through which Frances Trollope was passing; the young earl died from a hemorrhage, the wicked sister took laudanum, learned members of the Royal Society, such as Henry had longed to be, made their appearance, a clever but vulgar society woman represented what various critics had supposed Frances herself. These duplications were incidental. More surprising were the extravagant passages of great beauty devoid of sense; iambic verses which recalled the Elizabethan dramatists and were, it is safe to say, written from subconscious memories in intervals between drugged sleep and haggard waking.

Even if the therapeutic value of rest had been understood in the 1830's, it would have been impossible to restrain Henry. Thwarted in other directions, he turned carpenter, kept his room in the upper part of the house, whence he could be heard driving nails with feverish activity. He grew weaker but still rose daily, although at a late hour. Cecelia had been sent away to Uncle Henry's; Anthony, to Brussels. Emily was without companions, for her father had never been one, and her mother stayed with Henry and, with a care unusual in that day, would not let her join them except for a short time after tea. Then she was made to sit by the fire, the length of the room from her brother's bed. The mother placed herself between her children, where the wax end cast a dim light on the page from which her cheerful, reassuring voice read such words as she had long known by heart—"In my Father's house are many mansions. . . ." Her son had asked her to read the Bible to him. He uttered no complaint, suggested no fresh hope; but, as his vision darkened to the scenes of earth, seemed to attempt the exploration of a future in which all his family believed.

In Emily's case, the mother continued to deceive herself, and wrote Tom that the child would be well if only the house were not such a sad place. But "Henry is very bad. It is heart-breaking to watch him. God bless you, my beloved son. Write to me often. It is such a comfort."

Henry died at nine in the morning of the 23rd of December, 1834. It was the hour at which he had often wakened, and the mother trusted that his eyes were open to a day which promised better things. Immediately she wrote to implore Tom to come and bring Cecelia with him; but, made wary by her loss, she added that they must not sail unless "the weather were perfectly good." "We have suffered greatly" —thus courageously she thrust her anguish into the past. She asked them to come more for Emily's sake than for her own; Emily would be better for their presence. She sent a loving message to her other boy —now the younger son—he was her "dear, dear Anthony," to whom she could not write just then. But she had been able to write to Tom, and, reasonable as was her action, the letter and the summons expressed a preference to which Anthony was accustomed and which he could not easily forget.

Brother and sister reached Bruges too late for the funeral, but Tom went alone to Henry's grave near St. Catherine's Gate. As his pupils had been given up or had dispensed with his services, he spent the rest of the winter in Belgium, never exactly idle but seldom actively employed in his family's behalf. He did, however, consult a physician on the matter of his father's health, and cheerfully accepted the opinion that nothing serious ailed Thomas Anthony.

In February, 1835, Tom received a tentative offer of a place as master in King Edward's Grammar School at Birmingham. As he would not be eligible until he received his degree from Oxford, he crossed at once to make efforts to improve his unfinished status and to secure the position. In these laudable designs he was influenced by boredom, his mother's urging, and the fascination of travel, quite as much as by a virtuous ambition to maintain himself. He received his degree on April 29, 1835, and, while calmly awaiting the formal tender of the mastership, occupied his leisure in London in visits, desultory reading, and the unwelcomed supervision of his young brother, Anthony.

In the previous autumn, after Mrs. Trollope knew that Henry could not recover, she had sent both Anthony and Cecelia away from the Château d'Hondt. Anthony, who could understand a jest of which he was not the subject better than one on his affairs, was inclined to take seriously some family nonsense about his becoming an officer of the Austrian cavalry—provided he could learn French and German! His mother did seriously wish him to become something of a linguist, as well as to have him out of a house which was certainly melancholy and might be dangerous. One of that family of Drurys who had helped make Harrow famous kept an English school at Brussels; thither Anthony was dispatched to serve as an unpaid usher, whose recompense would consist of bed, board, and informal French lessons.

His size might have commanded the respect of small boys, for in his twentieth year he was tall, heavy, and admirably developed, but it was soon found that he was not a disciplinarian. On the two occasions when he took the pupils for country walks, he paid no attention to their scuffling. His inner life, enlivened by tales of his imaginary heroism and of the loves of beautiful young women, unrolled before him with such noise and color that he was entirely oblivious of his charges' yells and garments rent in warfare. The Drurys, down-at-heels themselves, sympathized with Mrs. Trollope and were correspondingly vexed with her loutish son. If the headmaster felt a qualm of conscience because Anthony received none of the stipulated French lessons, he could assure himself that the boy ate a great deal, was of no use to the school, and was at any rate not bothering his mother.

Mrs. Trollope had other and more influential friends. In late October, while Henry still lived, the Freelings sent word of an opportunity for Anthony to qualify as a clerk in the London Post Office at a salary of nearly £90 a year. Although the pay was small and the prospect of advancement far from brilliant, she could remember the time when her brother Henry had entered the War Office on the same footing, to commence a career as respectable as any Anthony was likely to attain. It was not a time to be nice, any pay was better than none, and her son would be employed instead of loafing.

Anthony, who had held few shillings in his palm, perhaps never more than one at a time, believed that £90 per annum would make a rich man of him. Leaving the Drurys, who rejoiced at being rid of their encumbrance, he paid his family a visit of leave. The wretchedness of the household shocked him out of his self-absorption. He saw them now, not as those who had of old thwarted and oppressed him, but as the suffering and oppressed. He fancied they were all dying. The strained exaltation on his mother's face terrified him; his father, entirely withdrawn from life, seemed a fit companion for the dusty churchmen of his *Encyclopædia*; Henry was lying, huge and gaunt, in an upper chamber, trying to find God; Emily was a transparent flower which must soon wither.

Sobered and sorry, he crossed to England for the first time alone, and put himself meekly in Tom's charge. His older brother took him to his lodgings in Little Marlborough Street, where he was living cheaply and well under the protection of an ancient domineering landlady. Next day Mr. Clayton Freeling was kind enough to escort Anthony to the grand, new classic Post Office at St. Martin's-le-Grand, and there Mr. Henry Freeling, son of the Postmaster General, conducted the private examination prescribed for all such candidates.

Anthony had not provided himself with a pen, and the one handed him was a wretched old quill. When, at command, he copied from a column in the *Times*, he blotted and misspelled. "That won't do, you know," objected the official, but the kinder Clayton, who was sponsoring the boy for his mother's sake, suggested that young Trollope was not doing himself justice and would be able to bring in a better sample of penmanship if he were allowed to prepare it at home. Mr. Henry Freeling agreed, but wanted to know the candidate's attainments in mathematics. Anthony said he knew a little arithmetic. Even this modest statement was an exaggeration, and he trembled, but luckily the examination was postponed until the next day.

He went back to Little Marlborough Street and implored Tom's help. The elder brother, glad to teach the humble, sat beside Anthony until, after many trials, he produced a fair copy of a passage from Gibbon. Armed with this specimen, but uneasy because he could not see any prospect of passing the examination in arithmetic, he returned to St. Martin's-le-Grand, to find to his disgusted relief that his testing was a farcical formality. No more questions were asked, no one so much as glanced at his beautiful "Gibbon." He was assigned a seat in the clerks' room and thus began his career.

At nineteen the junior clerk, A. Trollope, was strangely ignorant. He knew no language but English, in which his spelling and grammar were not faultless. He could have learned French, either at home in Harrow or in his six months abroad; Henry, with less schooling, was familiar with French, German, and Italian; Tom was equipped with French and Italian as well as the classic tongues. Music, science, the fine arts were but thinly represented in Anthony's vocabulary. He had read and reread Jane Austen, Cooper, Milton, Shakespeare, Scott, knew far more Latin than his grudge against his schools allowed him to acknowledge, and had had such scant practice in writing as an occasional theme and the keeping of a diary provided.

Yet the young fellow who came to London in October, 1834, was a great stride ahead of the boy who had driven his father to the Ostend boat in the preceding April. Journeys had been taken, alone or as a big brother in charge of a young sister. In Brussels he had caught tantalizing glimpses of a city second only to Paris in brilliance. At the Château d'Hondt he had realized how hard his mother worked and how the family depended on her. The belief that he would no longer be dependent on her, or on anyone, was immensely cheering.

His naturally acquisitive mind had taken in far less than its appetite needed, partly because he was shortsighted, but more because he was both obstinate and discouraged. What others thought either a vast mental leisure or the emptiness of the dullard was employed in that secret practice of embryo novelists, the systematic "telling stories to himself." He was ashamed of this habit, since it was absurd to play the hero, and felt an instinctive distrust of what might be permanently sterile. In order to lessen his sense of guilt, he would not allow himself to enjoy his tales too easily, and set himself tasks in the development of character, scene, and dialogue. A very sensitive mind had acquainted him with far more than he realized of human nature.

He was unhappy because his inner life was at variance with the outward forms by which he was expected to live. He felt confused and hypocritical. Conscious of disorder, he set himself a pattern to which he wished vaguely that he might attain. He would like to be a member of what he indistinctly imagined as the British aristocracy; a gentleman who had money but did not think about it, who lived on a country estate and belonged to London clubs, whose men friends were many; he was in Parliament; he rode to hounds in a pink coat: such a man Anthony would fain become.

In the Post Office he was at a disadvantage because he owed his place to influence. At Harrow neither "boarders" nor "day boys" would associate with the Trollopes because of their anomalous position as sons of a poor gentleman. The clerk, A. Trollope, was not shunned by his fellows, but his superiors and the Freelings soon had cause to criticize his behavior. He was untidy, his deportment shaded from the undesirably festive to the saturnine, his unpunctuality became a byword; nevertheless, when he exerted himself, he was more efficient than his steadier co-workers. In spite of the boy's yearning for order and stability, he ceased to visit his mother's friends, because they pleaded with him not to disgrace and disappoint her: Mrs. Freeling actually wept. At Christmas time, when news came of Henry's death and Tom went with Cecelia to Bruges to be absent many months, Anthony hid his grief and his loneliness under the behavior of a rowdy. An upstairs sitting room was reserved for the clerks, where they gambled surreptitiously for small stakes and gave occasional supper parties. He had little other social life.

In February, his mother, crossing from Ostend to see her publisher, was glad to find her boy still employed, but regretted his big cigars, of which he smelled abominably, and the fact that he was making no contacts which could be useful in his career. She had hoped that when he left the office at five he would find additional employment as a proofreader. Nothing had come of it.

She went back to the Château d'Hondt with the cheering news that Richard Bentley would finance her in a trip to Paris and publish in the coming October a book on Paris and the Parisians; she could afford to close the melancholy house in Bruges and transport its inmates to scenes of excitement and gaiety. It was her nature not to suffer a moment longer or a pang deeper than she must.

Seven years and seven months, like a period ordained in a tale of magic, had passed since Frances Trollope last had visited Paris. Twice since then she had crossed the Atlantic, and twice been dispossessed of her home; she had seen her children grow up and her husband grow old, she had passed the farther boundary of middle age; she had buried a son and become famous. Meanwhile the plastic hand of Time had been busy, and Paris too, was greatly changed. Frances Trollope had known the facts of Charles X's exile and Louis Philippe's accession to the throne, to which her old friend Lafayette—dead these three years—had helped to raise him. She could accept the new regime, but not the instability of social and political forms which confronted her within the well-loved city. She was really terrified at the sight of wild young figures in conical hats and extravagant costumes, inclined upon worse mischief than the American Indians—with whom indeed she had ardently sympathized. Yet in spite of such plagues, she found

Paris as charming as ever—the best place in the world, she said wistfully, for lightening a heavy heart.

She engaged an apartment conveniently near the best *salons,* and there installed her daughters, Auguste Hervieu, who was engaged to illustrate her book, and Thomas Anthony, who was included in the party because she was determined to have him treated by a good doctor. But the contribution of the Paris physician was largely an expression of surprise at learning that the patient was sixty-one and not the octogenarian he looked—an opinion gratifying to the young Trollopes, who felt that their parent had performed a remarkable feat in adding so considerable a figure to his age.

His ill health was an old story. She left him in the apartment and went out to look on Paris. In writing a travel book, she set herself a higher standard than she imagined necessary for the novelist, and with a business woman's acumen took notes of all that the prospective traveler or stay-at-home reader would expect to find in such a work.

In many distinguished houses she was an honored guest. It was a pity the "best people" of Cincinnati could not see her entrée, but, had they been permitted to do so, their experience would scarcely have qualified them to savor the distinction of such circles; it is to be feared that they would have criticized the slenderness of the collations. Her old friend Mrs. Garnett; Miss Clark, the English blue-stocking, soon to be the famous Madame Mohl; Princess Belgiojoso; and many ladies of the old regime welcomed her to their *salons.* It pleased her to see how each house offered a special attraction; here, the best professional musicians were heard, at another artists were lionized, a third featured the witty conversation of literary men, a fourth fathered political opinions in subtle disguise.

Charmed by the variety and cleverness of these soirées, Frances Trollope fancied herself presiding over a *salon* in London, where English humor might rival French wit. Heartier refreshments would be in order—hot suppers, not vulgarly ostentatious London dinners. Waking to her poverty and expatriation, she observed good-naturedly, "But I am not a great lady and have no power whatever to turn dull dinners into gay suppers, let me wish it as I may."

She was embarrassed by the broad talk of Parisians on subjects which she considered indecorous. Convinced that the French were as genuinely respectable as the English, she decided that their regrettable candor was due to their backwardness in drains. "When we cease to hear, see, and smell things which are disagreeable, it is natural we should cease to speak of them."

On every possible occasion she showed her reactionary political principles, carrying them into the realms of art and literature. She denounced the works of "the young men of Paris," of whom none was worthy to compare with her beloved Scott. The morrow, she said, would see Balzac dead and buried; Victor Hugo's wretched twaddle would never "heave the ground beneath the feet of Racine and Corneille." These young upstarts represented what she called "The Diabolic Age"—"The Idiot Era." Whatever they considered old-fashioned, they called *rococo*. "I am, I am rococo!" she boasted.

Tom, who delighted in surprise visits, appeared one May morning while the family sat at breakfast, with the news that he had taken his degree and did not expect to be needed at King Edward's Grammar School for some months, until a new building was finished. The Trollopes were again united, with the usual exception of Anthony, who was copying, loafing, dreaming at the London Post Office.

The mother was overjoyed to have a man of her family attend her on her jaunts about Paris. Unluckily invitations had already been issued for a morning party at Madame Récamier's. Tom's sisters had been asked, but neither Tom nor his mother thought it fair to substitute him for one of the girls. The occasion was really extraordinary, as Chateaubriand had promised to be present for a reading from his unpublished *Mémoires d'outre-tombe* and the number of guests was small but select, including the Duchesse de Noailles and the Duchesse de Larochefoucauld.

Although Mrs. Trollope dutifully described Madame Récamier as "the very model of all grace," and professed the greatest admiration for Chateaubriand, she reverenced these paling stars less for their accomplishments, for their conservatism, and for the soothing deference with which they treated her, than because they were the very epitome of cultured society.

One spring day she chaperoned a party of twenty young people, including her own, on a picnic at Montmorency. When luncheon had been eaten under the forest trees, picnickers explored on donkeyback the haunts of Rousseau and Grétry. Mrs. Trollope jogged on at the leisurely pace which suited her, talking to the old woman who owned the donkey, sympathizing with her troubles. She was feeling a British moralist's regret that Rousseau had not confined his literary works to the subjects of flora and scenery when her revery was brusquely interrupted by a wild-eyed boy on horseback who urged her to hasten back, as one of the party had been killed by a fall. While she had been indulging in good and even noble thoughts, the young men—son Tom among them—had been racing their donkeys. One of them, a certain William Makepeace Thackeray, had been thrown. A doctor was sent for and a near-by château opened its doors. Luckily the injury was not serious, and when Mrs. Trollope's party left Montmorency, young Thackeray's chance of recovery in such romantic surroundings made him more envied than pitied.

Frances Trollope could not always forget her sorrow. There were mornings when, waking early and unable to steel her will sufficiently for writing, she would walk to the Chapelle Expiatoire in the rear of the Church of the Madeleine, where she could count upon the solitude which was sometimes grateful even to her. The memory of the unfortunate king and queen over whose first obscure graves the memorial chapel had been built possessed for her a tender and romantic charm. Their tranquil statues reaffirmed what she was learning and had already learned, that all grief passes and the end is peace.

The Paris season was ending. Tom, with a plan of touring Belgium, was the first of the family to leave town. In June the others returned to the gloomy Château d'Hondt, where Mrs. Trollope compiled her book on Paris and the Parisians, and, when that was finished, began another novel.

Tom came and went all summer, bringing joy and taking it away. In early October he traveled to Birmingham to see how far the building of the Grammar School had advanced. Pleasantly assured that he would not be needed there for some time, he returned to the Château d'Hondt, to find that a grave change had taken place during his brief absence. His father was dying.

Morose and silent, the unhappy man had toiled until autumn over the hopeless task of his *Encyclopædia Ecclesiastica*. The *magnum opus* would never be finished. He knew no one else interested or qualified to complete his labors. To die thus was to consign not only his body but his work to instant oblivion: the living branch would perish with the dead tree. One little, desiccated lawbook, one published section of his encyclopedia, were the only permanent witnesses of his scholarship; the rest of his fortune was a mass of beggary and debts, exile, sons who had made poor use of their opportunity to become gentlemen and scholars. For Thomas Anthony, marriage had been a failure. His clever, too vital wife had reduced him to poverty, from which she could extricate herself and her children by the very qualities which had ruined them all; but he, an English gentlemen, could not survive his shame.

He took to his bed. Then the wife knew that he wanted her. She sat beside him and treated him with the tenderness she showed her ailing children. Words were not spoken, but the two at last understood each other. He, at any rate, loved her, and she knew her faults and recognized a generosity which uttered no reproaches. There was a deep honesty in the man, and on this she had built the family. Ill-matched as they were, neither could have found a better mate. Her restless brilliance would have polished to nothingness a weak man; his ferocious irritability have crushed or driven to fury a lesser woman. They had not been happy, but they had achieved more than either of them imagined.

He died October 23, 1835, at the age of sixty-one, after twenty-six years of marriage, survived by four of his seven children. The eldest wrote the epitaph for the grave beside Henry's in the Protestant cemetery of Bruges: it was in Latin with a subscription in Greek—*He has departed*. The family grieved at his passing, the more heartily because it was a great relief.

CHAPTER VI

The Break-up of a Family

1835-1837

THE grief which Frances Trollope felt at the death of her husband was for a past which no one else remembered—for the bright prospects of their marriage, hopeful days when the children were young, rare moments when the parents had been in complete sympathy, as used sometimes to happen when they made expeditions to picturesque scenes, or on those infrequent occasions when she had broken through his reserve and set free the love he bore her. Of such unshared memories she could not speak, and, otherwise, his death was but an end to suffering. His unhappiness had been dreadful, and his family were not callous; they had all had their share in his anguish, while her own distress had been intensified by the belief that the prolongation of his life endangered Emily's.

In the case of Henry, she had disregarded the doctor's warning against the dank Belgian climate and, blaming herself for this, she was agonized at the risk she ran by keeping Emily in the Château d'Hondt. Winter with its bitter weather was descending upon Bruges when she buried her husband. The funeral over, she fled with her little daughter from the melancholy house, leaving Tom to settle the business of lease and furniture at his discretion while they hastened to London. Schemes rather than purposes drifted through her harassed mind; she speculated on the advantages of a winter in Italy, or a cruise on any sea, to any port, if it might cure her child. She was eager to see Dr. Harrison, who seemed worthy of confidence because he had been right in Henry's case, but whom she valued more because he had formerly held out hopes for Emily.

Unless she made money Emily could not be saved. The expenses of her husband's funeral had greatly depleted her funds, while her last two books had brought in less than £200 each. A pressing London duty was to make new literary contacts, and her self-reliance, so necessary to such accomplishment, had never been less strong. She was not confident of possessing a public, she doubted her staying powers, and if Dr. Harrison were to give her no hope of Emily's recovery, she did not see how she could carry on the writing which alone could procure ordinary comforts for the child's last months.

The lodgings which Anthony had engaged for his mother were on Northumberland Street near his own, which provided a dismal view of Marylebone Workhouse. She greeted him with a cheerful face, assumed to spare her children's feelings, but Anthony, sensitive and inexperienced, supposed it imaged a hard heart and blamed, although he could not wonder at, her joy in release from his father's sickroom. He was almost surprised at his own grief; this was the end and he could never now be reconciled with his fellow-sufferer.

When Anthony had last seen Emily in Bruges, he had been convinced that she was dying. As yet she lived, but did no more. He was not well acquainted with his little sister, for he had been sent from the nursery to Sunbury, and then there had been Winchester for him, and for her the long years in America. He held a grudge against most members of his family, persisting in the not unjustified belief that they considered him a stupid, oafish fellow; but it was impossible for him not to be tender with this poor child.

For Emily was not to sail on sunlit waters or gather white violets in Italy. Dr. Harrison had said there was no need to take her out of England and, thus kindly, he bade the mother give up hope. All that remained was to secure Emily's comfort while she could, and she set out to find a house in the country. It could not be in Harrow, which had witnessed her husband's ruin, but it must be near her London publishers. Presently she told Anthony that she had decided on a house in Hadley, twelve miles from town; it would not be available until January, but as soon as she could occupy it, she hoped he would spend his week ends with her and Emily. Perhaps she added coaxingly, "I have only you to depend upon." In any case the barrier came down that winter, and he was good and loving to his mother and little sister. This was the first time he had been in a position of prime importance in the family.

Mrs. Trollope had other children for whom to plan, and as early as the end of November she realized that, since Emily's condition was hopeless, Cecelia must be kept away from her. To separate the affectionate sisters in the same house was unthinkable. Cecelia could not spend the winter in Belgium, where she was in Tom's way when he wished to relieve the tedium of business with visiting and walking tours. Fortunately she was charming to old people, and Lady Milman begged to have her for the winter at Pinner, near the Trollopes' former haunts. Thither went the docile girl, passing sorrowfully through London without Emily's suspecting that her sister was so near.

The mother had doubted her powers of sustained literary effort, but found she could write at Hadley for the old reason, that she must. There she finished her antislavery novel, *The Life and Adventures of Jonathan Jefferson Whitlaw*, dedicating it to the free states of the American Union. Although the "repulsiveness" of the subject matter and its propagandist aim brought a cool reception, the novel was vastly better than her earlier extravaganzas. The tone was deeply serious, the characters of the sadistic overseer and of Juno, the Negress "witch," were extraordinarily well developed. Fifteen years later, Harriet Beecher Stowe was to write in *Uncle Tom's Cabin* a simpler story with many points of resemblance. Hers was the better tract, but Mrs. Trollope's was the greater novel.

There was a rose garden belonging to the house in Hadley. The mother pleased herself by planning to have the invalid's bed drawn close to the window when warm weather came; on pleasant days stalwart Anthony would carry Emily out under the trees. But the child could not stay to count her mother's roses. She who, when a little girl, had watched in happy wonder the iridescent soapbubbles floating upward from her pipe, grew so ethereal that she seemed ready to rise with such celestial forms. Death had enraged Henry's haughty spirit, her father had turned from life in bitterness, but gentle Emily made no complaint. She died in February while the garden was frostbound; a hot wind passed through the chamber and the flax-flower withered.

Anthony was at Hadley, the man of the family, in a time when burials were exclusively the affair of men. He had never before seen

death, but conducted himself with decorum, attended to the distressing
arrangements, wrote to Tom and duly informed other relations, went
to Pinner to fetch Cecelia, attempted to console a mother whom grief
had broken.

Yet Mrs. Trollope's spirit had not, as she supposed, lost its
resiliency. Her world had so often crashed about her ears that she had
mastered a technique of recovery. It was necessary for a few days to
abandon herself to despair; then her will to live and to live joyfully
raised her up from the depths. To question the endurance of her affections would be idle: she only knew she had to live. The husband and
children whom she had watched over were exploring the wonders of
another land. She was convinced that the grave was but a portal, resting her hopes not entirely on the promises of Jesus as did the
Evangelicals, but on her own needs. God fulfilled every other craving
of the human heart; he would not leave this last and deepest hunger
unsatisfied; there must be life everlasting, because she wished to live
forever.

And she was free. Her three remaining children required neither
nursing nor her continual presence. Now she could speak as she
pleased without fear of frightening the sick or bringing on a dragging,
inconclusive argument with her husband. The repression she had
forced upon herself, although too often ineffective, had made her feel,
as she expressed it, like one "living in shadow, very deathlike
shadow." She had lost loved ones, but some were left to love: the
world was wide, and she had seen so much of it that strong assurances
of pleasure were added to the enticements of the unknown; she would
travel, write, sell her books. At fifty-six she wished to be under the
protection of a man, but not under his control: Tom could look after
her interests without interfering with her desires.

She wished heartily for his return from Bruges. The months after
Emily's death were lonely, for Anthony could come only for week
ends and, rather than allow Cecelia to stay in that dreary house, she
had courageously sent her to visit the Garnetts at St. Germains. Old
friends did not find Hadley too distant from London for occasional
visits, but it was Tom she wanted. Pleasure rather than business kept
him on the Continent, and when at length he reached the still un-

familiar house where Emily had died, his mother's greatest need of him was past. She was happily engaged upon her most famous novel, *The Vicar of Wrexhill.*

The enduring merit of this grimly uproarious tale of rural England is such as to suggest that Frances Trollope might have been a better novelist if she had never left Heckfield parsonage; there, pent within narrow boundaries similar to those which confined the Brontës and Jane Austen, she would have been compelled to concentrate her attention upon scene and character. Her travels, while deepening the culture of the woman, were disastrous to the novelist. The world had entertained her; and the instant a plot threatened to bore her, she picked up her characters and whisked them through foreign scenes, as much to refresh her own spirits as those of subsequent readers.

Nor was romantic love a congenial theme for a woman of her experience. Jane Austen respected decorous attachments; to the Brontës, passion was everything; but while Frances Trollope entertained the most cordial sympathy for young lovers, she thought of them as the beguiled, and could do no more for the enchanted than deck them with garlands of tender amusement. To Frances Trollope, sex was a homely and trying business. Indeed, the only passion she could deal with soberly was that of the will to power. She had no literary conscience, wishing merely to make money in an honest way and, incidentally, to establish British morality and Tory politics.

The Vicar of Wrexhill was her best book because she was suffering so greatly from Emily's death that, in self-preservation, she lost herself in her story. It had the merits of unity of time and place, simplicity of plot, and convincing characterization. Its satire was terrifying, and if, as was supposed, she used her friendly enemy—the vicar of Harrow, "Velvet" Cunningham—for the protagonist, outrageous. She was often insensitive to pain in others, though never to their bodily suffering, and it may have galled her pride to have Mr. Cunningham occupy the Julians she loved; but he was a genial, kindly man who in those early years had lost his wife and borne the deaths of many children.

The vicar of her novel was a rapacious and sadistic hypocrite. Evangelical readers were grieved or infuriated according to their dispositions at the delineation of the licentious parson and his female satellites; a "religious" poem set to the tune of a popular ballad revealed an erotic element in Evangelical worship which shocked the sincerely religious; satirical comments gleamed like ophidian eyes among the pages, and Hervieu's leering illustrations formidably enhanced the three-volume caricature. Toward the end of every novel Mrs. Trollope became deeply interested in her "good" characters and associated herself in their fortunes: the victorious close of *The Vicar* was heathenish in its fantastic suggestion of kettledrums and tomtoms.

By the time she had satisfactorily disposed of her villain, she had rid herself of the bitterness of her grief for Emily. Tom escorted her to London, where Miss Mitford, holding literary court in Russell Square, was surprised to see her old friend so blooming. She had indeed good reasons for feeling almost young again; Tom was with her, the new book was bound to sell, and, best of all, she was once again fired by the prospect of a change—she was going to Vienna.

When Henry died, she went to Paris; when Thomas Anthony died, she went to London; now Emily was dead, and she would travel farther and be long away. A fourth travel book would be the fruit of her journey. The facile Tom promised to be her courier; the Birmingham school was not even yet ready for his services, and, if he should be wanted, he protested cheerily that the authorities could summon him from Vienna.

He made himself useful. He offered to arrange in advance for the publication of the prospective book, and his mother, who disliked business, accepted gratefully. Whenever he went to London, he returned with books and pamphlets on Central Europe which they read with quickening hearts.

When Anthony came down to Hadley of a week end, his mother would descend to the nine o'clock breakfast, fresh after four hours of writing, bright with her old drollery. The talk centered tantalizingly on the journey down the Danube. He was not to see the great river with her, was unlikely ever to see it. Hervieu was going, Tom and Tom's college friend, Cecelia, even Coxe, his mother's maid, as a reward for her devotion through Emily's illness; but he, as always, was to be left at home. He could reflect dourly that he earned his keep, while Tom, his senior by five years, lived on their mother. But he must admit some justice in the dispensation, for Tom was a linguist, which he was not, and Tom had no position to keep him in England.

The large and cheerful party assembled at the disconsolate Anthony's lodgings on the evening of July 21, 1836, prepared to leave by the night mail for Dover. The array of luggage was formidable. German inns were reputed dirty, and Mrs. Trollope was carrying sheets and an ample supply of soap in addition to a generous store of tea.

After picking up Cecelia in Paris, the party crossed the border to Stuttgart, which Mrs. Trollope recommended to her countrymen at home as a city where everything but fuel was cheap and where Goethe and Schiller had been educated.

From Stuttgart on she yielded to the glamour of the past. She who was wont to call *romantic* "rather a silly-sounding word" was, except for her cynical view of young love, capable of intense romantic feeling. A picturesque scene, especially when it had been distinguished in history, enchanted her. Rising at dawn, she hunted down old castles with predatory zeal. In a locality where there was much to be seen, she broke her party into small bands which she dispatched on separate forays; the spoils of observation which they collected during the day furnished a feast in the inn at evening. To compare present scenes with those of earlier journeys was her special delight; the falls of Trenton, of the Genesee, of the Potomac were a gauge to measure those at Schwarzbach.

Yet she was physically a timid woman, terrified by thunderstorms, dizzied by heights, putty to the extortionate demands of innkeepers. Where dirt was found, she was squeamish, and much of Germany was excessively dirty. There were many things that Frances Trollope hated—tobacco, drunkenness, dirt, all allegories but Spenser's, prudery, going down ladders, Wesleyan chapels, decorated ceilings, poor cookery, camp meetings, the Young Men of Paris, Evangelicals —but the things she loved were so many that no one could count them.

During July and August the days were hot and bright, German summer weather with a swift evening chill. The Trollope party toured the country in horse-drawn carriages from which they descended to gather wild flowers, ripe raspberries, or the small sweet strawberries —often, to sketch a charming prospect.

At Salzburg Mrs. Trollope saw Marie Louise, no longer Empress of the French, but a shapeless, fat, and aging woman attended by a single maid and a lap dog the size of her dwindled fortunes. Mrs. Trollope hoped that Marie Louise did not know what she thought about her, but added that the ex-Empress did not look as if she were used to thinking about anything.

She was shocked to find no monument to Mozart in his native town; there was not even a tablet affixed to his birthplace. Having discovered the house, she made a point of pausing under the arch on her way to the hotel. Once when she was alone and night had fallen, the romantic old lady stood within the shelter of the courtyard and sang softly "La ci darem' la mano."

Yet even there she could not altogether forget old griefs, and there were new anxieties. Probably she reflected as little as possible on Anthony's insecurity; if he should lose his post, her brother could give him shelter—provided Anthony would accept shelter. Anthony's road would be his own; of all her children, he was the only one she could not influence except in the wrong direction. He had hinted at a longing to write, and she had advised him to read, meaning no insult, but trying to indicate a way to fill up the gaps in an education inferior to Tom's. He had been angry.

Yet on occasion she had been more stern with Tom; and Tom's problems she could not so easily put out of her mind, because he was constantly with her. He was an excellent courier, but could scarcely spend his life in squiring his old mother. He had only a shadowy position in view, coupled with antiquarian tastes and an unsubstantiated belief in his literary powers. The young man whose *Sketches by Boz* were making such a success in London was more than a year Tom's junior.

Of her three children, Cecelia worried her the most because she was so delicate. Mrs. Trollope admired Cecelia. Her heroines, well-bred, sensible girls, fragile, a little cold, a little remote, seemed patterned on her young-lady daughter. Although Cecelia was not much like her mother, they were a devoted pair and shared a trait more surprising in

Mrs. Trollope than in the girl—both were timid. When they felt
danger approaching, they met hazard hand in hand, Cecelia's pressure
meaning, "Are you scared, mother?" while the answering squeeze
conveyed, "Yes. But don't tell."

The three young men had their private adventures. Tom went to a
ball of shepherds and shepherdesses where the girls waltzed like
finished London belles. He visited libraries, and, his German failing,
held confabulations in Latin with the monks of Salzburg. In every
town it was understood that Tom was the leader of the party; he discovered himself on one register as "Mr. Passport—and Family." Yet
he was not always the most rational of guides. On the evening before
embarking on the Danube, he walked his mother down to the river
to see the boat. She was at once painfully reminded of the wooden
rafts she had seen upon the Mississippi. Here was a Noah's Ark cabin,
crammed with freight and crowned by a wooden bench precariously
nailed to the roof, whence one could dangle one's feet over the river.
Upon this Stygian craft her trusting son expected her to spend a week.

As she looked at the ladder descending to the cabin, recollections
of her dizzy spells and of the broken hips of other old ladies filled her
with dismay. At last she remarked ambiguously that if there were
"much real danger, we know that those who take care of us would not
let us undertake the expedition." Whether she referred to Providence
or to her son Thomas Adolphus, the latter was touched by her courage,
and was early at the wharf the next morning to construct a ten-foot pen
on the bow of the deck for his mother's accommodation.

The party of six set up housekeeping in this topless box. Tom im-
provised a cupboard in which they stored bread, fruit, and cold
cooked meats. Books, drawing-boards, paper were at hand. Nothing
could be more charming. The jolly crew beguiled their tasks with
song; an English naval officer appeared mysteriously and shared his
binoculars. There was much to see on either bank, while innumerable
cranes and wild ducks haunted the shallow reaches. A fleet of barges
for which thirty-two horses were counted approached and passed.

But toward the day's end the sky darkened and lightning shot from
the cloud fringes. The travelers were to pass the nights at inns, but
long before the boat docked the storm had broken. Mrs. Trollope's

little feet, less sure these latter days, slipped on the landing-stage; she was frightened and cold. At the inn, the young folk thought it great fun to sip hot English tea before the German fire, but Mrs. Trollope listened unhappily to the drumming of the rain. If they were in for what Americans called "a spell of weather," how could she keep Cecelia dry? How protect herself against the wrath of Coxe?

The morning realized her fears. Her party stowed themselves in the cabin among evil-smelling casks and tobacco-smoking Germans. Feeling ill, Cecelia sat outside on an overturned barrel where water-spouts from overhead and spray from the oars continually drenched her. Her little face turned blue and her mother was wondering desperately whether to drag her in to smother or leave her there to drown, when the English officer wrapped Cecelia in his cloak until she looked like Undine in the midst of her fountain. The young men slept on dizzy heights of packing-cases, Coxe sat in grim silence— Mrs. Trollope wrote her book.

That night was passed at a sinister-seeming inn. In the morning Tom settled the bill; but as the party embarked, the landlord demanded a second, much larger sum. When it was refused, he seized Tom's throat while villains sprang up about him, one armed with an axe. Mrs. Trollope screamed. She preferred to be robbed rather than sonless, and implored the captain to satisfy the villains. Payment was made, but at the next landing stage the captain told Tom how to lodge a complaint, and this in due time brought restitution.

The next day was fine, and Mrs. Trollope sat as regal as Cleopatra on her barge; the next it rained and she said scornfully, "how very unnecessary it was to float down the Danube in a deal packing-case." At night a niggardly landlady refused a fire and said it was not customary to change the sheets for new arrivals. But such deprivations were forgotten when they passed the fortress of Durenstein, where, beneath a turret window, Blondel the minstrel had sung to Richard the King. The English party indulged in romantic reveries on *Ivanhoe*, *The Talisman*, and the Wizard of the North.

Vienna, reached on September 1, proved the most elegant of cities. In those days, the inner walls provided a three-mile promenade dominated by the spire of St. Stephen's Cathedral. One of the buildings was eight-storied—high as Babel. The capital was reminiscent of New Orleans in its pageantry of costume and of race. The shadowed baroque grace of the palaces delighted Mrs. Trollope, but the gilded monuments of the Counter Reformation distressed her. She was a reactionary but no mystic, and Rome was as alien to her as the Evangelicals.

Even before their flat in the Hohenmarkt was ready to receive them, Mrs. Trollope conscientiously visited a kindergarten, a prison, a blind asylum, a school for deaf-and-dumb children, and the crypt of St. Stephen's, where thousands of mummified corpses were huddled, coffinless.

The music of Vienna disappointed her. The opera was not what she expected, and she judged that the best singing in the city was to be heard in the Jewish synagogue. But she had a treat in old John Cramer's playing the piano with exquisite precision in spite of stiff, aged fingers, and once more she told herself that she was "rococo, incorrigibly rococo."

The lady whom Cincinnati society had ostracized, and who had just floated down the Danube in a freight barge, was presently invited to dine at the British Embassy to meet Prince Metternich, Austria's greatest statesman, and his beautiful Mélanie, known as the haughtiest woman in the Empire. Tom and Cecelia were included in the small and select party. The Prince himself took Mrs. Trollope in to dinner: "She has made a conquest of my husband," wrote Mélanie, "and he appears to have made one of her." The Princess liked the little Englishwoman immensely, and wrote in her diary, "She is a good-natured woman, very simple and natural, an attentive listener, and grateful for every mark of interest. She is 45 or 50 years old [actually she was almost 59], and though she looks a trifle common, her conversation bears the marks of the best education."

Prince Metternich knew a good press agent when he saw one, and Mrs. Trollope did not disguise her sympathy with the absolutist principles he was striving to uphold in Europe; indeed, one of her varied reasons for wishing to visit Austria had been the desire to study the Metternich system in action. The Metternichs were all that was gracious. Princess Metternich set an evening early in the following week for her to dine at the palace. A portrait of the exquisite Mélanie by the inevitable Hervieu set the seal upon their intimacy, and Mrs. Trollope's access to the highest Austrian society—short of the Court itself—was assured.

Just before Christmas, Tom was at last summoned by the school in Birmingham. For his own sake, his mother could not be altogether sorry, and her new, great friends would look after her. Prince Metternich and the British ambassador, good-naturedly determined that she should miss nothing of Austrian pageantry, procured her an invitation to the installation of the Knights of the Golden Fleece, which provided as splendid a sight as Europe could offer. Innumerable festivities followed, ranging from Princess Mélanie's Christmas party for children to the celebration of a young archduchess's marriage; there were balls in great, glittering rooms beside which those of London seemed insignificant, and costumes which made her compare London fashionables to shepherds and shepherdesses. At a reception given by the Turkish ambassador, Cecelia won a flowery compliment from the host when he said to her mother, through an interpreter, that "Providence had accorded her great happiness in letting her see her daughter grow to such perfection."

The lavish attentions of Europe's highest aristocracy threatened, for a time, to turn her head. Her honesty had suffered a little from the painful experiences which followed *The Domestic Manners of the Americans*. When she admired, she tended to be too enthusiastic. A trace of snobbery pervaded her first accounts of the glittering balls at the French ambassador's and the dazzling receptions at the Princess Metternich's, although it is not improbable that she was less taken in by such scenes than she expected her readers to be. Happily, she remained long enough for her common sense to reassert itself—long enough to realize that even Viennese society could be tiresome and had its unpleasant distinctions.

The Trollopes were well placed for observing the gradations of society, since they had access to the aristocracy but were not, like them, debarred from contact with the wealthy bourgeoisie, the connoisseurs of art and music whose women wore magnificent diamonds, and whose men, whatever their business, were always known as "bankers." There were more Jews in Vienna than she had ever seen before. But Mrs. Trollope had never learned to feel at home with Jews and did not now choose to make the effort.

In every rank she found the passion for waltzing equally fervent. Even a middle-aged servant woman could, she learned, hire an escort to a ball; and cooks had been known to demand high wages on the grounds of the exorbitant cost of dancing partners. Mrs. Trollope heartily approved this universal gaiety and love of pleasure. She liked people to enjoy themselves, and looked on waltzing as the ideal antidote to political discontent.

Although she was opposed to the Roman Church, Holy Week in Vienna moved her deeply. On the Wednesday, she and Cecelia were among the small number of guests in the Court chapel. Next day they shared a bench with the Turkish ambassador, watching while the Emperor and Empress washed the feet of paupers. On Good Friday mother and daughter went to St. Stephen's and to the Court chapel, but the Easter parade was nothing; it was cold, they drove to the Prater, but the carriages of the nobility were closed.

May came and her lease expired. The last evening in Vienna was spent with the Metternichs. She left an amazing list of friends—the Archduke John, the Countess Zichy-Ferraris, Count Dietrichstein, Princess Odescalchi, Princess Vasa, Grand Duchess Stephanie of Baden, Archduke Francis, intriguing Archduchess Sophia, whose five-year-old son Franz Joseph was to rule the Empire far into the twentieth century.

Anthony supposed, a little enviously, that his mother had turned conservative because she had found Austrian archduchesses to be "sweet." He was too young to remember that her political conversion had taken place in America, where she had gone a radical to return a Tory. Since her experience of democracy across the Atlantic, her attitude had been entirely consistent.

The journey home occupied six weeks. On June 10, 1837, she found the roses blooming in her garden at Hadley. She had fled from grief, and returned to find that sorrow had not stayed for her.

CHAPTER VII

The Postal Clerk and His Relations

1837-1841

THOUGH it was long before he could recognize the fact, Anthony Trollope entered the English Post Office at the very moment when that remarkable institution, roused from decades of lethargy, was preparing to join and further the march of nineteenth-century progress. The fresh wind of reform which blew through England in the 1830's awakened in its course the Post Office from somnolence. But if Anthony perceived what was happening, it was with regret for the passing of the old rather than with enthusiasm for the new.

Two great innovations lay at the heart of the new process of growth and adaptation. The English mail coach, which, as if weighed down by its romantic encrustations, had never exceeded a speed of ten miles an hour, was being replaced by the noisy velocity of the steam railway. All English life was tremendously accelerated. The letters of London bankers and men of affairs, which had formerly spent days in transit, now reached their destination overnight.

Less spectacular but as far-reaching was the revision in the principles of postal finance. Traditionally, charges had been borne by the addressee, who paid a substantial fee on receipt of his letter, its amount determined partly by the weight and partly by the distance it had traveled. The system not only entailed a vast amount of bookkeeping but positively discouraged the public from using the mails. Poor folk could not afford to accept letters except in those rare instances when their correspondents had been able to get them franked by an M.P.; delicate-minded people hesitated to write what would cost an impecunious friend money to read.

But, in 1837, when the stubborn young clerk, Anthony Trollope, had been working for the Post Office for some two years, a retired schoolmaster, Rowland Hill, made his epochal recommendation of a uniform postal rate of a penny a letter, to be paid in advance by the sender, by means of affixing a stamp. This eminently practical scheme, although hotly opposed by conservatives in and outside of the Post Office, was so effectively backed by business and professional men that three years later the modern system of penny postage became an established reality. The volume of correspondence rapidly doubled, and the business of the Post Office continued to increase in almost geometric progression throughout the century.

A young man gifted with imagination and a desire to comprehend the changes which were transforming life in his native land could not have been placed in a more stimulating situation. But Anthony ignored his opportunity. In so far as he concerned himself with official matters, he stood with the reactionary bureaucracy which bitterly opposed Rowland Hill's beneficent scheme. He may have retained some romantic affection for the mail coach, although he had not, as a little boy, joined his brothers in their infant expeditions; but he would always be a man fated to take scant comfort in old ways, yet suspicious and hostile in regard to the new. In after years he grew sufficiently reconciled to change to call himself a conservative liberal and to become a follower of Gladstone. But long before he arrived at intellectual maturity, the realization was unconsciously borne in upon him that the most salutary reform is not all gain. In his mother's sense of the word, he was "rococo"—a lover of the old.

In these days he neither studied nor practiced philosophy but nursed his grievances against the world, clinging stubbornly to his role of a lower clerk in a hidebound government office. The inferior position which he occupied was due rather to his poor education and sullen manners than to deficient capabilities; if there lay concealed in him the talents of an executive, he had neither the opportunity nor the desire to display them. Impatient of routine, intolerant of discipline, he smoked and gambled many an evening with the office force, and thus lost money—to his deep disgust and shame.

Uncle Henry Milton seems to have told him rather sharply that he would be better off in his rooms, reading a good book and drinking tea of his own brewing. Anthony, who was at least twenty-one at the time, listened wrathfully to the avuncular suggestion and, without acting on it, stored it up for future repudiation. He had not learned to like tea, the light in his chamber was not good to read by, and he wished rather to live, and to write, than to read other men's books. But he was not altogether the Philistine he proclaimed himself; he studied a bit of French and Latin, and there were evenings spent in absorbed reading and long afternoon hours passed in the National Gallery, where he would have slunk guiltily out of sight had he encountered his connoisseur Uncle Henry.

Although he was not so hopeless a character as he fancied himself, his surly manners were enough to worry his mother's friends. He had heard a good deal of talk relative to the fine post in Birmingham to which Tom was destined, but he could take a bitter satisfaction in telling himself that Tom, five years his senior, was an idle fellow who lived on their mother. Anthony did not wish to be indebted to her, and when he lost money at cards, was furious because he knew that eventually the loss would be his mother's, since she would pay his debts; thus his superiority to Tom would be reduced and they would both be sons supported by a laborious old woman.

Anthony had two friends, two other outcasts, whom he organized into the Tramp Society. This was his first club. One member, John Merivale, had been with him at Sunbury, the school of grisly memories. To the brilliant Merivales and Drurys, John was as Anthony among Miltons and Trollopes—a lazy, unpromising misfit. What John's father had once said of his son would have been equally applicable to Anthony: "He is a dreamy, imaginative sort of boy—exorbitantly attached to the reading of novels and works of fiction, and excessively fond of his most intimate associates, whom he does not select from among those who are most exemplary either for school learning or strict regard to discipline, but chiefly for some resemblance to himself in their rambling pursuits and propensities."

Nevertheless, John Merivale was an engaging and vivacious boy. Indeed, the three members of the Tramp Society, slipshod as they seemed to their critical families, shared a cultural background of taste and breeding. But the lads at the Post Office came from a lower class, so that Anthony was as much out of place in the clerks' room as he had felt at Winchester and Harrow. Then he had been nobody, but now he was in the ridiculous position of a fallen lordling ignominiously condemned to labor.

His insubordinate manner, formed upon such models as his ancient bullies and the arrogant masters of Harrow, incensed his superiors. Colonel Maberley, the Chief Secretary, choleric himself and, unless Anthony maligned him, ungrammatical, once implied that young Trollope had committed theft: "The letter has been taken, and, by God! there has been nobody in the room but you and I!" "Then, by God, you have taken it!" bawled Anthony, thumping the desk with such vehemence that a bottle of ink splashed into the Colonel's eyes. The entrance of the private secretary with the missing banknotes cleared Anthony from the accusation, but removed neither the ink stains nor his superior's dislike.

When his mother returned from her year on the Continent, she persuaded Anthony to come and live with her and Cecelia at Hadley, refusing to accept money from him. If he had not been the most shiftless of boys, he would then have been comfortably off on his salary; but as far as her observation carried, he seemed no better off than when maintaining himself. She had no conception of the difficulties of a young man involved with professional moneylenders.

She had enough else to make her miserable that summer in the knowledge of her own debts and of Tom's dislike of the school at Birmingham. The clever mother was unlikely to realize that Tom's distaste arose from the aristocratic principles which she had done her best to inculcate, and Harrow and Winchester to foster. He had been bred up to believe that capacity was an inheritance of the upper classes; he judged his pupils incapable of becoming classical scholars because their fathers were tradesmen ignorant of Greek and Latin. It never occurred to him that he ought to prepare a lesson. In that period of universal condign punishments, it was his duty occasionally to thrash a pupil, and he could ill endure giving pain, especially to one who was not a gentleman's son. When the big fellow strode into his classroom with his academic gown proudly flapping, he was the Wykehamist doomed for a time to occupy a lesser sphere and give it tone; he felt that nothing more could be expected of him.

His mother was much disturbed when gossip reached her to the

effect that Tom contemplated resigning from the school. He had waited
years to obtain the post, he might wait years and not gain a better;
England was full of unemployed young men of good family. Unluckily, Tom's sweeter temper had little of Anthony's persistence.
She wrote her trying elder son: "I am fifty-eight years old, my dear
Tom. And although, when I am well and in good spirits, I talk of what
I may yet do, I cannot conceal from you or from myself, that my do-
ings are nearly over. Believe me, I should be perfectly miserable did
I look forward to your remaining where you are; for I see, and feel,
that you cannot be happy there. But give me the great comfort of
knowing that you have sufficient strength of mind and resolution to
stick to it for a little while, till we see our way clear before us."

Tom wrote promptly that he had never entertained the idea of
resigning. His mother begged his pardon, and spared him comment
on those traits of character which had made the rumor plausible. She
was continually propping him up against onslaughts of discouragement and sloth: when the manuscript he had written was rejected, she
wrote, "You must keep up your courage as I have long kept up mine
amidst very hard work, and much anxiety"; and after a little summary
of her literary disappointments—"All this I bore, and worked up
against it all;—with what result you know." He could more easily
accept the validity of her experience because, although she was
necessarily of an elder generation, her career was of the present; in
letters they were almost contemporaries, as she had herself been
publishing for only six years.

Tom came to Hadley that Christmas of 1837 to a house crowded
with guests. His mother was in debt, despite the success of *The Vicar
of Wrexhill*, but would not curb her hospitality. Anthony was there,
with a young colleague from the Post Office who was in love with
Cecelia. He was John Tilley, a merchant's son, in his twenty-fifth year,
who in his eight years in the Post Office had risen to be first junior
clerk at a salary more than double Anthony's. Everyone liked him,
and his excellent qualities lent a faint radiance to Anthony.

From Tom's conversation Mrs. Trollope learned that he had not
been altogether dreary at Birmingham. He was one who could follow
his uncle's recipe for a quiet life with placidity and enjoy sitting the

evenings through in his room with his pipe, a book, and a pot of tea.
He was never, like Anthony, uncomfortable in women's society, and it
was his great pleasure to dine at his headmaster's and talk to the
latter's wife, beautiful Mrs. Jeune. To the end of his life, Tom
acknowledged gratefully the charm of a small galaxy of lovely ladies,
such as the accomplished Mrs. Fauche of Ostend and the incom-
parable Mrs. Milman.

Mrs. Trollope did not like the house in Hadley enough to stay there
longer. It was too far from London, inconvenient to her publishers
and to the shops where Cecelia's trousseau must be purchased—for
Cecelia and John Tilley were to be married—difficult of access for
Anthony. In any case, she was not ready to make a permanent home in
England, certainly not until she had seen Italy, the country which
since her girlhood study of the poets had never ceased to tug at her
heart. The Trollopes' expenses were so great that even with constant
writing she could not keep her family free from debt. It was plain that
something must be done, something must be decided, were she to be
prosperous and her children happy.

Tom came once more to Hadley. It was in June of 1838 and the rose
garden was again in bloom. His long legs paced the trim walks, his
mother trotting briskly at his side. They discussed his career—that
future which at twenty-eight was as vague as any castle in Spain.
Neither felt it incumbent on Tom to continue in a field so ungrateful
as teaching. He admitted his love of foot-loose wandering and said
that, if he wrote travel books, they would provide him with the means
of travel. His mother spoke enthusiastically of the notes he had
gathered during a recent ramble in Brittany. He said he might return
thither with staff and knapsack and give the country a thorough going-
over; such an expedition would be too strenuous for her, but since his
mother was already famous, her name as editor of his book would
carry weight.

As they walked up and down the garden, they formed a partnership; vague assurances were wafted abroad to the effect that Tom
would henceforth be the mother's accredited man of business; if any
financial terms were decided upon, they remained a secret between
the principals. The son could assure himself that he would be giving

up much valuable time and some liberty; the mother was certain that she could support both of them, if he had overestimated—not his literary ability, but his powers of labor. She would get what she wanted, a reputable and pleasant way of life for Tom, and for herself freedom from loneliness. On this occasion her action was the result of careful thought and she would not have to conceal a foolish blunder with her unfailing wit. Few partnerships have been so justified by the results.

But Anthony felt her choice as an affront. Tom had been drawing more than twice Anthony's salary; why should he quit the school to batten on their mother? Perhaps he had been dismissed. Or, if he had left merely because he disliked teaching, did the family suppose that Anthony was enamored of a clerk's life? So Tom was to be his mother's literary agent; had not Anthony done his share of racing up the stairs of publishers with her manuscripts under his arm? He did not dream that the compliment was less to Tom's ability than to his own integrity; but the shrewd mother knew her boys and understood that easygoing Tom, with none of Anthony's bad habits, was a drifter, in need of constant encouragement and support. Yet at its root Anthony's charge of favoritism was justified, because she loved Tom more. He was charming, kindly, a great conversationalist, like her own people, the Miltons. Anthony was a dour fellow, regrettably like his unfortunate father.

Yet it was partly for Anthony's convenience that she moved from Hadley to London that summer, settling at 20 York Street, Portman Square. The three children were much with her, Anthony going each day to the Post Office, Cecelia and her mother collecting the trousseau, Tom in and out of the house. Mrs. Trollope entertained lavishly, friends of the family, friends of her children, literary folk. It became generally known that her elder son proposed a career similar to her own, except for the output of novels, although that veteran author, Colley Grattan, gave the tyro advice that Tom never forgot—and never followed—"Fiction, me boy, fiction and passion are what readers want!"

The marriage between Cecelia Trollope and John Tilley took place on February 11, 1839. The mother saw to it that the first wedding of the family, that of her only daughter, was done in style. The gaiety helped her through the occasion; her thoughts were less cheerful, because the young couple would not live in London but in Penrith in the Lake District, whither the bridegroom had been transferred.

But she was too busy to grieve. She had found a new Cause—her heart was set on the improvement of conditions among children employed in English factories. Lord Ashley (later Earl of Shaftesbury) was sponsoring a bill to shorten the hours of work for these unfortunates, who often began to labor in the mills at five years of age and were besides subject to gross mistreatment. Mrs. Trollope, a conservative with a sense of social responsibility and a love of children, proposed to Colburn that she write a novel on the subject. On his agreement to publish it, she set out with Tom within a fortnight after the wedding, armed with letters from Lord Ashley, and traveled to Manchester in search of material by the exciting and hazardous new railway.

The fruit of these researches, *The Life and Adventures of Michael Armstrong*, was marked by literary grace as well as by humanitarian zeal. Hampered by an improbable plot, by frequent dissertations on undigested political economy, and by an archaic tone, the book remains better than readable. Mrs. Trollope's portrayal of the little hero's bewilderment at the unequal treatment accorded him in public and in private was too poignant to be droll. She was fond of children. While Dickens lamented his own unhappy youth and Mrs. Browning grieved for children far away, and more like gnomes than humans, Frances Trollope wrote about them with the authority of the competent mother who had reared a family. In this novel she used the expulsion of the Trollopes from Julians Hill, as Anthony was to do in his own time. The latter part of the story was tiresomely impossible, but the happy ending, a double chorus of rejoicing, atoned for many frailties.

Lord Ashley's bill had been designed to limit these infants' working day to ten hours, but even so modest an object was not obtained until 1847, after Mrs. Trollope's passionate interest had long lapsed. Colburn had published her story first as a serial. By the time it appeared in book form, her conservatism had taken fright at the sullen temper of the working classes and she had resolved not to meddle further with social problems. A preface stated that she had given up her project of a sequel, because of the "scenes of outrage and lawless violence" by which the Chartists had meanwhile offended her.

Manchester's gloom had depressed her volatile spirits. With her partner and courier, Thomas Adolphus, she escaped to the Lake District to visit Cecelia in her new home. While they were in the region, they made a call on Wordsworth which Tom considered an unprofitable experience. Even before crossing the threshold, Tom offended the old poet by expressing surprise at a bay tree planted in a sunless spot by a doorway.

"Pooh!" ejaculated Wordsworth crossly, "what has sunshine to do with it?"

While Wordsworth droned to Mrs. Trollope, the bored Tom indulged in a *sotto voce* conversation with a nephew of Southey, an old schoolfellow who happened to be present. On the homeward walk, Tom made his mother admit that Wordsworth talked only of himself, but she said serenely that she liked to hear him.

Back in London, Tom left his mother busy with *Michael Armstrong*, and went with Hervieu to Brittany to begin his own literary career. He had succeeded in talking Colburn into advancing an expense fund for a walking tour. The two young men explored regions unknown to the British tourist, although even in the remotest villages they happened upon Oxford students, sequestered to read for their examinations. Tom and the faithful Hervieu rose before the dawn and walked long stretches to breakfast at some primitive inn. They hobnobbed with peasants, sketched and described the women's quaint attire, the relics of druidism, medieval chapels, village fêtes, and scenery.

The two-volume work which resulted from this delightful tour was written in Mrs. Trollope's manner, slightly modernized. This, which may be called the Trollope style, was a family possession. Henry had used it; it would be Anthony's; in a measure, Cecelia's; and both Tom's wives were able to produce it. In these early days Tom shared his mother's distrust of facile theories of moral progress; he too loved the "good old times"; yet his partiality was not rooted in political convictions, but resulted from his strong individualism and the inherent love for antiquity which Winchester had fostered.

He returned from his travels in Brittany July 23, 1839, to find his mother ill with tonsilitis. He offered to escort her on another visit to Cecelia in Penrith, and Mrs. Trollope, whose health was always better when Tom was with her and a journey was in prospect, found herself able to make a start in three days. Cecelia was settled in a charming house and gave every sign of perfect contentment with her excellent young husband. He was near her brothers in age and, like them, an enthusiastic walker. Mrs. Trollope used to waken John and Tom at half-past four in the morning so they could be out on a ramble and back again at the hour when her son-in-law must occupy himself with postal duties. She spent the hours of their absence at her desk. The family breakfasted together at nine, and Cecelia, Tom, and Mrs. Trollope passed the rest of the day in visiting and receiving guests from among the pleasant families in the neighborhood.

So cheerful was this summer visit, the way of life so congenial to the mother, who liked her early mornings free for writing and—her work out of the way—wished to be always occupied in society, that she was inclined to buy or build a house in the neighborhood. But as yet she was not ready to settle in England. This year she was going to Paris with Tom, next year to Italy.

The season of 1839–1840 in Paris was her most brilliant winter, surpassing even that spent in Vienna. Once more she had her niche in the *salons* of Madame Récamier, Miss Clarke, and Princess Belgiojoso; her circle of acquaintances widened to include Lord Granville, the British ambassador, and Lady Granville, Lady Caroline Bernard, the Princess Czartoryski. She was presented at Court, where the Duchesse de Nemours recalled meeting her in Vienna and said with flattering simplicity, "I have read all your books, Mrs. Trollope, and I like them *so* much." King Louis Philippe bestowed on her his famous half-grin and asked if she would like to revisit America: she suspected satire and thought up several witty retorts but was too prudent to give them utterance. On Valentine's Day Lord Granville gave a magnificent ball to celebrate the marriage of Queen Victoria to Prince Albert. Mrs.

Trollope regretted that she could not have Cecelia, who was near the royal bride in age, as her companion, and wrote, "I should like to have all my three sons"—for she counted John Tilley among them—"and my elegant daughter there with me."

One of her titled friends was not a social asset. It must have seemed odd to those who knew Mrs. Trollope's moral standards that she made no attempt to keep her sons from sharing her acquaintance with the beautiful, notorious Rosina Bulwer. But to Mrs. Trollope she seemed an affectionate, gentle creature who had been cruelly treated by her husband, Bulwer Lytton. Rosina Bulwer was trying her own hand at novel writing, and looked for assistance from the veteran and advice from the veteran's son, both of whom tried to instill some sense into her pretty, silly head.

In March Anthony himself took leave and came over to pay his mother a visit. She had never seen him so inclined to society. He squired her to party after party and, as far as she could see, enjoyed himself. Then he returned to office drudgery and Tom went down the Loire on a hunt for material for a second book. In June all three were in London, shrouded in gloom, for the youngest of them lay mortally ill at his lodgings.

Perhaps his gay mood in Paris had risen in despair rather than in gladness of heart. He had been having a very bad time. He felt that he was accomplishing nothing with his life and that, if opportunity arose to do better things, he had neither will nor energy to compass them. Without a decent income, he must remain a nobody; the only means by which he could make money was his mother's. He could not write history because he had no education; plays were doomed to failure when the playwright was ignorant of stage conventions; how could he, who never went anywhere, write travel books? There remained the novel. But he could not force himself to a start. This telling stories to himself was not a manly occupation; he had a suspicion that the characters were impatient to escape from the narrow confines of his mind.

Debts made him avid for money. A tidy gnome of a fellow who came to the office to dun him would sit patiently, murmuring now and then a dull refrain, "I wish you would be punctual." The neat little man was a usurer who extracted £200 for an original loan of £16.

Increase of salary could not stem the tide of a moneylender's calculations. In any case Anthony was already conditioned to think and care too much about money; it was to be a lifelong obsession.

He was shamefully entangled with a country girl. The innocent young fellow had called on her at her mother's, and the girl had suggested marriage. Scarcely liking to tell her that he did not care for her enough to marry her, he hung about the house hoping to find a tactful way of getting the notion out of her head. A few days later her mother came storming into the very Post Office, to demand in raucous tones, "Anthony Trollope, when are you going to marry my daughter?" His soul curdled at the roughness of her voice, at her monstrous bonnet, and the market basket on her arm. He saw himself in the dock, and heard the giggles of his fellow clerks.

Overanxiety about money had been his as long as he could remember, certainly since the time when he learned that his school bills were unpaid; here was a new preoccupation—the plight of the man who no longer wishes to marry the girl whom he has encouraged. His mother had written a book in verse on husband hunters, and he had shared the family mirth and disgust, but this was a little different: suppose one had allowed a girl to believe one meant to marry her and lacked the pluck to shatter her illusions? Out of such vexatious fancies, and from his attempts to rationalize his conduct, there gradually arose his unique understanding of human nature—his own and that of others—as something to comprehend, to explain, not something to be condemned except in those rare cases where the conduct was definitely ungentlemanly, un-English.

These miserable anxieties preluded his all but fatal illness. No one knew exactly what ailed him. The symptoms resembled asthma, but the doctors said it was not asthma. Often he was delirious, sometimes he seemed in a coma. Mrs. Trollope was wild with anxiety. In Paris a few months since, he had been a strapping young fellow; now he was as emaciated as she remembered Henry. Cecelia's baby was almost due, but she could scarcely think even of Cecelia while Anthony was so ill. She had as help in nursing him two young sisters brought by Dr. Elliotson, who attended Anthony. To have admitted them was but another of those injudicious actions with which her life was sprinkled. The Okey girls were hypnotic patients who had been dismissed from the hospital where they worked because of their highly unde-sirable gift of seeing a familiar called "Jack" at the shoulder of any patient who was about to die. "Jack" might be seen by an Okey in any place, at any time—on an omnibus, elbowing a stranger in the busy street. He was indescribable, formless; but "Jack" he was, and always fatal, if he appeared at the shoulder of the victim. To introduce the Okeys to the sick room of a sensitive young man was absolute folly. They reported "Jack" as being often at Mr. Anthony's knee, but never reaching the shoulder.

Whatever the nature of Anthony's illness, he began at last to recover. His mother was less willing than sensible Tom to admit the passage of the danger point. The older brother had been gravely anxious in the earlier course of the disease and had stayed much in the house, where he busied himself with the literary affairs of the lovely but exasperat-ing Rosina Bulwer.

When Anthony was obviously out of danger, Tom escorted his mother once again to Penrith, in order that she might see her first grandchild and namesake, little Fanny Tilley. Anthony followed in early autumn but missed Tom, who was off to explore unfamiliar re-gions in France. Tom had expected to take his mother to Italy, but events in the Near East made a general European war seem a prob-ability, and Mrs. Trollope, whose hardihood was nicely marbled with timidity, not only refused to adhere to the original plan, but said she was afraid to go even to France because of the anti-British sentiment prevalent there.

In spite of his mother's fears, Tom took two trips to France that year and on the second settled himself for the winter in a charming little apartment near the Rue de Rivoli, where he thoroughly enjoyed his first independent housekeeping. He neglected none of his mother's friends and made many of his own, going everywhere, chatting with and listening to persons of every class, critically observing the uni-versal anxiety behind the impenetrable front of the social structure. He accepted both the tense situation and its inevitable result with his customary benignity; the eventual overthrow of the regime seemed a pity, but he was not responsible.

His mother meanwhile finished two books of her own and edited his *Summer in Western France*, stamping the signet of approval on her son's denunciation of the modern Frenchman and even passing leniently over his allusions to the pleasures of a good cigar. She had not lost her dislike of tobacco, but this smoker was privileged.

Then, in her partner's absence, she found herself involved in a squabble with her publishers. She had, as so often, been in too much of a hurry and had placed one of her books with a rival firm; now Colburn, to whom she had originally pledged herself, threatened in reprisal not to publish the other, and added the hideous suggestion of printing the story of her nefarious conduct. She fell ill from worry, expecting to be branded as "a greedy, grasping, conscienceless woman." How could she explain to the world that she had not intended to defraud Colburn, but needed the money to build a house— for this was now her plan—near Cecelia in Penrith?

Henry Milton, himself the recent author of a clever and sardonic novel, read one of the books in question and pronounced it not worth getting into trouble over; he suggested that she lay it aside. But his sister had bought a building lot of three acres and intended that the book should pay for it. Her brother consulted a lawyer, who assured them that Colburn had no legal case and would have to publish; but, the crisis over, Mrs. Trollope's sluggish literary conscience was aroused; she sent *Hargrave* to Tom, begging him to read it and make what changes he thought advisable. Tom performed the task to everyone's satisfaction, and Colburn actually made a considerable sum out of the novel.

While the little tempest had been blowing over, the international crisis had been resolved and the way was at last clear for the long-dreamed-of Italian journey. Rather than make a start on April Fool's Day, she left Penrith on April 2, 1841, met Tom in London, and, not without trepidation, ventured to Paris, which she found to her surprise as safe and as charming as in old days.

Tom was able to secure only one seat in the Lyons diligence, so he stowed her inside and with hearty good cheer mounted to the top and the fresh air he loved. Sixty hours of incessant traveling brought them to their destination. The road over Mont Cenis had just been plowed through after the snows of winter. Tom left the diligence and strode ahead to await the party at the pass. His timid mother looked with delight at the magnificent scenery, and yet could scarcely subdue her terror lest the tearing wind or the missed step of a horse hurtle the carriage into the abyss.

Thus she entered Italy, the land toward which she had yearned since her girlhood in Heckfield parsonage. The poetry of Italy's sons had comforted her in exile, and solaced her in the more recent distresses of her troubled life. Yet the book she wrote on Italy was inferior to her earlier works of travel. At home there were people who had spent years to her weeks in the country, and she was afraid of expressing callow views on art and of subsequent attacks by hostile critics. Her remarks on architecture, sculpture, and painting were soundly conventional, but whatever charm her book possessed was due to her own little misadventures and the expression of those opinions which did not accord with those of other people; thus, she tried wickedly to whack off with a hammer a bit of Petrarch's house but, foiled by the excellence of its construction, contented herself with the appropriation of leaves of the passion flower which she hoped—but did not believe—had bloomed for the poet; she had an interview with the Pope, who, having been assured that she was really "the literary lady," sagely remarked that there were a great many books in England, but that he had not read them.

She did not neglect to seek out her Cincinnati protégé, Hiram Powers, the young sculptor who had been Henry's friend, and, through him, became acquainted with another sculptor, the superbly handsome Bostonian, Horatio Greenough. She wrote that such young men proved that, "however slow the progress of art may be in the United States, it is no want of native talent that occasions it." Zealous to admire Americans when it was possible, she sought an introduction to Edward Everett, the former governor of Massachusetts, and subsequently eulogized his poetry in her book. On him she made the customary impression of "a sprightly old lady, of very ordinary appearance, lively manners and conversation," who was "particularly civil and complimentary."

Of all the cities in Italy, Florence pleased her best, but if she dreamed of making a home there, it was a prospect for an old age which she thought privately would not descend upon her for many years. Though she was often weary and occasionally ill, though she spoke often of birthdays, she believed her resistance—and her legs—compared very favorably with those of her contemporaries.

Anthony's illness had prevented her from being with Cecelia during her daughter's first confinement. News came that a second baby was expected, and the grandmother, who had a poor opinion of the conduct of the earlier event, determined to hurry to Penrith. In February she recrossed the Alps on a sledge which she contemptuously described as "a miserable box half full of snow," and after a brief rest in Paris hastened to Cumberland. She did not, as she had expected, find Anthony in London.

CHAPTER VIII

The Son Is Reconciled with the Father

1841-1847

ANTHONY's illness of the early summer of 1840 was followed by increased depression. He feared that his personality was disintegrating, that ruin would be the final stage, and that not long deferred. Such hopeless discouragement resulted less from the petty faults to which he attributed his condition, than from the secret sense of guilt which the creative nature suffers while it remains sterile. At twenty-five it seemed to the young man that he had already thrown his life away.

That summer the office force gossiped about the forthcoming appointments of traveling clerks to the surveyors of the postal system in Ireland; the youths debated whether or not to apply for these situations. The positions held out the promises of change and increased pay, but there were those who said a surveyor, new to the dignity of keeping a clerk, would mistake him for a body servant and expect him to clean his boots. Anthony, convinced that if he asked anything for himself he would be rebuffed, kept silence during these discussions.

By August all the positions had been filled, but almost at once a report was received at St. Martin's-le-Grand that the clerk sent to the west of Ireland had been dismissed. It had been Anthony's duty to open and read the letter. Without pausing to reflect further on what he had been vaguely desiring all summer, he strode into Colonel Maberley's office to suggest, in his truculent way, that he should take the place of the incompetent clerk. Colonel Maberley was delighted at the prospect of being rid of him, but, as Anthony found later, he did not appoint him without sending a private letter to the Irish surveyor prophesying that young Trollope would not last long in the service.

The thing was done. There was no time to consult his mother and Tom, who were in Italy, nor did he wish advice. He went to the kind old family lawyer, John Young, a kinsman of Great-uncle Meetkerke, and asked a loan of £200 with which to buy an outfit and clean up his London debts. That the sum was immediately forthcoming suggests that Anthony's character in financial dealings was less shady than he fancied. His new salary would be a nominal £100, instead of the £140 he was now drawing, but the allowance for traveling expenses would raise it to £400. What he had heard of Ireland made him think it just the place for such a renegade as himself; he would fit nicely into that land of brawls and whisky.

On September 15 he arrived in Dublin, went to a dirty hotel, and after a wretched dinner, called for a bowl of whisky punch. The effect was pleasing while it lasted, but, like the rest of the Trollopes, he cared little for hard liquor. As the exhilaration wore off, he was terrified to think of himself alone in a strange country. But he assured himself that Ireland could hold no worse suffering than what he had undergone, and that if he could find anywhere on earth a fitting home it would be among these wild and wretched folk, infinitely poorer than himself. This difference was what he must count on; he would have more than twice the money he earned in London, and it was money which ensured the stability in life for which he hungered. The obsession grew stronger as his prospects brightened.

He was already a rich man among the Irish. Ireland's old evils, high rents and high taxes, had never borne more heavily upon the miserable peasantry. Population was growing, and small farms were being consolidated into great estates; the tenants were evicted and, moving on, were forced to compete for other land at still higher rents. Nearly a half of the rural population lived in one-room mud cabins, and fully half depended for existence on the potato crop. Violence and lawlessness were rife. England had sent over commissions of investigation and built workhouses. She had even granted political rights to the wealthier Irish Catholics. But Daniel O'Connell, the beloved leader of priests and peasantry, was teaching men to believe that there could be no lasting amelioration of the situation until union with Great Britain was dissolved and a parliament sat in Dublin. In 1841, the year of Anthony's arrival, O'Connell commenced an agitation for "Repeal" which swelled to vast proportions. Young Trollope, although never a believer in Irish Home Rule, saw the evils of the situation and realized that his countrymen ought to share his vision.

Dublin was the center of the Irish postal administration—a city of tall brick houses and quiet squares which had almost forgotten the bustle of fifty years since, when it had been a political capital. There centered also the culture of Ireland, with a bad theatre, a dull society, and one first-rate periodical, the *Dublin University Magazine*. Irish literature scarcely existed as an independent movement. Irish writers, from Maria Edgeworth and Thomas Moore to Charles Lever, had written primarily for London readers and left the treasures of Celtic legend and folklore to the ignorant Catholic peasantry. The idea of drawing upon this storehouse for a distinctively Irish literature in the English language was in its infancy.

Young Trollope discovered that he liked the Irish people. He liked them for the happy-go-lucky ways which made such infinite trouble for the Post Office—their habit of sending letters, often containing little gifts or sums of money, under long and indecipherable addresses, frequently ending in a direction to "any dacent neighbor"; the assurance with which they would requisition the services of the postman to write their letters from dictation. He liked the guard on the mail coach, McCluskie, who heard him discoursing on the merits of donkeys and remarked, "A fellow feeling makes us wondrous kind." The Irish treated him as a grown man and a gentleman. No one seemed to have any suspicion of the ignominy he had left behind him in London.

Neither incapacity nor lack of education had made him troublesome in the London office, but he had found the copying of other men's letters an irksome business, and any executive powers he might possess had not been tested. In Ireland he commanded men. He rode from one little Connaught town to another, on horseback or in a jaunting car, and in his progress he redressed wrongs. Arithmetic, dreadful in prospect, was not so bad when it took a practical shape; he stood over a wretched defaulting postmaster while the culprit taught him the necessary forms.

As for the gentry, he was amazed at his popularity with them. His chief duty was to investigate complaints. One bitter day of snow and sleet he drove up to a countryhouse in an open jaunting car to see if the owner could be pacified. He expected a tussle, for the man's letters had been hot and angry, but he was met with insistent hospitality; his bedroom was ready, dinner was all but on the table, brandy and water must be very hot, lest the guest take cold—as for complaints, the host said he had perhaps been hasty, and Mr. Trollope might say whatever he pleased about him in his report.

Anthony loved dancing, and the pretty daughters of the Irish squires liked the big young man as a partner. His chief was Master of the Hounds; with some daring Anthony bought a horse and began to hunt, thus asserting his social equality. The surveyor was not sure he approved of his clerk's hunting, but the young fellow was, of course, a gentleman, and in any case he did not know how to prevent him.

At last the boy who had never been allowed to join the games of Harrow and Winchester had found his sport. To ride with young men as an equal made him almost unbearably happy. The concentration demanded by the hunt freed him from the petty preoccupation with his awkwardness and from his inexplicable sense of guilt. And the effort to be first, the hope to pass all others and obtain the prize, seemed to gather together in one great burst the toil of a man's lifetime, to epitomize a career.

He fell in love, not with an Irish girl. When he met Rose Heseltine at the resort of Kingstown, near Dublin, she was on a visit from her home in Yorkshire. She was some five years younger than he and, like his mother, a little woman and splendidly healthy. She had a sense of fun and a certain decision of character. To call Rose Heseltine a woman of mystery would be absurd, and yet, historically, she remains a character almost unknown. She proved the very woman for Anthony. In his deep need to be established in the conventional sense, he could never have been happy with an exotic, an intellectual, or a girl of heart-shaking beauty. His darling must be poor, so that he could do everything for her; the more he did for her, the more secure would he feel himself. In spite of his burly appearance, he was chivalrous rather than passionate. In general he did not much like women, except when they were past the age of love-making.

In September, 1842, Rose and Anthony became secretly engaged. If there was romance in their courtship, they kept it to themselves. The revelation of personal tenderness was contrary to his nature. Very likely he had already arrived at the sound and essentially materialistic view of matrimony which he was to show in so many novels. A girl not conspicuous for wealth, family, or beauty, but sensible, healthy, intelligent to a point, and sympathetic—one who could be taken for granted and did not require too much of a busy man's attention—this was the ideal wife.

When he took his summer holidays at Penrith, he was careful not to mention Rose Heseltine's name to his mother. At Carlton Hill, the new house planned and built by Tom and Mrs. Trollope, there was so much to show him, so much for him to admire, that silence on his own affairs was not noticed. Yet he had much more to say for himself than in the old days. The brothers walked about the three acres of land, admiring the great numbers of trees Tom had planted with his own hands. Why, he asked, did they call it Carlton Hill? Tom did not know, but the owner of near-by Edenhall had said it ought to be called St. Michael's Mount, as the spring by that name was just at the foot of the hill. The old gentleman was superstitious; he had told Mrs. Trollope the house would be unlucky because a fairy-well had been disturbed by the builders. An American, a Mr. Longfellow, had just published a poem on the Luck of Edenhall—all wrong, too, as to sources. It was a question whether Mother would be contented to stay quietly in one house.

Anthony no longer envied Tom the privilege of being his mother's courier. He envied him nothing, and, secure in his own sense of worth, was surprised to see what a likable fellow Tom really was. The five years between them closed like a seam. When Anthony returned to Ireland, Tom went with him. Of Cecelia they had seen little because she was busy with her babies, but the families had frequently dined together and driven to more distant points, and John Tilley had shared Trollopean rambles.

From the very moment of landing at Kingstown, the usually imperturbable Tom was amazed at Ireland. It must indeed be a wonderful country which had so metamorphosed Anthony, and now that he saw it for himself, it had all the delicious foreign air of France, entered for the first time. He called upon his brother's chief, intending to do the handsome thing by Anthony and show the Master of the Hounds that the young man's relations were presentable. To his astonishment, no butler, but a bare-legged, very dirty servant girl opened the door. The family were pleasant, certainly, but their style of living not what one expected of gentlefolk.

Tom had wished to make a walking tour in the mountains, but as Anthony had work which must be attended to immediately, he suggested that Tom go on alone through Cliveden and they meet above the Killeries. Tom, impressed by the gravity of his brother's affairs—it was evident that the chief valued him partly because he did all the work— went ahead with a letter to a friend of Anthony's who immediately asked him to dinner and apologized for a perfectly good fish, saying he would have bought a turbot but could not give the absurd price of half-a-crown! Tom thought Anthony might be right in saying that the Irish, though desperately poor, were not so improvident as the British liked to call them.

In the course of their walking tour, the brothers went to an election at which a platform crowded with several hundred persons collapsed. The Trollopes speedily picked themselves out of the crush and began to help others, among them a small priest who was howling at the bottom of a heap of men. When they got him out, he cried, "Tell me your names, that I'll pray for ye!" They admitted cheerfully that they were Protestants, but he shouted, "Tell me your names that I'll pray for ye all the more!" Tom was never tired of observing the varied aspects of Catholicism in different countries. The Roman Catholic was more congenial to the High-Church Trollopes than the Evangelical of their own faith. On Anthony's first coming to Ireland, he had dined with a Roman Catholic family, and been warned next day that such a proceeding would bar him from Protestant society. Nothing could have made a Catholic connection so alluring as this ill-bred admonition.

A day of thick cloud and bursts of sunshine glorified the walk above the Killeries. Mist and sleet seeped through their greatcoats and back at the inn they sat, as Tom said, like Roman senators, wrapped in thick blankets, downing roast goose and whisky punch. Between the brothers, family feeling was henceforward reinforced by sympathy and affection. Tom had always liked young Anthony, and now he admired him. As for Anthony, it was healthful for him to be on the new terms with Tom by which he was accorded superiority in his own line and accounted a good companion.

Mrs. Trollope liked her own company only in small doses. When her sons went to Ireland, she began a round of visits, working, while her hosts slept, on *The Barnabys in America,* an extremely clever book with a flavor like Gogol's *Dead Souls,* and on *Jessie Phillips,* another novel of social implications which concerned itself with the Poor Laws.

Early rising gave her a long day which, after breakfast, ought, in her opinion, to be passed in such amusements as were enjoyed by other ladies who did not write books. At Penrith in winter, she could make a dress for her little granddaughter Fanny's doll, give orders to the cook, drive over to see Cecelia, dine out at one of the few houses within carriage distance; but all this was insufficient to appease her appetite for life. It was cold in Cumberland, and at sixty-two even the most energetic body suffers from icy draughts.

Worst of all, she knew perfectly well that even a new house could not keep Tom in Penrith. If he meant to write travel books, he would have to go on traveling; and, in any case, she knew she could not hold him. Nor did she wish to be imprisoned by her own house, which, new as it was, had its tenants of old ghosts. In public she could wear a gaiety which became her better than widow's weeds, but when she was alone, she thought of her griefs, of lost children and an unhappy husband; she was afraid of losing her memory and the countless calamities which overtake the old. When April came round, she told Tom she wanted to get rid of Carlton Hill.

Many people would have felt it necessary to apologize for abandoning a house which had been built at great expense, finished less than a year since, and set off by grounds in which innumerable young trees had been planted by a son's devoted labor. Not so Mrs. Trollope! Tom sent her off on a round of visits while he packed away the silver and china and made arrangements with the auctioneer. On May 11 he wound up affairs in Cumberland, and went to London to see Mrs. Trollope's publishers, his Uncle Henry Milton, and a few of the family's numberless friends, and on June 1 joined his mother down at Exeter at Cousin Fanny Bent's.

There, a week later, mother and son reached further momentous decisions. The old longing for Italy rose within them, and they determined to live in Florence for a year; then, if they liked the city sufficiently, they would settle there. Tom, English of the English, had no scruples about leaving his country. It never occurred to him that wherever he was could be other than England. As if to prove that she was not too old to start life again, Mrs. Trollope celebrated their pact by an eight-mile walk with Tom.

Before leaving England, they went with Fanny Bent to visit Frances' older sister Mary, who entertained them at an Exmouth hotel because her husband, old Commander Clyde, was either too ill or too cantankerous to have company at home. On September 1, 1843, the self-exiled pair left England for the Continent.

To Anthony, that same month of September, 1843, was even more memorable. Tom and his mother had merely changed their residence, but he had begun his life's true labors. John Merivale paid him a visit, and, as in the old London days, the two walked for many miles about Drumsna, where Anthony was stationed. On one such ramble, they came on a countryhouse fairly new but deserted, with the broken gate and grass-grown driveway which showed that life had gone away. The sight had a peculiar poignancy for Anthony. In his intense desire for security, a house had become a symbol. His neglected and distressed childhood had been punctuated by abandoned dwellings; and even when the home seemed most permanent, he had twice been reft from it, to be sent to Sunbury and to Winchester. The attachment other men felt for a mountain or a fair valley view he felt more intimately for the *house*, and to this peculiarity both his nearsightedness and the family taste contributed. As he looked at the sad, deserted home at Drumsna, he asked John Merivale to read its riddle: what ruin, what far journeyings, what tale of sons driven into exile by harsh fathers? The place continued to haunt him after John's visit ended, and very soon he was writing a novel.

The deserted house was not accountable for the entire plot. A chance encounter, another man's novel, and a true tale of the 1830's, each exerted its influence. Gerald Griffin's *The Collegians* had moved Anthony deeply; once, while walking around Lake Killarney, he called the attention of a companion to the spot where the murder on which Griffin based his narrative had actually occurred. The gentleman in whose company Anthony was rambling was a priest, a stranger. When he evinced no interest, Anthony began impetuously to relate the pathetic incident of Eily O'Connor's death. At this the priest turned on him abruptly, put both hands on his shoulders and said solemnly, "I stood on the steps while he was hung." He was the murderer's first cousin.

Anthony was more deeply indebted to another true story which went about Ireland by word of mouth: a good priest happened on a starving lad who had been in hiding a year because he had murdered a revenue officer. Utterly discouraged, the culprit was on his way to give himself up. The priest questioned him and, discovering his heathenish ignorance, told him bluntly that he was not fit to be hanged, but promised to visit him nightly in order to instruct him, so that eventually he would be prepared for that consummation. These visits the good man made at great personal risk, until he was able to utter an approving, "I never knew a man fitter to be hanged than yourself." The boy gave himself up, and was not hanged but transported.

Anthony made slow work of his book. After a day in the saddle, he could not drag himself out of bed in the morning, and there were letters to write to Rose and brisk plans to make for their future. In the next spring, 1844, after the engagement had lasted two years and a half, he intimated to his family that he was about to be married.

Although Tom and his mother planned to come to England in May, and the wedding day was set for June 11, Anthony made no point of their coming to the marriage. The ceremony took place in Rotherham in Yorkshire, where Rose's father managed a small bank. Perhaps Anthony did not wish to strain his new relations' resources by the descent of his family; perhaps he thought they might disapprove of his impecunious bride; but probably he believed that his marriage was principally his own business.

He took his young wife to Cecelia, now installed at Carlton Hill, when the roses which Tom had set out two years before were at the height of blooming. The whole family, John Tilley, Mrs. John, the children, Mrs. Trollope and Tom, were delighted with Anthony's

choice. In her turn Rose was charmed by her mother-in-law. She liked
to hear her talk, her industry gave Rose ideas for the management of
Anthony's literary career, and she was amused at the old lady's zest
in arranging picnics and pleasure excursions and quite won by her
kindheartedness when she fetched her daughter-in-law early morning
tea because she might have taken cold in the rain.

Everyone was polite and approving of everyone else; it was not yet
known that Anthony was writing a book. Mrs. Trollope had a great
deal to tell them all, which she had not wearied herself by writing.
There were ghastly details to add to Tom's brief account of her illness
in January; if he had not dismissed the doctor who was on the point
of applying leeches when she was all but dead from weakness, she
would not be sitting in Carlton Hill to tell Anthony all about it. And
the amazing thing was that the new man had cured her by almost the
same treatment which had saved dear Tom's and dear Henry's lives
when they nearly died from that *drain* at Harrow; port wine had saved
them, all three. And the doctor wouldn't take any payment.

She had gone to more balls and parties in Florence than ever before
and seldom got to bed until three in the morning, but she was always
up again and ready for her drive. She had seen a great deal of that
talented American sculptor, Hiram Powers, whom she had known as
a boy when he and poor Henry had such good times together in Cincinnati, and she had enjoyed the company of an American lady, a
Mrs. Brooks whose brother was Mr. Edward Everett. Socially, the
high point of the winter was, of course, her presentation at the Pitti
Palace to the Grand Duke and Grand Duchess of Tuscany, who paid
almost no attention to anyone else, not even to Tom.

Charles Dickens, whom she had met in London in 1837, had brought
his wife to call, and Sir Henry Taylor had visited her and they had
seen a great deal of Mr. Landor. She liked Rosina Bulwer; how could
she help it? She was so good-natured and so very beautiful, even if
quite devoid of sense. Let her hearers imagine this: the fair Rosina had
complained of being ill, and when she was advised to get a doctor, had
wept and called them *cruel*, saying they knew she had not a guinea to
pay him; and at that moment the jeweler sent in to ask payment for
the silver spurs and collar for her dog Taffy, who was to be *knighted!*

Their house in Florence was next to Santa Croce and they had watched Mr. Sloane's new steeple going up.

But, of course, the awful event of the year was the flooding of the Arno, a third of Florence under a yellow, turgid mass of water. Tom had seen strange sights from Giotto's Tower. There had actually been a cradle with a baby sailing along, until a rope was thrown to draw it in through a window. Their own house in the Via dei Malcontenti had been flooded to the depth of five feet.

After their return to Ireland, the Anthony Trollopes moved to the town of Clonmel, as he had been promoted to the southern district. He felt a lack of cordiality on the part of his old friends toward his young English wife, and saw that as a married man he himself was less popular. He had reached a stage where he could put up with a few slights, but it did not please him to have Rose unappreciated, and he was glad to leave, especially as Clonmel was a larger, more civilized place than Drumsna.

The young people could not afford a house, and spent the next few years in lodgings. Anthony hunted, traveled about southern Ireland on postal affairs—he was laying up an amazing knowledge of the country—and wrote. Rose believed in him. Even to her he did not read aloud the chapters as he finished them, but she read them to herself and told him her opinion. From the first, he put reliance on her taste and it is not unlikely that Rose had a share in pruning his work of the overexuberance of the mother and the rambling propensities of Tom —both of them natural to the Trollopes as a family.

In July, 1845, almost two years from its first germination, the book was finished. He took it with him to Penrith, told his mother in bleak tones that he had completed a novel, and asked her if she could dispose of it to her publisher. She was not to read it; he wanted her services as an agent, not as a critic. He fancied that the pleasant atmosphere of a year ago had grown chilly; he was not aware that the ice came from him. He thought his mother's expression dubious; John Tilley, Cecelia, Tom—and this especially distressed him—all looked as if he had walked with shoes on holy ground. It seemed that even Cecelia fancied herself as an authoress, and had written a High Church novel. Mrs.

Trollope promised cheerily not to read the manuscript and to do her best to place it in London. As a result of her efforts Newby agreed to publish on half profits.

The Macdermots of Ballycloran is a tragic, deeply moving story of Irish peasants and decayed gentry. It shows greater imagination than invention, and with good editing could have ranked among the very finest of English novels. Anthony, who became the chronicler of manners, began as an inquirer into the sources of life. He attempted to pull up the plant, root and branch, in order to trace and to reveal the processes of growth; later he was forced to content himself with the outline of leaf and flower.

It is possible that Anthony feared to have Tom or his mother read his novel lest they find in it a resemblance between Larry (the decayed gentleman) and his ignorant, luckless son Thady, and that other decayed gentleman of real life, Thomas Anthony Trollope, and his blundering son Anthony—although the persistent analogy may have been unperceived by the young author himself. The tragedy of hotheaded, affectionate, untaught Thady lay in the fact that his mental resources were not sufficient to enable him to deal with his circumstances. With a natural desire for order, his life was chaotic. When, after killing his sister's lover, he escaped to the mountains, he discovered that a masterless life among masterless men was more dreadful than any punishment which law could inflict.

Old Larry, imbecile from his misfortunes, turned against his son, drove him from his presence, openly hoped for his hanging. But the son was not vindictive; he pitied his father, and explained that ruin had robbed him of his faculty of judgment. Thady forgave Larry, and in this forgiveness Anthony drew a line through the debt his own father owed him. It was expunged forever and they were reconciled. But, though he had pardoned Thomas Anthony, he was not through with him. A long process of evolution would raise that gentleman to the peerage; eventually he would become England's prime minister.

Thady was hanged. Unconstrained by his public, Anthony would seldom have yielded a happy ending, and *The Macdermots of Ballycloran*, written before he understood the necessity of pleasing, draws to the pathetic close which Trollope's natural pessimism and his

sense of reality demanded. There was also a necessity, surely unconscious, arising from his identification with the hapless, ignorant lad,
which suggested the expiation of his own guilt in the death of Thady.
His insolence, his share in the contempt for his father which his
mother had inspired in the family, was thus purged. The reconciliation was complete.

The book still lay at Newby's when on March 13, 1846, a son, Henry
Merivale Trollope, was born at Clonmel, in an Ireland where all but
the rich were starving. The summer before there had been the familiar
rot on the potatoes, but worse and more general than in the memory of
man. No stores had been held over from the previous season, and
famine was abroad. Ireland knew well that face, but this was bleaker
than ever in her past. Its rigor changed her history. That year and the
next, tens of thousands starved to death. Men and women who had a
few dollars emigrated to America. Villages fled *en masse* to the workhouse. Fever attacked the starving peasants, and there was neither
medicine nor care to give them.

Such dreadful suffering helped Trollope to bear his private grief
at the postponement of his book and its unheralded publication in
1847—the year of *Wuthering Heights*. But the Irish famine ruined
any slight chance *The Macdermots* might have had of being a success.
The Irish had little money, at best, to purchase books, and English
readers, never prepared to welcome anything from that quarter except the humorous holding-up to mirth of Irish foibles, were deadly
sick with hearing of the suffering across the water. The government
had sent over food, and private philanthropy had done something;
but who wanted to read a book about the wasteful Irish?

Anthony received no statement from his publisher and, of course, no
money. Harper and Brothers republished it in New York, an honor
of which he was probably ignorant. He saw no criticisms—the only
English review, that in the *Athenaeum*, carefully sidestepped all the
issues he had raised—and no one wrote to him that he had read the
story. To himself he protested his complete indifference, but he would
not talk about it even to Rose, taking some comfort in the belief that
no one in Ireland knew he had written a novel.

CHAPTER IX

The Florentines

1847-1850

$\mathcal{B}$Y 1846 Tom Trollope and his mother were confirmed Florentines. Three winters spent in draughty palaces had made them at home in the small permanent colony of English and American residents, while they remained alert to welcome the more interesting of transient visitors to the Tuscan capital. In summer, like other foreigners, they left the city, going either to the baths of Lucca—where, as Charles Lever said, "cheapness and glorious scenery are happy associates"—or taking a more extended tour in cooler climes. In 1846, with one of the parties of congenial people dear to the mother's heart, they toured the Tyrol and Bohemia and stayed for some time at Gräfenberg in Silesia, where Tom took the cold-water cure for his rheumatism. Despite a vigorous constitution, Tom suffered from an arthritic condition and from headaches similar to those which had afflicted his father; he was also beginning to grow deaf.

In the following spring, Tom and his mother, who had not seen Anthony and Cecelia for two years, set out on a leisurely journey through the Riviera with England as their objective. They spent the first of May in Paris, and saw the last *fête du roi* in the garden of the Tuilleries—when the next spring came on, Louis Philippe was an exile. A fortnight in London was occupied with business, which included not only visits to publishers but formal dinners where literary celebrities mingled. Mrs. Trollope's friends found her changed; she was thinner, and showed that she was growing old. But she had not lost the faculty of startling society; gossip had it that the Bishop of Solway in her *Three Cousins* was actually Bishop of Winchester.

During their stay in England Anthony's first novel was published. Small wonder if she quietly tucked her author's copy of *The Mac-*

dermots of Ballycloran into her valise, intending to read it when she was home again in Florence. She could not gauge Anthony's painful eagerness to have his work appreciated; she cared little what was thought of her own many books, so long as sales were satisfactory.

She went eagerly to Penrith to visit her daughter in her own home among her babies. There was a peculiar tenderness between the mother and those children who had been with her in the awful straits of America; and Cecelia, her older daughter, who had patiently mended her poor clothes past recognition, understood better than her brothers the unselfishness of a woman who had not only earned money for them but denied herself pleasure—she knew how much "pleasure" meant to her mother—in order to secure it to her children.

Cecelia was so very glad to welcome her that the mother's bright eyes failed to see what she was determined to escape seeing—that her daughter was dying. Cecelia had lost her taste for joy. She loved her babies and her husband, but she was greatly altered from the excited little girl who had dealt out superlatives with a lavish pen. The deaths of Henry and Emily had lent a mournful cadence to her song; she had turned to religion and, going far beyond her family, who were content to observe High Church forms and fight Evangelicals, had become a Puseyite.

She had contributed a novel to the cause. There may still be found on the forgotten shelf of some old library an unpretentious little book whose title page reads, *Chollerton, a Tale of Our Own Times, By a Lady*. The Lady was Cecelia. It was a painful little book, whose clerical hero came home from Oxford resolved to make his family and friends either pious or miserable. The young divine recommended the Prayer Book as the "supreme guide," and stressed the fact that it ordained twenty-six fasts in addition to the regular Friday fasts and the forty days of Lent; had Cecelia worn away her slender strength by such rigors? Cecelia's mother's day "at home" was Friday, but Cecelia's hero forbade a picnic on a Friday. She had not as yet seen Theodosia Garrow, the young poetess with whom Tom was in love, but the words of a song in *Chollerton* were probably Theodosia's; Cecelia's conscientious note stated, "These verses are inserted by the permission of a friend."

When the excitement of her mother's visit was over, and the support which had upheld her girlhood was again withdrawn, Cecelia became so ill that John Tilley hastened to consult various doctors, on whose advice he decided to send her to Italy. He wrote his mother-in-law that Cecelia would set out as soon as he could find a suitable companion for her journey.

Frances Trollope was with Tom at Baden-Baden when the news came. She had been enjoying herself, going on picnics with British and American friends, and proving to everyone who took an interest what a good walker she was at sixty-seven. As usual, she was terribly agitated at the first shock of disaster and begged Tom to go instantly for his sister.

As a result of her precipitancy, Tom's journey missed its purpose, a fact which no one could lament less than that seasoned traveler. Learning that Cecelia had already sailed from Southampton for Leghorn, he returned to the Continent by way of Ostend and, continuing to Bruges, revisited the Château d'Hondt and the Protestant cemetery where two Trollopes lay buried.

Tom passed but a brief portion of his long, productive life in Bruges, but the old city held a fateful place in his philosophical development. This day in Bruges—and on a day to come—in the ancient square and in the Cathedral, he gave himself up to long reflections and the summing-up of life. Now he sat through a service thinking grave thoughts of time and change. He had again left Henry and his father near St. Catherine's gate; little Arthur and Grandfather Milton lay quiet in Heckfield churchyard; Emily in Hadley; would the white violets of Italy, which Emily never saw, bloom at last above Cecelia's grave? The Trollope children had uncommonly strong family feeling; Tom would be safe in saying, "Very pleasant were they in their lives"; but in their deaths, how far were they divided!

Many of his thoughts were of Theodosia Garrow, who had but a thousand pounds of her own, while he was still largely dependent on his mother. Marriage to Theodosia would be as strange as it would be improvident; he remembered her slim, brown hands, her amazing gray eyes, the rippling masses of dark hair which in some lights gleamed like copper; he considered her revolutionary fervor, which contrasted oddly with Trollopean conservatism. She was only twenty-two and he was thirty-seven; she was little and frail and he was big and powerful; according to hearty mid-century standards she was not in the least a beauty—Tom himself did not consider her beautiful. But Tom, who had been slow to grow up, was achieving maturity and was ready to make his own decisions as to what he wanted in a wife.

Theodosia's exotic appearance was less difficult to account for when one had seen her family. There was a certain vagueness about their antecedents, but Mr. Garrow was evidently the illegitimate son of an Indian civil servant and a native girl. The nephew of an eminent jurist, he was sent to England to be educated for the law, but being an indolent young fellow, he passed his days in pleasanter pursuits, such as playing the violin and drawing clever caricatures. When Tom knew him, it was as the man who translated Dante and monopolized his daughter. While comparatively young, Garrow had married a wealthy widow, Mrs. Fisher, born Theodosia Abrams. She was twenty-five years older than Mr. Garrow, with a grown daughter—plain, kind Harriet Fisher—and a grown son who annoyed his family by becoming a Catholic priest. It was less difficult to account for the expensive Mr. Garrow's marriage to an elderly, bad-tempered Jewess with a very comfortable income than it was to understand how he made her—at fifty-nine—the mother of Theodosia. Perhaps the very great affection between Harriet Fisher and her "half-sister" Theodosia provided a clue. Mrs. Garrow disliked this younger child, but Mr. Garrow loved her, because he found her so amusing.

The family lived near Torquay in a house named The Braddons, graced by a lovely garden. The Abrams sisters had been professional musicians, and little Theo inherited musical aptitude from both sides of the house. She made clever sketches, played the piano, sang in a voice of sweet exhaustion, and wrote verses. At thirteen she was a contributor to the *Book of Beauty*, that polite annual with engravings of England's Brightest and Best. Walter Savage Landor found the precocious little girl "more intense than Sappho," rated her higher than the much older Elizabeth Barrett, grieved that Byron had not known her, and implored his little friend "not to let Keats be our best poet."

Elizabeth Barrett, pensive and ill, was the child's idol. While the poetess was resting in Torquay, Theo dragged her half-sister on a visit to Miss Barrett but failed to see her. The little admirer gathered a bunch of violets and went home to write a poem on the proposed gift and its recipient, the verses studded with such consolatory lines as, "Thine innocent life, ebbing so swiftly away. . . . And thou, the gentle, the good, leavest behind thee in dying. . . . Innocent beings like thee fade with a gentle decay." Elizabeth Barrett thanked her for this mortuary tribute in a stiff little note, but conceded to Miss Mitford that the lines were "very sweet and touching."

The little girl and the poetess verging on thirty employed the same physician, who rashly drew comparisons: Miss Barrett, he declared, had the most excitable "system" in his experience—except Theodosia's. He predicted that the child would die in two years; but, as Miss Barrett later remarked with some acerbity, Theo "was dancing quadrilles then (and has lived to do the same by the polka)."

Later she tried to do justice to the young girl: "Very clever—very accomplished—with talents and tastes of various kinds—a musician and linguist, in most modern languages I believe—and a writer of fluent graceful melodious verses,—you cannot say more." In truth, Theodosia was a wonderful little imitator: she could outdo Scott in rhyming, though not in vigor; turn out a "Doom of Cheynholme" reminiscent of Coleridge; sound the voice of Byron in her "Cry of Romagna"; and admirably combine Shelley and Wordsworth in a romantic "Lady of Ashlynn." But Theodosia, for all her facility, could not improve.

It was with this gifted girl, whose misfortune it was to have both too much and too little talent, who was constitutionally too frail to make the most of what she had, that the healthy and sensible Tom Trollope had fallen in love. His mother petted her and called her Puss, and Theo, to whom no one but her half-sister Harriet had shown real kindness, was grateful. The Trollopes had such strength, such decision that it was natural for the subtle and vacillating girl to place herself under their protection. This was her fourth year in Italy, where her old friend Landor was living. The Italian patriot-poet Niccolini had translated her poem on the discovery of Dante's portrait, but did not like her manner of turning his tragedies into English, partly because he found her style of beauty antipathetic.

Mrs. Trollope returned to Florence, where she spent the week before Cecelia's arrival in getting her house ready for the invalid, for whose sake she determined to spend an unsocial winter. She soon found that the attitude would be general; the season promised to be bare of festivities because of the political situation, which became daily more uneasy. There was a popular demonstration at the Pitti Palace, and word came of dangerous times in Rome. Tom by chance met Dr. Jeune, who had been headmaster of the Birmingham Grammar School and now was head of Pembroke at Oxford, and invited him to dine with his mother. Dr. Jeune consented with reluctance, uneasy lest the lady bore him with epigrams, but reported her "clever, intelligent, and domestic." He wrote his wife that Tom looked well and was very busy starting the *Tuscan Athenaeum*, a "scientific, literary, theatrical and industrial journal" for the English in Italy—which was to last only three months.

No sooner was Cecelia settled at Casa Olivieri than the new doctor said she ought to spend the winter in Rome. The mother, again greatly agitated, assented anxiously to the suggestion and rented an apartment in the Via delle Quattro Fontane, but wondered whether she ought not to be permanently rid of the Florentine house and perhaps settle in Paris; Italy was on the verge of revolution, no place for an old lady and her sick daughter. Tom pacified her and prevented drastic decisions. He asked a favor: would she invite Theodosia Garrow to spend the winter with them in Rome?

Probably the question was no surprise. She consented, realizing that, if she were not both wise and lucky, she might lose Tom as well as Cecelia. Theodosia liked her, and took too little interest in household affairs to interfere unwarrantably; if ever a mother-in-law and a daughter-in-law could live peacefully together, their connection ought to be a success. Mrs. Trollope was exceedingly anxious not to lose Tom, her last unmarried child, and not to live alone. She could get along with Rose, but not with Anthony, and the Irish climate would not suit her asthma. What kind of a wife would Tom be getting? That was his affair, although she had a stake in his happiness and in the grandchildren; Theo was unlikely to have healthy babies. Tom's poverty and Theo's tiny fortune put her at an advantage because Mrs. Garrow, though rich, was not liberal, and the couple would have to depend largely on herself. When, on the last day of the old year 1847, her son broached the subject of the marriage, she had a cordial answer ready. She was delighted, she said, and as long as she lived Theodosia and he could be sure of a home with her. She had never behaved more wisely.

A few years earlier she would have questioned Tom's ability to support a wife. Now, however, he was at last giving signs of readiness to assume adult responsibilities. Like all the Trollopes, he had matured slowly, and it was not until his mid-thirties that he became a genuinely independent thinker. His earlier books had shown the influence of his mother's reactionary obscurantism and a tendency to belittle European progress since the French Revolution. But now, with his mother's influence supplanted in some measure by Theo's revolutionary ardor, Tom was making his début as a liberal. In a series of essays on Italian affairs which shortly began to appear in the London *Athenaeum*, he revealed himself rather surprisingly as a penetrating observer of social and political life, a forceful critic of conservative governments and Papal corruption, and a staunch believer in the political capacity of the Italian masses. They would never learn to govern themselves, he insisted, unless given the opportunity.

Even that arch reactionary, Frances Trollope, admitted that affairs in Rome were very, very bad, and that Tom, whose practical advice guided her in material matters, might also be right in public ones; but she was too old to change her principles. Besides, she was a woman to whom her children came first, and she was too much occupied with Cecelia to take a fervent interest in politics, except as they affected Trollope safety and comfort.

There had been anxiety lest Theodosia, who had no religion, and Cecelia, who had a very great deal, would not get on together, but the two young women became dear friends. When Theodosia was taken away from Rome by her father, Tom followed, and the mother was alone with her dying child, in a strange isolation which was yet no novelty. Cecelia seldom felt able to drive out; the mother tried to take exercise, but she had never enjoyed solitary walks and in the winter days the dull dread which hung over Rome seemed one more bruise upon her heart. She wrote Tom to send her several quires of paper, as the supply in Rome was expensive and poor, for she was about to try her usual panacea and start a novel. While she waited, she wrote pleasant notes to her friends who congratulated her on the approaching marriage of her "splendid son." Two old acquaintances, Lady Sevestre and her sister, begged her to find an apartment. She lightened her loneliness by taking them into her own, first imploring them to bring bedding, as the Roman pillows were "like iron." The ladies were not so energetic as their hostess, who wrote Tom sorrowfully, "I *cannot* walk alone."

Then she had a great fright. Tom was away and there came tidings of an insurrection in Sicily; the people had risen, driven out the royal garrisons, and set up a provisional government; the scared King of Naples had promised a constitution; in very Rome the Pope had called down blessings on the beloved and forbidden name of Italy. In Paris Louis Philippe abdicated and the Red Republic was declared. At Vienna old Prince Metternich, who had been so gracious to her a dozen years before, fled before the storm which he had striven to avert for thirty years. Surely this meant the end of civilization, they would all be guillotined, and the Dark Ages would return!

Tom came down to Rome, partly to reassure her, partly to gauge the prospects of revolution in the Papal States. From all sides a rising of the people was predicted. He explained to his mother that she was as well off there as elsewhere, since conditions everywhere were equally precarious. A letter from Anthony said that his English friends marveled at his keeping Rose and the little boys in Ireland in the teeth of impending revolution; but Anthony comfortingly—if cynically—added, "My own idea is that there is no ground to fear any general rising either in England or Ireland. I think there is too much intelligence in England for any large body of men to look for sudden improvement; and not enough intelligence in Ireland for any body of men at all to conceive the possibility of social improvement."

Thomas Adolphus Trollope

The marriage between Tom Trollope and Theodosia Garrow took place in Florence on the 3d of April, 1848. The bridegroom's old mother had lived through many ups and downs since the spring morning of her own wedding thirty-nine years ago, when her bridegroom had been the age that Tom was now.

The wedded pair set off on their wanderings among the hill towns of Tuscany. Then Cecelia, who was a little nearer home than she had been in Rome, protested that she must go all the way; if she must die, it would not be so difficult after she had again seen John and her little children. Once more Frances Trollope was greatly agitated; she feared Cecelia would die at sea, but the doctor advised humoring her, since her longing for home was insupportable.

Tom's money ran out, or Theo tired of his strenuous mode of travel; the bridal couple wanted to return, and had to be put off because Mrs. Trollope, not expecting so early an end to the honeymoon, had filled her house with guests. But the four met at Pisa before April was out, and Cecelia, very weak and ill, sailed for home just a month after the wedding. Her husband had a pretty house in London all ready for her. Her bed was placed in the back parlor; she begged to have the doors wide open.

In lowered spirits the three Florentine Trollopes went home without her to a Florence untouched by the convulsion of Europe. There was no quieter city in Italy; there was so little martial spirit that Tom could send the *Athenaeum* nothing but accounts of religious festivities and historical researches. News from the war in Lombardy was usually of Austrian advances, but when the Piedmontese won a rare victory, the Florentines courteously staged a sympathetic celebration. In July the family crossed the danger zone to summer in Switzerland. Here there were few tourists, but life in the Swiss cantons went on much as usual, and Tom enlightened the London public, through the columns of the *Athenaeum*, on such diverse topics as an institution for the prevention and cure of cretinism, and the boisterous jollity of a Bern music festival. Like his mother he was interested in everything, and had the gift of making everything interesting to others. He was making a praiseworthy effort to support Theo in a way pleasing to himself, but the readiness of the *Athenaeum* to print his articles provided an excuse for wandering hither and yon with a bachelor's freedom. His mother was busy writing *The Lottery of Marriage*, and Theodosia did not ask to be amused.

Then in September Mrs. Trollope was thrown into renewed panic by news of bloody fighting in the streets of Paris; out of Italy filtered rumors of fresh turmoil in Rome and Naples and of insurrection in Venice, where her old friend General Pepe commanded the revolutionary army. She felt that she could never again feel safe in Florence, implored Tom to hasten thither and sell the furniture for what it would bring; meanwhile she would fly with Theo and await him at Vevey. The obliging Tom set out at once, not loth to return to the disturbed area and see for himself how the revolution progressed. Perhaps he was surprised when, immediately on his arrival, his mother and wife put in their appearance; Mrs. Trollope had again changed her mind.

During the autumn the city remained tranquil. Mrs. Trollope was not sorry to know that Austria was reconquering northern Italy, and that radicalism had been vanquished in Paris; but Tom and Theo, who valued the liberal cause above personal convenience or even safety, were correspondingly discouraged. The mother fretted because it was difficult to get her manuscripts to England, and no easier to collect payments. She talked often of going home to live, but always ended by saying that her asthma would trouble her worse in the English climate; Italy had subjugated her.

Mrs. Garrow's good, plain daughter had died of smallpox, and the father and mother were going home to Torquay. Mrs. Trollope supposed that, much as she disliked Mrs. Garrow, she ought to seize the opportunity of traveling with them. But it was not until March, 1849, when the Garrows had gone without her, and republican dictatorships were functioning in Rome and Florence, that she could arrive at a decision. Then the three Trollopes closed the villa and started off together, she to gain a last glimpse of Cecelia, the others for a ramble in France.

They parted company at Aix-en-Provence, and Mrs. Trollope was alone. In all her travels she had perhaps never before been anywhere without a retinue of congenial friends, a servant or two, and members of her family. In Paris she failed to find John's letters; and, to the old and anxious, "no news" spells disaster. She hurried on, afraid she might lose Cecelia if she lost a day in Paris. Toward evening on her sixty-ninth birthday, the poor little woman crept into the house in Kensington. Cecelia was alive and able to whisper how glad, how very glad she was to see her mother. She lingered a month longer, until April 4, 1849.

During these weeks Mrs. Trollope did not break her habit of writing, for she could not sleep and dared not think. She sat at work in her cold room, leaving her fire unlighted against the colder morning. She worried over Cecelia and her devoted husband; the grandchildren were deplorably delicate, and she feared her own little namesake would shortly follow the mother.

After Cecelia's funeral, the old mother fell ill with bronchitis and, as soon as she could travel, left London for the milder air of Brighton where she visited her lifelong friends, the Garnetts, the family of that Mrs. Stone who had been her hostess in America. Mrs. Trollope took Turkish baths, discovered an appetite, and began to feel the relief of knowing Cecelia was at rest. When she returned to John Tilley's house in Kensington, she was well enough to entertain her brother Henry at dinner. He too was gaining after an illness, but the little festivity wearied him; he overtired himself in conversation but, as he wrote her, "Who can resist talking when *you* are there to answer him?"

Anthony and Rose, to whom a second son, Frederic James Anthony Trollope, had been born, wanted to adopt one of Cecelia's little girls, and John Tilley and Mrs. Trollope took the child across to Mallow, the pretty watering place in County Cork where Anthony was stationed. The father would not promise that the arrangement should be permanent, and Anthony characteristically dreaded the forced relinquishment of an object he might come to love.

At Mallow Rose Trollope did what she could to comfort and amuse the old mother, who, when some unusual exertion wearied her, was cross enough, not to those about her, but to *things*, scolding unmercifully the tea, the hard bed, the fire of peat. Anthony put her in a jaunting car which scared her mightily, though she lived to describe the experience as delightful. A young bugler was fetched in to make music, and his ancient father invited to play the bagpipes. When she saw from her window an old man breaking stones in the road, she pattered down to present him with a silver sixpence. The scenery charmed her and she planned a story, but she scarcely noticed the misery which in old days would have distressed her. Roofless cabins and potato patches running wild told the sorry tale of famine and mass emigration, but she thought only of her family troubles. She was restless, took it much to heart to hear that Tom was not coming, and at the end of a few short weeks insisted on going back to England.

It seems unlikely that in her uneasy and necessarily unsympathetic condition, Anthony brought up the subject of his own books—he had published a second and was at work upon a third—unless to ask of her experience some dry question concerning publishers and circulation. She could scarcely understand why he wanted to write when he had a salary. In her case life had satisfied the creative hunger, and she wrote not because she could not otherwise express herself, but because she needed money, liked to be busy, wanted to forget her troubles.

While at Mallow she heard that Mrs. Garrow was ill and had summoned Tom and Theo from Spain. Mrs. Trollope refused to believe that her ancient enemy was really sick; hurt at Tom's going to Torquay instead of to his own mother in Ireland, she wrote him: "I don't quite think it right that you and I should of necessity be parted forever. Do you?"

News came that Cousin Fanny Bent of Exeter was too much indisposed to receive visits, and, to crown her griefs, Cecelia's daughter, her own little namesake, was dying. These calamities were a little easier to bear when Colburn offered to publish the usual two novels next year, and it was discovered that Harriet Fisher's money was, surprisingly, coming to Theodosia. Exulting in Tom's luck, which was to mark the turning point in their collective fortunes, the mother wrote, "Not to be glad is, for me, absolutely impossible." She felt how very much she had liked poor Harriet, whose fortune was sufficient to relieve the family from financial anxieties for the first time in many, many years.

Very soon she had one of her scares: the cholera came to London, and, instead of pleading with Tom to come to her, she ordered him to keep away. But she herself fell ill and Tom did come, which made her tremulously grateful to a daughter-in-law who could easily become formidable now that she was rich. She wrote to Theo, "I love and bless you, dearly, dearly, for having spared my dear son to me for a precious week."

At the close of September Mrs. Garrow, in whose illness Frances Trollope had resolutely disbelieved, died in Torquay, and Mr. Garrow urged Tom and Theo to make their home with him at The Braddons. Mrs. Trollope could not countenance the arrangement, to which the languid Theo would have yielded, and wrote vigorously that her doctor said that if she, Frances Trollope, did not go south, she would be "a very suffering old woman for the rest of her life." After this strong hint of her claims, she concocted a second letter which cost her much anxiety; this was her supreme effort to hold the remnant of her family together.

Her only solution of the problem of the intransigent Mr. Garrow, the wedded pair, and herself was for all four to pool their resources and live together, which they could afford to do in style. She would undertake the onerous task of amusing the spoiled old gentleman. She dared not write this, lest Mr. Garrow should be apprised of her scheme and wreck it; but she urged Tom and Theo to meet her for a conference in London: "I write to make a request to you and Theodosia which I must say I think you *ought* to comply with. For very nearly forty years, my dear son, you and I have lived together in more perfect harmony than is often found, I believe, in any connection in life. And now, when I so very greatly need the comfort and support of your society, I am deprived of it. Having said this, I shall say no more. You and Theodosia must judge for yourselves."

She was successful in her scheme. The Braddons would be sold, and the four would make their permanent home in Florence. These points settled, Mrs. Trollope left England for Pau, where she spent a few lonely months among the resident English. Her much loved brother, Henry Milton, had seemed to be improving in health when she left him, and on the Continent matters were adjusting themselves comfortably; she had come to the place where personal and cosmic events seem of equal importance. Europe had been "pacified" by the armed forces of conservatism: Austrian troops had brought the Grand Duke home to Florence, French bayonets had restored Pope Pius, Venice had capitulated, General Pepe was again fugitive. Europe and she had weathered the crisis; there was every hope that the old Englishwoman would find a tranquil resting place.

CHAPTER X

Man of Affairs

1850-1857

ANTHONY'S second novel, *The Kellys and the O'Kellys,* was inferior to *The Macdermots of Ballycloran.* In the hope of pleasing a captious world, he had yielded to the characteristic extravagance of his family and set up two complete plots, one of Irish high life, the other of low. But the realist in him, or perhaps the contrary genius, had defeated his bid for popularity; his plebeian heroine was both ugly and old, and his patrician hero a fortune hunter. A host of virile characters enriched the book; there was a hunt as fine as he was ever to write, the ferocious brother of Anty was perfectly credible, the foul inn kitchen could be smelled and tasted. The work was admirably objective, although the insolvent hero recalled Anthony's masterless days in London: "He often felt that the kind of life [he was leading] —contracting debts which he could not pay, and spending his time in pursuits which were not really congenial to him, was unsatisfactory and discreditable."

A friend undertook to arrange for a notice of *The Kellys and the O'Kellys* in the London *Times.* After some thought, Anthony declined. If his book could not make its way on its own merits he did not care to have it promoted by artificial means, however usual. Then and there he resolved never to have any dealings with critics on his own behalf, a determination to which he adhered through life.

At the end of 1848, Colburn wrote him that *The Kellys and the O'Kellys* had put the firm out of pocket and that he could not encourage him to continue his efforts. Undefeated, but accepting the obvious truth that Irish novels did not pay, Anthony took the French Revolution as the background for his next work.

Less good can be said of *La Vendée,* which came out in June, 1850, than of its two predecessors. Even the *Athenaeum,* which had cautiously praised *The Macdermots* and *The Kellys*—perhaps at Tom's instance—was noncommittal. A tale of adventure in the tradition of Scott, the book had neither Scott's virility nor his pictorial power. The persistent hope of gaining a public had led Anthony aside from his true course into a form which never permits what was to be his supreme achievement—the leisurely development of character. The book might never have been published, had not his brother good-naturedly undertaken to act as agent; as it was, it brought him only £20.

In the self-mockery which aims to forestall criticism, he wrote his mother, whom he hoped to meet at the forthcoming Exhibition of 1851: "I mean to exhibit four 3 vol. novels—all failures!—which I look on as a great proof of industry at any rate." This third rebuff, fortunate as it was for his future development, shook him, and he could not speak of his bitter disappointment even to his wife. His disposition could endure failure only when it could be blamed upon extraneous causes, and as a writer he was still a humble man, ready to believe that some of the fault was in himself. In his anxiety to make money and redeem his promises to himself, he was determined that his own sloth should not vanquish him. If he could not succeed with a novel, he had already experimented with other forms which might serve. There was no one to tell him he was a born novelist, and his active and still flexible mind ranged in many directions.

Despite his abandonment of Ireland as a subject for novels, he hoped to turn his knowledge of the country to account. In his constant traveling he had seen dearth, famine, and pestilence, and observed the efforts of the British government to relieve distress of unexampled intensity. In 1849 he had succeeded in publishing in the London *Examiner* an able analysis of the Irish question in which the policy of the administration was shrewdly defended. He had not silenced the government's critics, however, and he felt that a more detailed examination of the problem would serve not only the cause of justice but his own fortunes. When in London he had called on John Forster, editor of the *Examiner*, proposing a further series of Irish letters for his paper. The great man—only three years Anthony's senior—had taken his time and had hedged his assent with so many cautious restrictions that Anthony formed the mistaken hope of generous payment.

The five letters which appeared during that spring of 1850—signed with the initials A.T.—were admirable in their accuracy, their force and grace, and their practicality. It was evident that he had expended much pains upon them. His object was to show that the public money had been spent to preserve life in the most effectual way possible, under the peculiar difficulties of the case. He defended Lord John Russell against the abuse of the Irish gentry—"a class of men not to be surpassed in the pride of station or in the want of refinement"—and made specific recommendations in the matter of rentals and of encumbered estates.

In his final letter he made the too characteristic mistake of the Anglo-Saxon in passing judgment on less favored peoples: "I find it impossible to believe that the Irish are gifted with those qualities, which are required to support a stern struggle for constitutional liberty." They were a people "not naturally prone to political excitement," and a wise government need not despair of restoring tolerable conditions by able administration.

Aside from this misjudgment, the letters were shrewd, well-informed, and healthily optimistic—not the work of the discouraged man he was sometimes inclined to think himself. In politics he was still an optimist, though he had lived amid scenes as depressing as any it was possible to conceive and had seen human nature under dire stress. His personal life was contented, and he was beginning to make a name for himself in the postal service—though the modest salary of a surveyor's clerk made the hope of literary remuneration important. Yet with much to make him happy, he found that without literary success it was impossible for him to be at ease. The virtual failure of his Irish letters intensified his distress at the almost simultaneous misbirth of *La Vendée*.

Meanwhile he had been working the Irish vein at another point. Recalling the success of the travel books which Tom and his mother had written—Tom's pleasantly complacent sketches from the *Athenaeum* were even then being reissued as *Impressions of a Wanderer* —he had approached John Murray with the proposal to write an Irish guide. The publisher did not offer him a contract, but agreed to let the young surveyor submit a sample, upon which he undertook to report in a fortnight. Anthony spent several weeks upon Dublin and the Lakes of Killarney, and dispatched a roll of manuscript to Murray's office— where it lay, unopened, for nine months.

Anthony made an attempt at drama. To write a play had been an early ambition, stimulated by the frequent theatricals in his mother's drawing room, in which as a clumsy boy he had been allowed only minor parts or none. He had the gift of writing spontaneous conversations and the will to labor at the polishing of his lines with infinite care; but he was hampered by an inborn distaste for plot and, in a smaller measure, for action.

The Noble Jilt was a historical comedy, laid in the time of the Flemish struggle for independence, and written in a mixture of blank verse and prose. Where *La Vendée* had shown the conservative influence of Scott, *The Noble Jilt* had some of the revolutionary fervor of Sir Henry Taylor's *Philip van Artevelde*, plays which had stirred his enthusiasm since his school days. Shakespeare's influence, too, was evident in the conventionalized alternation of serious and comic scenes and the occasional set pieces, such as Upsel's soliloquy in the second act.

The play was by no means without merit. The comic portions revealed more imaginative power than he has usually been conceded. But the main idea—that of a girl who jilts a perfect suitor for a man she does not love, only because she fears she cannot live up to him— was basically unconvincing. It was the first evidence of the lifelong self-deception with which Anthony Trollope tried to evade the problem of what to do with the woman of intellect who is capable of passion.

More damning to the play's success was the fact that historical romances had gone out of favor on the London stage. His mother's old friend George Bartley, the manager of Covent Garden, whom he asked for an opinion on the finished manuscript, minced no words in telling him that his dramatic effort would not do. Anthony knew that he had done his best; perhaps he felt that no one is less likely to sympathize with an unknown author than the old friend of his mother. But, as he told Rose, Bartley knew what he was talking about. The veteran had sentenced his characters to remain imprisoned in the manuscript, instead of permitting them to be born into the world like those of the three novels. *The Noble Jilt* was laid aside, but not destroyed.

Still experimenting, he wrote for the *Dublin University Magazine* a long, unsolicited review on the first two volumes of Charles Merivale's *History of the Romans under the Empire*. Because of the old family friendship, a book by a Merivale was almost as near a thing as a book by a Trollope. The review was published, doing some service to the historian and more to Anthony, because the research it necessitated aroused his interest in Latin antiquity as it had never been kindled by Winchester or Harrow. But when he asked the editor for payment, he was told none could be made.

While thus proceeding from one failure to another, he must often have pondered on the contrast between his own life of toil and frustration and his elder brother's easily won successes. He had resented Tom's unfair prominence in the home and his occasional persecutions at school; but he was not envious of his accomplishments. Anthony's letters to Florence were easy and affectionate: Mrs. Trollope was his "dearest mother"; he and Rose would like "nothing on earth" better than coming to visit her. Hearing that the Florentine Trollopes had spent such inordinate sums on their new house, the "Villino Trollope," that they could not visit England for the Great Exhibition at the Crystal Palace, he wrote, "I cannot tell you how I grieve at this." Rose was exhibiting something or other at the Exhibition and getting a new silk dress; he himself was contemplating the purchase of a hat; John Tilley had studied up the whole Exhibition. "Will there be no such thing as a cheap trip from Florence by which a man could come to London and go back within a fortnight or so?"

The mother, who had been ill, was in no fit state to travel, but Tom, unable to resist, left her with Theo at Lucca while he took the "cheap trip" to England. He found Anthony, Rose, and the two boys at Exeter visiting Cousin Fanny Bent, the old companion of his early travels, grown dismal with years and feebleness. The older generation was passing away. Aunt Mary, the Commander's wife, still lived to be visited, but Uncle Henry Milton had rallied in the previous December only to die in January—less, Anthony thought, from illness than from a weariness of spirit. Nor was the younger generation, except for his own children, remarkable for health. During the year two little Tilley boys had died of measles and whooping cough. Tom and frail Theo, married three years, had had no children.

Official business kept Anthony from literary work during 1851 and most of 1852. It was an opportune interval in which he dropped his feverish experimentation, regained perspective, and gathered his strength for a more auspicious attempt. Meanwhile the great work of expanding the postal service fully occupied him. There were still large rural areas in the British Isles where no service was available, and free delivery was ordinarily provided only in the neighborhood of a post office town or village. His superiors in St. Martin's-le-Grand felt that a rural post should be established wherever there was a reasonable prospect that it would pay its way by increasing the volume of postal business, and on this basis had undertaken a long-term reorganization of the whole service.

Anthony was directed to reorganize his district in Ireland and, having done this to satisfaction, to perform a similar service in southern England and Wales. The lad who ten years before had gone to Ireland in disgrace thus returned, an official of recognized competency, to those rural scenes which had been familiar to him since childhood. Months of traveling among the thatched villages, commons, rolling hills, and cathedral towns of the southwestern counties fixed in his memory the scenery and manners of that imaginary county of Barchester which he was soon to people with the creatures of his mind. Meanwhile Rose and the two little boys, Harry and Freddy, were uprooted from the comfortable house in Mallow to follow him about the country from one temporary lodging to another.

Hating to relinquish anything to which he had grown accustomed, he devoted much thought to means of continuing his hunting in his new mode of life. The government allowed him sixpence a mile as travel allowance, and he calculated that by traveling forty miles a day—and earning his money—he could keep two hunters and a groom on his expense account. Clad to save time in pink coat and hunting boots, the big, black-bearded man zealously searched out short-cuts for underlings to follow with their mail bags, and descended on farm or rectory to frighten the truth about local conditions out of the residents by a rapid fire of questions—stand-and-deliver methods which he justified by affirming that it was the only way to learn the facts: if he gave time for reflection, everyone would lie for fear of getting into trouble with the postman. This strenuous life delighted him. He was combining business and pleasure in a way for which few men would have found either initiative or strength.

The business was so urgent that the long-planned visit to Florence had to be postponed for another year. Meanwhile, late in September of 1852, John Tilley told him that he had met a man—in Kensington Gardens, of all places—who had divulged the information that Theodosia Trollope was expecting a baby. This was a peculiar way of getting family news. Anthony complained that neither Tom nor his mother had written for two months, and demanded the facts.

The rumor proved true: Tom's letter to Anthony, the mother's to Rose, established it: after five years, a child was expected in the coming spring. Anthony's congratulations were no less strange than the manner in which he had learned the news. Still smarting inwardly from the poundings the elder brother had given him at Winchester, he wrote in pseudo-humorous vein that it would be delightful for Tom to have a small creature on which to wreak his spite. "One wants someone to exercise unlimited authority over. . . . The delights of flagellation, though less keen [than murder], are more enduring. One can kill but once; but one may flog daily. . . ."

Amid occasional blunders of taste in personal relationships, he was already immersed in preparation for the book which was to reveal to all the world his faultless tact in moving among imaginary people. The enforced holiday from writing had the salutary effect of making him scrutinize his ideas before carrying them out. When a good subject like that of *The Warden* occurred to him, there was ample time to weigh and reflect upon it, examining it from every angle, before investing his labor in it.

A midsummer night's stroll about the precincts of Salisbury Cathedral—a scene bewitching to the most nearsighted eyes—had given him the close for a setting and the clergy as characters. To people the scene with churchmen and others normally associated with clerical affairs would not be difficult for one who had known so many of them—old

Dr. Nott of Winchester, the masters of Harrow, "Velvet" Cunningham, Grandfather Milton, Aunt Diana's husband—all were in holy orders and familiar to him from his youth. Yet it was a novel venture, not to say a bold one, to treat these reverend persons like ordinary human beings, with the foibles that flesh is heir to. Except for the curates in Charlotte Brontë's *Shirley*, together with one or two of his own mother's novels, there was hardly a precedent for it since Jane Austen. George Eliot's *Scenes from Clerical Life* did not appear until two years later.

A batch of letters to the *Times* on a matter of church patronage furnished his theme—a good man in a false position. The wind of reform, which had swept clean the dusty corners of the Post Office administration, was blowing insistently against that accumulation of worldly vested interests represented by the English Church. Anthony saw the need of reform, but he saw too the injustice it could work in actual cases. He was a little uneasy about the situation of the Warden of Hiram's Hospital, supposing that he needed a clear-cut moral issue such as that of a good man in a correct position, or a bad man in an incorrect position. He was, indeed, a poor critic, and scarcely more a conscious artist than his mother; and he sensed and all but shared the feelings of his readers, who were puzzled that so excellent a man as the Warden should be liable to attack. Nevertheless the book gained immeasurably from the subtlety of the problem, which established a characteristic ethical atmosphere well suited to the tolerance and half-humorous resignation of his maturer temperament.

The writing proceeded slowly, but was very pleasant. When he complained to the Florentine Trollopes of tardy promotion in the postal service, he could add, "However, this does not really annoy me," because he was happily preoccupied with his clergyman, whose daughter had engaged herself to the chief of her father's enemies—a young fellow named Johnny Bold; and Johnny, a mixture of principle and bumptiousness, was attacking the Warden for enjoying what he could not earn.

Toward the end of 1852 his promotion came, and he repaired with Rose and the boys to a new home in Belfast, an orderly city of red brick, girdled by spinning mills. It was Anthony's first assignment to the north of Ireland, and writing was completely interrupted for two months while he mastered the details of his new surveyorship. Once fully familiar with the local delivery routes by rail, coach, dogcart, and foot-runner, with the wage scales and the contracts with private carriers, he returned to work on *The Warden* without further interruption until the spring.

In April, 1853, he took Rose on the long promised visit to Florence, where Tom's new house and a new Trollope baby awaited them. Letters had not prepared them for the magnificence of the Villino Trollope— Trollopè, the Italians called it—which outran their most extravagant fancies. A noble marble staircase led to vast reception rooms; the rare volumes in the long library were numbered in the thousands; there were suits of armor, Florentine bridal chests, a terra cotta Virgin attributed to one Orgagna. A marble balcony overlooked a garden with fountains, statues, cypresses, and orange trees, with the old crenelated, iris-decked walls of Florence in the rear.

Certainly a great deal of money had contributed to such excellent effects, and Anthony must cheerfully admit that Carlton Hill was nothing to the Villino Trollope; even the memory of Julians paled before such grandeur. He and Rose, fresh from a succession of dreary lodginghouses, admired without envying. Perhaps they saw too much of the petty economy which the possessors of such houses frequently practice in private. Their own tastes were different. Of all the homes he had seen, the pleasantest in Anthony's opinion was English Julians Hill, where his mother had taken the family from doleful Harrow Weald.

The visit was almost purely a family affair. Little "Bice"—Beatrice Harriet Catherine Trollope—was only a month old, and Theodosia had not regained her strength; besides, the spring was advancing and people were going out of town. Frances Trollope took her young daughter-in-law about, showed her the sights and shops of Florence and bought her a handsome silk dress. Further, she presented Rose with an exquisite brooch which Princess Metternich had given her in Vienna almost twenty years before. "I thought her," asserted little Mrs. Anthony, "the most charming old lady who ever existed."

Frances Trollope, when she wrote to English friends of her love for the blue Italian sky and the pale gray-green of the olive, assured them that she was well content. Yet her courage often faltered in these latter days. She was troubled by asthma and bronchitis, her teeth had been extracted, and the replacements pained her. Tom was often away, and Theodosia's chronic ill health was depressing. Devoted as she was to her exotic daughter-in-law, she was glad that Anthony had such an "admirable" wife as Rose.

The three-volume novels which she continued to publish every year told the story of her slow decline. *Petticoat Government* in 1850 had shown no sign of senility; rather it benefited by the waning of the author's exuberance. But *Second Love* in 1851, suggested by her visit to the Lakes of Killarney, had been almost too much for the old lady. Pithy observations abounded, but she tired of her characters and occasionally forgot them. Since then another three-volume novel had come out, and four more were to make their appearance before she finally laid down her pen.

Florence, with its brilliant and cosmopolitan society, was a wonderful place for a novelist. Charles Lever boasted that he found most of his characters at his own receptions, and some people felt that satirical Mrs. Trollope was prone to do the same thing. "Of course, I draw from life," she once admitted, not very reassuringly. "But I always pulp my acquaintances before serving them up. You would never recognize a pig in a sausage."

During the season she was at home to the general English-speaking public—resident and transient—each Saturday morning, and she had many cordial friends. Even Browning, who "had made a sort of vow never to sit in the same room with the author of certain books directed against liberal institutions and Victor Hugo's poetry," had been melted by her kindness and good nature. The Brownings had decided that they could afford to "be quite friends, and lend each other books, and forget one another's offenses, in print and otherwise." A less exacting friend was straightforward, black-eyed Hiram Powers, the sculptor, on whom she took Anthony to call.

Rose and Anthony were chary of expressing their opinion of Theodosia, who seemed touchingly happy with her small daughter, already much more like her than like the Trollopes. Anthony, the shrewd observer, who had heard of Theo's expectations in so roundabout a way, may have caught a smile, a whisper, or a shrug exchanged in some small group. Theo, an exotic even among exotics, still young, married to a man fifteen years her senior, left alone in Florence before her child was born, although in extremely poor health and in low spirits: was it not perhaps remarkable that the couple should have a baby at all, after being childless so many years? Anthony's keen ears might have been quicker than his brother's to catch some of the mischievous, irresponsible chatter by which Florence lived.

Soon after the Anthony Trollopes returned to Ireland, he was transferred from Belfast to Dublin, where the family settled in the suburb of Donnybrook. That autumn saw the completion of *The Warden*, which William Longman agreed to publish for him on the basis of half-profits. The book appeared at the beginning of 1855, and it was soon evident that at last he had made a modest success. The *Athenaeum*, though troubled by his "perfect indifference" to right and wrong, found him "extremely clever and amusing"; the public, eager to be diverted from the miseries of the Crimean winter, agreed. The men at the Post Office began to be aware that their noisy, efficient colleague had written a book.

Anthony realized that he was exceptionally able in characterization and that he had lighted upon a rich field. The public, who refused to read about the wild Irish, liked characters who resembled themselves and the people they met at parties—with slight improvements in the wit and beauty of the good; with delicate deepening of shadow in the dishonesty and impropriety of the less good.

To write thus to order was immensely better than not to write at all; yet it was not quite what he wanted. His desire was to probe deep into human nature and to publish his discoveries, unrestrained by the shabby-genteel limitations of his age. Such writing, he began to realize, would leave him a poor man and an unread author. And, although he scarcely wished to establish himself as the father of mild comedies of English rural life, he did care very much to establish himself as a country gentleman with his own stable—perhaps later as Sir Anthony Trollope, or Anthony Trollope, M.P. To gratify such ambition required plenty of money, which his pen must earn.

The choice was clear, but he was slow to make it. To the end of his days, he never quite abandoned himself to the second-rate career he now chose to follow. In the midst of the success of *The Warden*, a momentary discouragement caused him to speculate whether the career of a publicist or a philosopher might not possess a dignity and security beyond that of a romantic novelist. In *The Warden* he had clumsily satirized Carlyle under the name of Dr. Pessimist Anticant; now he dashed off a trial manuscript in Carlyle's own manner on the evils of the state, labeled it *The New Zealander*, and submitted it to Longmans. Decision took but five days: the reader reported that it was very bad— a "most feeble imitation" of Carlyle. Trollope, docile under criticism, swallowed his pride and fell to work upon a new novel in continuation of *The Warden*.

Barchester Towers, which was to make his name known to all the English-speaking world, occupied his spare time for the next eighteen months. As yet he had set no clock upon his writing; the number of words exacted from himself in the morning task was not a matter to ruin or glorify his day. The work proceeded pleasantly and without bustle, a second visit to Italy occurring within a few weeks of its beginning.

This time he and Rose did not go to Florence. John Tilley traveled with them to Venice, where they met Tom and his mother; Theo was not one of the party. Mrs. Trollope walked briskly on the Lido sands and climbed many steps with her old bright pride. But the younger generation feared "mamma" was beginning to break up; she was terribly frightened when a thunderstorm broke on them in a gondola. They forgot that she had always been almost as timid as she was plucky, and that she found electrical disturbances especially trying.

The party of five traveled to England, the men making a detour, Rose keeping the mother company until they met again at Innsbruck. It was Frances Trollope's last visit home. Many, almost all, of her old friends were dead, but she took an interest in their children's children and went to visit a small girl of the Drury family who was away at boarding school. When the child was called out of class, she found a little old woman in a frilled cap and a black bonnet, drinking tea at one end of the long table. Someone said, "Come and speak to Mrs.

Trollope." The old lady did not wait for the little one's cautious advance but jumped out of her chair, ran to meet her, and with both arms around her neck said, just as a fairy godmother would, "You darling child!"

Sensible Rose was sure that her mother-in-law was failing, else she would not take so avid an interest in spiritualism. She had come to England less to meet her grandchildren than to see the famous medium, Daniel Home. Tom was there with the same avowed object, though his attitude was entirely different. Mrs. Trollope wanted to know about her dead children; her positivistic son wanted to know how the tricks, if such they were, were managed.

The 1840's had been colored by mesmerism and animal magnetism; the 1850's were enlivened by spirits, and Tom and his mother were in the forefront of the interest in both movements. For the past two years the Trollopes' Florentine friends had quaked at walking chairs and galloping tables. From Connecticut in America, region of amazing spiritualistic phenomena, had now come Daniel Home, a tubercular young fellow who had wanted to be a minister or a doctor, until his efforts to lead a normal life had been frustrated by the concentration upon his bewildered person of the full force of spiritualistic influences. Wherever he went, he was attended by spirit hands, rappings, and violations of the laws of gravity. Brought over to London, he was installed as guest of a reputable solicitor, a Mr. Rymer.

To Mr. Rymer's house at Ealing flocked scientists, the curious, and the empty-hearted who longed for news of their lost ones. Elizabeth Barrett Browning visited the medium with her incredulous husband, who was violently annoyed to see a chaplet of flowers placed by invisible hands upon his wife's head. Bulwer Lytton was presented with a cardboard cross and admonished in a ghostly message to believe in it. Accordion or guitar discoursed celestial music, and bodiless hands and arms appeared in unexpected places.

Mrs. Trollope went with Tom to Ealing. Among the guests was Sir David Brewster, the eminent scientist. High tea was served on Mr. Rymer's lawn, where Mrs. Trollope watched the red-headed, consumptive Daniel making himself as agreeable as if he were a normal youth. She liked young people—this boy was the age of Henry when he died—and she pitied the medium, whose face bore obvious signs of suffering. When it was time for the manifestations to begin, they trooped into the house and took seats around a massive dining table.

Presently the table was levitated. Tom and Sir David Brewster instantly threw themselves to the floor to investigate. Tom, observing that the heavy table was actually suspended five and six inches above the floor, said in choice Trollopean language to the great man groveling at his side, "Does it not seem that this table is raised by some means wholly inexplicable?" "Indeed, it would seem so," admitted the erudite Sir David—but went home to write to the papers that he had seen nothing unusual. Tom, equally baffled but more honest, kept careful records of his observations, and permitted their publication for what they were worth.

Tom's interest was coldly scientific; his expressions of "doubt and incredulity" at last resulted in Home's begging him to stay away from further séances. But the mother was a bereaved old woman who missed her children and pined for news of them. Disappointed at Ealing, she invited the famous young medium to be her guest in the Villino Trollope, where, in October, he appeared at Florence for a month's visit.

Theo thought the young man odious, but the sensation he created among the Florentine expatriates was immense. The house became enormously popular; séances were held almost nightly, and the Trollope furniture whisked about amazingly. It was whispered that Mrs. Trollope received visits from her dead children. Theodosia, though she did not once succeed in tripping Home, was certain that such a detestable creature must be a counterfeit. Tom, respected as a man of sense in that exotic society, distinguished between the physical phenomena and the alleged communication with the spirit world. As to the former, he was convinced that they were not produced by any "fraud, machinery, juggling, illusion, or trickery" on Home's part. But as to the intercourse with spirits, Tom "doubted."

Anthony Trollope never expressed himself publicly on the matter of spiritualism: he made it a kind of rule not to encroach upon his brother's bailiwick. Only a faint echo of the impressions his late Italian experiences had left upon him found its way into the new novel; An-

thony was disgusted and amused by the Italianate Stanhope family of
Barchester Towers.

Eleanor Bold, widowed daughter of the Warden, was again his
heroine—as charming but a little sillier than in her virginity, and
destined to be even more obtuse before Trollope finished with her. The
Barchester company was augmented by new friends: Mr. Slope was
an able scalawag; Archdeacon Grantly had "improved upon acquaintance"; Mr. Arabin, who married the widow Bold, belonged to the class
—rare in Trollope—of men of intellect. The disagreeable but not inhuman Mrs. Proudie could be considered a caricature only by those
whose experience of life had not led them into the circles where Mrs.
Proudies are bred. Among the many excellencies of *Barchester Towers*
was the first of the inimitable Trollopean parties; as admirable in a
different sense was the quiet deathbed of Bishop Grantly, in which the
worldliness of the archdeacon was conquered by the affection of
the son.

The book progressed slowly and with many interruptions. During
the whole of July, 1855, Anthony had to be in London twice a week
for the hearings of a select committee of the House of Commons which
was inquiring into the postal arrangements in the south of Ireland.
Trollope, as the official most thoroughly conversant with the locality,
was selected by the Post Office to attend all the sessions and bear the
brunt of the questioning. His own examination occupied the greater
part of four sessions, in which he displayed an impressive mastery of
every detail within his broad jurisdiction. He answered 1,673 questions put by honorable members, and the printed record of his testimony occupied 102 pages in the official Blue Book of the committee.

His attitude toward the committee was respectful but by no means
submissive. The printed testimony did not conceal his contempt for
the Irish members, whom he suspected of putting themselves forward
on behalf of special and probably corrupt interests. Yet he chose his
words with extraordinary care and successfully eluded all the self-
contradictions into which his inquisitors sought to entrap him. He insisted that the record be kept straight on behalf of the Post Office, refused to answer the same question more than once, and generally let it

be known that he understood the business of parliamentary inquiries at least as well as did the members.

The committee ultimately decided by a narrow margin that no change in the present postal arrangements was called for. Trollope was inclined to think the whole proceeding had been a mere political maneuver leading to a foregone conclusion. Perhaps it would afford suitable material for a future book. Meanwhile he had a right to feel that he had performed an arduous duty with enormous credit to the Post Office and to himself.

Anthony's regular postal duties now required him to use the railways instead of the horseback travel he so much enjoyed. He took to writing bits of his story as the carriage rattled over the Irish rails, later handing the sheets to Rose to copy legibly. Sometime during this busy period he came to the resolution that he ought not to take time for research or even for general reading at the expense of his service to the government—an ominous decision, since it implied no diminution in the literary output he intended to exact from himself. Here was the beginning of that false standard which vitiated so much of his future work. Confronted with a choice between mere quantity and the quality which only time and reflection can give, he made the sacrifice which came easier to him. Not self-cultivation but the production of millions of printed words became the ruling object of his life.

Before *Barchester Towers* was finished, he had published in the *Dublin University Magazine* a review of three more volumes of Merivale's history and an anonymous article in opposition to the principle of Civil Service examinations. Here again he found himself in sharp opposition to England's doctrinaire mid-century reformers. Mindful of the way in which he himself had come into the government service, he strongly repudiated the notion that public offices were staffed exclusively by "the idle, the weak in mind, the infirm in body, the unambitious, the jolterheads, the ne'er-do-wells, the puny, and the diseased," insisted that the faults lay in the unattractiveness of a civil service career, and poured ridicule on the eminent men who hoped to cure them by forcing boys of seventeen to take an examination which few Oxford graduates could pass. Sly digs at Rowland Hill, the head of his own office, who had "brought himself into place" by inventing penny postage, contributed nothing to Trollope's popularity at St. Martin's-le-Grand, although the chiefs of the postal service could not fail to recognize his value for all kinds of official assignments. Early in 1857 they employed him to write a brief "History of the Post Office in Ireland" which turned out to be as interesting as the subject and his materials would permit, and was printed as an appendix to the annual report of the Postmaster General.

Barchester Towers was finished in November, 1856, and published by Longmans in May, 1857. Mr. Longman had conceded him slightly better terms—half profits and an advance of £100—but had insisted on certain changes of a kind to leave Anthony in no doubt as to the bondage a genteel novelist must suffer. His mentor had objected to the "low mindedness and vulgarity of the chief actors." There had never been such a Bishop and his wife "in our time." The Signora Neroni was "a great blot on the work." No exception was taken to his frequent reference to Barchester bosoms, but "foul breathing" had to be struck out, and "fat stomach" must be altered to "deep chest."

But the criticism which most enraged the author was the very reasonable observation that the book would be improved by condensation; the reader suggested that it be cut from three volumes to two. Anthony, already too much inclined to think of industry as a mere matter of filling pages, could not tolerate an attack on his literary principles. He felt that he had done his duty if he reread the stint of the previous day and then went over the proof of the finished book, some two, or even three, times. His indifference to the need of real revision and excision was as remarkable as the facility and clarity with which he wrote his first drafts. Now he professed to understand that he was asked either to strike out two words from every six, or to burn the manuscript and write another book. He blustered loudly, but complied with at least some of the suggestions. Physical details were softened, several passages were rewritten, but *Barchester Towers* was not cut.

He had reason to feel his judgment vindicated by the book's reception. The faithful *Athenaeum* immediately gave him its customary warm review. In August the London *Times* broke silence with a complimentary notice a column long. In October the *Westminster Review* pronounced *Barchester Towers* "decidedly the cleverest novel of the season." All the reviewers found faults as well as merits; but each implied a recognition that he was becoming supreme in his special field. The public had begun to expect from him what the *Westminster* called "delineations of modern life in a special class of society."

Long before the *Westminster* came forth with this sententious utterance, Anthony had begun and finished another novel—his sixth. To have written one promising book earned him no respite; he must immediately justify the anticipated success by demonstrating that he could repeat the performance. *The Three Clerks*, written in less than five months and completed on August 18, 1857, set the seal upon his tendency to place speed and quantity ahead of quality.

Longmans proposed to publish the book on the half-profit basis, but Trollope wished to dispose of it for a lump sum. There was some haggling; Longman spoke of the value to an author of the firm's name upon the title page. Anthony said, either then or when he thought of it, that in his opinion the name of Longman had its greatest value at the bottom of a check. He was huffed because one of the firm had told him that *so and so* had "spawned" three novels on them in the year; was the fellow hinting at him? He determined that, since Longmans would not agree to his terms, he would try his luck elsewhere; with two successes to his credit, the firm ought to realize that his work was not speculative—it would sell.

The Three Clerks, although a good story, was not the equal of its immediate predecessors. The young hero, Charley Tudor, was the boy Anthony supposed himself to have been, and much of the book was autobiographical, even to the entanglement and the fear of a breach of promise suit. But what is so real is rarely true, and his memories had an artificial ring. The writing actually enabled him to pay off many old scores against civil service reform, Rowland Hill, and parliamentary investigations. Alaric Tudor's disgrace was a further illustration of his delicate understanding of the way in which a man whose intentions are on the whole good may, through blunder or circumstance, find himself in a false or even criminal position.

The scenes in the widow's home at Hampton were very pleasant, and there was a droll picture of young men in the domesticity of a public house bar where the landlady sat darning stockings; Mrs. Woodward was the first of the charming, sour-sweet, middle-aged mothers of whom Mrs. Dale would be the loveliest; and tough old Uncle Batt was an amusing fellow. But the two young couples were not amusing, edifying, or convincing. Katie, whom Trollope loved for Charley Tudor's sake, seems to have been his little sister Emily, who died at Hadley. "I had not the heart to kill her," Anthony admitted, "I never could do that."

CHAPTER XI

British Agent

1857-1859

BECAUSE Anthony was eager to start with Rose toward Italy, he allowed but one day in London for negotiating a contract for *The Three Clerks;* he had written from Ireland for an appointment with one of the partners of Hurst and Blackett, successors to Colburn, so that no time should be wasted. But the representative of the firm which he had decided to favor with his wares broke the appointment without notice. After fuming in the office for an hour, Trollope rose to go; the foreman, uneasy lest the house be losing a valuable connection, suggested that he leave his manuscript. This Trollope pronounced quite out of the question. The foreman, attempting to delay the impatient author in conversation, hazarded a guess as to the subject of the novel; he trusted it was not historical, adding reflectively, "Your historical novel is not worth a damn." Without stopping to satisfy the man's curiosity, Anthony hurried out to seek his mother's old publisher, Richard Bentley, who accepted the book immediately, paying over the considerable sum of £250. By thus flouting two of London's most important publishers, Longman and Hurst and Blackett, Anthony concluded with the third an arrangement greatly to his advantage.

Rose and he spent a few days of their holiday in Switzerland; then, since a visit to his mother was their principal object, they went on to Florence.

They found the mother sadly altered. The whist-table and the daily drive tired her, and she was now a stay-at-home with her grandchild, little "Bimba," as Uncle Anthony called her, and Tom's querulous old father-in-law. Mrs. Trollope was very deaf and very quiet. The diagonal folds of a plaid shawl were pinned around her shrunken shoulders, and her nose loomed large above the drooping lip. Her

Frances Trollope

memory was fading. Her thirty-fourth and last novel, *Fashionable Life: or Paris and London,* was flaccid and lifeless. With unconscious pathos she had written of her own characters, early in the third volume: "I really feel at a loss what next to tell my readers about them." Slips in grammar were no worse than in earlier work, but there were more contradictions and repetitions. The dialogue, once so sprightly, was wordy and highflown, and in her characterizations appeared the desire of the aged to oversimplify human relations.

The small section devoted to spiritualism, in which Home the medium figured, was more vivid. Mrs. Trollope, putting what she had to say into the mouths of her characters, made it evident that, like Tom, she believed in the physical phenomena, but unlike him, wistfully desired to credit the metaphysical as well. Yet she cautioned against acceptance of what was not proved. As for the moral right to investigate occultism, she made this pronouncement through her good old clergyman: "As far as my eye can penetrate, I can discern no law in Nature, nor recognize any principle in ethics, which can lead me to doubt that every effort to acquire knowledge, is in manifest obedience to the laws of God." Other brave old women might long to penetrate the secrets of a future whose existence they had never doubted, but the search was peculiarly important to Frances Trollope, for she had not outlived her rare curiosity. She was the more restlessly eager to enlarge her scope because her spirit was cramped, as it had never used to be, in a deaf, rheumatic body.

She knew that she was through with writing novels, and if her family troubled to read *Fashionable Life* they must have known it too. With a new mildness, she told Anthony how pleased she was to have him begin when she left off. Almost extinct as she looked, huddled in her high-back chair with her small feet hanging limply, her eyes, glancing over the rims of her spectacles, had lost neither their curiosity nor the shadow of laughter. Anthony's old sense of injustice was aroused; he told himself that she talked as if he were a beginner, ignoring the labor of twelve years; such was the treatment his family had always accorded him. But Mrs. Trollope had become forgetful, nor do a dozen years seem long in retrospect when one has grown so old.

She had relinquished her title—Mrs. Trollope of the Villino Trollope. Theodosia, poet, musician, accomplished translator, was the lady to whom Florentine visitors referred in letters home when they glowingly described an evening in Mrs. Trollope's delightful *salon*. But no more money would be coming in from new books by the veteran novelist, and the want of it would be felt in the sumptuous villa.

The two sons of the veteran had been slow to reveal their literary powers. Not until this year 1857, when Anthony was forty-two, had he been able to lay indisputable claim to the name of novelist; in the same year Tom—T. Adolphus Trollope, as he styled himself—at forty-seven, made his first important historical contribution in *The Girlhood of Catherine de Medici*. Although neither man had as yet reached the height of his powers, they could secretly compare their achievements. The elder brother, a traveler even in babyhood, had chosen the world view of history; Anthony, whose observation had been restricted both by eyesight and by environment, found his field in the intimate character analysis of the novel. Humanity in action was the concern of both, but their approach differed.

Tom was a positivist and a determinist. To him Catherine de Medici, the girl born in a Florentine palace to become queen mother of France and instigator of the St. Bartholomew's Day massacre, was "a penetrating intelligence wholly devoid of moral ideas"—a typical product of heredity and of the brilliant and corrupt society of the last days of the Florentine republic. Too much the scholar to invent where sources failed, he spent his energies in re-creating the political and social atmosphere in which she developed. But Anthony, had he by some strange chance been attracted by Catherine de Medici, would have been interested primarily in the woman; her origins and circle would have been dealt with only as they directly illuminated her character.

The brothers differed in their approach to religion. Tom's was that of the historian and sociologist. The march of science, with its inherent challenge to revealed religion, had no power to distress him; he felt himself superior to both. Religious sentiment, whether High or Low, Protestant or Catholic, was a social phenomenon, the infinite variety of its manifestations determined by race and circumstances. Every creed was capable of analysis and sympathetic comprehension, each filled its place in the unfolding of the historical panorama. Thoroughly alive to ethical considerations, he perceived that the moral order of the world was manifested in no nice apportionment of individual rewards and punishments.

But Anthony had wished to accept the teachings of the English Church. The pattern of his life, his conservative preferences, and his public all demanded it. He took a refined pleasure in the ritual; church bells and children's voices in the choir aroused nostalgic memories. With few illusions about the Anglican clergy, he was none the less a man capable of mysticism, a potentially spiritual man, and throughout his writings is scattered evidence of profound spiritual unease. He dreaded reverses and had no confidence in his power to sustain them, but at the same time endeavored to persuade himself that, if a man did right, he must receive a material reward.

Fearing to probe his own beliefs, he observed that if a man once began to doubt, he was unable to check himself and became lost in speculation. Even a slight change in religious views was attended by danger. "No one becomes an infidel at once. When the first step has been taken, the pace becomes frightfully fast." He hoped that he believed, but did not know either what or how much: "Is there, one may almost ask, any man who has such knowledge?" There were times when he thought wistfully of the beauty of the Roman Church. Sometimes when he inveighed against the overly religious, he was hitting out not only at Evangelicals but at received religion and the society which backed it.

He was less preoccupied with sex than with religion, but even more afraid of it. The son of Thomas Anthony was shy and sensitive. A popular Victorian novelist could not divulge all that he knew about his lovers, and his unconscious resentment at this restriction increased his dislike of marriageable young women. Not the springs of individual feeling, but the working-out of standardized emotions amid the endless complexities of human relationships, became his chief concern. He seldom cared enough for his girls to consider how they looked. Frequently he provided merely a decorative frame which the reader might fill with a portrait of his own ideal Victorian maiden; but this he did with such tact as to secure him a general reputation for charming heroines, deserved in but some half-dozen cases. Many of them were as pliable as rubber, and as obstinate.

Yet he was a master of old women, especially horrible old women; and exuberant, loud-mouthed spinsters who did not wish to marry were his delight—Miss Dunstable and Miss Todd were as cheerful and hearty as the mother of his early memories. He was faultless, too, in his delineation of old men; and his young men, no matter how rapid and few the strokes, are differentiated by their personal traits more than by their circumstances. But his marriageable girls, except for Lily Dale, Laura Standish, Mary Lowther, and the young Glencora, can be told apart rather by the little which happens to them than by inherent characteristics.

Tom, unlike Anthony, was fond of women and a general favorite with them. His geniality, balance, and sincere kindness charmed them all, regardless of age or condition. The "fallen woman," from whom Anthony shied nervously, was one of Tom's best subjects in history and later in fiction, and was treated with sympathetic detachment as a phenomenon natural in the circumstances which produced her.

Both brothers had a love for society. Anthony liked best to be with men, but, when Rose was present to protect him, could be extremely cheerful in a drawing room. In Florence in 1857 he had both his wife and Theodosia to take care of him. The Brownings were away that autumn, but the Charles Levers were there, and his acquaintance with his mother's old whist partner deepened almost into friendship. The corpulent Irish novelist had at first been afraid of old Mrs. Trollope lest she put him in a book, a habit of his own with acquaintances, but at Lucca, where they had spent the hot weather at the same hotel, her inexhaustible good-humor had won him over. She had been constant in attending his whist parties, to which she brought fresh packs of cards as her way of showing appreciation of his hospitality. If she intended Mr. Richards in her *Life and Adventures of a Clever Woman* for a caricature of Charles Lever, he did not know it.

Now that old Mrs. Trollope had given up whist, he devoted himself to her sons, enlisting their help in various projects for amusing the

English and American residents of Florence. Lever himself was amusing enough to those who did not see the melancholy beneath the surface. He fenced, shot, and rode with his children, but all exercise left him appallingly fat. The wittiest of men, he kept the whist table in an uproar of laughter—a good person to rouse Anthony. But Lever privately thought the Englishman Trollope insensitive, and, like many others, wondered that he could write with so much delicacy.

Before Anthony left Florence, he asked Tom to suggest a plot—a strange request for the shy, proud novelist, if it was seriously meant. At any rate, the plot of *Dr. Thorne* was proposed and accepted, and the resultant novel became the most popular in Anthony's list. Yet the circumstance was unfortunate. Not only did Anthony chafe over an indebtedness which he was too proud not to acknowledge, but the plot was unsuited to his genius. Arranged events could not, in his point of view, possess reality. Characters, when properly conceived, necessitated action, but the action must not dominate the characters. His refusal to keep secrets from his readers sprang from this distrust of prearrangement and surprise. Tom, who had the historian's mild contempt for the novel, provided a plot loosely in accord with his own thesis that human behavior is the product of circumstances, but too melodramatic and improbable to be congenial to his brother.

The novel hung upon a secret which could never have been kept. Murder, illegitimacy, a *cause célèbre*, the adoption of the slain man's child by his brother, the amassing of a great fortune by the murderer, and a whole county's supposed ignorance of the strands which connect past and present—these were heavy handicaps for a realist; and it was not the plot, but the magnificent delineation of character, the charm of country life, and the hearty love of traditional England which made *Dr. Thorne* a fine novel. Its position in a popular series was another advantage, but its greatest claim on public affection was the delightful doctor himself, although, from an artistic standpoint, the unhappy, ambitious Lady Arabella was a greater achievement.

On returning to Ireland, Anthony devoted himself to *Dr. Thorne* until early 1858, when an important event occurred in the other branch of his dual career. The Post Office, whose head had professed a complete lack of faith in him a dozen years since, now entrusted him with an important diplomatic mission. He was to leave his routine duties and travel to Egypt, with power to negotiate a treaty for the better conveyance of the Indian and Australian mails. This was a signal honor and, aside from its public significance, occasioned great private satisfaction; for if he had been envious of Tom's voyage to America and his innumerable rambles on the Continent, it was he himself who would have the glory of being the first of his family to set foot in Africa and Asia.

Although *Dr. Thorne* was far from completed, his growing confidence in his power to command a market determined him to attempt disposing of it for cash in its unfinished state. Passing through London, he offered it to Bentley, his latest publisher, for £400—an advance of £150 on his demand for *The Three Clerks*. His assurance temporarily convinced Bentley of the desirability of the bargain, but only until the pressure of Anthony's presence was removed. Next morning the publisher tracked his peremptory author to the Post Office to tell him that he had changed his mind.

Anthony clapped on his hat and tore across London to Tom's publishers, Chapman and Hall, in Piccadilly. He had, he shouted, only an hour at his disposal; did Mr. Chapman want a book of his enough to pay him £400 down? Before he left, the agreement had been satisfactorily concluded, but Anthony retained an amused impression of Mr. Chapman's grasp on a poker, and of his most uneasy countenance. Thus highhandedly was arranged the publication of the first of thirty-one books by Anthony Trollope under the imprint of Chapman and Hall.

The February voyage from Marseilles to Alexandria was stormy, and Anthony suffered from seasickness. He sat at a table in the saloon, trying to forget his misery while he filled out page after page of *Dr. Thorne,* according to the specifications in his little notebook—so many words an hour, so many hours a day, so many days a week. He was fiercely proud at the evidence of physical fitness and of the inflexible will which could overcome both his present squeamishness and the sloth of his long immaturity. Unlike his mother, he did not need to write for a living; but quantity was his goal, and his self-sufficiency was so great that he thought the quality was sure to be good.

He finished *Dr. Thorne* in Egypt, and, on the very day following, began *The Bertrams;* but his self-justification shows an uneasy conscience: "My novels, whether good or bad, have been as good as I could make them. Had I taken three months of idleness between each they would have been no better." Not three months of idleness, but three months of painstaking revision, would have improved them. But Trollope would not rewrite. A word changed here, a spelling there, and he felt he had done quite enough and was ready to begin again.

The object of his present mission was to expedite the transit of the mails across Egypt on their way to India and Australia. The Suez canal was still no more than a speculation—a dream, so Anthony thought—and the British mails had to be unloaded from the steamer at Alexandria, sent by rail to Cairo and thence by camel to Suez on the Red Sea—a two days' journey across the desert. But now a railway from Cairo to Suez was nearing completion, and the Post Office was eager to secure an economy of twenty-four hours in the long chain of its Eastern communications.

The Egyptian official with whom he had to treat was young Nubar Bey, an Armenian Christian who was to become one of Egypt's outstanding statesmen. Anthony admired his colleague's dignified and agreeable manners as much as he underestimated his intelligence and diplomatic skill. At stated intervals Nubar visited him, bringing his servants, his pipes and his coffee. In unessential matters the two men readily agreed, but Anthony, whose desire for speed was almost an obsession, insisted that the mails should pass through Egypt in twenty-four hours, while Nubar, true to Ottoman custom, maintained that double the time was required.

Anthony suspected that the steamship company preferred the slower schedule and was backing the resistance of the Egyptian government. He became more aggressive, hectoring his oriental colleague as though he were a delinquent publisher. But Nubar, who had enjoyed a European education, understood his suspicions perfectly and was tolerantly amused by them until, having played out his little game, he was ready to capitulate.

While waiting for the slow fruition of his diplomatic efforts, Anthony found time to see the pyramids and to effect various improvements in the post offices at Alexandria and Suez. His business done, he paid a flying visit to the Holy Land, leaving a letter for his young postal colleague Edmund Yates with such laconic advice on sight-seeing as, "Hear the howling dervishes of Cairo at one on Friday. They howl but once a week."

He was glad to be spared the company of clever Yates in Palestine, where he looked forward to a momentous spiritual experience. What Anthony asked of the Holy Land was profoundly simple; he wished to become as a little child. He longed to believe that every word in the New Testament was literally true, to believe that he was seeing with his bodily eyes the places where Jesus had walked and taught. The Armenian and Russian pilgrims at Jerusalem filled him with loathing, and he could see for himself the absurdity of the alleged scriptural sites within the city. But the Mount of Olives was uncontaminated, and, as he pondered there alone, he could imagine his Lord walking and talking with His friends. Much of this nostalgia went into the book he began in Egypt. He underrated the novel, partly because of its restless tone, due in some measure to constantly changing scenes, but more because he would gladly have disowned its revelation of himself.

The worst which can be said of *The Bertrams* is to repeat that Trollope confused humor with burlesque, adding that the novel would have been better for reworking and that it contained occasional improbabilities in character. These were minor faults in the book which, of all Trollope's works, has remained the most modern in tone and the most haunting in mood—one which in the nomenclature of a latter day might well have been called *Requiem for Youth*. For *The Bertrams* is a story of disillusionment, in which only the humblest find happiness, while the beautiful and gifted—those who ask much—are wounded in their idealism and, though they linger long, cannot recover.

The tact with which Trollope made the cousins resemble each other in exactly the right degree, the gradual disappointment of the son as he realized the venality of his father, the high level of conversation suitable to a young man of genius—never pompous, never verbose—and the impression of emotional immaturity in the young lovers, gave indications of the psychological powers and extraordinary sensitivity of the novelist. The familiar Trollopean prejudices found their place, the dislike of Evangelicals and of the French, the admiration for coarse, jolly women who were not hunting husbands, the wry absorption in money problems.

In the card party of the ancient ladies of Littlebath, at which Lady Ruth Revoke was scolded into a fit, he surpassed his mother in satire. The scene was so perfectly pitched that one shudder of Trollope's vast shoulders would have transformed Miss Todd's drawing room into a cave and the players into Goya's witches; but he did not shudder, he was calm and even amused; he had known just such old ladies—and the gruesome never resolved into the supernatural.

He returned to Great Britain by way of Malta and Gibraltar, where he accomplished further improvements in the postal service and gathered impressions which he could use in future short stories. By the end of May he was on another, less distant mission, into Scotland, where he spent two months in settling various disputed questions, especially that of mail delivery in crowded sections. In heat peculiarly trying to one of his heavy build, he walked, beside first one grumbling postman and then another, to the top flats of tall Edinburgh houses. The reflection that he was suffering twice as much as his companion and would, when the exertion was over, be writing love scenes at his hotel instead of resting like the humble postman, filled him with pride in his superior strength and ambition.

The late summer and autumn of 1858 were spent quietly in Ireland, but *The Bertrams* was not yet finished when, in November, the Post Office asked him to undertake a third and more distant mission, this time to the West Indies. It was believed that the postal service in far-away colonies could be managed on the spot by colonial governments with greater efficiency and economy than from home. Besides his investigation of this problem, he was empowered to conclude postal treaties—as in Egypt—with officials in Spanish Cuba and in Panama; as he had been successful in earlier missions and was recognized as an able administrator, his superiors could conscientiously employ him abroad while at home they enjoyed a vacation from an often troublesome subordinate.

Anthony's mission necessitated a change of family plans. He must postpone the yearly visit to his mother, which was regrettable in view of her age and failing memory, but he tried to make up for her disappointment by writing unusually affectionate letters. Harry and Freddy were in school and Rose would have to remain at home without him, since much of the trip would be too difficult for a woman. As for his literary work, he believed he could finish *The Bertrams* on the westward voyage, and Chapman and Hall assented to his proposal to pay him £250 for a travel book on the West Indies. The sum was £150 less than his demand for *Dr. Thorne*, but the work was to fill only one volume instead of three.

He sailed from Southampton on November 17, 1858. The passage was rough and Anthony found more than weather to grumble at, as walnuts were wormy, claret warm, apples withered, and lights went out at eleven no matter how exciting the whist. His traveling companions were Spaniards, bound as he was for St. Thomas in the Virgin Islands, the jumping-off place for all points in the Caribbean region. There the "Atrato" docked on December 2. Among the blacks who came on board to solicit laundry, a Negress in pink gloves and stiff white muslins diverted him by the gift of a rose with a sentimental, "That's for love, dear." Anthony observed throughout his travels that the Negresses were neatly and fashionably dressed and moved with consummate grace, qualities which he greatly admired in women.

As for St. Thomas, to which he was fated to return three times, he called it "a Niggery-Hispano-Dano-Yankee-Doodle place; in which, perhaps, the Yankee-Doodle element, declaring itself in nasal twang and sherry cobblers, seems to be of the strongest flavor." His first objective was the British colony of Jamaica, from which he was to go on to Cuba.

He found Kingston a hot, sorry town, well-planned, but never finished. The brick buildings were defaced with cracks where mortar had crumbled away, and the wooden houses had not been painted. The streets had neither lights nor sidewalks, nor was there drainage, so that one must walk either through sand or rivulet.

Spanish Town, seat of the Jamaican government, was even more forlorn. Heedless Anthony took the train from Kingston without inquiring as to the timetable, only to find at the other end that the distance was covered but once in four hours. From high noon until 4:15 he was a most unhappy man. His business at Government House occupied only twenty minutes; then Anthony went out to wander through blazing deserted streets, until by bribery he persuaded a Negro to direct him to a tavern where he sat and waited for train time.

The West Indian hotel diet of beefsteak, cheese, pickles, bread, and beer struck him as indiscreet. The Negroes stood upon their dignity when he ordered them about as one did English servants. When Anthony complained that the price of gloves was exorbitant, a colored clerk retorted airily, "We consider it rather cheap. But in Kingston, sir, you must not think about little economies."

Anthony did not believe that the Negroes deserved their reputation for thievery. Certainly they never robbed him, and as he was culpably careless with money, this established their honesty in his opinion. But they were vain and lazy, religion had not improved them, they aped their betters and had a snobbishly low opinion of late arrivals from the African jungle. Anthony was anxious to correct the ideas spread about by more or less ill-informed English humanitarians. Observing that in England it would be considered wrong to despise the Negroes, he added with Trollopean aplomb, "I can hardly think that anything so natural can be very wrong."

The brusquerie which made the home government glad to employ him overseas did not endear him to the colonial authorities. O'Connor Morris, Postmaster General of Jamaica, made this comment on his dealings with the special emissary: "I believe Mr. Trollope had a thousand good qualities of head and heart, which were disguised in a most unfortunate and repelling manner"—an observation reminiscent of those applied in earlier times to the father, Thomas Anthony Trollope.

He was less truculent on his visits to the homes of Jamaican planters, who lived as English gentlemen ought to live, hunting, fishing, and performing the magisterial office. The mountain and forest scenery charmed him. Life was leisurely; at six, coffee and toast arrived in the bedroom, one bathed and dressed slowly because of the heat, rode for an hour or two, ate a huge breakfast. The ladies were seldom visible until dinner time, then a little music, a stroll in the garden—but unfortunately everyone went to bed at nine, before the evening was well begun. When a Jamaican invited a house guest, he used the formula, "Come and I will give you a cool bed."

Beneath this tempered existence, so charming to the casual visitor, lurked the dread of ruin. For slavery had been abolished in all British colonies, and Jamaica could no longer compete with Spanish Cuba or with Louisiana, where slaves worked the sugar plantations. To make the situation more difficult, the home government had removed the protective tariff. The Negroes did not furnish sufficient paid labor, as they cared little for money and could practically live off the fertile country. Half the sugar-cane fields, more than half the coffee lands had been allowed to revert to bush. Politics were abjured by the whites because an English planter was unwilling to sit in a legislature where the emancipated slave appeared as his equal. Gentlemen segregated themselves on their estates; thus the towns decayed and the blacks gained the ascendancy.

While Anthony was in Kingston, the Negro Soulouque, ousted dictator of Haiti, fled to Jamaica. Refugees from his tyranny already settled there celebrated his downfall by a three days' revel across the street from the hotel where Soulouque and his family took refuge. The amusement with which Trollope observed the rejoicings, and the hauteur with which he guarded himself from any personal contact with the fallen tyrant and his adherents, were those of a Gulliver in Lilliput. His racial tolerance, unlike his mother's chivalrous, involuntary alliance with the oppressed, was that of a man so sure of the superiority of his own strain that he could afford to judge leniently of others.

In February, impatient to get on from Jamaica to Cuba, he refused to wait for the passenger boat and took passage on a brig from New Brunswick. He paid heavily for his precipitancy, as there was a horrible smell left by the late cargo of salt fish, the heat was terrific, and the skipper so incompetent as to run his vessel aground.

On board the sweltering, motionless craft, Trollope commenced the volume which became, next to his mother's *Domestic Manners of the Americans,* the best-known travel book by one of his family. His theory was that such a work should be written under the stimulus of travel, with every impression fresh on the unjaded eye. There were, in his opinion, two kinds of truth, and that resulting from the scholar's painful research was not his. He reckoned himself an observer, recorder of the changing scene; his judgments were swift, not deep, but he believed them sure.

He thought Havana a wretched town. The streets were poorly lighted by oil lamps, and the fashionable drive, in which the citizens took consummate pride, was of such inferiority to those upon the Continent of Europe that he passed over it without realizing he had seen it. The population were naïve in their pleasures and, though the women were better behaved than those he had seen in Spain the year before, they were ugly and ungraceful, with big noses and backward sloping brows.

He was eager to compare slaveholding Cuba with free English Jamaica, and gladly accepted an invitation to a large sugar plantation. No evidence of cruelty fell under his eyes, nor was there any attempt to keep him from seeing all that was to be seen. The slaves worked sixteen hours a day in the busy season, during which they were allowed six hours for sleep and two for meals. They were well fed and well cared for, not as human beings, but as property. Infants were baptized into the Catholic faith; animals were not baptized, and this rite marked the chief distinction between beast and black. The Church took no further interest.

All Cuba was seething over President Buchanan's famous message to the American Congress, advancing claims to territory in Mexico, Panama, and Cuba itself. Trollope, though shocked at the "out-spoken insolence" of Buchanan's tone, was none the less convinced that Cuba ought to belong to the United States. The decadence of Spain was hastening toward ruin; when Cuba was no longer Spanish, British traders would engage in Cuban enterprise. More important, if it became a part of the United States, Cuba must abolish not only slavery but the slave trade; and the ships which still carried the hateful cargo from Africa to the island were the ships of United States citizens flying the American flag.

Returning to St. Thomas, Anthony next set out to visit the Windward Islands, British Guiana, Barbados, and Trinidad. He found a higher range of prosperity in French possessions, such as Martinique, than in those belonging to the British crown. The explanation lay, he thought, in the realism of the French colonists, who wasted no vain regrets on the home they had left but, realizing the permanency of their separation, set themselves to making the best of the new world. But the English heart was eternally set on England, and English dreams were always of the Homeland.

Trinidad moved him to further pronouncements on the racial question. Humanitarian sentiment in England had much deplored the importation of coolie labor from India into the West Indies; but Trollope saw in it the one means of salvation for many of the islands. Labor was scarce, and he believed that nothing but life and death competition would induce a Negro to work. The emancipation of slaves had been quite right, but the blacks were incapable of the higher pursuits of civilization. Hence he promulgated a comfortable theory that the intermarriage of Negro and coolie stock would instill conscience and energy into the black and improve the physique of the East Indian.

He was now to visit Colombia, Panama, and Costa Rica, but had first to return once again to the fever-ridden harbor of St. Thomas. He went out of his way to see the wretched villa where Bolivar had died in exile, and grieved to view the mean memorials of so great a man. One section of his journey customarily required three days for its performance, but he determined to make it in two in order to prove that a mounted mail carrier could expedite his deliveries by a day. The postman and he started at daybreak, Trollope's two-hundred-odd pounds mounted on a wicked brute with a saddle devised for torture. The first day caused him excruciating pain, which he could endure better than the thought of confessing himself beaten. After pondering the question, he ordered two bottles of brandy, poured the contents into a washbasin and sat in it. The heroic remedy was just within the margin of endurance, but it cured him, and he was able to finish the route on the second day.

In Panama the heat was unbearable, the laundress sent back his shirts in worse condition than she had received them, and the style of the church buildings resembled "that which is so generally odious to an Englishman's eye and ear, under the title of Renaissance." Crossing the isthmus by rail, he pronounced that it would be as impossible to construct a Panama canal as for de Lesseps to succeed at Suez. God did not ordain isthmuses between continents without a purpose; railways were righteous, because they hastened the mails, but canals were the nearest things to blasphemy.

He was the first of the Trollopes to see the Pacific. He had known that the actual sight would bring no joy comparable to what he had felt when, in his study at home, he had pored over the map and told himself that he should soon behold what Magellan had seen. Yet he was disappointed because he could think of nothing but the fearful heat, the careless laundress, and the horrid food. "Oh, those weary clothes!" he exclaimed as he packed for his next stage. "If a man could travel as a dog, how delightful it would be to keep moving from year's end to year's end."

The grueling journey across Costa Rica by mule was full of strange encounters amidst magnificent scenery. He went to sleep, accidentally, in the crater of an active volcano, became acquainted with German savants, muleteers, filibusters, clergymen and naval officers, and gathered material for later tales, less strange than his own experiences. It was May when he returned to St. Thomas, for the third and last time. Thence he proceeded to Bermuda, where he remained for two weeks, feeling uncommonly indolent, and much disgusted at the sentimental kindness shown to convicts.

His many months of travel were not to close without a glimpse of the land which had inadvertently made his mother's fortune. Some day he hoped himself to write a volume on the United States, whose government and social life afforded, he believed, "the most interesting phenomena which we find as to the new world;—the best means of prophesying what the world will next be, and what men will next do." For the present he contented himself with a hasty trip from New York to Montreal and back. He grew lyrical over Niagara, as his mother had done, but grunted contemptuously at the Thousand Islands and the rapids of the St. Lawrence, and judged that Saratoga, then in her palmy state, must be "a very dull place for persons who are not invalids."

In New York he had a fruitless interview with Harper and Brothers, who had been reprinting his novels for the past dozen years, paying a small sum to his London publisher for the early sheets but nothing whatever to the author. Trollope had made a point of keeping the American rights of *The West Indies* in his own hands; he now offered them to Harpers, but they declined, alleging that the subject "did not suit" them. Anthony thereupon surrendered his rights to Chapman and Hall, from whom Harpers nonchalantly acquired them for the trifling sum of £30, leaving Anthony empty-handed as before. The experience did not predispose him in favor of American business methods.

The Post Office regarded his mission as highly successful. Lord Elgin, in the annual report of the Postmaster General for 1860, departed from precedent by devoting several paragraphs to his achievements. "Mr. Anthony Trollope, as mentioned in the last report, had, on a previous occasion, ably discharged a similar duty in the Mediterranean and in Egypt, and performed the new work assigned to him with even greater success. Not only did Mr. Trollope devise many improvements in the details of the service, and effect a considerable saving, but, although a landsman, was able to propose a scheme of routes for the mail packets, which, while better adapted than the present to postal purposes, would be attended with a great saving of mileage, and is pronounced by Captain Washington, Hydrographer of the Admiralty, to be superior to the existing routes, even in a nautical point of view," etc., etc.

Quite as gratifying proved the reception of the hastily published travel book. The *Athenaeum* spoke of him as "a cultured and a scholarly writer, with a bright imagination and large experience of the world." The *Saturday Review* observed, "Mr. Trollope gives us exactly what we want, and he gives it us in a shape which we cannot praise too highly." The *Times* in various issues devoted seven and one-half columns to the book and to the special problems on which Trollope had written. "We looked for amusement only from Mr. Trollope," wrote the reviewer, "and we are inveigled into instruction.

If by means of Mr. Trollope's pleasant pages attention is turned to these islands, and some encouragement is afforded to our planters, the author may regard his book of travels as the most useful, if not the most brilliant, volume which he has yet published."

This made very pleasant reading to Anthony Trollope, Esq. He betook himself at once to Chapman and Hall's offices and informed them that he must have £600 for his next novel—an increase of fifty percent over anything he had hitherto received.

CHAPTER XII

The Ripening

1859-1861

ANTHONY was not satisfied with his life in Ireland. When he had been stationed at Mallow, Dublin had seemed the world's center, but since his establishment in the Irish metropolis he had come to regard it as being, for his purposes, a place outside the universe. Only a London residence could satisfy his ambition and his needs. He had been in the postal service for twenty-five years, and no man could rival him in knowledge of the Irish mails; but Ireland in postal matters as in literature was only a backwater. There was little more for him to do there—his talents could find their proper scope only at the heart of the postal system, where the mail trains went out twice a day and the whole space of St. Martin's-le-Grand had become barely sufficient to accommodate the administrative offices.

Moreover, beyond the narrow sea many literary men, younger than himself, surpassed him in reputation; he was too far from his publishers, out of touch with English periodicals to which he ought to contribute; above all, he was hungry for the society of men with the same interests. He would not, like Tom, seek his good companions in continental expatriation. Even Tom found it necessary to make a long annual journey from Florence when a new book was published. Nor would Anthony, who was neither historian, poet, nor writer of *belles-lettres,* be satisfied with the polite Florentine circle. If he were to write English novels, he must live near England's heart. He would even give up hunting if it stood in the way of his ambition.

His successes with the English scene could not reconcile him to the failures of his two Irish novels, and, even while he made his preparations for leaving Ireland, he planned a third attempt. His long residence had not altered his impression of Ireland as a romantic country peopled by romantic folk; he knew that among fiction writers no one

was his peer in comprehension of the Irish and their social conditions
—he considered Lever inept in characterization—and he could not understand why a public which demanded romantic novels should not
be satisfied with what he was willing to provide. *Castle Richmond* was
his farewell to the country which had welcomed and cherished him;
when in his old age he wrote *The Landleaguers*, he was actuated by
motives quite unlike this mixture of pertinacity and charming gallantry.

On August 2, 1859, Chapman and Hall agreed to publish the spec-
ified Irish novel, and two days later Anthony began *Castle Richmond*.
The theme was one which Adelaide Proctor had used in the previous
year in *Homeward Bound*—a shipwrecked sailor returned after long
exile to find his wife married to his friend. Tennyson was to use it in
Enoch Arden, but in Anthony's hands it was considerably altered: the
husband in *Castle Richmond* is a rascal who rises from his alleged
grave to blackmail the family of his supposed widow.

The dignity and unselfishness of the defrauded lady, the chivalry
of the man who has believed himself legally married to her, the integrity of the threatened household, produce a situation full of anxiety
which keeps the reader in poignant suspense. This domestic drama
was played before a drop curtain of famine with starving peasants as
chorus, for *Castle Richmond* was a tale of Ireland's worst days. Anthony had seen and tasted hunger; its memory drifted like murk
through the pages. A quiet sorrow, a delicate restraint exalted scenes
over which his mother would have poured vitriol. Without a misspent
word, he showed a stripped hut, a dead baby on the knees of a dying
woman, a naked child dead in a corner.

Such bitter food was not relished in England. Had Ireland been in a
less unhappy state when *Castle Richmond* was published, English
readers could have been comfortable in the thought that twelve years
had passed since these poor wretches starved to death. As it was, they
could not pick up a daily paper without seeing reference to current
evils in that luckless country. Rents had continued to rise, landlords
to be extortionate, taxes to increase, and the endless quarrel between
Catholics and Protestants had waxed in bitterness. A strong police
force was ineffectual in subduing malcontents. Across the Atlantic,

especially in New York, Irish emigrants who had left the country in the dreadful years of dearth had grown rich and were sending money home to foment disorder. The Fenian Society had declared its purpose of setting up an independent Irish republic. Victorians disliked depressing novels based on truths which pricked at conscience.

Perverse Anthony thought better of the plot which he had developed from Miss Proctor's than of his own admirable characterizations. Of his little heroine he remarked contemptuously, "The girl herself has no character," and thus libeled his own creation. He was even more severe on the unfortunate, still youthful woman who was in love with her daughter's suitor: "The mother, who is strong enough, is almost revolting"—an injustice which had its origin in his secret dread of the woman who wishes to marry the man who has changed his mind.

The progress of the novel was retarded by a holiday in the Pyrenees, where he worked irregularly and collected material for several mediocre short stories. On his return he asked the Post Office to transfer him to England, and applied to Thackeray, the recognized leader of English letters, for admission to the charmed circle of London's literary élite. The great novelist, he heard, was to edit a new magazine, the *Cornhill*, slated to appear on the first day of 1860. He did not know Thackeray; he had not been on his mother's Parisian picnic which had nearly deprived England of *Vanity Fair;* but as early as October, 1859, he wrote to ask whether he would be welcomed as a contributor.

Thackeray's reply was genial but indefinite—although fiction was of course necessary, he would prefer articles. But Anthony had already been in touch with Smith and Elder, the proprietors of the new magazine, and had extorted from them the sumptuous offer of £1,000 for the copyright of a novel to be published in the *Cornhill*, the first installment to be in their hands by December 12.

It was a day of triumph and anxiety. He could not think of refusal. The price was almost double any he had hitherto received, the recognition it implied gave him exquisite delight. But November was upon him, and he had no novel except the half-finished *Castle Richmond*, which belonged to Chapman and Hall. Could he take *Castle Richmond* away from Chapman? Would the *Cornhill* be likely to accept an Irish story?

It was clear that *two* novels were wanted at once, and that in the allotted weeks he could not complete even one. The splendid hazard excited him; thus had his mother taken her swift, and sometimes ruinous, decisions. He went to London to negotiate, thus spending the beginning of the all too brief period. He would ask Chapman to release *Castle Richmond*; if he refused, or if Smith would not take an Irish story, he would have to do what Dickens, Thackeray, and Mrs. Gaskell did habitually—to publish as he wrote. A momentary compunction touched him at the thought of delivering installments of a novel whose end he could not foresee; frequently his characters diverged from his original conception of them, and one could not alter chapters once they were in print.

Mr. Chapman obligingly agreed to surrender *Castle Richmond*, and even promised to take it back if the *Cornhill* could not use it. And Mr. Smith felt that they could not—he said frankly that he dare not risk an unpopular subject at the commencement of the enterprise: he had hoped for a novel on the order of *The Warden* and *Barchester Towers*. Anthony was disappointed but not discouraged by a decision which he had expected. The Irish novel was restored to Chapman, and next evening on the train he began *Framley Parsonage*.

He realized what his public wanted, and was half reconciled to their will. They wished him to write about themselves, about dinners they might give or go to, about love affairs they might have, if they were lucky; the people and the incidents must be raised above the flat familiar level, but not to such a height as to cause readers a painful feeling of inferiority. And he was expected not to deal with unpleasant subjects.

Framley Parsonage required little invention, beyond imagining a young lord and his proud mother at the great house, a young clergyman and a sister quite as proud at the rectory across the park. Each of these principals had relations who appeared almost without effort on the conjuror's part, and to sustain them a half-dozen characters were brought forward from earlier stories: the Proudies, the Grantlys, the patent medicine heiress. Because, as he phrased it, "There must be love in a novel," Lucy Robarts, the clever "little brown girl" in the parsonage, was wooed by Lord Lufton, whose mother thought he could do better. On this frail life line hung the weight of three volumes.

Trollope considered Lucy his "most natural" heroine. She was genuinely charming and intelligent, notwithstanding the silly obstinacy necessary to the author in completing his tale of pages. But the chief interest lay, not in the love idyll, but in Mark Robarts, his debts and his excursions into the hunting society of Gatherum Castle. The distinction between Mark and his friend Lord Lufton was maintained with delicate precision; the aristocrat was as handsome, better born, enormously richer, but less intelligent and less fine than the young clergyman.

More important to Trollope subjectively was the perpetual curate and martyr Josiah Crawley. The bitterness Trollope felt toward his own father had been purged away in his treatment of the suffering Larry Macdermot, but the problem of his parents continued, perhaps unconsciously, to occupy him. He showed consummate art in revealing the spiritual pride and worldly envy which had cankered the essential goodness of the erudite clergyman, who was never less than a gentleman in his awful poverty and who was amazingly like the unfortunate barrister Thomas Anthony Trollope. Mrs. Trollope also played a part in *Framley Parsonage* in the familiar figure of Emily Dunstable, of whose humor he managed to convince his readers, although they could not see the play of feature and the mimicry which had delighted Anthony in old days, when his mother amused the family. More and more images of the past dominated his writing. He allowed the bailiffs to take possession of *Framley Parsonage*, but would not permit them to work the mischief wrought at Julians Hill.

While working at top speed on *Framley Parsonage*, he was making powerful efforts to secure his transfer and promotion in the postal service. Rowland Hill, the Chief Secretary, could not be asked to aid an active enemy, but Cecelia's husband John Tilley, who had married again and had risen to be Assistant Secretary, exerted his influence, and in December Anthony was appointed Surveyor General of the Eastern District of England, at a salary of £700 plus travel allowances. This made it possible for him to settle within easy reach of London, and before the waning year was out he had leased a large, rather imposing Georgian house at Waltham Cross, twelve miles from town.

All the Trollopes were fond of gardens, and Anthony, looking about his estate in bleak December, imagined Rose pouring tea under the giant cedar on the lawn when summer came, and literary men out from London, sampling fresh-picked strawberries and cream from his wife's dairy. The vegetable garden was extensive; he boasted that he grew peas, beans, broccoli, cauliflower, celery, beets, onions, carrots, parsnips, turnips, sea kale, asparagus, French beans, artichokes, vegetable marrow, cucumbers, tomatoes, endive, lettuce, herbs, cabbages, and potatoes—a nurseryman's catalogue. The stables were roomy enough to tempt him to keep hunters—the Essex pack was kenneled only ten miles away—and he decided he could afford to hunt two days a week.

He was now a country gentleman, far less insecure than that gentleman-farmer, Thomas Anthony Trollope, who had built Julians forty years ago. The younger Anthony held what he wanted, one hand grasping Rose, his boys, his estate and the delights and duties which went with it; the other clutched on his position in the Post Office, his writing, the society he intended to enter. Not a finger could slip without the loss of something precious. The actuality of success was in his grip, but to keep what he had captured meant constant exertion and vigilance. Every morning at half past five his Irish groom brought him coffee. Half an hour was spent in suffering over yesterday's stint of writing, and the remainder of the three-hour period was devoted to the new assignment. He had a fetish which kept him to his work: it was a notebook with lines and dates, less picturesque than Balzac's purple dressing gown.

Yet he was not altogether happy. His driving energy was too often a flight from thought. While he was writing, or pounding along after a fox he seldom saw, or shouting with laughter among men friends, he was content; but when the day's assignment was done, when he jogged home from hunting through the mist, when someone seemed to slight him, he would be depressed and angry, both at the trivial cause and at himself for a lack of fortitude.

His inner uncertainties showed in his ferocity toward subordinates. A postmaster mouthed a grievance; Trollope growled, "Why don't you pay an old woman sixpence a week to fret for you?" He was able, he was never slack in duty—and he was generally disliked. It was horrible for underlings to watch him at work; he would stand at his desk and write in a frenzy, his sparse hair on end, a handkerchief stuffed between his jaws to choke back imprecations. He got on badly with colleagues who were on his own level, disliking Scudamore, who wrote poetry for *Punch*, and detesting Yates, who was becoming known as a critic and feuilletonist. Toward his chief, his attitude was perverse. He and John Tilley were leaders of the faction which opposed Rowland Hill, "that man from Birmingham," whom younger men in the service considered an ideal secretary. Anthony had had a hand in the bureaucratic obstruction which kept Hill from the direction of postal affairs for fifteen years.

Yet as a public servant he was so able that his services would have been sorely missed. He took a genuine interest in the welfare of the Post Office personnel, served on a committee to investigate grievances in the circulation department, went with John Tilley to speak for the Post Office at a parliamentary investigation on civil service appointments, and interested himself in the Post Office Library and Literary Association, which had been formed by some of the junior clerks who showed more taste for mental improvement than had been customary in his own day.

A month after Trollope had triumphantly settled in Waltham Cross, virtually announcing himself an established London author ready to enter literary society, he made his bow to his compeers at a dinner given by George Smith, one of the proprietors of the new *Cornhill*. He was extremely pleased at Mr. Smith's invitation, expecting the affair to put him at once where he had long wished to be. A brilliant assemblage of journalists, critics, and freelances had been invited. Thackeray would be there, and Trollope was prepared to like the man whose letter had been so charmingly friendly. Two of the other guests were destined to become his warm friends—G. H. Lewes and the painter Millais.

But in the event the dinner was a disappointment. Thackeray presented an impressive appearance with his height, his dignified carriage, and the thick white hair which belied his forty-eight years. Unfortunately, he was suffering acutely from his painful chronic complaint and gave the new acquaintance only a curt "How do!" upon which Trollope sulked throughout the evening. In time, and with reservations, the two men surmounted the bad beginning and became friends. Anthony grew familiar with Thackeray's house in South Kensington and came to love his charming and talented daughter Anne, who acted as her father's hostess and secretary and wrote delightful articles and stories of her own, against which nothing worse could be said than that she loved adjectives too well to choose between them.

Inwardly Trollope, the blustering official, and Thackeray, the polished man of the world, had points of resemblance. Both lacked self-confidence, both suffered from melancholy, and Trollope felt himself peculiarly liable to the indolence he condemned in Thackeray. But Thackeray sometimes chose to show his weakness to the world, and Anthony was inclined to despise this self-revelation. He thought Thackeray incapable of anything but the life of a littérateur; and even as a writer—though he admired his work, especially *Esmond*—he held him scarcely deserving his signal success.

With G. H. Lewes, another guest at the *Cornhill* dinner, there was nothing for Anthony to envy and all to admire. Lewes's wretched health, his puny ugliness, his miserable first marriage, his failure as an actor, the poverty which forced him to write dramatic and literary criticism and attempt the novel when all his aptitudes and interests lay in science, biography, and philosophy—all such griefs and disadvantages were borne, not so much with patience, as with an actual gaiety at which Anthony marveled. Six years had passed since George Eliot, that "wonderful woman," as Anthony reverently called her, had joined her life to that of Lewes. For her, Trollope made an exception to his usual detestation of intellectual women; he was her friend as much as her husband's. The Leweses valued Anthony's "straightforward, wholesome *Wesen*" and made him a welcome guest. Whether or not he asked permission to bring Rose is unknown; it seems unlikely. But he made a return for their hospitality when he assisted Lewes's son Charles to a position in the Post Office.

John Everett Millais, the artist, was a much younger man than Lewes or Trollope, only thirty at the time of Smith's dinner; tall, curly-headed, handsome, and unaffected. His straightforward friendliness charmed Anthony, who took umbrage at any sign of preciosity. As a boy of nineteen Millais had joined the Pre-Raphaelites, but, as there was nothing of the mystic in his matter-of-fact temper, he had separated from the group in order to paint literary subjects with photographic accuracy. He had just emerged, cheerful and with undiminished popularity, from a terrific battering by the art critics, urged on by Ruskin. Millais was admirably fitted to illustrate Trollope's novels, because his aim, like the author's, was to present a pleasing, recognizable picture, neither commonplace nor over-refined. Trollope himself could understand and enjoy such work. He asked from an illustrator what his readers wanted from him—a well-told tale.

Dickens, who published his own magazine, *All the Year Round,* was not at the *Cornhill* dinner. Neither was Wilkie Collins, nor any other of the prominent novelists whom Trollope soon met and with whom he had occasion to compare himself. Dickens and Thackeray shared the zenith of England's literary firmament, toward which George Eliot was rapidly rising. The men were the same age, three years older than Anthony and two years junior to Tom Trollope, with whom Dickens had long been acquainted. The period was momentous to Dickens, for he had begun his inimitable readings, left his wife, and was about to buy Gadshill Place. He was not on speaking terms with Thackeray because of a recent squabble at the Garrick Club, occasioned by a satirical description of Thackeray which Edmund Yates, Trollope's Post Office colleague, had published in his scandal sheet.

Indeed, Anthony found that London's literary circles were frequently disturbed by silly wrangles. Charles Reade, who scandalized the Garrick Club by parading the rooms in slippers, insisted on an apology when his opponent at whist said, "Now, old Cockamaroo, play something," and was mollified only by the assurance that he had misunderstood, and had been called nothing more insulting than "old cockawax," a term inexplicably innocuous. Reade, at forty-six, was working on his *Cloister and the Hearth*. He had held an Oxford fellowship, studied law, and attempted drama before he began novel-writing.

Highly educated, but captious in temper, he was frequently involved in lawsuits—not a man with whom the irascible Anthony could expect to keep on friendly terms.

Wilkie Collins was only thirty-six when Anthony came to London. He had not been writing long, for he had commenced life in the tea business, changed to the law, and only recently, with Dickens's encouragement, diverted his career to literature. *The Woman in White*, to be published during 1860, assured his reputation. At thirty-two, George Meredith had asserted his claim to consideration by the publication of *The Ordeal of Richard Feverel*. The stars of Collins, Reade, Trollope, and Meredith were rising in various orbits, but the reading public was in those days so limited that a collision of interests was certain to follow. Collins was superb as a designer, Meredith as a stylist, Reade consummate as a dramatic teller of tales; but Trollope had no reason to feel himself their inferior in knowledge and exposition of character, in control of situations, in veracity and quiet humor.

Anthony's personality was sufficiently conspicuous to lend excitement to the gatherings of London authors, whose first impression of the newcomer was always one of bigness, loudness, and insensibility. Some never got beyond this; others gradually became aware of his benevolent expression, and a few perceived the self-distrust which lay at the root of his bad manners. All agreed, however, that his behavior was not in the best of taste. At Chapman and Hall's the office boy reported that he "splashed around like a Triton in a school of minnows" and swore "like a sergeant major." Fellow authors were exasperated by his boasting over his mechanical methods. Affecting exaggerated contempt for artistic standards, he would tell new acquaintances that he always "chose the words that would fill up the pages quickest." It was felt that such revelations not only violated convention but by implication reduced "genius" to a question of words per hour. It harmed him, too, by diverting attention from real merits which had nothing to do with his rate of production.

The success of the first *Cornhill* dinner led to monthly repetitions. When the series ended, Anthony was uneasily afraid that his own indiscretion had put a stop to what he had greatly relished. It happened one evening that Thackeray called across the table, interrupting

George Smith's talk with his neighbor, to ask if Dr. Johnson was getting his dinner behind the scenes—a facetious reminder of the old story that the famous lexicographer used in the days of his poverty to hide his shabbiness behind a screen when dining. As Smith was too deep in conversation to hear the allusion, Thackeray repeated it. At that, Smith observed vaguely that he did not think anybody by the name of Johnson was present.

It amused Trollope to see Thackeray's small jest flatten out. Perhaps he wanted his colleague Yates to realize how much he missed by his exclusion from the *Cornhill* dinners; he may have enjoyed the telling of a little story which made Thackeray appear importunate and absurd; whatever his motives, he told it as an anecdote in Yates's presence. The delighted Yates dispatched an article to a New York paper, ridiculing the bright yellow *Cornhill* with the ornate cover-design, and retailing the tidbit of gossip which put two men whom he disliked in a ludicrous position. The diatribe was noted and reprinted with enlargements by the London *Saturday Review*, whereupon Thackeray, in the August *Cornhill*, bitterly attacked the eavesdropping "Mr. Nameless" who had given the story currency. Anthony, obliged to recognize himself in the abhorrent "Mr. Nameless," took the wise course of confession. "I told the story not against you, but against Thackeray," he told George Smith ruefully.

As he had returned to his early arrangement with Chapman by which *Castle Richmond* had to be completed in March, 1860, he could not give his complete attention to the installments of *Framley Parsonage* but had to work on both books at the same time. He rationalized the procedure by the airy observation that a man did not confuse his town and country neighbors, and an author could no less easily keep in mind the distinction between two sets of characters. When he sat down to write, he summoned the denizens of the parsonage or of the Irish tale as he required them; the characters were all he needed, for: "I have indeed for many years almost abandoned the effort to think, trusting myself with the narrowest thread of a plot to work the matter out when the pen is in my hand."

The confession sounds more shocking than the reality, for when he spoke of "thinking" he referred to the exigencies of plot, and to plot he was a natural enemy. "Thinking" in another sense, as of brooding over the consistent playing out of a scene, was still his chief occupation. As he rode or walked, the event unfolded, and when he was ready to set it down upon paper, his characters had successfully rehearsed the piece. As to diction, he troubled himself too little. If he avoided repetition and rank grammatical errors, if the sound did not strike harshly on his not too musical ear, if he used the sturdy *do, begin, read* for the languid *perform, commence, peruse*, he felt that nothing more should be required of him.

Framley Parsonage was finished on June 30, 1860, when the Trollopes had been six months at Waltham Cross, and the wished-for strawberries were ripening along their beds. Anthony did not, however, intend by his settlement in the English countryside to renounce the pleasant inconveniences of travel—not while great events were simmering in so many parts of the world. There had been talk of a visit to India and a book on the reconstruction which was healing the scars of the great Mutiny. He thought of revisiting the United States, to examine for himself the precarious balance of slave and free which the outcome of the next election would certainly destroy. The Italian situation would more than justify a visit during the autumn holidays. That summer, however, he stayed at home to work on a new novel called *Orley Farm*, a name substituted for the "Julians Hill" where his mother had taken the family when she began to make money.

In October he and Rose went to Florence to visit the Tom Trollopes and Anthony's mother. The separation had been long and eventful for both branches of the family. The dream of united Italy had been realized since his last visit. Full eighteen months earlier, while Anthony sweltered upon the Spanish Main, Theo and Tom had witnessed the outbreak of the war for Italian independence. While writing of the worldlings at Gatherum Castle, Anthony had been able to prime himself on the development of the Italian question by reading Theo's impassioned articles in the *Athenaeum*. He must have smiled to see how thoroughly Trollopean her style had become. Her sentences were more elegant, more ardent, and less satirical—otherwise Tom or his mother might have written them. She had shown amazing energy—had actually achieved a "scoop." From her own windows she had seen history made in Florence's rechristened "Piazza dell' Indipendenza."

The *Athenaeum* also printed extracts from Tom's new book, *Tuscany in 1849 and in 1859*. Anthony observed that his temperate brother too was roused almost to passion in the cause of Italian liberty; he had imbibed Theodosia's enthusiasm while she assimilated his style. Both were declared Italian patriots of the moderate stamp. They were indignant at the lukewarm attitude of the London government, and stressed the prospects of British advantage through the creation of a free, united Italy.

At the culminating moment of Garibaldi's grand exploit, when, in epic phrase, the bearded hero greeted his sovereign as *primo re d'Italia*, Anthony was already in Florence. Theodosia, exultant, was collecting her sheaf of essays for book publication—*Social Aspects of the Italian Revolution*. The others seemed less moved. The elder Mrs. Trollope had outgrown all politics, whether conservative or liberal; and Tom, satisfied that Italy had gained what he desired for her, was returning to his normal interest in her past. Since his brother's last visit he had published two serious historical works, *A Decade of Italian Women* and *Filippo Strozzi*; a third, *Paul the Pope and Paul the Friar*, was ready for the press. Beneath the trivial titles, each was a highly creditable piece of scholarship. T. Adolphus Trollope never claimed to be other than a popular historian. He was no man of parchments and musty cartularies; hard worker that he was, he wrote for a wider public than that of the collators of manuscripts. Not the less, however, did his work conform to the canons of historical method. *Paul the Pope and Paul the Friar* was by far the best book he had yet produced. In the resistance of Venice to the Papal interdict of 1605 he had found a theme congenial to his liberal convictions and a hero whom he could judiciously admire. The dramatic conflict of civil and ecclesiastical pretensions gave him full scope for exercising, in a style generally of sustained and harmonious dignity, his rich gifts of narrative, description, and psychological insight.

Tom was now fifty years old—high time to be thinking of his *magnum opus*, that history on the grand scale which every historian wishes to leave behind him. In this case the choice could not be difficult. The historical labors of the next five years were devoted to *The History of the Commonwealth of Florence*. Meanwhile there was need for another kind of writing: that of the historian turned novelist. His mother had given up work, and the expensive way of life of the Villino Trollope—its proprietor a known and valued buyer of rare editions and art objects—required plenty of money. And so a novel called *La Beata*, a slight but charming story of studio life in contemporary Florence, was already appearing as a serial.

Tom was at home among artists, as Anthony would never be, and in his first novel the descriptions of interiors and of persons were more subtly suggestive. A broader culture and a judicious habit of mind made themselves felt in his writing, but did not actually benefit his novels, because his attitude was that of a master of puppets, in whom he took only a business interest. In his frequent digressions, when he would record odd matters of research, his enthusiasm mounted, and what was out of place in his novel became its pleasantest reading.

Anthony and his wife were impressed by Tom's and Theo's popularity and importance. The Villino Trollope was recognized as one of the centers of social and literary life in Florence. Under its stately colonnades Italian radicals argued with double firsts from Oxford, and the poets of the new Italy, for whose verses Theodosia offered matchless translations, exchanged courtesies and sipped the famous Trollopean lemonade. English and American notables passing through Florence—Mrs. Somerville, Harriet Beecher Stowe, William Wetmore Story, the Leweses—would have felt their visit incomplete had they not passed an evening with the cultured Trollopes. Tom was known throughout Florence as "dear old Tom Trollope," not because of his age, but because everyone was fond of him.

From the family gatherings at the Villino one face was missing: old Mr. Garrow had died. Walter Savage Landor, who had always made a pet of Theodosia, had offered a quatrain to her father's memory, in sending to ask for some of her famous sweet pea seeds—a naughty boy's verses, written on a scrap of paper and thrust into a black-edged envelope:

> "Many has been the pleasant day
> We spent together at Torquay;

Now genial, hospitable Garrow,
Thy door is closed, thy house is narrow.

"Anticipated answer to the enclosed:

"And have you, then, the face for these,
To ask two pods of my sweet-peas?"

But Theodosia's efforts for Italian unity summoned more excellent
lines from the old poet:

"Nobly, O Theo! has your verse called forth
The Roman valor and Subalpine worth."

Two years earlier, Landor had fled from a libel suit in England. His
family, whom he detested, were at Fiesole, but he refused to live in
their company. He was eighty-five, had no money, went poorly clad,
and had grown an immense white beard on a face hitherto clean-
shaven. He was deaf and cantankerous and shockingly neglected until
the Brownings took charge of him and installed him in a neat little
house under the city wall. There Anthony was taken to call, and "A
clever man he appeared to be," was Landor's verdict. Like Mrs. Trollope, he took to reading Anthony's novels. The great classic poet, who
had years before proclaimed with noble dignity his readiness to relinquish life, was living on alone, to tend his flowers, make wry jokes,
and fly into tantrums.

He still loved and admired Theo, but she was much occupied, and
the young American girl Kate Field was a novelty in Florence and very
submissive to him. He was innocently flattered when the pretty, talented Kate wrote down his aphorisms. She was petted by all the little
group, for she had a charming voice and was ambitious to become
either a singer or a writer. Since she was familiar with the teachings of
Swedenborg, it had been easy for her to please Mrs. Browning by an
ardent interest in spiritualism.

Tom and Theo had settled Kate Field and her faded, ineffectual
mother in a flat opposite their own house, and lent them what furniture they needed. Theodosia was writing a series of articles on studios
in Florence and took Kate with her as she gathered her material. Kate
was young enough to be the daughter of Robert Browning or either of
the Trollope brothers, and Robert's "love" and Tom's and Anthony's

"dearest Kate" meant very little in a period when men in their forties spoke of themselves as elderly. Nor was she given to flirtation, being more interested in trying to choose between her talents and deciding how to exploit them. All the coterie except perhaps Theo, of whom Kate observed she did not go far in anything, expected the young girl to have a brilliant career. Mrs. Browning did not live to be disappointed, nor Theo to be justified.

Like everyone else, Rose and Anthony, who had no daughter, were charmed by the pretty young American. When Anthony heard that she had not read the *Arabian Nights*, he assured her that he was their author and would send her a copy.

Anthony and his wife made other acquaintances in Florence. Isabella Blagden, for example—Isa to the little group—was a woman well worthy of her friendship with Mrs. Browning. Like Theodosia she had Indian blood, but in a nearer degree, being the daughter of a Hindu princess and an English gentleman. Her origin was evidenced by her tiny frame, sparkling black eyes, and a bird's delicate alertness. Bright colors and gaudy garments fascinated her, and she fitted into natural beauty like one who has not strayed from home. From her little villa on the Bellosguardo she enjoyed views of the Arno valley, Fiesole, and the city; her housemates were the dogs she had rescued from the streets.

She had a host of friends and was as practical and kind as she was gifted. When they were ill, she nursed them; when they were miserable, she listened to the recital of their griefs; when they were absent, she wrote them voluminous letters. But what she was to them, they could not be to her, nor had she any Lewes or Palmer to aid her talent and extoll her gifts. Her richly sensuous poetry, impassioned as Keats's or Rossetti's, was not collected while she lived, and, when posthumously published, made only a slight volume.

Her friends were concerned about her finances, and as she had a finished novel, Anthony promised to take it with him and do his best to place it with Smith and Elder. Ivory Beryl was her pen name, preserving her initials according to mid-century taste. But practical Rose sniffed at Isa's writings, which seemed to her so precious as to be devoid of sense.

Anthony received other commissions; he was to buy an English saddle for the *Bimba*, as he called Bice, and the *Arabian Nights* he had promised Kate Field. With his little gift to the American girl, he sent a letter—in care of Tom as he had not remembered her address—urging her not to waste her time, but to see and to hear all that she could while she was given such unusual opportunities.

For his mother, there was nothing he could do. On this last visit she had no longer the strength to go out in the carriage. He had to bawl in order to make her understand him, but she could always hear when Bice sang, and would hold up a finger for silence with a murmured, "The little darling!" She sat with one of Anthony's novels open on her lap, not reading much. Once or twice a day she would quaver, "Take me out for a trot, Tom," and on his arm would promenade the garden walks. But Anthony could not recognize, in the withered creature who awaited the fall of the splitting husk, either the flashing wonder of the nursery or the celebrity who had been his rival.

On his return to London, Anthony fell into a minor dispute with Thackeray. He sent to the *Cornhill* a short story, fruit of his Italian visit, under the title "Mrs. General Talboys." A frigid *poseuse* had, notwithstanding marriage, been kissed upon a picnic by an American author. Rose had told him it was ill-natured, and Thackeray may have decided to reject it lest the originals be guessed and the magazine find itself in difficulties. Rather than incur an argument, he sent it back with a hint that it was immoral.

But Anthony would not rest under such an imputation. He wrote Thackeray an excellent letter, admitting an editor's right to judge such questions, and the duty of the author to accept his verdict peaceably, but protesting against the bondage of Victorian morality. If "Mrs. General Talboys" were impure, what could not be alleged against Effie Deans, Hetty Sorrel, "the illegitimate brat" in *Jane Eyre*, and Thackeray's own Beatrice, her naughtinesses "all the more naughty in that they are told only by hints"? His irritation was but thinly concealed as he recalled this cleverness of Thackeray's in hinting at what he did not venture to describe. But he could scarcely expect Thackeray to take seriously the protestation that he blushed for what his mother and sisters had read in "that very fie-fie story," *Oliver Twist*. His mother would not have blushed for herself or her daughters; in *Jessie Phillips* she had ventured far beyond Dickens.

Thackeray was ill when the letter came. Dreading the violence of Trollope, he asked his daughter to read it to herself and decide if he could bear it. Yet he did not reconsider "Mrs. General Talboys," and his languid reply begged the questions which Trollope professed to raise. Neither of the gentlemen had been straightforward.

Anthony was the more eager to justify himself with Thackeray in his role of critic because he was collecting his own travel stories of the past three years under the title *Tales of All Countries;* Italy, however, as Tom's province, was excluded. As short stories they were not even second-rate, since they were neither cleverly plotted nor sufficiently rapid in character development; but as indication of the author's psychology they were delightfully rewarding. The hero was usually the disguised Anthony, coping ineffectually with an awkward situation; the humorous tone of the relation aimed to excuse or justify his lack of adroitness. Everyone knows the blunderer who hastens to point out a comic element in his behavior in order to prevent unsympathetic notice. The author who thus explains away his folly enjoys special advantages of anonymity and of ability to invert or transfer his misdeeds, while he benefits by the act of confession. Anthony was often embarrassed by his own behavior, but gaucheries, not sins, were what oppressed him.

At Waltham House he spent the winter and spring working with brief interruptions on *Orley Farm*, which began in March to appear in monthly parts. Trifles carried over from his past gave him a lively interest in the new novel: the farm was Julians Hill, where his mother had made the family comfortable after the wretched years at Harrow Weald; in Keppel Street the lawyer and his wife loved each other and were happy, just as were the Trollopes, until his mother's ambition soured their lives; at Judge Staveley's were played the Christmas games for which Waltham Cross was beginning to be famous.

The book was rich in character and, in the quality of suspense, surpassed all his other works. Although Lady Mason's guilt was never in doubt, the outcome of the trial and the impact on her elderly lover and son provided intense psychological uncertainty. Trollope's own regret at what he considered a premature *dénouement* showed how superior was his practice to his theory: had the crime been concealed, the novel would have been one of plot rather than of character.

The mechanics of the trial scene have been harshly criticized, but it would require a cool observer to fix his attention on points of legal procedure while Lady Mason was at the bar. Anthony could not but admire his erring heroine; in the bitter brew he measured out for her, there was less gall than he was wont to pour for erring women.

As if unable to avoid quarrels, he emerged from his literary seclusion to deliver a lecture on "The Civil Service as a Profession" before an audience of postal employees and their families. His remarks were little more than an undisguised attack on the Civil Service regulations, under which both he and his hearers were working, and on their mutual chief, Rowland Hill. He strongly criticized the exclusion of government employees from the parliamentary franchise—a condition which persisted until 1868—asserting that he had himself more than once "applied to some big wig—to Lord John Russell, or some other such powerful person, asking him to liberate us from our bondage." He inveighed against the system of promotion by merit: "I think that it behoves the Civil Service as a whole to see that the rule be abrogated." The speech bristled with such ferocious bits of insubordination as "Men will not now be browbeat"; "No man in the Civil Service need bend his neck to any yoke"; "Such improvements do not descend from the few to the many. They ascend from the many to the few." In particular he decried the system of placing outsiders —like Hill—in "seats which should afford the appropriate rewards of the Civil Service."

Rowland Hill, the Chief Secretary, who had put up with many an insult from his surveyor, said with justice that Trollope ought to be dismissed. The Postmaster General, Lord Stanley of Alderley, sent for the lecturer and told him how his superior had expressed himself. Anthony asked bluntly if he were to be got rid of; at this, the Postmaster General laughed. To go unpunished and even uncensured was nevertheless a sorry triumph, owed largely to the influence of his brother-in-law John Tilley, and to his personal friendship with the Postmaster General.

A further detail of his life's pattern was successfully traced when on April 5, 1861, he proudly joined the Garrick Club, sponsored by Thackeray. He who had been left out in the games of Harrow and had never belonged to any club except the Tramp Society formed by three lonely lads in London, was henceforth to associate on intimate terms with men worth knowing, to play whist in the little room upstairs, or to talk over the opening incidents of the American war with the authority of one who seriously intended very soon to visit the United States.

Orley Farm was finished June 15, 1861. A week later he resumed work on an old book called *The Struggles of Brown, Jones, and Robinson*, which he completed on August 3. The title was a borrowed one; the subject, the methods of advertising, which had been a source of caustic mirth through the 1850's; and Trollope's aim was to establish himself as a humorist while striking a blow on behalf of the good old ways of business. However, *Brown, Jones, and Robinson* proved neither humorous nor satirical. Today its interest lies only in Trollope's strange conception of humor as of something rowdy, grotesque, and even brutal. No one was eager to publish the little book, but, after some hesitancy, George Smith accepted it for the *Cornhill.*

Anthony went to dinner at the Leweses, bringing them the sad news of Mrs. Browning's death, and let them take him on to tea at the Carlyles' in Chelsea, because Carlyle had forgiven, if he had ever known of, the satire in *The Warden* and had spoken well of *The West Indies and the Spanish Main.* The visits of the day were curtailed because Anthony was busy preparing for his American journey. Lewes prophesied that as a Britisher he would find considerable unfriendliness.

Chapman and Hall agreed to publish a book on the United States, but the Post Office was less complaisant when he applied for nine months' leave. His friend, the Postmaster General, inquired skeptically if Anthony were ill. Anthony, conscious of looking perfectly sound,

mentioned tranquilly his intention of writing a book. Rowland Hill
observed that if Trollope's leave were granted, he ought to feel that
any claims for former special services were canceled. So vindictive in
his desire to beat his superior that he was willing to disadvantage himself, Anthony refused to go under such conditions; and the Postmaster
General again sustained him, if only for the sake of overruling his
pedantic Chief Secretary.

Rose was to accompany him, but planned to return before the winter
and his entrance into the war zone. A letter was dispatched to Florence
asking Kate Field to recommend a Boston hotel. Her reply, mention-
ing the Tremont, was sent on with his request for reservations. Kate
herself, he advised, should stay in safety in Florence. On August 24,
1861, a month after the Union defeat at Bull Run, the Trollopes
sailed from Liverpool.

CHAPTER XIII

American Manners—
Revised Version

1861-1862

Anthony's second visit to America was the first of his journeys undertaken with the specific object of producing a book of travels. To write a book about the United States, he said, had been the ambition of his literary life; he had formed his design before the outbreak of the Civil War, and did not intend either to be deterred or to be unduly influenced by the existence of that conflict. Without claiming to be a political sage, he thought he could add something to the familiarity of Englishmen with Americans, and to "the good feeling which should exist between two nations which ought to love each other so well."

This virtuous intention was obscurely related to an unfilial desire of showing that his mother had been wrong in her *Domestic Manners of the Americans*. He admitted that her book had produced a good result in the amelioration of social absurdities in America, but it belonged to a class of travel literature which had created as much soreness on one side of the Atlantic as laughter on the other. His task should be to mitigate the soreness, to explain the political system which had produced the deplorable manners of his mother's day, and to show how its defects had passed away while the good had remained.

He was not ill-qualified for such a mission. In political matters, though not infallible, he possessed insight, judgment, and strong common sense. He had seen much of the world, and his Post Office work kept him abreast of the tide of progress. His knowledge of the United States was substantial, if not profound. Before the "Arabia"

steamed out of Liverpool, his mind had been made up on most aspects
of the American crisis, and his eight months in the States seemed only
to strengthen the validity of his conclusions. In '61 and '62 it was
still reasonable to expect a Northern victory and yet to believe that
a beaten Confederacy would succeed in maintaining its independence.

Such a division of the country, he thought, would "give the North
new wings, and leave the South without political greatness or commercial success." The opinion corresponded not only to appearances
as they then were, but to the psychological necessities of his own
being. His natural sympathies might have led him to side with the
romantic South—he remarked that if he had lived in the times of
Prince Rupert he would have been a hard-riding Cavalier, though he
ought to have followed Cromwell. But in the Northern States, labor
was honorable, and work, according to his own life's practice and
theory, must be successful; in the romance of the Southern cause his
determined realism scented the odor of decay.

There could be no doubt as to the success of his projected book;
the war might make his travels difficult, but would well reward his
pains. Englishmen took the deepest interest in the struggle, although
few of Anthony's associates shared his enthusiasm for the Union. Many
resented the attitude of the Washington government toward neutrals;
other potential supporters had been alienated by the defeat at Bull
Run; the blockade and the fear of Northern designs on Canada increased the tension. Conservative Englishmen believed that republican
institutions had finally demonstrated the fatuity of which Frances
Trollope had accused them three decades earlier. But everyone was
interested. Everyone would read what Anthony Trollope had to say
about the war.

The "Arabia" touched first at Halifax, where a Trollope cousin
who commanded the fort asked Anthony and Rose to dine with him.
Even in Anthony's opinion the eight hours ashore did not warrant
a chapter, and he handsomely contented himself with a paragraph.
Two days later they docked in Boston. He had looked forward to
the experience with a certain dread. Constitutionally pugnacious as
he was, he had always wanted everyone to like him, and he feared
that a city crammed with abolitionists would regard an Englishman

as an enemy. But these fears were never realized. Throughout the North he found a bitterness against England amounting almost to passion; but his nationality occasioned no personal discourtesy, though at times he felt that he was "walking over smothered ashes." The best way to avoid unpleasantness, he found, was to begin by declaring himself an Englishman.

The first visit to Boston lasted but a week. To find so many better-class people in the city before cold weather surprised him, until he learned that the war was partly responsible and, for the rest, that even well-to-do Americans seldom maintained both a town and a country residence. Boston could be summed up as "pleasant," but not "fine"; Beacon Street was like a little Piccadilly, and the Common reminded him of Green Park.

The literary circles of Boston and Concord accepted Anthony with reservations. He was accustomed to society, and the formality of the dinner tendered in his honor impressed the guest less than it did the little coterie, for whom refinements of table service retained some of the charm of novelty. When Oliver Wendell Holmes informed him that connoisseurship in Madeira wines was held a fine art among them, Anthony retorted, "They might be better employed." It was natural for them to suppose that an animal which roared so loudly would have an impervious hide; the Autocrat did not suppose his clever little darts penetrated to injurious depths, and shot them to amuse the tableful. Lowell condemned the guest as "rather under-bred," but decided that he "rather liked" him.

Anthony, sensitive and observant, missed neither the half-resentful humor nor the covert amusement. He bombarded their delicate preciosity with shouted praises of English grapes and peaches, knew that Emerson and Lowell on his right were discussing matters too high for him, and noted the preoccupation of Hawthorne in getting all the good of his canvasback duck. It was Anthony's first meeting with Hawthorne, who had made Tom's acquaintance in Florence and thought him "a very sensible and cultivated man"; in his vague way, the mystical novelist had "suspected" Tom of being an author.

When the Trollopes had been in Boston a week, the mosquitoes drove them to the Ocean Hotel at Newport—a gloomy place, built to accommodate six hundred, in which the footsteps of a scattered twenty-five re-echoed hollowly. The Southern clientele had stayed away, and the season was over, but Anthony could not believe that so dead a place had ever been lively. Rose and he went riding on hired horses; they voted them wretched beasts. He could have bathed but would not, because he liked neither to wade through shallow water nor to wear a bathing suit. They took the two-mile drive past the pretentious estates along the shore, observing, not without gratification, how little Americans understood the art of landscape gardening.

At the hotel the ladies' drawing room was draughty and vast. A pitcher of water stood on a table in the exact center, symbolic of cold purity. Occasionally a guest would sing, with shrill screams struggling to subdue the awful spaces. There was conversation of a kind—American women could "always talk and often very well"—and a deplorable custom of bringing children to the table, where they ate pickles. Anthony did not like children. His scenes of "baby worship" were noisome; the children tolerated in his books were such starved intellectuals as the young Crawleys, the unpleasantly sly Henry Grantly, or the preposterous daughter of the Neroni.

From these unfestive scenes the Trollopes fled to Portland, intending a six or seven weeks' circuit through Canada and the northern United States which would take them as far west as Minneapolis. They traveled by train, but did not enjoy it. Anthony protested that the best way to bring about equality was to begin by admitting the existence of classes—political equality was one thing, social equality quite another. The long, common railway car was an abomination, and he was seldom quick enough to get a seat with Rose. When he gave up his place to a woman bowed down with boxes and babies, she did not thank him. Probably she was afraid of him—a big, well-dressed foreigner with an elegant lady at his elbow.

Portland proved to be the most charming town they had yet seen. The streets curved as streets ought to do, the elms were magnificent in their yellowing foliage, and the houses dignified and large, but not pretentious. Those were the times of which Louisa Alcott wrote in her *Garland for Girls;* Anthony, who had no daughters of his own, admired the pretty young creatures as they walked home alone from their tea parties at nine in the evening, neat workbaskets at their sides, secure in innocence.

From Portland the visitors went on into the White Mountains. For scenery, the Rhine valley could not be compared with them, and the autumn foliage was amazing. He could see the straggling trees through the wild beauty of tangled colors, but their trunks were lost in scrubby undergrowth. The sight vexed him as it had his mother, whose eyes, like his, had been educated by park land and royal forest.

He found the same difficulty she had experienced in securing private room service; hotelkeepers were as easily offended in 1861 as in 1827. He discovered a "surly independence" which he could understand as an assertion of political equality, but found annoying. He did not like to have loungers look over his shoulder as he wrote "A. Trollope" in the hotel book; he did not like being ordered to "wait for that gentleman" or "follow that young lady" when the gentleman and lady were the boots and chambermaid. The food was excellent, although sherry was "not understood"; but he objected as vigorously as his mother to the regimentation which forced a guest to sit at a common table thrice daily at rigidly fixed hours. When he asked for a guide to conduct them up Mount Washington, he was brusquely informed that no idle boys were kept about the place. But people in the New World were not inhuman, for when he and Rose were lost on Owl's Head, in the rain and night, a search party was organized for their rescue.

Though not on an official mission, he was eager to investigate the American postal service, and heard with anguish that a Vermont carrier refused to set forth in a rainstorm. Nowhere was there free delivery, and at the post offices the rich and privileged unlocked their private boxes while the poor stood in line before a window. This, he felt, was not good business. The percentage of literacy in the United States was far higher than in England; therefore more letters should be written, not only to augment the Federal revenues, but to lend the charm of correspondence to arid lives.

After brief visits to the cities of Canada, where the attitude of the "lower classes" differed little from what they had encountered in New England, the Trollopes reached Niagara in the second week of

October. On his previous visit Anthony had pronounced the falls more graceful than Giotto's Tower, comparing them to the building he most admired, and using the adjective which expressed the quality he valued most highly in women, scenery, and architecture. He found that the sight lost nothing through repetition. Forgetting Rose, he luxuriated in a state of unaccustomed mystic exaltation.

From Niagara they went on to the Great Lakes, which appalled him; they were "cold, cumbrous, uncouth, and uninteresting." Detroit looked "harsh and crude"; Grand Haven was "a place such as might break a man's heart." By Anthony's requirements, an American town ought to resemble Portland, and possess fine old trees, large but unpretentious houses—he could not forgive the Americans for building Grecian porticoes of painted wood—broad, well-kept lawns, and a picturesque irregularity. Notwithstanding his lack of training and his nearsightedness, he was an industrious and conscientious critic of architecture. He had learned to think poorly of Sir G. G. Scott's pseudo-Gothic and even doubted whether English perpendicular were able to express the height of the sublime. But art and nature were chiefly significant to him as the background of the human drama.

Impelled by the surly comments of railroad officials, he had suggested to Rose—in vain—that ten pieces of luggage were rather too many, and that she might perhaps dispense with her bonnet box. As they traveled his respect for the American system of checking increased. Not one of the ten but followed faithfully; once the little writing desk with all his money lagged behind for a day, but reappeared intact. Nor was he ever robbed, although in spite of repeated warnings he refused to lock up his possessions.

Americans, then, like West Indian Negroes, did not steal. Yet he would not call them honest. The slogan of the West, "It behoves a man to be smart, sir," disgusted him as deeply as the spirit behind the words had affronted his mother. Like her, he was indignant at the exploitation of immigrants. The pioneer spirit which made men clear the land appeared less noble when one saw how little they loved the soil, and how quick they were to leave it. Their labor was speculative; they cleared to sell—and to move on. In the cities, he was shocked at the risks which crude financiers took with capital and contemptuous when he learned that they lived entirely in the present, without a wish to secure their families. It was the hazard which they enjoyed; when one fortune crumbled, it was easy to build up another.

At La Crosse, Wisconsin, the first real sign of war was encountered, when a regiment of volunteers came down the Mississippi on their way to Washington—a fine set of men, with faces far more intelligent than those of British recruits. Some of the men were certainly thirty-five, forty, perhaps more, for here and there he caught sight of a gray beard. They would suffer under the discipline essential in an army; it was evident that they considered themselves the equals of their officer, who, on his side, was uneasy because he felt that the relation with his men was incorrect but did not know how to mend it. The volunteers bore themselves like heroes, but Trollope feared they would soon lament as slaves. They had enlisted for three years, and left at their backs the vital task of settling a new world.

His reflections were profoundly melancholy as the steamer continued up the river to Saint Paul. He had been told over and over again that the North must control the Mississippi, and that if the South could not be coerced back into the Union the route would be closed to Northern commerce. The idea depressed the civilized Englishman of the nineteenth century. "The days are gone," he felt, "when any country can interfere to stop the highways of the world." He did not see why an independent Confederacy should not learn to live on terms of amity with its Northern neighbor; he thought the attempt to impose one government on distant peoples, with different habits and expanding interests, was contrary to all the lessons of economics and history. "The North and South are virtually separated, and the day will come in which the West also will secede. As one thinks of the all but countless population which is before long to be fed from these regions, of the cities which will grow here, and of the amount of government which in due time will be required, one can hardly fail to feel that the division of the United States into separate nationalities is merely a part of the ordained work of creation, as arranged for the well-being of mankind."

He was sad, and no one but Rose would talk to him. Other women on the boat distrusted the English foreigners and occupied themselves

in seeing that their precocious infants were not defrauded in the allot-
ment of pickles and beefsteak. At twenty-five the mothers' faces were
old and strained; it was a pleasure to see how fresh and well-dressed
Rose looked, in sight of forty.

Moving swiftly from city to city with the untiring Rose, he collected hasty impressions, often of an apparent triviality, but really
indices of the American way of life. In Dubuque he ate the perfect
apple; in the grandeur of the Chicago hotel, cold-water pipes ran
hot, while hot refused to run. Americans were unaccustomed to use
their legs and invariably overheated their rooms; their great glory
was in their "wonderful patent contrivances." Cleveland was a pleasant
town, with its public park bestowing a gracious freedom which London might well copy; in Buffalo there were enormous grain elevators,
about which he jotted down many figures; Pittsburgh was to be remembered as the place where he stepped from his tub onto a green
carpet and turned the soles of his feet to burnished black.

By the time the Trollopes reached West Point, Anthony had ceased
to take the silence of his fellow travelers as a personal affront; even
among themselves Americans did not talk. The Military Academy
made him uneasy by its high requirements and strict discipline; he
thought the boys were overworked. When told that two-thirds were
dropped because of inability to keep up, he positively suffered. He
could remember his ignominious career at Harrow, and thought it
hard that so crushing a misfortune should be inflicted at an age when
the capacity for suffering is greatest. At Sandhurst boys could be
boys; at West Point they must be men. He groaned again when in the
chapel he saw two British flags among the captured trophies. He wished
heartily that England would bundle up all the prodigious number of
banners she had acquired in battle and send them back by parcel
post prepaid, in exchange for those two emblems of her rare defeats.

He was not half so pleased with New York as his mother had been.
Except for a superior school system, a "perfect" insane asylum, and
the "almost alluring" hospitals, there was little to see and scarcely
any means of seeing, since there were no cabs, carriage fares were
exorbitant, and the technique required of travelers on the horsecars
and omnibuses was beyond him. He did not understand that he was

expected to put the fare in "a little hole behind the driver's back," and when he passed by it, "bells used to be rung" at him which made him "uneasy." When he received his change, he dropped it in the straw: from his awkwardness came "trouble and unhappiness." The women in omnibuses behaved abominably. Enormous in trailing, dirty hoop skirts, they crowded into all the available seats and talked to each other at the top of their lungs, while their ferocious glances dared any man to insult them. The English visitor whose book was intended to soften the memory of his mother's harshness pronounced their manners "more odious than those of any other human beings that I ever met elsewhere."

He found New York the most American of cities, but not on that account the most agreeable. "Free institutions, general education, and the ascendancy of dollars" was "written on every paving-stone along Fifth Avenue, down Broadway, and up Wall Street." Fifth Avenue was "as grand as paint and glass can make it," but the magnificence did not extend to the poorer streets. Central Park, stretching away to the northward of the city, would doubtless become one of its great glories. But when he was "expected to declare that St. James's Park, Green Park, Hyde Park, and Kensington Gardens, altogether, were nothing to it," he "could only remain mute."

He preferred to talk about the war, and lost no opportunity of making clear his own attitude and that of England. He believed that secession had been unjustified, and that the North had had no honorable alternative to fighting, but that England's strict neutrality between the two belligerents was the only course open to her, just as a neighbor was not supposed to take sides in a quarrel between husband and wife. The Union was unlikely to regain its prewar extent, but military victory would enable it to determine the fate of the border states, from Maryland to Missouri, and to rescue them from slavery. The loss of the slave states would not really be an evil to a people which was proving its ability to weather a crisis. "They have the great qualities of the Anglo-Saxon race,—industry, intelligence, and self-confidence; and if these qualities will no longer suffice to keep such a people on their legs, the world must be coming to an end."

Anthony had an important matter to settle in New York regarding the unauthorized publication of his books by the firm of Harper and Brothers. Since Harpers' near piracy of *The West Indies*, he had been determined to put an end to their practice, copyright or no copyright, and had with much difficulty obtained from them £100 for the American edition of *Orley Farm*—his first American earnings in thirteen years of American publishing. On that occasion Harpers' London agent had not concealed the firm's intention of republishing the book in America whether or not the author agreed to their terms; and Anthony was eager to find some other American publisher who could rid him of the Harper incubus.

But Harpers was the country's most powerful firm, and rival publishers were loth to compete with them for a valuable author. If they published an authorized edition of an English book, Harpers could bring out an unauthorized edition, undersell them, and drive them from the market. "You are Mr. Harper's property," one of them told Anthony, "and we don't dare touch you. He has put his hand upon you, and we cannot interfere." Before he could hope for an alternative arrangement, he must persuade Harpers to give him up.

Mr. Fletcher Harper, youngest of the four brothers, was pleasant, energetic, and competent, and far too shrewd to permit the lucrative Trollope to slip away from him. Anthony made his complaints and, brushing away the cobwebs of diplomacy, asked Mr. Harper point blank what they would do if he arranged to have his new book brought out by another publisher. Mr. Harper did not believe that any competitor would venture to "steal" this angry Englishman; therefore he suavely indicated that if Mr. Trollope could make a more satisfactory arrangement elsewhere, Harpers would not interfere. He did not commit himself as to what he would do if Mr. Trollope contented himself with an *unfavorable* bargain for the sake of being rid of them, but permitted Anthony to leave the building under the delusive impression that he was free to sell his books to whom he chose, and that Harpers would refrain from bringing out an unauthorized edition. He could not have been more mistaken.

It was good to be back in Boston, whither the Trollopes returned before the middle of November, 1861. The city he had first called "pleasant" was, by comparison to others he had seen, a most delightful place. Yet Bostonians were too much addicted to lectures; to attend "a course" was the diversion of the staid. Prices for this esoteric amusement were high, and stage effects superior to those at home; music, correct lighting, a platform graced by dignitaries provided the proper setting. Anthony was one of an audience of three thousand who heard Emerson lecture upon the war. He had read *Representative Men,* and "feared much that there would be a lack of common sense." But the Concord sage disappointed him pleasantly by speaking not only lucidly but in a vein of which Anthony approved. "Your American eagle is very well," said Emerson. "Protect it here and abroad. But beware of the American peacock."

At a lecture by Edward Everett, Trollope was asked to sit on the platform with the worthies. He observed, as they filed along together, that the six or seven ministers of the gospel were quietly segregated and seated in a little group near the speaker. When, in his discourse, Everett came to the words, "the prayers of these holy men whom I see around me," he turned to them with fine, theatrical effect which much disgusted the English gentleman on the platform. Although Everett was a family friend, Anthony did not approve of him, and squirmed upon his seat of honor as the ex-minister to the Court of St. James ranted on about the English "wallowing in their misery."

A third famous lecturer, Wendell Phillips, by the bitterness of his attack on Lord Palmerston put an end to Trollope's attendance on Boston's evenings of diversion. He commented ruefully that there sometimes seemed "no being so venomous, so bloodthirsty as a professed philanthropist." Trollope was not a friend of abolitionism. To him personally the name of slave was odious—"I would not own a negro though he could sweat gold on my behoof"—and he looked forward to the emancipation of all slaves in some more or less distant future. But to preach abolition during the war was "either the deadliest of sins or the vainest of follies." The Negroes who had been slaves were not ready for the responsibilities of free men; the idea of transporting four million souls to Liberia was fantastic, and the most likely outcome of such talk would be a bloody servile insurrection.

Kate Field and her mother were now in Boston, and their presence added something to the enjoyments of social life. Boston society was easily classified. "The bald and hoary-headed and superlatively wise" sat on platforms at the back of the lecturer; the people with whom he and Rose associated listened from the front and attempted to be "studious without any of the labour of study." Their houses were comfortable and they gave dinner parties with canvasback ducks and champagne at half past two in the afternoon; a guest could not go home after dining, but stayed on with steadily diminishing spirits until time to attend the evening lecture. Sunday was rigidly kept, but Sunday evening was "quite a good time."

The institution which most won his admiration was the Public Library. The liberality which permitted the free use of books, the honesty of a public which could be trusted with such privileges, the excellent staff management, made an ineffaceable impression. "It was all *couleur de rose*; the librarianesses looked very pretty and learned, and, if I remember aright, mostly wore spectacles; the head librarian was enthusiastic; the nice instructive books were properly dogseared; my own productions were in enormous demand; the call for books over the counter was brisk, and the reading room was full of readers."

Throughout the East all laborers read, some of them three newspapers a day. Books and magazines were peddled through the trains, and, though the novels were of the most flimsy, their sale argued the general literacy. As to religion, Americans must certainly be counted as church attendants, but individuals roved from sect to sect and appeared indifferent to doctrine as long as they found entertainment and a vacancy in a pew. There was, he felt, a "rowdiness" in American religion. As if with reluctance, he admitted that these people possessed the three rudiments of civilization, for they ate and drank, wrote and read, and said their prayers. "I do not like the Americans of the lower orders. I am not comfortable among them. They tread on my corns and offend me. They make my daily life unpleasant. But I do respect them."

By horsecar he went to Cambridge, to stroll about the unkempt grounds and view with dismay the seven "very ugly red brick" buildings of Harvard College. At Lowell he made a genuine effort to study the living conditions of factory workers. Lowell was more like a college than a mill town, with well-shaded streets and decorous boardinghouses supervised by the owners—a philanthropist's Utopia which could not permanently withstand the effects of competition. As he returned in the smoker, an aged Canadian surprised him by detecting his nationality. "There is no mistaking you," he said, "with your round face and your red cheeks. They don't look like that here." Anthony "felt quite fond of the old man," and offered him a cigar.

The crisis which brought England and the United States close to the verge of war occurred during the Trollopes' stay in Boston. The famous Captain Wilkes, relative of an old Trollope acquaintance, removed two Confederate agents from a British mail steamer and brought them triumphantly into port, in defiance of international law. Immediately a great clamor of justification and recrimination arose on both sides of the Atlantic. Trollope found it pretty "to hear the charming women of Boston, as they became learned in the law of nations." But his own patience was exhausted. "Up to this period my sympathies had been with the North. But this stopping of an English mail-steamer was too much for me."

In the midst of the crisis, on November 27, Rose sailed for home. Anthony believed he would soon have to follow her. He paid a visit to Longfellow—who showed him, "with an honest cheery pride," the English editions of his works—and then started for Washington. He missed his wife, and was depressed by the increasing probability of war. He "began to believe that the world was going backwards." "These people speak our language, use our prayers, read our books, are ruled by our laws, dress themselves in our image, are warm with our blood. They have all our virtues; and their vices are our own, too, loudly as we call out against them. They are our sons and our daughters, the source of our greatest pride, and as we grow old they should be the staff of our age. Such a war as we should now wage with the States would be an unloosing of hell upon all that is best upon the world's surface."

He stopped at Philadelphia, where for the first time he "came across live secessionists," and at Baltimore, where martial law prevailed and ladies wore the forbidden red and white, filling their windows with Confederate colors. Even in the confusion and stress of war and divided sentiment, he felt the charm of the city as his mother had done, observing also that the country looked "as a hunting country should look."

One of the charges he had made against his mother was her unfitness to judge the prospects of a young nation. But his opinion of Washington proved to be less sound than hers. Familiar with Versailles, she had been delighted with the plan of the capital and prophesied that in time the spacious outlines would be filled by fine buildings and a numerous population. Anthony, with the trained eye of a Post Office surveyor and a practical man, condemned the plan as confusing and inconvenient. Moreover he did not believe Washington could remain the capital after the war. The city would stay as he found it—"a ragged unfinished collection of unbuilt broad streets. . . . Of all the places that I know it is the most ungainly and most unsatisfactory; —I fear I must also say the most presumptuous in its pretensions."

All was not utterly condemned; the White House was "neat and pretty." He did not believe the Monument would ever be completed, and he had reason for this suspicion: peeping into the box which contained contributions, he had seen only two half-dollars—both counterfeit.

The mud was dreadful; the morale of the capital was despicable; people did not seem to care who won the war; the boundless cynicism was appalling. He was thoroughly miserable, with a great carbuncle on his forehead. He did not see Lincoln, because someone spoke of such an interview as a *favor*, and Trollope would not press for one. The military filled the city. They pelted furiously along the muddy thoroughfares; but when he trotted his horse, he was shouted at.

He attempted to go to Mount Vernon in a government boat with several adventurous ladies. Someone told the commander that the Confederates would carry off his passengers if he landed them. The women were not averse to playing the role of the Sabines, but the unromantic commander sent his passengers back to Washington. Determined to visit the shrine, Trollope tried again with better success. He dismissed the house as "comfortless and inconvenient" and hurried to the tomb, where he paid a tribute to Washington as a great and good man—exactly as his mother had done thirty years before.

When he came to Washington he was certain there would be war, and was preparing for a quick return to England. A senator assured him that the government would have "no great objection" to taking on a new antagonist, and tension mounted when it was known that England had demanded the surrender of the two Confederate captives. A British man-of-war stood in the Potomac, ready to take away the ambassador and his suite. Lincoln's cabinet met on Christmas Day and again on the day following, and Trollope was informed that he might have to leave at an hour's notice. That evening he dined at the house of Mr. Seward, the Secretary of State. Rumor had it that a decision had been reached. Friends came in to inquire, and as the guest was leaving the dining room it was announced that the two men would be given up. The crisis was past. Anthony acknowledged that the American government had "behaved well."

His book was growing rapidly. With his personal impressions he interspersed long chapters on American political and social institutions and on the war. In addition, he was indulgently corresponding with Kate Field and sending her painstaking criticisms of her literary effusions, mingled with the half-amused gallantry of a man who was no longer very young and whose friends had told him that he showed strongly "that steady married appearance of a paterfamilias which is so apt to lend assurance to maiden timidity." Kate was stepping forth as an advocate of women's rights; and Anthony, not content with the gentle ridicule of his letters, inserted in his book a special chapter in opposition. "Let women say what they will of their rights, or men who think themselves generous say what they will for them, the question has all been settled both for them and for us men by a higher power. They are the nursing mothers of mankind, and in that law their fate is written with all its joys and all its privileges. That women should have their rights no man will deny. To my thinking neither increase of work nor increase of political influence are among them. The best right a woman has is the right to a husband, and that is the right to which I would recommend every young woman here and in the States to turn her best attention."

He spent four days in camp with the Army of the Potomac and was shocked by the wretchedly dirty sentries mounted on muddy horses. The long, tangled locks of the men dropped filth, and they swore horribly. Although sure that the North must conquer, he was more and more convinced that the position of the abolitionist was unsound. An abolitionist would not eat with a Negro—unless in England at the table of a benevolent duchess. Anthony kept his faith in the congenital inferiority of the black race, but did not shrink from contact with its people, and was touched when his colored landlord said he was sorry to lose him. He agreed with his mother not only in feeling that the Negresses made excellent domestics but in deploring the attitude of white servants. "An American woman who is paid in some shape to supply your wants,—whether to sell you a bit of soap or bring you a towel in your bedroom at an hotel,—is, I think, of all human creatures, the most insolent."

After being bogged for a month in Washington mud, he set out on a second western tour, which was to take him through Pennsylvania, Ohio, Kentucky, and as far as Saint Louis. He found Baltimore knee-deep in slush, and went on to Harrisburg, where he visited the legislature and marveled to see lawmakers dirty and unkempt. At Cincinnati he went to see his mother's bazaar, "Trollope's Folly"—a sorry building in these latter days. The proprietor expatiated on the ill-luck which had always attended its possession. "I believe, sir, no man or woman ever yet made a dollar in that building." Its spacious saloons housed a quack doctor and "a college of rights-of-women female medical professors"; yet a few years, and the temple of the arts and graces was to become a house of ill fame.

Anthony shared his mother's admiration of Kentucky; the fertile meadows reminded him of England; it was good hunting country, and the trees were magnificent. Then he saw the Ohio in flood, and the dreadful plight of homeless settlers in want of shelter, food, clothing, but uncomplaining, until he exclaimed, half in vexation, half in admiration, "Surely there is no other people so passive under personal misfortune!"

In Saint Louis the prisons were crowded with Southern sympathizers; he heard that there were twelve hundred in jail, all noncombatants, on whom were inflicted penalties usually reserved for captured soldiery. He visited the Benton barracks. No one tried to hide conditions from him; indeed no one seemed to feel that apology or concealment was necessary, but he had not believed that humanity could be degraded to such depths.

At Rolla, the headquarters of General Curtis, a correspondent associated him with the memory of Frances Trollope and told him, ambiguously, that her son was an "accession." He dined with General Ashboth, the Magyar, who had come to America with Louis Kossuth. Trollope admired him and was touched when Ashboth showed him, in his tent, his little treasures—his chess-men, his sword, the daguerreotype of a beloved friend in his own country. Anthony was frightfully uncomfortable in the mud and filth. He had to carry his own bag up a hill in the dark and fell face down in muck. He imagined that he was traveling light, but on that sad occasion bore a load of twelve shirts, a dress suit, a set of maps, several heavy books, three pairs of boots, a box of cigars, and a bathtub. "No American of my age and weight will ever go through what I went through then."

Arriving at Cairo, Illinois, at 4:30 A. M., he had to roll his trousers up to his knees in order to reach the hotel, where there was neither place nor means of washing except in the men's room. He was afraid to brush his teeth, because even the use of his own comb excited adverse comment. He had to share a room with an English friend, who justified his existence by producing certain "comfortable tin pots from Fortnum & Mason's." The friend said cheerfully, "It is a new phase of life," and Trollope was too depressed to comment.

Cairo—Dickens's "Eden"—was like a port upon the Styx. The spectral faces of malaria sufferers peered from the windows. The travelers went to see the gunboats moored along the Ohio, and shuddered at the desolation of the muddy, wintry prospect. Two regiments passed. All wore blue greatcoats, and boots which hunting men might envy, but there was neither discipline nor cleanliness; many, very many, were drunk. He and his friend were invited to dine with two officers. At the door of their shanty the landlord ordered them to scrub themselves with the stump of an old broom; Trollope's trousers looked like bread spread with molasses. They partook of squirrel soup, prairie chicken, brandy, and champagne, and their spirits revived.

His mother had said frankly that she disliked the West. Anthony, who had expected to soften her pictures, deepened their somber tones. The women of the Middle West were "as sharp as nails, and as hard." The men were intelligent; they had energy and endurance. But "dirt, dishonesty, and morning drinks" were prevailing vices. Worst of all was the filth. "I have eaten in Bedouin tents, and have been ministered to by Turks and Arabs. I have sojourned in the hotels of old Spain and of Spanish America. I have lived in Connaught, and have taken up my quarters with monks of different nations. I have, as it were, been educated to dirt, and taken out my degree in outward abominations. But my education had not reached a point which would enable me to live at my ease in the western States." His mother, ill and defenseless, had served no apprenticeship in uncouth ways of life, but her indignation had been less bitter and lacked the sour ferment of her son's.

He did not pass within the Southern lines. If he left his baggage, he might succeed in crossing the frontier on foot, but the prospect was too uncertain. If he went by water and was captured, he would have to appeal to the British minister and perhaps fray the strained bond between his and the Federal government. He went back to Washington by way of Cincinnati and Baltimore, which he now considered the pleasantest town of the country next to Boston. At Philadelphia he called on Lippincott, the publisher, who agreed to bring out the American edition of his new book. The terms were not favorable, but he had the satisfaction of believing he had vanquished Mr. Fletcher Harper.

He had promised to spend a week in Boston before sailing for England. The city shone all the more by contrast with his late experiences. Massachusetts was "the noblest of the states," and he felt himself a friend to all its citizens. "Even the State House, with its great yellow-painted dome, became sightly." Everyone was on runners; he took a lady sleighing, but the horses ran away, to his "grief and shame." He could write a story about it.

His book was practically finished, swelled out by bulky chapters on the Constitution, the government, the judiciary, and public finance. It was long and repetitious; nor did it live up to its title, *North America;* he had said nothing of conditions in the South, next to nothing of the westward movement. Yet it was a book worth reading and has remained so. Though he miscalculated the outcome of the war, he never faltered in his conviction that a great destiny awaited the Union of free states. He perceived that the condition of the masses was superior to that in his own country, and believed that free education and natural wealth would raise them higher still. The war would teach them to purge their government of corruption. "If the American people can learn the necessity of employing their best men for their highest work,—if they can recognize these honest men and trust them when they are so recognized,—then they may become as great in politics as they have become great in commerce and in social institutions."

His incidental criticisms, though he could not disavow them, made him uneasy; he feared that his friends in Boston would close their doors against him when they read his book. On the personal side a compound of trifles had overcome him, and he was bowed down by the recollection of dirt, pickle-eating children, handsome but shrewish faces of women, and the persistent dearth of conversation.

His mother's wits were too far gone for her to find vindication in her son's revised "American Manners." She had prided herself on having done something to better American behavior; when men slouched in public places, the battle cry "a Trollope!" had been known to pull up back and down feet into decent positions. When she had been in America she had been little and almost old, shabby and ill-attended, and people had dared to be rude to her; they had not been intentionally insolent to the important-looking, well-dressed English author, Anthony Trollope; thus his ire had less excuse. Yet it must be admitted that he was the better able to differentiate between what annoyed him personally and what was in itself an evil.

CHAPTER XIV

Height of the Harvest

1862-1864

THE outward massiveness of Anthony Trollope in middle life mirrored his inner solidity; he believed that he would be able to shape his career as he wished it. Detail after detail had been etched in the pattern, until even the crowning embellishment of a seat in Parliament seemed not too difficult to the craftsman at work upon his destiny. He was a high official in his country's service; a novelist acclaimed on both sides of the Atlantic, sure of a market for whatever he cared to write; a well-to-do gentleman with a good house in a hunting country, who was able without stinting himself or his family to save a third of his income. He kept dogs, horses, a dairy, maids and men-servants, had a wife known for her fashionable clothes, and supported her little niece, Florence Bland, who might make herself useful by-and-by.

As for his looks, he liked them. His color was good and his beard magnificent. True, he was bald; but, as he naïvely expressed it in *Ralph the Heir*, "There is a baldness that is handsome and noble, and a baldness that is peculiarly mean and despicable." His was the former, and the contours of his skull were grand. His friends compared him, when he laughed, to Silenus; both Tom and Anthony were beginning to resemble wise and benevolent satyrs.

The artist Samuel Lawrence was engaged by George Smith of the *Cornhill* to paint Trollope's portrait as a publicity feature. The idea was gratifying to Anthony and he was delighted with the finished work, but the seven or eight sittings bored him and he fidgeted and scowled while the artist tried to keep him entertained. Rose was given a drawing from the portrait, which she treasured, and a duplicate was presented to the National Portrait Gallery. Anthony pronounced the painting "solid," a word he much liked when applied to him.

The face in the portrait was an assurance that the pattern neared completion. Cloudy hair fringed the bald brow and skirted the hollow cheeks to join the fine, soft beard. The temples had a "hammered" look, the full lips were melancholy. The great, straight nose was broad at the base, with narrow, pointed nostrils and deep furrows running to the corners of the mournful mouth. Only the small, bright eyes beneath strong brows showed that the man was not old. Under the bounce and volubility, the artist had seen sadness and a quietude which was not peace but motion held in equilibrium. He did not look like one who would undervalue his deserts. The face was haughty, almost arrogant.

Such was Anthony Trollope caught by the anguished artist in rare moments of repose. But the man in action was, as an acquaintance put it, more like "a frantic windmill." Though he insisted that his height was but five feet ten, everyone thought him taller; he held his broad shoulders erect, was florid of face, with gray-blue eyes behind gold spectacles. Not wishing to look the dandy, he wore his fine clothes with a carelessness that never touched the slovenly. He favored a black kerchief knotted twice about his thick neck. He had many awkward mannerisms; like his Archdeacon, he would stand with his back to the fire and his feet far apart, thumbs tucked into the armholes of his waistcoat; he would worry his silk handkerchief with his teeth, as a dog worries a bone. Much shouting had made raucous a voice in which at times an early sweetness still sounded. He looked cross, except when he smiled or spoke; but he had a charming, flattering way of looking directly at the person with whom he spoke and giving him his perfect attention.

The house at Waltham Cross afforded him great happiness. Now that he was settled in a home of his own, he exhibited Grandfather Milton's taste for "au-mieux-ing." He added rooms and in the fall and winter of 1862–63 kept carpenters at work, postponing the usual visit to Florence. Since he hunted throughout the season, he suffered less from the alterations than did Rose, who filled the blanks of his absence with letter-writing and household duties; the hour of his return was never certain, and he was very sad when he came in to learn that she had gone out. Usually he brought friends from the meet; his boys were also much at home and hunted too, so that both house and stable were full.

All this was satisfactory to a man who remembered that forty, even thirty years ago he had been like a wretched little beast shivering in the sleet without intelligence to foresee a better future. As a boy, he had supposed that he would always be poor and dirty, that he must be forever scorned. The prosperous Anthony Trollope could rejoice when he looked back upon that most unpromising of children, while he recalled with exaggeration his past miseries, using them as an index of the improvement in his fortunes. Yet his complacency was tinged with fear. He looked forward as well as behind him, and knew too many maxims and moral tales wholly to trust the present good.

Even within his gates there were signs of disintegration. Until his children were grown boys, he had paid them scant attention; but now when they were old enough to hunt and be his companions, it appeared that one of them was determined to go away. The younger, Frederic, was learning nothing in school; he was miserable, and longed to try his luck at sheep-raising in Australia. Anthony could not but sympathize with a lad whose school experience was in some ways a replica of his own; with sore hearts father and mother yielded to the pleadings of their sixteen-year-old son and permitted him to emigrate. If there was any more urgent reason for his departure, it was well concealed.

This domestic grief was not the only obstacle to Anthony's contentment. A disappointment in his public career awaited him. Sir Rowland Hill retired and was replaced by John Tilley; Anthony, next in line, confidently expected promotion to his brother-in-law's vacated post of Assistant Secretary. Perhaps because this pleasant prospect disposed him to be more genial to his ancient enemy, or because he hoped by tardy diplomacy to secure Sir Rowland's backing, he wrote the inventor of penny postage a handsome letter: "I cannot let your resignation from office pass without assuring you of my thorough admiration for the great work of your life. I have regarded you for many years as one of the essential benefactors, not only of your own country, but of all the civilised world. I think that the thing you have done has had in it more of general utility than any other measure which has been achieved in my time."

But Scudamore the poet, whom Anthony had never liked, was promoted over his head, a source of wrath unspeakable. He would have thrown in his resignation, but could not, because he was too firmly committed to the pattern he had plotted for his career. Long since he had determined, with his wife's assent, not to leave the service until he had put by an income equal to the pension for which he would be eligible in 1875. He calculated that it would take another two years to reach the designed position, independent of Post Office pittances; and swallowing his chagrin, he clove to his old seat.

His passion for popularity had hurried him into two of the wrong clubs, from which he resigned shortly. A more complimentary election admitted him in 1864 to the Athenaeum, where he enjoyed playing whist and writing letters on the club stationery with the delicate pale crest of Athena. After Thackeray's death at the end of '63, he was appointed to fill the vacancy on the Committee of the Garrick Club. This was a source of great happiness until the novelty wore off; that tarnished, the connection remained a solid satisfaction. To dine at the Garrick, to play whist in the little room upstairs, to be recognized as a fixture by the attendants and younger members, gave him the feeling that at last he had become popular among men.

North America had been hurried through the press, to meet a generally favorable reception. Anthony undervalued the work, taking too seriously the trifling errors which were called to his attention, and not knowing that so great an authority on American matters as James Bryce would pronounce it excellent. When Kate Field complained that he had not sent her a copy, he soothed her by writing, "One gives presentation copies to old fogies and such like," and confessed that he objected to paying £1 4s. for his own book.

The maddening thing to him was that Kate or any other American could buy a copy for sixty cents! Harper had published a pirated edition four days in advance of Lippincott's, which had been sanctioned by Trollope, and was selling it at a price which injured not only the author but the authorized publishers. Anthony had never had more justification for his wrath. He wrote an open letter to James

Russell Lowell, published in the *Athenaeum*, in which he rehearsed his wrongs at the hands of Harper: "They undoubtedly have been very smart"—he did not know a more despicable quality than Yankee smartness—but "the possibility of such tricks takes away all security both from the author and from the publisher."

Mr. Fletcher Harper replied in an insolent manner; Anthony, he asserted scornfully, was "not the first man who, in the hope of selling his wares for a sovereign, has refused ten shillings, and has at last grumblingly agreed to accept a crown [a reference to the American edition of *Orley Farm*] . . . If Mr. Trollope has lost instead of making money by the transaction, he has at all events learnt by experience the useful lesson, that the gratification of pique and passion is an expensive luxury."

Anthony's rejoinder to this rough schooling did not lack dignity. "The Messrs. Harper affect to deal with the English authors and publishers, but they do so with a threat in their mouth. 'If you do not sell to us at our price,' they say, 'we will take your goods without any price.' This is what we call piracy." As for certain doubts which Mr. Harper had cast on his veracity, he stuck to his guns: "I repeat this assertion on my own personal credit, and I think that I shall be believed in England: I am very sure that I shall be believed in America."

No reply from Harper appeared in the *Athenaeum*. Small wonder that the promotion of an international copyright agreement became to Trollope an ever-increasing interest, fed from his deep sense of personal injury.

Kate Field had sent him a batch of American newspapers, for which he returned thanks with a lugubrious, "They are, however, very bad." In his letter he affirmed his stand against military conscription: "My feeling is that a man should die rather than be made a soldier against his will. One's country has no right to demand everything. There is much that is higher and better and greater than one's country. One is patriotic only because one is too small and weak to be cosmopolitan. If a country cannot get along without a military conscription, it had better give up—and let its children seek other ties." And then, "I am now writing a letter to be published about that beast Harper. But as

I write it I cannot but feel that this is no time for such matters. Why don't they draught him & send him to New Orleans?"

Since the time when Anthony had established moral equality with his gifted mother and brother, he and Rose had taken pleasure in maintaining the family associations, and the links with Florence were not allowed to grow rusty. The circle of the Trollopes in Italy was constantly altering, as guests came from home and intimates returned to England. A friend of one brother was welcome in the house of the other, although Anthony never reached the high level of hospitality maintained in the Villino Trollope. Tom himself came to London nearly every year, and Anthony was almost as pleased at his brother's success as by his own. The Italians set great value on Tom's historical writings. In 1862 the King of Italy created him a Knight of the Order of Saints Maurice and Lazarus, conferring the privilege of the white and green cross of Savoy. Few Englishmen had been thus honored.

But in personal affairs, Tom, the lucky Trollope, was no longer so enviable. While Anthony, at home in England, was secure and pros-perous in spite of family changes and disappointments in the Post Office, the elder brother was experiencing poignant anxiety darkening to grief. Shortly after Anthony's return from America in 1862, Tom had arrived in England in time to see his latest novel, *Marietta,* through the press. Early in July word came that Theo was danger-ously ill, and, cutting short his stay, he had hastened back to Florence, to find her in a precarious condition. There were four doctors, and for a time Tom was, in Anthony's words, "nearly crazed." Not many months before, his mother had suffered a shock, and, though she was up and about, her mental state was such that she could give him neither comfort nor help.

Tom did not give way to pessimism; but from that time Theo's rallies and setbacks deceived no one else. The disease from which Henry, Emily, and Cecelia had died was ravaging Theodosia. In Sep-tember she was strong enough to go with him and her adored Bice to the Italian Lakes, where she rambled with her little daughter and fatigued herself beyond reason. The woman whose frailty in the past had inclined her to indolence now worked at her writing with pathetic energy, perhaps with the hope of leaving behind her memorials for her daughter to cherish after the mother's voice and face had faded. Her clever sketches were published regularly in the *Athenaeum*.

In December she was again very ill, but by the middle of January, 1863, had sufficiently recovered to send an article on the commemorative tablet with which the Florentine municipality had honored her friend, Elizabeth Barrett Browning. She too was shortly to be thus commemorated. Robert Browning found Theo's article "quite perfect in its way," and wrote to Isa Blagden, who kept him informed of the sad progress at the Villino Trollope, "She has true tact and taste and feeling. She and her husband would smile if they heard the real affection I have for them."

Tom had been dear to both the Brownings because of his sound scholarship and his integrity—Mrs. Browning had dubbed him Aristides the Just—but his spurts of industry when he needed money and his habit of buying and selling exasperated her widowed husband to the point of writing, "I never knew the chaffering spirit so strong in a gentleman and person of culture."

It was not uncommon for Tom to be impecunious in the midst of his magnificence; a state which would have mortified Anthony but did not embarrass Tom, if it resulted from the pleasures of a journey or the purchase of a picture; it was his jolly boast that he kept his bank under his hat. After the December crisis in Theo's illness, the doctor advised Tom to take her away, but Tom was just then quite out of funds.

He wagered with himself that he would write a two-volume novel in twenty-four days, and went to work, standing at the high desk on which so many thousand words had been penned. The mental exertion can scarcely be gauged; the indefatigable Anthony, when he came to Florence in the summer following, protested that it would have killed *him*. When *Beppo the Conscript* was half done, Tom took a day's respite, but finished the book in less than schedule time, the actual writing of six hundred pages having been the work of twenty-three days. The novel written at such breakneck speed, and under no creative urge except the wish to make money for Theo, presented an interesting and authentic picture of the effects of military conscription upon a group of Italian peasants. The love story was pleasing, and the style of writing excellent. True, it ranked below *La Beata,* and the characterization was not equal to that of *Marietta,* in which Tom had furnished excellent materials for a study of ambition, avarice, and deferred hope, only to spoil what might have been a great novel by his curious levity of treatment.

If his books were to sell, he was forced, like Anthony, to make concessions to the public taste. Unfortunately these did not hurt him enough. He wrote novels for money; his profession was the writing of history; when he undertook fiction, it was for the sake of his family, and was covertly regretted because it meant postponement of his work on Florence. His attitude toward the novel was never nearer than that of an indulgent step-father to an engaging but sometimes tiresome child. He was most interesting when he digressed from the story to explain the history or customs of a period.

Anthony, very soon after his return from America, had set to work on a new novel for the *Cornhill. The Small House at Allington,* which began to appear in September, 1862, introduced Lily Dale, the heroine with whom everyone but himself was to sympathize. In those early days she was really charming; she had wit, never doubted that everyone loved her, and was charmingly inexperienced. Anthony in later years ungallantly called her "a French prig," but he stood within his rights when he obstinately forbade her to marry loud-mouthed Johnny Eames. Her popularity was rooted in her constancy to the lover who jilted her, and, moreover, a union between the fragile Lily and the boobish Johnny would have had implications unsuited to the comedy of manners. Trollope's commercial sense and his instinctive good taste prevented such a mismating.

The past was surging up through the texture of the novels in accelerated measure; Johnny's father, like Thomas Anthony, had impoverished himself in farming; Johnny had a pronounced resemblance to himself, and like himself had been too gentle with a female who wished to marry him and threatened a breach of promise suit; the lengthy disquisition on hobbledehoys read like a rationalization of his own unpromising youth, and his attack on Lily's perjured lover had the epic quality of the Harrow fight. Of signal importance, although not for his undignified share in *The Small House*, was the introduction of Plantagenet Palliser.

Some time before *The Small House at Allington* was completed, Anthony had allotted five days to the writing of a Christmas story for *Good Words*, on the theme of a bride who gave the price of her wedding dress toward relieving Liverpool factory workers thrown out of employment by the American war.

Good Words was a respectable family magazine edited by Dr. Norman Macleod, a Scotch Presbyterian and one of the Queen's chaplains, a philanthropist who, among other exemplary projects, had established the first penny savings bank in Glasgow and opened schools and refreshment rooms for workingmen. He was a sincere Christian, a charming person with an excellent sense of humor, a friend of Trollope, to whom he had turned in his desire to raise the quality of his magazine and draw his readers out of the narrow evangelicalism promulgated by other publications in his own field. He wished, he explained, to publish reading matter "much wider, truer, more manly and more human,—i.e. more really Christian in its sympathies." Would Anthony write him a novel? He wanted Trollope's "best," but a best which the *Cornhill* would not care to publish—in a word, less "worldly."

"The Widow's Mite" had proved Trollope's perfect understanding of what was expected, nor was there anything in Macleod's specifications to affront an author who frequently aired his belief that narrative ought to have a moral purpose. He demurred at Dr. Macleod's proposal, then reconsidered, and, thus virtually put upon his honor, fell to work on *Rachel Ray*. He had been ill in February, 1863, suffering from what his doctor diagnosed as liver trouble, a complaint conducive to low spirits and bad temper. It left Anthony in a cantankerous mood, reflected in his attitude toward his assignment.

Early in June, when Dr. Macleod read several of the serial lengths in print, although as yet none were published, he told the author apologetically that the novel would not do—it was too harsh against religion: "It is the old story—the shadow over the Church is broad and deep, and over every other quarter sunshine reigns."

Anthony, who no longer had any difficulty in placing manuscripts, at once demanded £500 compensation in lieu of the £1,000 for the completed story, and, without allowing Dr. Macleod's publisher time to answer the proposal, added a threat to bring suit if he did not accept it. The sum was paid on the day it was requisitioned. Macleod, although the injured party, would not quarrel with Trollope, who, most discreditably, made a virtue of not himself breaking off their friendship.

For Trollope was decidedly to blame, and could not have failed to see that his treatment of religious persons, for such an audience, was offensive in the extreme. All characters who bore the Christian label cast a dark shade on daily life and over Rachel, his heroine, and her love. Odious Mrs. Prime and grasping Mr. Prong, the Evangelicals; prejudiced Dr. Harford and feather-headed Parson Comfort of the Established Church; the heroine's weak mother; the gossiping congregations—all were invidiously attacked as "Christians."

Thus was expressed Anthony's half-formulated revolt against society. *Rachel Ray* was in essence a plea for youthful happiness and, even above that, for freedom. Why should youth be denied the right to ramble and make love at twilight among the old graves in the churchyard? Anthony's morose mood did not blemish a primrose beauty in the little idyll.

Among many excellencies was the family resemblance between the heroine and her avaricious, self-righteous sister; Rachel, thwarted in her love, behaved like a pale reflection of sullen Mrs. Prime. Anthony's understanding of life in half a hundred households showed clearly that as a child he had intently observed the ramifications of interests and personalities among his own relations; no amount of study in later years could account for the consummate art which was so germane to him as to be unconscious.

The popular novelist, to whom failure and waste were abhorent, disposed of *Rachel Ray* to Chapman and Hall and spent the period from August, 1863, to April, 1864, in building a novel upon the salvage of his only play, *The Noble Jilt*—metamorphosed into *Can You Forgive Her?* Added to its considerable intrinsic merit was the position of the new book as the first of the parliamentary series: it offered Trollope's public the advantage of following the pilgrimage of Mr.

Palliser and Lady Glencora, his two greatest characters, as it occurred in time.

The past meant more to all the writing Trollopes than the future; the mother had wanted the good old days back again; Tom, free from such romantic longings, had a historian's interest in the panorama of earlier times; but Anthony was haunted by his childhood, the problem of his parents baffled him, and, in his efforts to make right what had been hopelessly wrong in their relation, he spent the greater part of twenty years refashioning his father into a perfect English gentleman and his mother into a warmhearted but shockingly indiscreet duchess.

In *The Macdermots of Ballycloran* Anthony had purged his heart of bitterness toward his father and expiated vicariously his own guilt. Probably after that he more or less forgot him, except for his revival as Joshua Crawley, until in middle life, with grown boys of his own, he began, as men do, to review his relations with his father and, when the need of comprehension and love had long been over, to sympathize and to admire. As yet Anthony himself could have no idea what Plantagenet Palliser would mean to him, but the figure tardily introduced at the fag end of another's love affair in *The Small House at Allington* was to undergo an evolution which in time would console the son for the suffering of the father.

In the writings of a creative mind, it is these subtly disguised and often unconscious resemblances which reveal the author's inmost compulsions. Thus it is of small importance that in crude outline Johnny Eames resembled either Anthony or Frederic Trollope; but that Thomas Anthony Trollope should be recreated Plantagenet Palliser, Duke of Omnium and prime minister to her majesty Queen Victoria, is as wonderful as true, and reveals the lavishness, romanticism, and sweetness of filial love in a man to whom such qualities were seldom attributed.

In order to recompense Thomas Anthony for his misfortunes, it was necessary to give him a very great name and a bottomless supply of wealth; the essential character of the man must not be altered, but the harsher traits could be softened—as was legitimate, since his asperity was attributable to the exacerbations of poverty and ill-health. Mr. Palliser was not robust, but he was above those mean domestic difficulties and dosages which brought on Thomas Anthony's headaches.

Anthony Trollope did not err in his presentation of his parents. Mr. Palliser, pattern for English gentlemen, was unlovable in spite of his absolute virtues; he could not get on with people; he was so meticulous in trifles that his wife laughed at him and made others laugh too; he was a pedant upon whom the habit of quoting Latin gained alarmingly; he loved his children, and they respected him, but kept their distance and their secrets from him and confided in their mother; he was a tremendous worker; he was patient with his wife's follies and seldom checked her extravagances; he overlooked her lack of taste and the commonness of her ambition; but with innumerable good qualities he remained a repellent figure.

Lady Glencora was charming and generous but frightfully indiscreet; more clever than her husband, but shallow and imperfectly loyal; she could not forgive him for his understanding of her, and could not love him because he would not approve of her; she attached their children and separated them from their father; she was not, horrible to relate, quite a lady. Either because her identification with Frances Trollope was not intended in the beginning or because Anthony feared the recognition—or perhaps only as attributes conveying the sense of an inferiority he consistently maintained—several characteristics inapplicable to his mother's life were advanced, such as Lady Glencora's extreme youth, her great wealth, her rescue from a marriage with a ne'er-do-well.

While her husband's apotheosis was thus in its earliest inception and her own lower spiritual plane had scarcely been assigned to her, the mother in Florence, whom he had resented rather more than loved, died in his brother's house, at the age of eighty-three years and six months. Her mental decline had been long, but her physical death was brief and easy; she kept her bed only a day or two. Of the gay household set up in Keppel Street more than fifty years since, two only survived her, the eldest and the youngest of her sons. Her grave, near to Elizabeth Barrett Browning's, was a great way from those of the husband and children she had buried here and there, against the resurrection, as a sower sows his seed.

Her death could not much affect Anthony, though he felt kindly toward the quiet old woman of the past eight years, whom he had ceased to associate closely with his clever mother. Rose, who was given to the trite, felt it sad that one who had lived such an active life should have become imbecile. The boys, Frederic and Henry, had not those associations with their grandmother which Bice and Cecelia's children had enjoyed. As for her books, they were forgotten.

But Tom, well into his fifties, loved and missed her, although he was too sensible and honest to be sorry she had gone. To Kate Field he wrote, "In all probability, my dear Kate, you will have seen in some paper or other the fact of my dear mother's death, & will have understood that that has caused my silence to have been longer than it otherwise would have been. I do not mean that the shock of her death was such as to incapacitate from writing to you; but simply that the mass of letter writing which it has thrown upon me in addition to my other work has been very great. Nevertheless, though we have been so long prepared for it, and though my poor dear mother has been in fact dead to us for many months past, and though her life, free from suffering as it was, was such as those who loved her could not have wished prolonged, yet for all this the last separation brings a pang with it. She was as good and dear a mother as ever man had, and few sons have passed so large a portion of their lives in such intimate association with their mother as I have for more than thirty years!"

The mother would have asked nothing better than his honest, affectionate praise—"as good and dear a mother as ever man had." Anthony's measured phrase lacked the intimate charm of Tom's blunt words: "Of all people I have known she was the most joyous, or, at any rate, the most capable of joy." Neither of her sons made much of her extraordinary talents; in their opinion, the epitaph which could be carved on the monument of many a lesser woman suited her life and works: She was cheerful, industrious, and affectionate.

Anthony was still smarting from the promotion of his competitor,

Scudamore, when, in the summer of 1864, he wrote the harsh little novel *Miss Mackenzie*. He had threatened to leave out the love interest—partly as an experiment, because he found it increasingly difficult to write conventional love scenes; a little because of his special wrath at an old cleric who had been scandalized by certain passages in *Can You Forgive Her?*; a little because of a general disposition to be disagreeable owing to his pique over the postal appointment. Deciding that love could not be eliminated, he selected as heroine "a very unattractive old maid" who turned out, in spite of his malevolence, a pleasant, sensible young woman, blooming and healthy even at the advanced age of thirty-four. As she was an heiress, she had to be supplied with suitors, and a motley group was provided by her cross-grained creator—an Evangelical minister with a squint, a rogue, a dilatory acquaintance who had not wanted her until she was rich, and a parsimonious old cousin with nine daughters and a shrewish mother.

Toward the close the perverse Trollope softened toward his ill-treated heroine, and the completed tale, while lacking the charm of the youthful lovers of *Rachel Ray*, was not otherwise inferior to it. Two or three old friends stepped into the pages of the little book; Littlebath society was enlivened by the parties of Miss Todd, and Lady Glencora patronized a bazaar for the benefit of the orphans of Negro freedmen.

He began a greater book, *The Claverings*, for the *Cornhill* on August 24, but interrupted its progress for three days in September to write a story called "Malachi's Cove." Of all his brief tales, this was the best worth remembering. The elfish girl who gathered seaweed for her living, the scent of "the long, soft, salt-bedewed trailing masses," the glimmer of "the dishevelled hairs of the ocean," the poetic imagery and the economy of phrase combined to produce a story not inferior to one of Turgenev's.

The Claverings marked the zenith in Trollope's scale of prices, with a single check for £2,800 for a novel of two-volume length. The plot was of more importance than was usual with him: Julia Brabazon broke her engagement to Harry Clavering and married the rich roué Lord Ongar. Harry consoled himself with Florence, "a little brown girl" with the tenacity of a limpet. Lord Ongar died and Julia, his young widow, uninformed of Harry's engagement to Florence, was given reason to hope that her wretched experience was the prelude to a happy second marriage with him; although chastened by her woes, she saw no reason why a woman should not eat her cake and have it. Harry, however, unlike the majority of Trollope's men in the same predicament, remained true to the girl to whom he was most deeply committed.

Julia was the second of Trollope's potentially tragic women; her easy acceptance of the dissolute Ongar, her dewy repentance and gracious hopes, and the measureless remorse which followed her disillusionment when the likable but vacillating Harry was lost, would have made her great had not the cause of her prolonged penance been sentimentally slight. If Trollope's sympathies were occasionally with the fox, he usually hunted with the hounds, and concurred in the Victorian verdict on the girl who thoughtlessly preferred an old man's money to a young man's love. There was unscrupulous brutality in the way he forced Julia to lose her lover, to strip herself of Ongar wealth, and to go into permanent seclusion with her weak, querulous sister.

Of the "fun" in *The Claverings*, of which he thought highly, it must be admitted that the antics of the monkeyish Sophie Gordeloup in dealing with Captain Boodle had a certain finesse. Count Pateroff, although an English conception of a continental adventurer; sadistic Sir Hugh; the vulgar Mrs. Burton, who so wonderfully married off her flock of daughters; Mr. Saul the curate, whose poverty and gawkiness did not conceal the Christian gentleman—among these shining minor lights there was not one which fell short of perfection.

The folk of the Barset tales were excluded, although Clavering was in Bishop Proudie's diocese and it was the Bishop's edict against hunting parsons which was the source of Mr. Clavering's absolute idleness. Thus in its entirety *The Claverings* became a novel which a man might do worse than have chosen were he determined to read one, and one only, of the tales of Anthony Trollope; but it would have been fair to warn him that he might find himself committed to half-a-dozen others.

CHAPTER XV

The Hardening Crust

1865-1866

THACKERAY's sudden death strengthened the intimacy between his family and Trollope's. Anne Thackeray could easily believe that Anthony was as heartily grieved as everyone was shocked. She was touched by expressions of sympathy which may have been in part due to relief, and to remorse that this should be so with him. Early in 1865 she visited the Trollopes at Waltham Cross, feeling her own sorrow scarcely lessened by the passing of a year. It was a place to ease the sense of suffering; the old house stood lapped in snow, the halls were chilly, but one smelled the wood fires before crossing the threshold; they burned in bright, warm rooms uncluttered by Victorian plush and ormolu. Anne lay quietly thinking in her bed during the darkest hours and felt less lonely when she heard Anthony's groom rouse him, as the clock solemnly struck four.

Anthony's stumbling up long before dawn was symptomatic of the life he was leading. He had arrived at the peak of his activity, and a fever of haste was discernible in every endeavor. As though his duties at the Post Office, his hunting, the writing of two lengthy novels a year were insufficient to absorb a man's energies, he was wildly striking out into new fields. During the subsequent four years he would be instrumental in founding and editing a famous newspaper and an influential review and would establish his own magazine, for which he was to function as editor and principal contributor. Unable to force back the creative tide surging within his unquiet being, he would create new literary *genres* and publish anonymously in order not to overwhelm a public which could not be expected to read with the speed of his writing. He could not stop writing; beyond action lay emptiness—a sterile void in which he dreaded to hear the dismal whirling of his thoughts.

At the time of Anne Thackeray's visit he was engaged upon *The Belton Estate,* a nineteenth-century landscape of a story, where the autumn sun slanted over stubble fields, farmhouse, manor, and woodland. He had employed his usual innocent triangle—the girl, the first lover who was not to be her husband, the second lover; and, as always, made the old theme appear spontaneous. Among Trollopean ladies, his heroine shone as a woman of intelligence, dignity, and unselfishness. But the third volume, necessary to complete the tale of pages, did her injustice by forcing her into a false and wearisome indecision over accepting her lover.

The lowered pitch of *The Belton Estate* was largely due to Anthony's anxiety. His new manner of life required a large income, which he doubted his power to maintain if he confined himself to the domestic novel. Love interest had never wholly absorbed him, and, as he grew older, he was inclined to scamp the scenes of dalliance. He had an uncomfortable feeling—which none of his bluster could exorcise—that it was silly for mature men to write love idylls. As he wrote the pages of *The Belton Estate,* he pondered the problem of the continuance of his present vogue and the possibility of finding a new *genre; genre* it would have to be, for he had begun to shrink from the universal. The old affirmations sprinkled the pages of *The Belton Estate:* to nurse a sorrow is but folly; grass growing between the cobbles is a sign of evil; effort brings success—familiar mottoes these, written without much thought. But his touching words on prayer were an indication of his pressing anxieties: he wrote, as with a heavy sigh, that it was the most difficult "of all works in which man can engage himself." The desolation of Clara's father recalled the heartbreak of Thomas Anthony. No novelist ever dealt more tenderly with suffering old men than did Anthony Trollope.

He was continually making efforts to secure new markets. It may have been the recollection of the family magazine at Harrow—whose youthful editor had not solicited his contributions—which made him so determined to assist in the founding of the *Pall Mall Gazette.* London, as well as Anthony, had need of a newspaper of the projected kind, an afternoon publication furnishing pungent and penetrating comments on the morning news. George Smith backed the enterprise,

Frederick Greenwood of the *Cornhill* was the editor, the name was chosen as a compliment to Thackeray's memory, because in *Pendennis* he had conceived a *Pall Mall Gazette* "written by gentlemen for gentlemen."

Anthony was a frequent contributor of brief sketches which were later collected in book form. The first series was on hunting. The little papers were only pleasantly informative, but contained several memorable gems such as, "Always shake hands with your friend the farmer. It puts him at his ease with you." In their entirety, the effect was oddly neutral: the man who disliked hunting might enjoy collecting equipment; the man who loved hunting would seldom see a good day's sport; there was no valid reason why a parson should not hunt—but he had better not; ladies were not unwelcome—but let them ask no favors. He had little to say of the wild rapture, the ecstasy of yielding to the primitive urge. He was puzzled himself to account for the fascination which the hunt had for him; an inexplicable sense of guilt, quite apart from the cruelty of the sport, which he was able to rationalize, made his explanations clumsily inept. He phrased his pleasure awkwardly—"Always to excel and to go ahead of everybody." To write of days in the saddle was his delight; his objective descriptions relieved an inner tension, but the muddiness of his mental processes made it impossible for the general reader to share his enthusiasm. Charles Lever's Galway hunt in *Charles O'Malley* quite outdistanced any of Trollope's.

Later, in 1868, Anthony, still vainly attempting to account for the irresistible attraction of the sport, wrote two more essays on hunting. He mentioned the charms of nature and of convivial society, the happy initiation into the secrets of the English countryside—then broke off, as if baffled by his inability to find the true source of his addiction. Yet he confessed candidly that to him the present ecstasy possessed value surpassing that of an uncertain heaven: "We are told that the great happiness of life is to have lived well and to have done with it. There is in the idea of this theory the necessity of a standing ground outside the world which looms to us cold and uncertain. But there is no doubt about the joy of having ridden well to hounds."

When these later sketches were republished in book form as *Eng-*

lish Sports and Pastimes, Anthony furnished an introduction which showed his amusing deficiency in forecasting the future. Football had not been included, he explained, because of "its irregularity and lawlessness"; golf was known too little beyond Scottish bounds to warrant giving it a place; the public had lost interest in prize fighting; tennis was not "widely known." But after such miscalculations occurred a sentence which proved him possessed of a far-reaching if narrow patriotism: "That English Sports may remain among the descendants of Englishmen to days in which perhaps England herself may exist no longer, is our wish as sportsmen."

Even more important to Anthony than the *Pall Mall Gazette* was the *Fortnightly Review*, that stand-by among English periodicals, which made its first appearance on May 15, 1865. Indeed, he was prime mover in its inception. Intending to make use of it as a vehicle not only for his own serials but for articles and book reviews, he invested in it £1,250 of his capital. Its distinguishing feature was to be the exclusion of anonymous contributions; the tone was to be liberal, the style intellectual, and the writer would be permitted to say whatever he pleased over his own signature. Anthony, however, laid an odd restriction upon the contributors. At a board meeting where the new principle was formally promulgated, he blurted out that nevertheless no one should be allowed to question the divinity of Christ. It was a betrayal of his own disquietude, and resulted in alienating one or more of the scheme's supporters, besides giving rise to several pleasant anecdotes in which Anthony figured surprisingly as a defender of the faith.

Among the staunch remainder were several men well fitted to increase Anthony's understanding of politicians and intellectuals; Charles Waring knew "everyone worth knowing"; Danby Seymour, who had been in Parliament, was familiar with current publications and contemporary history; John Morley was as able as, in Trollope's opinion, he was "advanced."

The board were desirous of securing George Henry Lewes for editor, and it fell to Anthony to attempt persuasion. Lewes protested that he had not the health for such a venture, and Trollope, looking with horror at the lank face framed in long hair, the straggling moustache, the brilliant, hollow eyes, was half ashamed to press him. Lewes promised to think over the offer and accepted it on May 15, the day of the first issue.

Although Lewes's health forced him to resign at the end of 1866, the warm friendship between the two men continued until Lewes's death. They had private confabulations over coffee and cigars, and when they made part of a group, Trollope listened to Lewes without interrupting him, something he could seldom force himself to do when other men were talking. Lewes, the grandson of a famous comedian, had acted in his youth; he possessed a fine sense of drama, and in telling a story used his body as well as his voice. Trollope admired him, but was continually perplexed by his enjoyment of life; Lewes was always tired and very often in pain, he had had outrageous domestic troubles, and yet, when he said he was happy, Trollope knew he was sincere.

The many special articles and reviews which Trollope wrote for the *Fortnightly* voiced opinions common to intelligent Englishmen in the 'sixties, but showed no advance over them. A keen observer, shrewd in appraisal, he went straight to the core of any question he chose to treat. He was able not only to see both sides of the question but to feel both, recognizing at once the need for reform and progress, but touched by an affectionate regret for that which must be changed.

His friend Charles Buxton had published a book called *Ideas of the Day on Policy;* Anthony reviewed the work from the realistic standpoint that Buxton was a "black sheep," because he was a nonpartisan; if a man did not join a party, he could be neither popular nor effective. Buxton's dilemma furnished a precedent for that of Anthony's Phineas Finn. Goldwin Smith lectured on the American Civil War; Anthony, who had not believed the South justified in secession, observed that, "Rebellion may be, and in our own days has been [in Italy], the highest duty of man." In his review of a longer work on the resources of America, he pronounced the Civil War an accomplished blessing, praised the obedience to law and the educational system of the United States, but reprehended its antipathy to free trade. In an article on the Civil Service, he forcefully restated his belief that higher posts should be filled by men promoted from the ranks, and that employees ought to be allowed to vote at parliamentary elections.

"The Irish Church" questioned the principle of Irish support of the Established Church; Anthony agreed that it was contrary to the principles of religious liberty to tax an entire population for the benefit of a communion to which only one tenth belonged. Another article on a religious subject revealed Anthony's shrinking from the harsh code of the Old Testament. Dr. Macleod, to whom Trollope had behaved badly in the affair of *Rachel Ray,* but with whom he remained on terms of distant friendship, had courageously attacked Sabbatarianism in Glasgow, its very citadel. Macleod charged that the conventional strict observance of the Sabbath transformed the "Day of Rest" into "a day of torment." Anthony endorsed Macleod's opinions and added daringly that "the lessons contained in the ten commandments were not lessons given to us."

Among his book reviews were two on Ruskin's *Sesame and Lilies* and *Crown of Wild Olives.* Anthony abhorred "fine writing" and considered elegance un-English if not unmanly. He could not avoid praising the charm of the moralist's language, but speedily reduced his arguments to absurdity by stripping them of their pretentious imagery. "That such a man should write on Art may be well, but that he should preach to us either on morals or political economy is hardly to be borne." Thus was Anthony the spokesman of his class and great among the Philistines.

While Anthony busied himself with numberless literary activities, his sister-in-law, Theodosia, was dying in Florence. Tom could scarcely believe that he was losing her, for she had always been fragile, and her tubercular condition had been so protracted that she seemed invested with a strange immortality which held her poised between both worlds. She was wearied with coughing and her fingers trembled uncontrollably when she attempted to form words for her poetic fancies, or for those letters she still directed to the outer world. Her sensitive spirit suggested that her lingering put a blight on her darling Bice and wearied her husband. Early in that April of 1865 Isa Blagden wrote Robert Browning that Theo would never be better, and Brown-

Bice and Theodosia Trollope

ing passed the news to Anthony, who could scarcely credit it. On that same day, April 13, she died in her husband's arms.

Isa had been very kind. At the beginning of March she had moved into the Villino Trollope and constituted herself chief nurse. The night after Theo's death she sat up with Tom, who was much shattered, and the next day took motherless Bice to her little house on Bello Sguardo. The old-fashioned garden with its golden oranges was walled in by solemn cypress trees; the lizards sunned themselves. Bice felt at home there, but Uncle Anthony suddenly appeared and snatched her away to English wholesomeness.

Left alone in her garden, Isa wrote letters to Robert Browning. She was a charming little woman, but perhaps she had been jealous of Theo, perhaps she would have liked to marry Tom herself. She and the poet exchanged gossipy letters; in answer to his excited demands, she admitted there was renewed talk about the dead and gone Theo—the old question, whose child was Bice? Isa staunchly defended her friend's memory, protesting too stoutly.

Anthony had not come to Florence when his mother died, but immediately on hearing of Theo's death, he came to console his brother and to rescue Bice. He visited the Protestant cemetery and saw the new grave beside his mother's, close to that of Elizabeth Barrett Browning, near to Landor, the great poet who had loved and valued Theo since her girlhood.

Propriety had driven Isa Blagden back to her villa, but Anthony found with relief that Tom was not living alone. For some months young Alfred Austin, the journalist and aspiring poet, had been Tom's companion on the long walks which had been his only relief from the sight of Theo's anguish or his own struggles to finish his history of Florence. When the funeral services were over Austin left the cemetery at Tom's side. After silent musing, the older man said that he would be glad if Alfred would share his villa. Austin was delighted, not only because he was attached to Tom but because the garden at the Villino Trollope was already full of roses and the house itself "a happy combination of English comfort and Italian art."

He played his part loyally, doing what he could to distract his

host's mind from his grief, and keeping him at work on the history
whenever such application seemed possible. Tom had been sleeping
on an average only five and a half hours of the twenty-four; the
practical need to finish his book and the harassing conditions of his
private life had made this the most arduous of his tasks, in a life in
which effort had been singularly spontaneous. Two volumes were in
print, but the remaining two were written in most unacademic haste—
a fact which may have been known to the *Spectator* critic who, on their
appearance, urged him to "devote himself to works which, with a
little extra care [!], will hand down his name to posterity." For the
period, *The History of the Commonwealth of Florence* was, in the
words attributed to the great Italian historian Pasquale Villari, "the
best work on the subject"; but within a few years the patient research
of other scholars caused it to be first superseded, and then forgotten.

Anthony carried off Bice, the "wonder-child," saw to it that she
had a riding horse, and, his avuncular duty thus nobly done, handed
her over to Rose. In his large house, from which he was absent during so many of the little girl's waking hours, she could not be in his
way: he did his writing long before she was out of bed in the morning.
Once, when a third niece was visiting at Waltham House—Florence
Bland had made her home there for several years—he offered a five-
pound note to each of the girls for the learning of "Lycidas," his
favorite poem. It never occurred to Bice that she would do well to
memorize the lines. The others duly recited it and received the prize,
but Bice was not disturbed.

She was twelve, exquisitely proportioned, but very small. She may
have missed "Pen" Browning, with whom she used to ride her pony;
Pen's mother had delighted to watch them, "side by side like two
butterflies." The little girl grieved for her mother, who had taught
her in that charming fashion which asked no effort from the pupil.
Bice's voice was famous in Florence, where the best teachers had
begged the privilege of taking her as a pupil. Jenny Lind had told
her that if she would study professionally she could rival her, but
Bice's great eyes had darkened uncomprehendingly. It seemed she
had a prescience that she was among those whom the gods loved.
Wholesome as was the regime of Aunt Rose, it could scarcely be grate-

ful to the precocious little girl; in Florence she not only had friends of her own age, but was treated by all the grown people like one of themselves, only better, because, being so young and little, she was really more wonderful.

Her father came for her in the summer. He was cheerful, quite changed from her last sight of him. Everyone in Florence had tried to console him; he had been dining out much more frequently than during the last years of Theo's life. He did not perceive the plans for his remarriage. The gossip about Theo had put him in a martyr's niche; dear old Tom Trollope, whose wife had long been an invalid, deserved a second chance—a happier wedded life. Robert Browning wrote wryly to his informant Isa, "Lord love us, how little flattering is woman's love— It seems he may throw his handkerchief to anybody in Florence." In England Rose planned to do a little matchmaking on her own account, lest Tom be caught by some designing Florentine. He was a desirable *parti* in spite of his deafness and his five and fifty years, for the ugly young fellow had grown into an imposing man; he had a European reputation, was well-to-do, possessed many beautiful bibelots and a magnificent library, and was the kindest of men and a delightful host and guest.

Full of schemes and enterprises, he suggested himself as Italian correspondent for the *Daily News* and was accepted, but soon gave up the post—later he would serve briefly as the Italian correspondent of the *Times*. He told Rose and Anthony that he had sold the Villino Trollope because life there was unthinkable without Theo; he could not go in or our without seeing the mournful memorial tablet which the city had placed there in honor of her efforts for Italian freedom. He had bought an old house—Ricorboli—on a hillside outside Florence. But he had made money on the sale, as property was rising on the chance that Florence would be the capital of Victor Emmanuel's new Italian kingdom. Anthony said sardonically that whatever Tom had realized on the Villino Trollope he would spend on Ricorboli—and more too.

Tom had indeed begun to plunge into the extravagances necessitated by his own ideas of what was required to transform a tumbledown old house into a gentleman's estate. Unrestrained by the fastidious

Theodosia, he was "au-mieux-ing" on a grand scale. By what he considered Machiavellian intrigue, he had purchased ten pillars of purple marble with pure white bases and elegantly cut capitals which had once enclosed the choir of the cathedral. It was his intention to employ them in the foyer of Ricorboli, an octagonal hall lighted by eight lancet windows filled with stained glass and separated by niches each of which was to contain a complete suit of armor. His library would be fifty feet in length, his gardens would outclass those of the Villino Trollope. Dealers in antique furniture considered him their lawful prey; vendors lay in wait to show him extraordinary "finds."

But Bice was on his mind. He wanted her back in Florence, but admitted the necessity of engaging a governess. After some insistence he persuaded a young French girl, a teacher in her own mother's school at Brighton, to take the post; but she was lonely in Italy, and the winter less benign than she had expected. The next spring she returned to England, and Rose and Anthony were free to send out their own candidate—ostensibly as governess, in reality as the future Mrs. Tom.

It was not easy to persuade Fanny Ternan—she had been christened Frances Eleanor—to accept the position. Charles Dickens, her mother's friend, had introduced her to the Tom Trollopes when, as a young girl, she had been studying voice in Florence. The mother, Mrs. Ternan, was a beautiful and charming woman, a talented actress in Shakespearean roles, and Fanny, her oldest daughter, had been born in Philadelphia some thirty years before while her parents were touring the United States. Irish Tom Ternan had been jealous and conceited. Before Fanny was ten he had died, so it was said, in an insane asylum at Bethnal Green. The three little Ternan girls were pretty and good and much attached to one another and to their mother.

Unsuspecting Tom supposed that Fanny had been devoted to Theodosia. It was not so; she had admired her for her musical and poetic gifts and pitied her for her frailty; she was too healthy herself and too young to sympathize with her extraordinary lassitude, and yet not young enough to escape the Florentine gossip about Bice's paternity. Of Bice, however, she was extremely fond.

But she made difficulties about going back to Florence as Bice's governess and said she was writing a novel; the family friend, Mr. Dickens, believed her to possess literary talent. Anthony and Rose persuaded her; they were convinced that her clever talk was exactly suited to Tom's tastes: in beauty and goodness she was everything one could ask, and for her own sake she ought to be out of England and away from the scandal which linked her sister Ellen's name with that of Charles Dickens. Her younger sister, Mrs. Rowland Taylor, lived in Florence, so that Fanny would not be wholly separated from her family.

More was done for her by way of propriety than had been thought necessary for the French governess; she was chaperoned by young Mr. and Mrs. Alfred Austin, who were living, or rather camping, in Ricorboli, which was in an appalling state. The flooring of the second story had been removed for the construction of twin staircases, and unwary exit from a bedroom might result in a broken neck. Tom's fourteen thousand volumes waited the completion of the library; but the garden, although not yet in order, was a place in which to linger, and, as Tom liked the custom of dining out of doors, the simple meals he favored were served there. A bottle of Chianti in its straw cradle, sausage, black bread, and fruit spread the rustic table. Friends from the city or from the palace next door came very often to see how the house progressed. As the evening darkened, there were walks through the vineyard where they picked the clusters of ripening grapes.

Tom had been very fond of Theodosia, but, though he never said so publicly, the sensible Fanny was far better suited for marriage with a Trollope. No doubt she understood that she had been dispatched to Florence less as governess than bride; she liked Mr. Trollope extremely, said she would marry him, but preferred not to do so in Florence; it was too far to ask her mother and Rose to travel. Nor was England chosen—ostensibly because of its distance, more probably because of the difficulty occasioned by the whispers about Ellen and Charles Dickens—and the couple decided on Paris.

Maria Taylor, the youngest of the sisters, was staying at Ricorboli and would travel with them; Rose, Anthony, and Mrs. Ternan planned to meet the party in Paris. Anthony, informed of the engagement, issued a triumphant, "I told you so," and, after reading a paper on "International Copyright" before the Association for the Promotion of Social Science at Manchester, came out to Florence to join the escort. He suggested taking Bice to England for a visit during the honeymoon, but Bice did not feel equal to the proper English atmosphere of Waltham Cross and said serenely that she preferred to stay with Isa Blagden.

Isa herself was not favorably impressed by Tom's choice; she knew of Fanny's literary ambitions; no doubt Mr. Charles Dickens would find room in his columns for the sister of his protégée. Nor was Dickens enthusiastic over the match, although he wrote Tom a civil letter of congratulation. To a woman friend, he confided that he did not "in the least care" for Fanny, whom he judged, with evident misgivings, to be "infinitely sharper than the serpent's tooth"; he cautioned his correspondent to "make no reference to me which either [Fanny or Tom] can piece into anything." But Browning, who, dearly as he liked a choice bit of gossip, had no reason to fear Fanny's deductive powers, wrote to Isa: "I am glad to learn that T. Trollope is about to marry happily, quite right in him to try. I think him affectionate, good, full of various talent, all which his wife will soon find out."

In mid-October, 1866, Anthony and the youngest of the Ternan sisters, Mrs. Rowland Taylor, chaperoned the elderly bridegroom and his young Fanny to Paris, where they met Rose and the bride's mother. Immediately after the simple wedding, the pair went to Chartres, first stopping place on a long ramble similar to those Tom had enjoyed as a boy with his mother or Fanny Bent, and in his maturity with the frail Theodosia.

Having done his duty by Tom, Anthony could return to work with an approving conscience. Matchmaking had been the sport of idle hours, and his life's business of writing was progressing in yet another path. During an autumn holiday in Bohemia he had fallen under the spell of Prague, and had written *Nina Balatka,* a novel of the witch city. Unwilling to be known as the author of so unconventional a book, he published it anonymously in *Blackwood's* after George Smith had refused to bring it out. Anthony offered a far-fetched reason for his resort to anonymity, protesting that it was unfair for sales and criticism to depend on established reputation rather than on actual merit—he was, he said later, making a test case. With this absurdity the man who was capable of explaining his characters' most delicate impulses rationalized his own uncomplicated motives. He was no altruist, and his choice of a new personality was obviously due to the overfrequency of his own name on publishers' lists, his wish to exploit a new field, and a desire to air opinions and prejudices which would offend his stable public. In some quarters Tom was suspected of writing *Nina Balatka*, although clever Mrs. Oliphant recognized Anthony's hand.

When the novel failed, he protested angrily, "Prague is Prague," which was quite true as far as background went. The Hapsburg palace frowned by day and laughed by night, John of Nepomuk guarded the bridge from which an angry king had flung him, the rain pelted the soughing elder bushes and the wry tombstones in the ancient Jewish graveyard; the smells, the sombre colors, all proclaimed the authenticity of Anthony's Prague.

But English readers cared very little for Bohemia, and the theme of the story was one to puzzle or affront the general public. Nina was a Christian girl, and her lover was a Jew. Her relatives opposed the marriage with insolence and knavery; the lover's kindred, equally disliking the match, behaved honorably and at length yielded through compassion for Nina. Few readers objected to what was said against Bohemian Catholics, but there must have been some who sensed the author's irritation against all organized Christianity and who resented the contrast of the Church with the dignity and nobility of the Ghetto—not that Anthony liked Jews; he was merely very cross with Christians.

His growing store of foreign observation and experience—Italy almost always excepted—was put to literary use as rapidly as it accumulated. A new series of short stories, the successor to *Tales of All Countries*, appeared in 1867 under the title *Lotta Schmidt*. With the exception of the haunting "Malachi's Cove," it was remarkable only for the light it shed on Trollope's materialistic standard of literary honesty. Strahan published the collection and set up the proofs for a two-volume work. Trollope, who held that there was

material for only one volume, was appalled at the "desert of margin":
he refused to cheat the public by selling them so much blank paper;
and the type was broken up, Anthony sharing the expense with Strahan.
According to his own standards, Trollope was as honest a man as
could be found in England: he insisted on giving his readers the
quantity for which they paid; he was pleasantly sure that the quality
was good enough for them.

From this period dated an agreeable series of *Travelling Sketches*
on the subject of English types abroad, which made their first appearance in the *Pall Mall Gazette*. But another series of *Pall Mall*
sketches appeals more strongly to modern Trollopeans who are not
members of the English communion and who may consequently be
unfamiliar with its usages. In *Clergymen of the Church of England*,
the title under which the collection was republished, they will learn,
among other answered riddles, why the stately archdeacon did not
derogate from his dignity when, upon his marrowbones, he bored
with an awl into the flooring of St. Ewald's parsonage. These papers
showed once more how greatly Trollope's attachment to the past of
the Establishment was at variance with his common-sense conviction
of the necessity of reform. More poignant was his nostalgic longing
to believe as he had once believed in all the tenets of the Church.

After these trivial sketches flowed in amplitude *The Last Chronicle
of Barset*. The ambitions, greeds, and passions of the fabulous, but
solid, county of Barset surged around the question of a good parson's
honesty in a business matter. From the bricklayers of Hogglestock
to the Proudies in the palace, every inhabitant was interested; and
the last of the concentric circles, arising from the plunge of such a
stone, washed as far as Lily Dale, fragile and sweet in spinsterhood.
By a touch of genius on her creator's part, the Warden's daughter
caused the disaster; few but Nelly Harding-Bold-Arabin could have
meant so well and been so silly. Mr. Crawley himself had grown
nearer to the image of Thomas Anthony Trollope.

When Anthony confessed that he could not comprehend Mr. Crawley's ignorance of the source from which he received the check, he was
probably thinking to himself that his own father had been quite as
mad in his methods of managing his wife's estate: he could scarcely

understand either of them; but thus both bitter, learned men had acted. The book seethed with life; the Proudies are with us yet, Griselda Grantly, who had *not* been jilted by Lord Dumbello, took a hand in her brother's affairs; Johnny Eames made an epic journey; Cousin Toogood quoted Dryden in the wrong places and worked marvels; the Quiverfuls paid the butcher for the stew. Best of all was the Warden's passage in the sweetness of a ripened fruit long left hanging. No taint of sentimentality touched the quiet deathbed, but tender justice was rendered to a good old man.

Even while Anthony was doing what lay so beautifully within his power, he was making an abortive effort in a form for which he was singularly ill-qualified—he was trying to write a history of English prose fiction. He was not notably well-read and had neither time, eyesight, nor patience to make him so; his insistence on Victorian morals would have made his work useless to future students, and his idea that good style consisted in an absence not only of ornament but of definite characteristics would have made him a very odd critic. His true aim, however, was not objective history but the old unhappy urge for self-justification: "I intended to write that book to vindicate my own profession as a novelist [Tom looked down upon novel writing], and also to vindicate that public taste in literature which has created and nourished the profession which I follow." The effort came to nothing, but he was able to use his introductory pages in an article written a dozen years later for the *Nineteenth Century*, and his meditations in defense of the modern novelist gave him material for a popular lecture which he repeated, with variations, on half a dozen occasions. The "chaffering spirit" which Browning deplored in Tom was not lacking in Anthony, who bargained and sold when he could, and, when his wares were not marketable, refurbished them and tried again.

CHAPTER XVI

Fame Is Not Enough

1866-1868

Can You Forgive Her? had been an experiment in which the political element overbalanced the romantic—the loves of the ladies depending largely upon elections and cabinet meetings. Trollope's urgent interest in politics and his tepid feeling for romance, combined with the pressing need of a fresh field, suggested that his success in *Can You Forgive Her?* could be urged further in a novel whose chief theme should be political, while the love motif sounded as faint, occasional music. Variety could be gained through the use of house-party and hunting scenes, in which the ladies might bear a share. To write this kind of book would be delightful; it would be about places and people, diversions and affairs which were precious to him.

"Of all the studies to which men and women can attach themselves, that of politics is the first and the finest," wrote Anthony, with a liberality which falsely promised to atone for a fining down of his heroines' affairs of the heart by allowing them a share in the political game. Actually, Lady Laura in *Phineas Finn* was the hostess of a political drawing room—until she married for power and was immured by the jealous Kennedy; Lady Glencora entertained lavishly while her husband was prime minister—but made herself ridiculous by her hospitality without increasing his prestige; Alice Vavasour's candidate was defeated, she was married against her will and buried in Persia; Lady Eustace's money would have helped the impecunious Lord Fawn in his career—but being frivolous, she threw away her opportunity by marrying a murderer. In contrast to these presumptuous ladies, Madame Goesler, who proved her humility by refusing to marry the duke, was rewarded with Phineas, the nonpareil. Thus it appeared that women might "attach themselves" to the noble science only in a wholly subservient way; Madame Goesler, who claimed nothing, achieved the only substantial success.

Anthony happened to be in Ireland while he planned his next novel, and without much reflection he decided to take an Irish hero, handsome, fickle Phineas Finn, who gave the book its title. His success with the character was extraordinary; through the novelist's easy affection appeared his amused understanding of a young man who owed his fortunes not to his native talents but to personal beauty and a charm which antagonized few men while women found it irresistible. Very subtle was the slow deterioration of the impulsive, lovable young man into the pompous politician; so subtle that it is possible it escaped the conscious mind of the author.

His hand was less sure in painting the enigmatical Madame Goesler, an exotic a little out of place in his gallery, nobly as she adorned it. Anthony seemed afraid of breaking one of the tiny treasures in her little drawing room, where young Henry James would have been in his element. But the red-haired, angular, aristocratic Lady Laura Standish was within Trollope's scope, and he understood her as James could not have done; James would have raveled out the pattern and rewoven it with clever deviations. Trollope felt a sympathy with Lady Laura, akin to that with which he regarded Lady Mason; because of this latent compassion Lady Laura's wretched frustrations appeared due rather to Fate than to Victorian conventionality. When Trollope disliked a woman, he hounded and harried her—reduced her to rags. He liked Lady Laura, and created a tragic figure. Such compassion, devoid of sentimentality on the part of an author, tends to remove the character from the prison of the period to a universal and timeless plane.

The book finished inconclusively with the Irish member back in Ireland with his little Irish sweetheart, but Trollope knew that it was not an end; Phineas would soon return to England. He could envisage a series like the Barchester novels in which these representatives of the ruling class would appear and reappear, always recognizable, and yet subtly altered by the passing hours and by their personal fortunes. Like the tales of Barset, the novels would be straightforward, revealing men and women as they appeared to their own circle

—in this case a higher one; there would be very little tittle-tattle and positively no peeping through keyholes.

Yet he wanted more strings for his bow, and the failure of *Nina Balatka* had not cured him of a yearning for the foreign scene and a new personality. His successful management of background and color was proved by the fact that many readers supposed Tom to be the author of *Nina Balatka;* everyone knew that Tom could write foreign tales with authority. Anthony would make another attempt.

The scene of *Linda Tressel* was laid in Germany; the story ended unhappily; and, except for Linda herself, the characters were types rather than individuals, a fault to which Trollope was prone in writing of "foreigners." *Nina Balatka* had been a story of Christians against Jews; *Linda Tressel* was the story of innocent, pliable youth against society.

The Ghetto had saved Nina; Linda was hunted to death. Her religious aunt, an Anabaptist as was "Old Farmer" of the Trollope nursery, symbolized the tyranny of home; the old man who was bent on marrying Linda embodied lust and greed; the rich burgher who counseled her submission spoke for the world of conventional morality; the serving maid betrayed her—even her lover lurked in shadow and, phantom-like, leaped the stream below her window. This lack of substance in the girl's only hope was indescribably painful; it was as if Linda only dreamed that he existed. Significantly, she found refuge in a Catholic home, but there she died—so that Anthony could satiate his fury against her persecutors. Nor did he wish to save her; he had both run with the fox and hunted with the pack, and she, "the precious victim," must perish. This little story, lugubrious more often than pathetic, was packed with sinister revelations.

Fewer than five hundred copies of the anonymous *Linda Tressel* sold in the six months following publication. But the weeks spent on the plaintive little story had dislodged, for the time being, his morose spirit, and the rest of the summer was unusually happy. Amid this all-pervading mental toil, he was leading with Rose the busy social life of well-to-do English people. In spite of the host's odd habit of going to bed at nine of an evening and rising at four, visitors delightedly accepted invitations to house parties at Waltham Cross. Professing not to know his near neighbors, Anthony would say, "We have our old friends down in batches, which we like best."

Often he and Rose would plan for their guests a drive or a ramble taking in some favorite scene. Anne Thackeray liked to recall a picnic with Mr. and Mrs. Millais and the Trollopes when in their pleasant strolling they had come upon a painter in the wood; Millais had corrected the bewildered artist's brushwork and at last each in turn had told the poor man, not without laughter, the names of the others who had distinguished him by their notice. Another lady remembered going to Harrow with the Trollopes; Anthony had shown her Julians Hill—his "Orley Farm"—and pointed out, "with many chuckles," the hedge through which the young folk had smuggled their mother's treasures when the bailiffs were in the house in 1834. But he did not chuckle when he told her of his shabbiness and sufferings at Harrow School.

People who made Rose's acquaintance either at Waltham Cross or at other people's country houses seldom found much to comment upon, except that she was very fashionably dressed and "very nice indeed." One lady remembered her beautiful white hair above a youthful face. Probably few realized how essential she was to Anthony as a fixed point in a shifting world. Neither she nor Anthony were brilliant talkers; at dinners they said little except to their next neighbors. Anthony, indeed, was known in social circles as an unsatisfactory conversationalist. Alfred Austin called him "a delightful companion, and brimming over with active intelligence," but "in no accurate sense of the word intellectual, and as unhelpful and impatient an arguer as I ever met." A pious Scot remembered him as "the only man I had heard swear in decent society for uncounted years."

"However much you might like his bluff, hearty, resonant personality," wrote Frederic Harrison, "you would have said he was the last man to have any delicate sympathy with bishops, dukes, or young ladies." Yet his rollicking, boisterous manner concealed a keen observer, a man of deep and subtle feeling, which was hoarded up and subsequently lavished on the creatures of his mind. If he appeared insensitive to natural beauty, it nevertheless had power to awaken his emotions and renew his spirit: to betray these emotions would have seemed unmanly.

Sometimes, with a young companion, he would raise a corner of the veil which hid the creative process from mistrusted eyes. "One of the first things he asked," wrote the American Walter Herries Pollock, "with regard to a story which I was then wanting to write, was whether I thought of it all day; whether when I walked the characters were always in my mind; whether my whole attention, when not given perforce to other things, was devoted to them and what might possibly befall them. This, he said, was the only way in which the people and events of a novel could be made to live, and in this way it was that every one of his own characters was so life-like."

But in general company he continued his boastful shout, lauding himself as a pattern of industry, the earliest up in the morning, the man who could earn a day's hunting before breakfast. To his lasting detriment, few of his listeners had the perception to see that he was hiding himself behind this afflictive barrage. A typical story was told by a gentleman who met Trollope at a country house whither he had brought his hunters. Anthony played cards, smoked, and got to bed in the small hours. But at breakfast he announced that his pen had earned him twenty pounds that morning. The next night the same gentleman met him at another country house, where the procedure was repeated.

Actually Trollope's self-depreciation was the most disingenuous form of brag. He was protesting his own superiority in strength and perseverance. He considered the man who could write only when everything about him and within was at peace as a poseur or an enervated rag of masculinity. When Carlyle bade the universe hold its breath so that he could write in quiet, Trollope judged the "Chelsea sage" deficient in power of concentration; nor did he think the philosopher's output sufficiently distinguished to warrant such parade. When he tolerantly assured George Eliot that imaginative work like hers could be done only in short stretches, he was leniently taking into consideration her sex, her physical frailty, and perhaps her age. But when the author was a man, how small a rill of inspiration his must be which had now and again to be dammed up in order to form a pool deep enough to hold the slippery fish of his ideas! Trollope could feel that he had never needed to create an artificial reservoir.

In his investigation of channels for his almost unparalleled literary fertility, it occurred to him to emulate Thackeray and Dickens and publish his own magazine. The *Fortnightly*, which he had been instrumental in founding, was now firmly established as a thoroughly respectable Liberal periodical. However, despite its name, it appeared but once a month; and this infrequency, together with the impossibility of anonymity, set an arbitrary limit on the amount which he could contribute. A magazine of which he was editor would enable him to publish more of his own unsigned work, and he could extend his columns to the other writing Trollopes; it would afford scope for the political interests which had been quickened by Disraeli's new reform bill and the writing of *Phineas Finn;* he felt that "the good old Liberal cause" stood in need of support; his intended retirement from the Post Office would leave him free to assume new burdens; the name *St. Paul's* appealed to him; the publisher Virtue was definitely interested.

The talented Robert Bell was at that time in financial difficulties after a library speculation. Anthony offered him the post of assistant editor of *St. Paul's* at a salary of £250, a quarter of the remuneration intended for himself; thus the terms, if adequate, were not generous. But Bell died in April, 1867, without accepting, and Anthony bought in his fine library. He wished to assist Mrs. Bell, and he had not forgotten his brother Tom's library of fourteen thousand-odd volumes. Although his Post Office colleague Edmund Yates professed a belief that no man of his time was "more heartily, more thoroughly, more unselfishly charitable," Anthony's donations were seldom lavish and sometimes originated less in pure kindness of heart than in a sense of propriety, very compulsive under his bad manners.

That year he took his holidays earlier than was his habit in order to rest before assuming his editorial duties. Thus he was in France when Tom came to England to enter Bice in the Brighton school. Fanny could not be expected to teach Bice, write novels, play the part of hostess of Ricorboli, and participate in the social life of the

Florentine circle. Besides, Bice was a difficult pupil, not because she was bad-tempered, but because she preferred parties and overnight visits to the routine of lessons. Such a life was too stimulating for Theo's delicate, sensitive daughter. Fortunately she agreed to try Brighton; Fanny would not, and her father could not, oppose her.

But under much outward decorum and good will, the newly married Tom Trollopes were in trouble. Of the now long forgotten storm the principals allowed little to escape at the time, and, in their subsequent writings, they concealed the very existence of the scandal.

This much, however, is certain: Robert Browning met Tom near the Athenaeum and, in view of his deafness, gave him the address of the aurist who had operated on Lord Lytton. He noticed that Tom looked very wretched but supposed this was the result of a rough Channel crossing; he said, quite honestly, that he wished he could see more of Tom, and added, "for politeness sake," that he was sorry not to see Tom's wife. Tom smiled and said nothing. Silence in the Trollopes was an oddity, and Tom's look struck him as peculiar. Browning left him and stepped jauntily into the Athenaeum, where the story met him. Its source was unimpeachable: Anthony Trollope had told the tale in Paris to a fellow clubman! According to him, there had been a great quarrel, "revelation of the past misfortunes of which T. had been ignorant altogether"—and the upshot was that Fanny had left her husband.

Because Isa Blagden always knew everything, Browning wrote her for further information, explaining that he felt it would be indelicate for him to inquire of Dickens's friend, Forster. Isa's reply was destroyed, but in his next letter to her Browning gave vent to this impatient outburst, "What is the amount of evidence people *do* expect in such cases? The seventy-two eye witnesses which, it is said, are required to prove the adultery of a Cardinal?" Poet and poetess discussed the two wives, the dead and the living, Theo and Fanny; Isa said spitefully that Browning ought to have known for himself that Dickens published Fanny's stories for other reasons than their pure merit. But the unproved scandal concerning Ellen Ternan and Dickens was no secret from Tom, and it seems certain that the "revelation" concerned the old story of Bice's paternity. Fanny was altogether too good-natured to have wanted to make Tom unhappy, and, if she told him what his deafness and his complacency had spared his overhearing, it was probably to keep him from making unguarded remarks. But the Tom Trollopes had parted company.

A few weeks passed, and in mid-August, Fanny and Tom were together again in Bruges. But he had had a blow, and at fifty-seven even his stout spirit was less resilient than in earlier days. He quarreled with Anthony, who had gossiped on his affairs; he loved poor Theo more than ever, and began to speak of Theo's daughter as *My Bice.*

While Fanny wrote in their hotel room, he sat day after day in the square in Bruges, listening to the carillon while the great bells seemed to toll the fortunes of his family, of whom two lay buried just beyond the town; seemed to ring out Theo, his past, and his too brief future. He walked beyond the walls, found again the graves of Henry and of his father, and took some pleasure in observing that the inscription he had composed was still legible. An incident at the Post Office would have made him laugh more cheerily if his heart had not been made sore by the explosion of a cruel secret; the clerk refused to hand over a letter addressed to Fanny, because to have a husband read his wife's mail might cause domestic difficulties.

But Tom soon grew tranquil. Fanny was not always writing, nor was he long idle. She listened with flattering pleasure to stories about what happened to the Trollopes before she was born. At Waterloo she was charmed to learn from their guide that more than thirty years ago he had piloted another Madame Trollope over the battlefield, a lady who had asked numberless questions and taken notes. "The Americans," he added reflectively, "don't like her."

Fanny could climb the spire of Antwerp Cathedral as nimbly as Cousin Fanny Bent had done three decades ago, and she was ever so much prettier. As they journeyed, they recited Lear's limericks and, when the stock ran out, made their own. When two months were over, they returned to Ricorboli at peace with each other, secrets shared, ready to stand together against slander.

The erring Anthony, whose Paris chat had spread the story of his brother's domestic problems, spent September and October of 1867 in Waltham House writing *The Golden Lion of Granpère,* the insipid fruitage of his vacation in the Vosges. It was intended to be the third in his series of anonymous foreign tales but, after a first rejection by Blackwood, Anthony made no further attempt just then to place it, and the little novel was laid away in the small body of unpublished work. That he did not press its marketing was due to events of such importance that the fate of one book, where there were already so many, seemed insignificant.

He was leaving the Post Office to take up the editorship of *St. Paul's*, for the long-awaited time had come when his yearly income equaled the pension he would receive if he remained another eight years in the service. He had not forgiven Scudamore's promotion over his head, although he had not allowed his wrath to lose him money. As he was only fifty-two, his resignation could not pain him as it might have done at sixty; there was regret, but there was also excitement and expectancy.

In behalf of the Duke of Montrose, Postmaster General, Anthony's brother-in-law, John Tilley, wrote a letter of appreciation couched in fine though ironic language. Anthony's old colleagues gave him a farewell dinner at the Albion Tavern, at which Mr. Scudamore presided. Trollope professed melancholy at leaving the Post Office, and doubted "whether inspecting Post Offices were not better work than delineating character"—a comparison which the reporter understood was ironically intended. The "sadness of farewell" afflicted Trollope more than it could the service. He was a very able administrator whose headstrong ways had impaired his popularity. After the severance, the department paid him an honest compliment in asking him to perform a final service; he was requested to visit the United States to conclude a new postal treaty. He accepted, and the journey was slated for the spring of 1868.

His introductory editorial for *St. Paul's*, the first issue of which appeared in October, 1867, was scarcely calculated to establish its success; he claimed for the new magazine no special merit whatsoever. The Trollopes never grasped the fact that self-valuation has a share in the price the public places on a man's work. It was not only unnecessary, it was foolish of him to call his *Phineas Finn* "a slight story," to admit that the hero was "not very heroic," that readers would be "lifted into no heaven of admiration or of wrath by the virtues or by the vices of their new acquaintances." Much of this was not only true, but what he had intended as a natural development of a realistic view of life; but as an editor, who presumably wanted his magazine to sell to the general public, his admissions were indiscreet, and the publication's ultimate success was commensurate with Trollope's underpraises.

He had no conception of the proper editorial "front," was disposed to a fussy overconscientiousness, hesitated to reject any contribution, but showed himself too ready to buy manuscripts from himself and the Tom Trollopes. He had many other good names on his list— George Macdonald, the Scottish author of excellent religious novels; Allingham, the Irish poet, who, however, produced little after he settled in London; the peerless Margaret Oliphant; Mrs. Craik, author of *John Halifax, Gentleman* and many lesser sanctimonious novels; Charles Lever; Sir Charles Trevelyan; and Austin Dobson—while a homely grace was given the magazine by the pleasing illustrations of Millais.

Austin Dobson, then in his mid-twenties, was a very charming fellow whom Anthony could not but like; that he should admire Dobson's poems offered a fresh proof of his mother's lasting influence. By adoption, Dobson belonged to the Georgians as certainly as Frances Trollope's birth had ranked her with them. She would have applauded his delicate, fastidious verses and pushed his fortunes, as she had enjoyed doing for many young men of talent besides Hervieu and Hiram Powers. Anthony took a different tone when he suggested alterations in Dobson's lines from that in which he advised changes in Kate Field's effusions, where humility would have been misplaced. When he criticized Dobson, he did so not because he felt qualified, but because as an editor he knew that his subscribers demanded "clearly intelligible" verse. "I know I am sticking pins into you by my remarks; but whatever is an Editor to do?" Again he wrote humbly, "I hope you will forgive me, if you do not agree with me." "Une Marquise," which first revealed Dobson's mastery of the exquisite *genre* of his choice, appeared in the March, 1868, number of *St. Paul's* and was not published in volume form until five years later, when his *Vignettes in Rhyme* was dedicated to Anthony.

But the function of critic was performed privately. Literary judgments were excluded from the pages of the magazine with a brusque statement that they would require the undivided attention of the editor and all his staff if they were to possess any value.

The subjects of the editorials were chosen from political scenes at home and abroad, with special emphasis on reconstruction in the United States. Trollope provided a leader, "The Uncontrolled Ruffianism of London, as Measured by Rule of Thumb," the fruit of his investigation of the current crime wave, which he decided regretfully had been overrated. As far as he could determine, a virtuous citizen could go about armed only by a watch which would satisfy his wife as to the hour of his return. But he found out certain methods of thugs, instances of garroting and murderous attacks, which were utilized in *Phineas Finn* and *The Prime Minister*. The urge to make information play double duty was characteristic of all the Trollopes.

He was fully alive to the monetary advantages of editorship. His editorial salary of £1,000 could be augmented by the writing of articles at twenty shillings the page and serials at twenty-five shillings. A monthly installment of *Phineas Finn* averaged twenty-seven pages and netted the tidy sum of £35 15s. With Napoleonic liberality he provided a market not only for his brother but for his brother's wife, whose novel, *The Sacristan's Household,* ran throughout a full year. In the September and November issues of 1868 the Trollopes filled more than half the magazine; in the latter month the family earnings amounted to £83 5s., of which Anthony pocketed the lion's share. But even the combined talents of the family could not make the venture a permanent success, and Trollope relinquished it in 1870.

The contract for Anthony's next novel, *He Knew He Was Right*, was signed with Virtue on November 15, 1867, at a figure equal to the top price received for its immediate predecessor, *Phineas Finn*—£3,200. The new book was not so much as begun when the papers were passed, but within six months a huge manuscript was going to press. No previous work had stood so much in need of excision, but neither had any previous work been so extraordinarily rich in inimitable shapes. The madness of Mr. Kennedy had not injured the popularity of *Phineas Finn*, because Mr. Kennedy was a minor character whom no one was asked to like: in the new book Anthony, as a popular novelist, made a mistake when he chose as protagonist a gifted young man who, from being difficult and jealous, progressed into insanity. Louis Trevelyan inspired the casual reader first with anxiety, then with dislike, afterward with an irritated desire to have something done by somebody to save the poor fellow's reason, but at last the chief sentiment was a wish to have him die and stop causing the wretchedness of all the people about him.

The book was prodigiously rich in life and color. The reader was made at home in the society of London, Florence, and the cathedral city, and was diverted by four marriages. Considerable acidity went into the composition of characters; the innocent wife was pig-headed, the governor of the Mandarin Islands was mischievously ineffectual, the flirtatious capers of the elderly beau augured a degree of malice even greater than his vanity, the minister who did his duty was revolting in his lack of charity, the detective was disgusting, Miss Stanbury (who resembled the lamented Cousin Fanny Bent) was cruel in her caprices, the episode of the rival sisters and their clerical demi-suitor was as satirical as if Mrs. Trollope had written it. All this is not to say that *He Knew He Was Right* was not a prodigious work; such elements were, however, destructive of its popularity.

The mission to the United States which Trollope had agreed to undertake on behalf of the Post Office was primarily concerned with the establishment of a uniform rate for postage between the two countries. Anthony was given full power to negotiate a new postal convention to replace one concluded the year before, and the American Postmaster General promised to extend every facility which would enable him to finish his business with a minimum of delay. At his own request he also received authority from the Foreign Office to deal with the question of international copyright.

Whatever gratification he derived from this dual mission lay in the personal distinction and the early hopes with which he set forth, in the first spring of 1868, on what was from beginning to end the most vexatious of his journeys. In Egypt he had suspected the Peninsular and Oriental steamship company of double-dealing; but such mistrust was confidence compared to his doubts of the officials he met at Washington. They broke appointments, a fault peculiarly abhorrent to him; he feared that he would yield too much for England; questions arose over which he had no authority to treat; he threatened to write home and say that negotiations should be broken off; although all pending issues were satisfactorily settled by correspondence after he returned home, in the end he suspected that Yankee cleverness had been too much for his British guile.

Nor was he more successful in his attempt to establish the copyright. He did not blame the American public for Harpers' piracy, and said rather handsomely that he thought the average reader was willing to pay a fair price for an English book. He exonerated the small publisher; the "Leviathans" were the thievish rascals who stole his books with the right hand while the left waved aside the smaller fry who were willing to deal honestly with English authors. He tried to make it clear to American writers that they were the worst sufferers; who would pay money to one of them, when he could get an Englishman's book for nothing?

The heat of summer, the plague of mosquitoes, to which he offered special attractions, and perhaps the added weight of six years, made him excessively unhappy in Washington. He was making desperate attempts to finish *He Knew He Was Right*, while he accomplished little in his public mission.

In New York in April he learned that Charles Dickens was sailing for Liverpool after his exhausting series of readings in American cities. Anthony came aboard in the mail tender with just time to locate Dickens, shake hands, and dash off again before the ship got under way. "It was most heartily done," wrote the elder novelist.

Next month in Washington it was very pleasant to stumble on Kate Field and call on her the same evening. She wrote a laconic line in her diary, "Met Anthony Trollope. Same as ever." They had another chance encounter, he called again, and accompanied her party to the Capitol. Kate too was the "same as ever," but Anthony was not pleased to find her so. That she should be as pretty, as enthusiastic, as youthful was, of course, delightful, but why had she not married, or settled on a career? Though she was perpetually in motion, he feared that she was essentially idle.

She asked Anthony to criticize her story, *Love and War*. He was polite, but less gentle than with her earlier efforts. He told her that she had an easy, pleasing style—but she was didactic, egoistic, had not learned "the knack of story-telling"; her plot was pretentious. In a moment of weakness he suggested that she try to write something for *St. Paul's*, where she had probably hoped to see *Love and War*. He wanted her to make something of her life—"and then you are so young," he wrote in tender pleading, but could not keep back a vehement postscript, *"The end of your story should have been the beginning."*

Rose had teased him by saying, "Don't you wish you may get it?" when he entreated her to join him in America, but she relented and met him in New York in June. He had to return to Washington for a few days, on July 14 went to Boston, and on the 15th sailed with Rose, home, to England. Kate was in Auburndale; he made no effort to see her, but wrote a note stating firmly the exact length her story must be, if she wanted to see it in *St. Paul's*.

In the heat of summer and the rage of official negotiation, he had finished *He Knew He Was Right* and begun *The Vicar of Bullhampton*. If anyone had a right to preach industry, it was he who so fervently practiced it.

CHAPTER XVII

The Servant of His Youth

1868-1869

ANTHONY must often have been conscious of the gulf between what he knew about women and what he was permitted to say of them. Very frequently he showed an understanding of the painful situation in which penniless girls of his own class found themselves when no suitable lover appeared. Among such girls were Dorothy in *He Knew He Was Right*, the loving sister Kate in *Can You Forgive Her?* the wretched American girl in *The Eustace Diamonds*; in such cases his attitude varied from the simple acceptance of a trying situation as insoluble, to a brutal satisfaction in it.

To husband hunters he was merciless, even when admitting that no other course lay open to them. But on no class of women was the effect of his personal bias so strangling as upon those of high mental gifts. His resentment against his talented mother vented itself in depicting the clever and warm-hearted Lady Glencora as a ludicrous figure in society and a troublemaker: Alice Vavasour, the intelligent young woman who longed for a political career, was herded into the bonds of conventional marriage: Lady Violet Effingham, the London belle, was given a brutal booby to tame and a full nursery to keep her quiet: the able Madame Max Goesler married her inferior, handsome Phineas, and asked little better than to supply his creature comforts; and Julia Brabazon took her beauty and her brains into hopeless exile. Instead of allowing Lady Laura Standish to rule over a diminished political drawing room, a course which would have made it possible for her to recover from her unlucky passion, Anthony banished her to Dresden; and Lady Carbury, who, like Frances Trollope, wrote in order to support her children, was a butt for his ridicule.

He did not avoid the insistent question: What is a woman to do with her life? But his inexorable answer, "Let her fall in love, marry the

man, have two children, and live happy ever afterward" could not
dispose of every spinster. Even when a young woman suited him by
being sufficiently pretty, well born, and unintellectual, he found it
increasingly difficult to follow her love affair with cheerful ease, because in his private opinion romantic marriages were undesirable.
Sometimes an odd confession would slip past the guard of the popular
novelist, taking shape in such dubious pronouncements as that, in
view of the uncertain results of love matches, humans might do worse
than choose partners "as the birds do by force of nature."

In the case of the unfortunate girl whose misstep had been discovered by implacable society, he was disposed to a cautious humanity.
Her fall had put her entirely out of the world of polite Englishmen
and women; in consideration of this detachment he could afford to
be merciful. He attributed the harsh judgments of society to virtuous
women, and, while he admitted that severe treatment must be accorded
the sinner, he thought that, if she repented, something ought to be
done to ameliorate her lot. Each of his two novels which employed
the theme of the fallen woman commenced, contrary to his practice,
with a preface. In the case of *The Vicar of Bullhampton*, begun in the
United States in 1868, the import was apologetic, almost pleading;
Anthony, whose chief aim was "the amusement of the young of both
sexes," confessed that he had ventured to treat of the fallen woman
because he wished to arouse sympathy for her sisters in misfortune,
whose fault was "often so light in itself," whose punishment was
"horrible beyond the conception of those who have not regarded it
closely."

The brutal old miller, Carry's father, who had, in an excess of
paternal virtue, "broken every bone" in the body of his daughter's
seducer and turned his victim out-of-doors, was the stock cruel father
of mid-century fiction. But while Anthony was pleading for mercy on
the erring girl, he could not conceal his approval of the cruel old man.
As in the tale of *The Macdermots of Ballycloran*, the image of the
unforgiving father fascinated him; when he described the miller in
the act of pardon as feeling "degraded, not so much by his daughter's
fall as by his concession to his fallen daughter," a note of admiration
was not wanting. Besides, old Brattle was a stoic, and Anthony envied

such philosophers. Trollope's own attitude to the touching child whom he had chosen for his "sinner" was, however, that of the intelligent observer; he summed up her problem expertly as that of a pretty, resourceless girl who was expected to do without amusements; "the utterly purposeless tenor of her day and of her whole life" was too much for virtue.

He had anticipated—wrongly, as it turned out—that his preoccupation with Carry and the family at the millhouse would result in their overshadowing the vicar, the lovely lady, the squire and the rest of the gentry. But it was here that the main interest of this almost matchless tale resided. Bullhampton was a perfect English village; it was both masculine and feminine, differing thus from the creations of Mrs. Gaskell, which were almost entirely populated by ladies. So surely did the mental map provide directions that, if Bullhampton had actually existed, a reader could have found his way through the unlighted streets to the house of the disappointed squire, to the vicarage, past the odious Methodist chapel, down to the mill, along the sinister hedge which skirted the property of the murdered man, further, if one had courage, to the mansion of the vainglorious grandee.

In Mary Lowther's love story, Trollope, whose dislike of interference in the fortunes of youth balanced his respect for authority, described the course of an engagement into which an overly conscientious girl was persuaded by her friends. The reader's sympathy was gradually withdrawn from her jilted lover, because of his weak sensitivity to public opinion and his assumption of authority over the reluctant Mary.

There was never a more delightful vicar; the unalloyed virtues which made prigs of George Macdonald's ministers were humanized by recklessness and good nature; if Trollope did not quite like his poor Carry Brattle, the vicar did. The friendship between clergyman and squire was sweetened by Anthony's wistful regret that such a relationship had been impossible for him: "That undemonstrative, unexpressed, almost unconscious affection which, with men, will often make the greatest charm of their lives."

The novel had been slated for publication in *Once a Week*, but in March, 1869, E. S. Dallas, the publisher and a Garrick Club acquaintance, asked Anthony's permission to bring it out in the *Gentlemen's Magazine*, a distinctly inferior periodical. The reason he alleged was not one to appease Trollope: Victor Hugo had been dilatory in submitting his *Man Who Laughs*, but had at last delivered the manuscript, which Dallas intended to print immediately; since both serials could not to be published simultaneously, the English author was asked to give place to the French. The offense went deeper because of Trollope's dislike of Hugo's politics and sensationalism, while the delicate nature of *The Vicar of Bullhampton* made it peculiarly galling to have it ousted by the work of one of those very libidinous "Young Men of Paris" whom his mother had reprobated over thirty years before. He refused to yield, and the new novel was published in separate numbers at great financial loss to everyone concerned.

In the Dallas controversy, justice was on Anthony's side. When treated with proper consideration, he was not a difficult author in his dealings with publishers. John Blackwood and he were always warm friends. In that summer of 1868, while everyone was still reading *The Last Chronicle of Barset*, he and Rose paid the Blackwoods a visit at Strathtyrum. Anthony was the lion of the hour. His popularity went to his head and Rose was powerless to control him. One of the guests chronicled sourly that Mr. Trollope "tried to play golf" at St. Andrews. After "a somewhat worse shot than usual," he pretended to faint but, falling heavily on a golfball secreted in his pocket, he let out an "unfeigned yell." In addition, Anthony swore in the presence of clerical gentlemen. But his worst crime was depreciating Sir Walter Scott. He told the company of Scotsmen that, if one of Sir Walter's manuscripts were sent in to a London publisher of the day, it would inevitably be rejected. Someone asked incredulously whether Scott had become old-fashioned. "Not a bit," said callous Anthony, "it is just because they are so dull." Such behavior was rather naughty; he would never have offered up his own cherished Sir Walter, had he been able to find any other reputation with which to plague the company. But John Blackwood saw through his maneuvers and enjoyed them.

Anthony was thinking seriously of entering Parliament. One by one he had fulfilled his boyhood ambitions and, in doing so, wiped out old scores against relations who had undervalued him. But Uncle Henry Milton's satirical reply to his boyish confession that he would like some day to be in Parliament had not lost its sting, though Uncle Henry had long lain in his grave: he had said few clerks got into Parliament—Anthony had always intended to be one of those few.

There were half a dozen arguments against his making the attempt. He was not actuated by any strong wish to serve his country, nor had he any important measure to propose. He was fifty-three years old; on the whole he preferred keeping his money to spending it, and the election would cost heavily; it was improbable that he would gain a seat; if he did, he would be bored by his duties; he was by no means a good speaker, since he was incapable of extemporaneous efforts and, when he had committed to memory what was to be said, suffered so deeply in imagining the unhappiness of his listeners that he was likely to rattle off the words too fast for anyone to understand them.

In the matter of political principles, he proudly affirmed that he stood where he had been standing for thirty years; not to have progressed seemed to him a positive merit. His mother had once remarked that if some fine morning all classes were leveled, by night half the people would be making beds for the other half. He would never have admitted even to himself how complete was his agreement with her. God had made the Haves and the Have Nots—although occasionally there was some straying over the boundary. Anthony hoped for a gradual amelioration in the condition of God's unfavored children, foresaw the slow dissolution of the Empire without distress, and proclaimed himself an advanced conservative Liberal. His ideal was, "I will not say equality, for the word is offensive, and presents to the imagination of men ideas of communism, of ruin, and insane democracy,—but a tendency towards equality." He was confident it would not come in his day.

In 1868 he became a Liberal candidate for Beverley in the East Riding. His agent told him frankly that he would lose; not only was he entirely unknown, but Sir Henry Edwards, the Conservative, who had represented the borough for ten years, could not conceivably be unseated. Sir Henry was the chairman of the Beverley Waggon Company, Ltd., manufacturers of railway cars and agricultural machinery, and the company's managing director was also the manager of Sir Henry's political interests. A great deal of money had been spent on local charities by the Conservatives over a long period of time, and individual voters were accustomed to substantial bribery.

Trollope persisted stubbornly; he gave his agent the £400 he asked for current expenses, and on November 1 went down to Beverley to canvass. His running mate in the Liberal interest was Marmaduke Maxwell, later Lord Herries, who had read Trollope's novels and was glad to be associated with him. Their supporters included several newspaper men, a Baptist minister (on whom Trollope took vengeance in *Ralph the Heir*), a Colonel Hodgson who was an employer of labor, and a very few other "gentlemen." The county families were solidly entrenched behind Sir Henry Edwards—he had spent money on Beverley.

It was not an affair for an honest man. The municipal elections were held on November 2, and Sir Henry's manager prepared for the day's business by drawing £800 from the bank. With the bag of gold coins on a table before him, he settled himself at the Golden Ball tavern, while his assistants installed themselves at other strategic points. The voters entered singly or in shy groups; the agent doled out the bribe of fifteen to twenty shillings and wrote down in his notebook the amount and the name of Sir Henry's adherent. As he did so he explained that the rate of payment was higher than usual because it was a "double event"; the payee must vote Conservative not only in the municipal elections on that day, but again a fortnight hence at the parliamentary elections. The number of these purchased henchmen was somewhere between 800 and 1,000.

Anthony was too shrewd to believe unreservedly in the purity of his own supporters, but the atrocity at the Golden Ball was so flagrant as to purge his side of reproach. In disgust he abandoned the field to go hunting with his fellow candidate. Anthony loathed all that fortnight's dingy work; he was dragged up and down miry lanes to solicit votes; the weather was rainy and he felt bedraggled; the autocratic hand of the committee gave him no peace. The Conservative opponents kept out of town until the day after the great bribery, and then came down to triumph. Anthony, though he finished at the foot of the slate, made a surprisingly good showing, with 19.7 percent of the total votes polled.

Early in the following year there was a trial at law, at which bribery was adduced. The election was declared void, the Conservatives lost their seats, and Beverley was disfranchised altogether. Anthony, however, was bitterly vexed. He had failed in an important detail of the tapestry he had long been weaving; he would never sit in Parliament, never be made free of the admirable little door reserved for members. It was exasperating to remember the mortifications which had not brought him what he wanted. From that time forward he had his heroes elected to Parliament with increased frequency.

He did not immediately set down his own experiences in the form of fiction, but mulled over them as he wrote the brief tale of an ethereal gentleman, *Sir Harry Hotspur of Humblethwaite.* The short books of Trollope were nearly always better constructed than the three volume novels, because they provided scant rope with which to dangle his characters. Most of them were written upon a slight or an ungrateful theme; some were ungenial, others sorrowful.

Sir Harry Hotspur was an austere version of Sir Peregrine Orme, and, like Sir Peregrine, a near relation of Dickens's Sir Leicester Dedlock. Sir Harry bade his daughter Emily love her cousin, and Emily was obedient. When Sir Harry was apprised of the cousin's unsavoriness, he ordered Emily to un-love him. She could not; was silent, turned to religion, pined, was taken to Italy, and died, constant as any Trollopean maid and as unfortunate, except for her maidenly satisfaction in breaking the heart of the father who had helped to break hers. Emily's mother was genteel and silly—a Mrs. Ray in high life. The cousin's mistress was a more solid character, whom Trollope wronged when he represented her as the actual author of the letter which killed Emily. A tiresome repetition of *black sheep* and *wolf* marred the diction of a book which was flaccid rather than pathetic.

He arrived in February, 1869, at the doleful moment, long foreseen, when he had undeniably outrun his market. Two novels were in the process of publication and three more lay concealed within his study, finished and waiting to be delivered. His position was so sobering that he manfully abstained for two months from beginning a new novel. But he was not resting. The labors of an editor and his own voluminous contributions to *St. Paul's* occupied many hours, and he made one more attempt to write a play, this time a dramatization of *The Last Chronicle of Barset*, which a theatre manager had requested but failed to approve. The play was never performed but was privately printed under the title *Did He Steal It?*

In part inspired by Dickens's readings and the recollection of Thackeray's lectures, he was accepting invitations to occupy various platforms from which he read lectures on such favorite topics as copyright, the writing of novels, and the place of women. His "Higher Education of Women," dedicated jokingly to his niece Florence Bland, evinced the old feeling that the present state of affairs was highly unsatisfactory but that he would be reluctant to see it changed. A few months later he spoke in Edinburgh on "English Prose Fiction as a Rational Amusement," and revealed his painful anxiety to justify the profession of novelist—one upon which his own family had traditionally looked down and which was open in these Victorian days to doubts on the score of purity.

Amid his other pursuits, he occasionally read—less for recreation than because he feared his stock of ideas might prove inadequate to the demand put upon it. A regular supply of books from Mudie's lending library accompanied him wherever he went. If he did not look into them himself, he expected Rose or Florence Bland to read them and acquaint him with their contents at second-hand.

Anthony had been an indifferent father; his boys had grown up without the painful and strict association of the earlier generation with Thomas Anthony, without the tender companionship which existed between Tom and Bice. Henry, the elder son, was called to the bar in 1869, when he was twenty-three. He had never felt drawn to the law and very possibly had been propelled thither by the desire of Anthony to please his own long-dead father, the ruined barrister. His aspirations were literary, but Anthony thought they were not likely to justify themselves. Yet when Frederic Chapman suggested that the father buy his son a partnership in the publishing house of which Anthony was already a director, the thing was soon done. There is no record of Henry's three years' activity in the publishing business, except that "an office life did not appeal to him" and he felt that the great John Morley employed hyphens too abundantly.

Frederic Trollope, Henry's young brother, had already passed some years in Australia. He had been an over-grown boy and not a clever one—the Trollopes were never precocious—and had exchanged his unhappy life at school for the hazards of sheep raising. That the parents should have permitted this venture argued trust and liberality on their part; the roughness of the existence to which the boy was committing himself, his extreme youth—he was but sixteen—the chances of illness, the gossip of friends disposed to hint that he had been sent off in disgrace; these and worse had to be endured.

Rose and Anthony had stipulated that when Frederic was of age he should come back to them for a year and decide while at home upon his future career. True to his word, he returned in 1868 to his family. His mother renovated his wardrobe and planned his favorite meals, while his father provided him with a hunter and saw to it that he did not lack amusements. Such wiles were vain. Frederic had never been in doubt, and in the spring of 1869 went back to his sheep.

The novelist, disappointed in both sons, was able to embody his own frustrated wishes in permanent form. In early April, 1869, he assuaged the pain of Frederic's departure by commencing the four months' labor of *Ralph the Heir*, in which the despondent, oddly attractive Sir Thomas bore burdens of character and incident similar sometimes to Anthony's own and again to those of his unfortunate father. Sir Thomas, a lawyer like Thomas Anthony, cold and formal in manner, detached from society, had for many years been engaged on a great work, a life of Lord Verulam, which, like Thomas Anthony's *Encyclopædia Ecclesiastica*, would never be completed.

But Sir Thomas's objective experiences in his attempt to enter Parliament were a transcription of Anthony's at Beverley; and in a subjective sense, Sir Thomas, moody, sensitive, and shrinking, was very like the inward Anthony. Sir Thomas had erred in neglecting his daughters, as Anthony had neglected his boys; his uneasiness of conscience made him hate to go to church; his real motive in attempting to get a seat in Parliament originated in the suspicion that he was out of touch with life. A sense of futility spoiled all that he did, and he supposed that he had been foolish to try to live "above and beyond the common lot." He had "ventured to think that he could think—and had been ambitious. So idle as he had been in thinking, so inconclusive, so frail, so subject to gusts of wind, so incapable of following his subject to the end, why had he dared to leave that Sunday-keeping, domestic, decent life?" Ten years had passed since in *The Bertrams* Anthony had told the story of a young man vanquished by the problem of his relation to the universe; in *Ralph the Heir*, the sufferer was old and weary and the vexed question had shrunken until it concerned scarcely more than the tribute due to Caesar; it was rather one of convention than of philosophy. Should a man believe what everyone else in his world believed?

So small and personal a matter as whether he erred in writing on Sunday exercised Anthony; he blustered about his practice of doing so, as if the noisy admission justified the action—which, however, continued to rouse a sense of guilty discomfort. He looked at the shelves where his many works were standing and wondered if they proved nothing more permanent than his industry. He had written out his mortification at Beverley, but continued to dislike his failure; besides, he had lost his confidence in a great English institution. Troubles were coming: Rose or one of the boys might die; he would have to die himself some day; he could not forget that his father had not lived to a great age and that his mother had become senile. He thought much of his parents and his youth while he wrote *Ralph the Heir*: the "kill" of a great hunt took place near Grandfather Milton's churchyard at Heckfield.

Victor Hugo had seemed to Anthony a vile intruder when he usurped the columns in *Once a Week* which had been designed for *The Vicar of Bullhampton*; but in the autumn of 1869 rebellion raised its head even in the *Fortnightly*, where Trollope felt he had proprietary rights. Edward A. Freeman, the historian, published an article on fox hunting, condemning it as a savage sport; the editor, John Morley, upheld this philistine judgment, and, what gave Anthony an even deeper sense of injury, Cicero, his own peculiar friend, was quoted as saying, "Was it possible that any educated man should find delight in so coarse a pursuit?" Trollope replied to Freeman, Freeman replied to Trollope,

Trollope wished to continue the controversy, but was dissuaded by Morley. Freeman wrote two long letters to the *Daily Telegraph*, and a lady by the name of Helen Taylor backed up Mr. Freeman in the *Fortnightly Review* with convincing logic and the charitable comment that Mr. Trollope showed a "confusion of ideas."

Anthony's arguments were indeed based not on reason but on preference. Fox hunting, like bearbaiting, cockfighting, bullfighting, and kindred pleasures, have their origins in atavism modified by contemporary morality. It may be possible, as Trollope said, to hunt with the hounds and suffer with "the precious victim," but it is not possible to avoid liking one better than the other. Anthony knew a vast deal about hunting the fox, perhaps almost everything except why he enjoyed it. To be called "cruel" pained him excessively. He protested that as a boy he had never taken a nest or worried a cat, but Freeman would not excuse him so easily and blandly mentioned that there were degrees of cruelty. Anthony took the discussion far more seriously than did Freeman, who not only had the historian's objective outlook but was not, like Trollope, at the bar of conscience. When the urbane Freeman suggested that Trollope's article should be published with his own in a little volume, Anthony refused in haste, explaining that he would be proud to do so, but only if Freeman would let him have the last word.

The Eustace Diamonds, a gay novel with a captivating title, occupied most of Trollope's writing hours from early December, 1869, until the following August. It was now his confirmed habit to write without prescience of coming events; as each incident occurred to him he added it to the last recorded, somewhat in the fashion of a picaresque novel—his characters meanwhile so firmly kept in mind that their behavior maintained rational consistency. These slight uncertainties, little as the method which permitted them was to be recommended, prevented his becoming jaded with the task. He acknowledged that the love element in *The Eustace Diamonds* was too slight to carry it to success, but protested that what it furnished was excellent—that Lucy Morris was a "pretty" heroine. But Lucy Morris lacked the dignity of her predecessors; she was altogether too ready to be made a convenience. The real heroine was the tough, the vulgar, hypocritical, shabby but delightful Lizzie Eustace. Trollope worried, as he wrote the novel, lest he might be plagiarizing Becky Sharpe. This anxiety was unnecessary, for Lizzie was subject to the moral law beyond which Becky freely ranged. Becky did not deceive herself, but Lizzie tucked her head under sentimental feathers. Anthony had more reason for anxiety lest he be accused of plagiarizing from *The Moonstone*, which Wilkie Collins had published in 1868; but the superficial resemblances between the two books seem never to have occurred to him. The hilarious adventures of Lizzie against the law and its staid defenders rang like hunting music and, bad as were her principles, few readers were inclined to wish her properly punished.

Lady Glencora romped in and out of the story, championing Lizzie and ridiculing her husband's absorption in decimal coinage. A certain fashionable Preacher Emilius, late of Prague, habitation of the wicked Christians in *Nina Balatka*, was Lizzie Eustace's punishment; but Trollope's personal distaste for the converted Jew was too evident for artistry. The minor episode in which a penniless American girl of eighteen was forced into marriage with the brutal Sir Griffin Tewett shed a strange light on Anthony's inner life. The girl went mad on her wedding morning, not quite in the style of *The Bride of Lammermoor*, for she had no other lover, but through absolute horror of the groom. Anthony had always insisted that the first essential of a novel was the quality of pathos. Here was such a situation, below the tragic plane, but pitiful, very touching; yet he made no proper use of it. There was cruelty in his attitude toward the young girl's despair; Lucinda was the fox, and her creator pursued her with the hounds.

CHAPTER XVIII

A Few Books and a Long Journey

1870-1872

The *Eustace Diamonds* would have been finished in six months instead of eight, had it not been put aside in favor of other projects, among them *Tales of an Editor*, and a *Caesar* for Blackwood's series of "Ancient Classics for English Readers." "I do not know that for a short period I have ever worked harder," was Anthony's comment on the three months' labor which went into *Caesar*. Longer, rather than harder, the labor should have been. Twice he read over Caesar's *Commentaries* and followed this initial step by examining the works of Plutarch, Longinus, Napoleon III, and his own friend Charles Merivale. He was also familiar with Mommsen's writings. Such far from prodigious feats constituted all his preparation for writing a history. An unwieldy approach and a disorderly arrangement marred an introduction whose twenty-seven pages bulked too heavily in a total of one hundred eighty-two. The preface naïvely concluded: "Then it is that we remember that the coming of Christ has changed all things, and men now—though terrible things have been done since Christ came to us—are not as men were in the days of Caesar."

Caesar's conquests were related in the half-joking style of a clever schoolboy. Anthony's horror at the ruthless methods of the conqueror was almost amused; he professed not to know whether to marvel more at Caesar's genius or at his simplicity. Censuring Caesar for acting from political motives, he asserted that his conquests furthered civilization. He refused to credit the picturesque story of Vercingetorix surrendering on his marvelous steed, because all the horses of Alesia must have been devoured by the besieged. On the authority of Cicero, Anthony believed Caesar and not his secretary to be the author of the *Commentaries;* but the admission was made grudgingly, as if he felt it almost a personal affront that a politician and a general should have added authorship to his pursuits.

The finished book was an admirable little work for young people's supplementary reading, one which he hoped would furnish all a "well-educated girl" needed to know about Caesar. His "well-educated girl" of the period needed to know so little about Caesar or about anything else in history that this hope was not immodest. The publication date was June first, and as it was John Blackwood's birthday, Anthony made him a present of the book. "I send down the whole work corrected," he wrote, "having, as I think, complied with every suggestion made by you or Collins. It is a dear little book to me, and there is one other thing to be said about the little dear. I think the 1st of June is your birthday, at any rate we'll make it so for this year, and you will accept it for a little present."

There had been mixed motives in the writing of *Caesar*; he hated to remember that he had been considered a dullard in his school days, and had hoped to wipe out the slights of forty years since; his father had been ambitious for his boys to become classical scholars, and Anthony, himself a father of sons, had reached the period when a man reflects with sympathy on the desires of those who tried to shape his youth. Perhaps more conscious was the wish to show the world that he was not only a novelist but a scholar. But he was unaware of the youthful quality of the little book he had written. Textbooks were seldom favored with learned reviews, and *Caesar* was mentioned in passing or ignored by the lay critics. Charles Merivale offended him by returning thanks for the gift of his "comic Caesar." The adjective was not strictly apropos; amusing, diverting, lively, vigorous, possibly droll would have been a better choice; to Trollope *comic* meant *funny* in a grotesque, extravagant sense. He thought of humor as the antic quality in *The Struggles of Brown, Jones, and Robinson*, the buffoonery of his widow Greenow, the crude, blunt candor of Emily Dunstable; he made nothing of the great gift which lay in his quiet appreciation of the foibles of his delicate creations, a humor sympathetic, pervasive, implied in his natural point of view. So Charles Merivale said he had written a "comic Caesar"! He began to study the Latin authors, an hour daily, sometimes several hours.

The stories collected as *An Editor's Tales* were published in rapid sequence from October, 1869, to May, 1870, in *St. Paul's*. Their length was sufficient to obviate the clumsy approach which was his principal difficulty in the short story, and to provide space for the development of three-dimensional characters, in which lay his superiority. Stories told by an editor when based on his professional experiences have a permanent interest for writers; but as such readers are necessarily biased, it would be unwise to conclude on their testimony that Trollope was a great short-story writer. He was not.

Trollope confessed his partiality for "that dearest of little women" whom he called "Mary Gresley"; he taught her painstakingly the storyteller's method but, when he pronounced her ready to publish, her sickly clerical lover exacted from her a promise "never to sin by writing fiction." Through the concern of a literary man over wasted talent slyly peeped the satisfaction of A. Trollope, champion of domesticity. Fully aware of the cruel limitations which the period imposed on women, he was in the main in sympathy with such restrictions. Girls who married, widows who were "widows indeed," mothers who lived only in and through their husbands or children; upon these props rested England's social structure.

A better story was "The Spotted Dog," in which a triangular figure was developed, at the apex the drink-ridden scholar, at opposite angles the editor and the kind-hearted publicans who attempted to save him. Later the situation was rendered more complex—indeed almost universal—by the indication of the miserable drunkard wife and the wretched children. Trollope refrained from stressing moral implications.

In mid-April, a month before the last of the *Editor's Tales* appeared in *St. Paul's*, he wrote Kate Field, evidently in reply to her submission of a manuscript, that he had resigned his post as editor. Conscience constrained him to add a candid, "or rather am now just giving up my magazine, and therefore have no longer any power in that line." As a matter of record, the July number was the last to be published under his aegis, so that had he wished to purchase Kate Field's contribution, he could probably have done so. Financially, *St. Paul's* had not been a success; the high rates paid to contributors were unwarranted by the circulation, there had been too many Trollopes in the ranks, and Mr. Virtue, an honorable and intelligent printer and engraver, was inexperienced as a proprietor. The magazine needed great names, but Anthony wished his contributors to be anonymous, a short-sighted measure, for though the Trollopes could thus publish incessantly without appearing to overload the columns, the general public believed that unsigned stories and articles were probably not by eminent authors. In breaking off from Smith and the *Cornhill* Anthony had injured himself financially.

In that spring of 1870 he delivered four addresses on the art of fiction, for which he received a total of £50. The sums which were being paid for Kate Field's lectures in America had an almost fabulous sound in England. He wrote her that she must not hope for such prices when she came over; the rooms lacked the capacity of those to which she was accustomed, and the audiences were holders of season tickets and would not pay highly for special attractions. His letter, written at the Athenaeum on the small sheet of club paper adorned with the pale, charming head of the goddess, suggested the vexation of a busy man teased over some trifle: "I never said you were like W. Petrie. I said that that woman did not entertain a single opinion on public matters"—after which the pen ran on into irritated illegibility.

His literary life was punctuated by sharp skirmishes with his publishers. In April Edmund Routledge asked him for a Christmas story, offering £100 in return for an engagement to write no other Christmas story that year. Trollope replied bluntly, calling himself "a punctual workman" and refusing point-blank to make any such commitment. Pacified by Routledge's reply, he wrote that "stories do not come as thick as blackberries," and that he did not, in fact, expect to write more than one. A few months later he forced a publisher to print *Sir Harry Hotspur* in one volume instead of the intended two, lest the public be asked to content itself with "literary short measure."

He spent a day or two with Alfred Austin down at Swinford Old Manor just after the outbreak of the Franco-Prussian war. Austin was waiting for the requisite authority to proceed to German headquarters as war correspondent for the *Standard*. "If you can get permission," observed Anthony, "you will be a lucky fellow, for there is not a man in Europe who would not like to go to the seat of War"—a sweeping statement he would have found it hard to prove. His brother Tom was one of the exceptions. Fanny and Tom had been contemplating the sale of Ricorboli and a settled life in England; but the war was to make such a change in their fortunes as to necessitate a complete reconsideration of their future.

In the early autumn Anthony spent less than a month in writing *An Eye for an Eye*, a work which scarcely exceeded the limits of a novelette. He was nervously eager to clear his desk before sailing with Rose to visit Frederic in Australia, and had in mind a longer book in the parliamentary series which he hoped to write before he began to take down his travel notes. *An Eye for an Eye* was an Irish story on the familiar theme of an irresponsible young man who thought a girl fit to bear his child but not to be his wife. The weight of family prestige crushed out Fred Neville's good intentions, and the girl's mother— one of those Medea women by whom Anthony was fascinated—killed her daughter's false lover.

Trollope's reverence for the institutions of the past was always at odds with his resentment against family and social interference in human action; such mischief was the theme of *Rachel Ray*, *Linda Tressel*, and *Nina Balatka* and a secondary theme in *The Bertrams* and *The Vicar of Bullhampton*; in *Linda Tressel*, where its result was most nearly tragic, he exclaimed, "Are we to believe that the very soul of the offspring is to be at the disposition of the parent?"

An Eye for an Eye would have been more plausible had Fred Neville been less of a "bounder"; it was impossible for the reader to think him better suited to succeed an earl than Kate to be a countess. "Father Marty," the good priest, was a fresh instance of Trollope's affectionate regard for the defenders of the old faith to which he could not adhere. Contrary to practice, the little book had both introduction and conclusion; these were two scenes staged in a madhouse, which produced the effect of solemn music ushering in and out the action. *An Eye for an Eye* was a lament, not for lost honor, not for young love, but for the death of good intentions.

Although he had hastened to finish the little book and was hurriedly setting to work on *Phineas Redux,* he did not intend to have either published in his absence; they were packed away at Chapman and Hall's in the special custody of his son Henry, as yet a partner in the old family firm. Anthony had more than a little difficulty in determining the title for the new parliamentary novel. Five years since, Phineas Finn had been banished to Ireland, which was, in view of his ambitions, practically a death sentence. To summon him back from the shades required the sound of a tucket, and this title, *Phineas Redux,* had a martial ring. Ignorant readers would no doubt misunderstand and call him Mr. Redux, but it was not to such a public that Trollope addressed himself. The gentry in the new novel were not those gentle girls and manly young squires and curates whose love affairs beguiled the long evenings in country parsonages while dutiful daughters read aloud the tales of Barset. These men and women belonged to the "leisure" class, they were "aristocrats," and, though Trollope cunningly muted the strings when their passions were the theme, it was not difficult to catch the overtones of jealousy, hatred, ferocity— the undertone of dull stupidity. The music of their virtues was played louder, as very probably truth demanded.

Very delicately did Anthony indicate the alterations five years had effected in his characters; Phineas, handsome as ever, immensely attractive to women, had lost the charming modesty of youth and gained in self-importance. After he had openly boasted that he would like to kill a political opponent, the man was murdered and Phineas was tried for his life. He was bewildered, considered himself affronted, sickened with self-pity. The ladies did not desert him; the men were on the whole surprisingly loyal. The subtle Madame Max offered herself and her fortune to him, the red-haired Lady Laura smouldered in her passion, and her hapless husband, Mr. Kennedy, became a homicidal maniac without loosening his Scottish grip on money matters. Lady Glencora, now Duchess of Omnium, was said at the clubs to be rather more dairy maid than duchess; the exquisite Lady Violet had domesticated the brutal Lord Chiltern. There was good sport for horse and man in *Phineas Redux.*

Scant time was spent on refurbishing for publication another novelette, *The Golden Lion of Granpère.* Trollope seems to have supposed that if he made English people stupid enough they would turn into Alsatians. Except for Madame Faragon, one of the right Trollopean crones, a duller cast could be found only among cows in a pasture.

A visit to Australia had been planned ever since Frederic's stay in England in the winter of 1868–69. His marriage to Susannah Farrand was to take place in December, 1871, and his parents wished to be present at the ceremony.

No previous journey had required such elaborate preparations. To secure a contract for a travel book was routine business; Chapman and Hall agreed to pay £1,250 for a two-volume work, two months after publication, and a London daily bargained for a series of letters. What differed from the preparation for other voyages was the disposal of Waltham House and the acknowledgment that an era had ended. The home had been purchased in happier times; in the diminuendo of life it had become too large—no hope remained of Frederic's settling down as a gentleman-farmer, Henry preferred the city. The situation which had been desirable when the boys were young, when Anthony was in the postal service, while he could hunt with a good conscience, had altered altogether, even in the matter of maintenance; he was growing older and his vogue, if not his earning power, was beginning to wane. Rose and he agreed on the advisability of freeing themselves from the house before the mournful events of old age fettered them to it. The furniture was sold and the estate placed with an agent. Anthony lost eventually some £800, but he had spent twelve good years under his own roof.

The "Great Britain," on which they had taken passage, was scheduled to sail May 6, but an accident to the line postponed the date until the twenty-fourth. After the hurry to have everything done, the Trollopes found the delay extremely vexing, and Anthony wrote Alfred Austin that the "very worst phase of life" was trying to be jolly "with nothing to do." He observed that his only anxiety about a future existence lay in the doubt lest the denizens of Heaven were too happy to care to read novels: "For your sake I trust that there may be left enough of the prevailing spirit of our present nature to make satire still palatable."

During the tedious wait, he lunched with the Leweses at The Priory to meet Turgenev, the Russian novelist, and dined with Charles Lever, who described the event as "a feast of Lucullus, capital talking." Lever himself had but thirteen months left of life. His wife was dead, he disliked his consular post at Trieste, he suffered desperately from gout, but his courage sustained his wit. Anthony liked Lever better than Lever liked him: "I don't think Trollope pleasant," he observed critically, "though he has a certain hard common-sense about him and coarse shrewdness that prevents him from being dull or tiresome. His books are not of a high order, but I am still always surprised that he could write them. He is a good fellow, I believe, *au fond*, and has few jealousies and no rancours; and for a writer, is not that saying much?" But Lever had never excelled in the study of character.

As was Anthony's custom, he had a desk installed in his stateroom on the "Great Britain" and on the second day out from Liverpool he commenced *Lady Anna*, finishing it before docking at Melbourne. The novel was in two volumes; its brevity was due not to excision, a virtue foreign to him, but to his arrangement of the daily task to fit the duration of the voyage. "Every word was counted," he announced as one proclaiming a meritorious action. Many careless repetitions marred the pages, but the plot was clever; the interest which Lady Anna and her crude lover were designed to attract centered rather on Lady Anna's tigerish mother, and in a less degree upon the rival claimant, the meek old tailor, and the wicked earl.

Anthony's concern with young love, never very warm, had grown tepid; he was inclined to venture into morbid psychology. The Countess of *Lady Anna* was pathological, the daughter "faithful," but with that rubbery constancy which in Trollope's girls was too often sheer obstinacy; the young tailor alone, who was there merely to be loved at the price of propriety, was free from the taint of the sickly or unnatural. Trollope showed his perversity in fixing on a tailor when a bank clerk, a curate, or a young farmer could have met all the requirements without offending his readers; but it was something of a sop to convention that the lady abandoned her title when she married her tradesman, and instead of braving English society sailed with him to Australia—very probably on the "Great Britain" with the Trollopes.

They reached Melbourne on July 27, 1871, after a voyage of a little over two months. Anthony had finished his novel and was ready to begin his thousand-page travel book. Daily he recorded his experiences and the information he had collected, boasting that freshness and accuracy resulted from his method, and ignoring the fact that a day-to-day transcription should be carefully edited.

On August 11, he was in Queensland, where he had been advised to arrive before the period of greatest heat. Of the seven members of the Queensland cabinet he learned that six were squatters; the name, less opprobrious than its sound, was used to designate the aristocrats whose unnumbered flocks cropped vast tracks of unclaimed land. Frederic Trollope too was a squatter, but in a small way, as he owned only ten thousand sheep. Throughout the colony the squatters were recruited from the sons of English gentlemen. Their lives were necessarily lonely, and they married young for companionship and for help in running their enormous concerns. At fifty they were ready to retire, either as wealthy men or as failures who had to acknowledge that there was no further hope of success. In these lonely stations there were many books; Dickens, Macaulay, Shakespeare could be found in almost every house. There was no churchgoing because of the vast distances; when guests came, they made long visits.

The squatter's life was enlivened by his feud with the free-selector, the little man, who, unlike his great enemy, owned his small holding. He had purchased it from the Crown and paid perhaps all that he had, so that his desperate poverty and his remoteness from law and order inclined him to petty thievery; he would filch a sheep or, more daringly, lift cattle, and when he was detected, might turn sulky and set fire to his neighbor's fences; no evil could be worse dreaded. Anthony's sympathies were all with the squatters, both because Frederic was one of them and because, although they owned no land, they represented the landowning class of England; but he felt that Australia would be better served by encouraging the small free-selectors, because as farmers they would form a settled rural population such as the young country most needed.

Frederic's station was two hundred and fifty miles west of Sydney, and the Trollopes spent three days traveling in a buggy through woodland before they sighted it. Some fifty acres along a creek had been cleared, and here the young man had built his house and his woodshed. The house had three rooms and no upper story, but the wide verandah, hung with trailing vines and furnished with comfortable chairs and tables, was the real dwelling place. Servants' quarters and kitchen were in separate buildings at the rear, and there was a bachelors' house for the young men who worked about the place. Twenty horses ran in the large paddock, a cow was kept for butter and milk, a young orchard was growing with the rapidity of the tropics, and the opossums had eaten all the vegetables in the garden.

The father found time heavy in the solitude, after the novelty had worn off; he tried to institute a whist table in the verandah, but he could see that the young men played only out of good nature; they would not learn the rules, and regarded the game as a childish entertainment fit only to amuse the old gentleman out from home. Anthony took to long, solitary rides along the forest glades, where a kangaroo would leap across the track, startling horse and rider, or he would pull up to listen to a bird he had never heard sing before; the bush was unending, it hemmed him in on every side like life itself. But he felt it regrettable that no clearing suddenly arrived at would reveal a house, that there was no likelihood of a group of human beings meeting him in the narrow way.

He was more sensitive to scenery than readers of his English novels realized, for when he wrote of the home country he did not wish to bore them by describing what they ought to have seen for themselves; in his works of travel he recorded many a fair sight and, like his mother, loved to draw comparisons with other scenes in faraway lands. What had pleased her, gave him pleasure: "Unless it can convey this vague feeling of distant, unapproachable, and almost mysterious delight, scenery loses half its charms." Either the mother or the son might have written these romantic lines.

He was the visitor from England—from Home. Such loyalty to the Mother Country as he found was almost troublesome; the colonists were positively angry in their protestations against being cast off and repudiated. England was Home, although many of them had never left Australia. But they had another patriotism equally touchy; it was not safe to criticize the ways and works of the colonies: Australian sheep were the finest in the world, the native wines the best, the tables most bountifully provided; when he complained that cockroaches had eaten a hole through his coat, he was severely told that, if so, he had brought the cockroaches into the country with him.

The education offered in the colonies was of a character to make youth develop early, but this precocity was followed by an overlong maturity. The universal standard was, as in the United States, much higher than in England, but far below the flower of civilization produced by the great public schools and universities in the homeland. As for the aborigines, he had no sympathy with missionary efforts; if anything could improve the natives it would be work. No doubt they could be taught to sing hymns in record time, but in adolescence they would escape to the bush and revert to savagery.

His dislike of what he saw at the gold mines at Ballaarat strengthened his conviction that labor, not luck, was what a man needed for success. There in the Chinese quarter, where gambling, opium-smoking, and unmentionable sins were practiced without check, white women and young boys, who had themselves been enticed, were decoys for the miners with money to spend. All Australians were gamblers; even the most respectable ladies in colonial society gambled in mining shares. The women were too sure of themselves, too untender; they had no patience with age and infirmity; he saw more than one reduced old man whom he thought of as a humble Lear.

Although he did not dislike Australia as he had the United States, and saw nothing quite so awful in the way of towns as Cairo, Illinois, there were some, especially inland, whose wide, straight streets struck him as excessively ugly. The Australians were certainly great braggarts, the climate was hot, the mosquitoes wicked; but the convict element had been absorbed by later generations, so that a question about a man's grandfather was merely rhetorical. If a laborer would save his pay instead of going on a spree, he could live better and eventually rise higher than he could ever hope to do in England: gambling and drink were the ruin of gold miners, sheep shearers and workers in every trade, even of the lordly squatters.

When the Trollopes took the steamer for New Zealand on July 29,

1872, they had spent a year and two days in Australia and seen Frederic and his young wife, Susannah, established in their lonely station. No doubt Rose would have been glad to wait the birth of her expected first grandchild, but Anthony wished to finish the journey and complete the book which had been its excuse. The first great-grandchild of Thomas Anthony Trollope and his wife Frances would be followed by seven brothers and sisters in rapid succession; on this prolific branch of the family devolved the title which had been so far removed at the beginning of the nineteenth century.

It was mid-winter in New Zealand; the roads were rivers of mud and the mountains glittered with snow. This was not the season for the few tourists who visited the islands; Anthony was amused to hear his landlord remark in a reflective tone, "So this is Mr. Anthony Trollope. He must be a damned fool to come traveling in this country in such weather as this."

In New Zealand the strife between squatters and free-selectors was more bitter than in Australia, the attachment to England stronger; every sentiment he had taken note of earlier seemed intensified. Many other books based on the islands had preceded his, but undismayed, he did sufficient research into the records of history and physical geography to provide a background for his picturesque observations, and ended with a stirring exhortation to English men and women who were not afraid of work to emigrate to New Zealand.

On the Pacific voyage to Hawaii and San Francisco he put together the two volumes, republished as four, of *Australia and New Zealand.* They were furnished with excellent maps, bristled with statistics, and yet were vigorous in style and readable, although less entertaining than his *West Indies* and inferior to his mother's fascinating work on Austria.

On his journey across the United States he called upon Brigham Young, who received him with marked disfavor and suggested that Anthony was a miner. Anthony said he was not. With some contempt, Brigham Young inquired if Anthony earned his own living. Anthony said he did. "I guess you're a miner," was the Mormon's considered opinion.

The Trollopes arrived in New York on November 25 and put up

at the Brevoort. Anthony discovered in the *Morning Herald* a statement to the effect that he had compromised his lawsuit with Baron Tauchnitz, the German publisher of his works, "for an enormous sum of money." He sent a correction to the newspaper and wrote Tauchnitz, with more complacency than exactitude: "I never had any contention with any publisher though, either on my own account or that of others, I have perhaps had more dealings with publishers than any man living."

In December the Trollopes were back in England, the new book all but ready for the publisher. Anthony had kept three of his hunters when, twenty months since, he had vacated Waltham Cross; two of them had been idle for the period of his absence. Now, instead of giving up hunting as he had planned to do, he bought another horse. Thrice weekly during the season a cabman called at the London house at seven in the morning and ate his breakfast in the hall, after which he drove Anthony to the station, whence the old sportsman traveled to the meet. Such a day, with its uncertain promises of pleasure, entailed the pains of a dozen hours on wheels besides the train journey, but he rated the difficulties inferior to the joys and thus spent four more winters, absent from home three times weekly, but invariably trying to reach the house for an eight o'clock dinner with Rose.

Not long before leaving England, Anthony had told Austin with enthusiasm that there was "not a man in Europe who would not like to go to the seat of War." During his absence in Australia, his brother Tom had undergone experiences qualified to give a more realistic sense of the unromantic nature of international strife. With his daughter Bice and his wife, Tom had spent the latter part of the summer of 1870 in a Heidelberg *pension*. The family had many friends among the professors of the University, all of whom detested the militarism of Prussia; these gentlemen conceded superior talent and culture to the Prussian state, but feared and abhorred the political aspirations which ruled it. German unity, it seemed, could be achieved only by the loss of liberty, and unity was not worth the price. The Shakespearean critic Gervinus phrased it thus, "People say that Germany will swallow Prussia. But it will not be so; Prussia will swallow Germany."

Tom, like the rest of the Trollopes, liked Germans and sympathized with their cultural aims. When war with France was declared, he had Fanny and Bice to think of, and he put no trust in French chivalry; if the vaunted *marche à Berlin* came off, he wanted his women safe in Switzerland. The Trollope refugees followed a pattern already familiar in Europe, faring better than most because Tom was a shrewd and practiced traveler. Fanny reported that the laundry had not been returned; someone hurried to the washerwoman's door and took the clothes as they came from the tubs. The trunks were squeezed shut on wet and dry, and the little party made a dash to the railway station, where, as Tom had expected, they found that all the other transients in Heidelberg had been inspired with an identical ambition of getting to Switzerland. Fanny and Bice were small and young, Tom's shoulders were massive—it was no time to show gallantry outside the family. They managed to board the train, luckily indeed, for it was the last going to Switzerland.

In Bern they made themselves comfortable in a suburban *pension* where Tom had stayed before. There the war seemed far away; they took long walks, went to hear the organ at Freiberg, placidly removed to Thun. On September 3, they read the news of Sedan in a Bern newspaper, and Tom at once realized that he was ruined. It was clear to him that the crushing defeat of France would result in Rome's becoming the permanent capital of Italy; property in Florence would depreciate in a landslide, and the house in which he had invested all his money would have to be sold for the little it could fetch.

The family, neither stunned nor mourning, stayed on in Thun until September 12. They took walks, they went on steamboat excursions. The greatest happiness of Ricorboli had been in the collecting of treasures and in the "au-mieux-ing"; and, though it was a pity to lose and to lose thus heavily, Tom consoled himself with the recollection that his greatest wealth was hidden under his hat—he could go on writing, Fanny could go on writing, and at sixty such a man as he was not an old fellow. They decided to return to Italy, hot as it was there, and see what could be done. Milan was reached at midnight after a fatiguing journey; Bice lay down at the hotel to sleep, but her father and Fanny went to the Cathedral and climbed to the very height.

On the morning of the nineteenth, at seven o'clock, they re-entered

Ricorboli, which already looked strange to them, as if the whole which they had so happily put together waited only the signal for flying apart. But nothing decisive was done about the house that winter, while Tom looked cautiously for a buyer. It would not be wise to show panic, as the optimistic believed that all Italy would prosper greatly under Victor Emmanuel and even Tuscany would not suffer; others thought that the King would not wish to make Rome the capital because of friction with the Vatican. Tom shared neither delusion. In June he took his family to Venice, where he rented a hotel suite and made both ends meet by bringing on his Tuscan servants, whose provident purveying made the vacation almost an economy. Among his own enterprises was the verifying of Ruskin's reports of extant Byzantine architecture.

After the October plebiscite came the financial crash which Tom had foreseen a year earlier; the day of Florence was over, mortgages were called in, and, as the nibbling buyer had swum off, Ricorboli was advertised for sale and its treasures catalogued. The library consisted almost entirely of rare books on Italian subjects which in those days would have fetched little of their value in London. An Italian bookseller proposed to buy the entire 14,000 volumes for £2,000 which, although very short of the library's worth, was an offer Tom would have accepted, if by poor judgment the auctioneer had not refused it without referring the matter to the owner. Broken up, the library brought in only half that sum. Not only in Italy—in England, France, and in the United States—much interest was felt in the sales of Ricorboli; requests for catalogues were many. When affairs were finally wound up, Tom had lost the residue of Theo's estate and all his life's earnings, a sum amounting to £10,000, but retained an income of £300.

In 1872, after a summer in Switzerland with Fanny, he packed her off on a visit to her mother so that she might be spared the misery of the actual break-up, and returned to Florence, where he hired rooms and moved out of the villa what few treasures he could afford to keep. He behaved admirably, but perhaps he did not suffer very much. He noticed that his friends were as cordial as ever; during the intervals of activity at Ricorboli, he dined out with the old gusto, went to spiritualistic parties, and wrote articles. Of all the Trollopes, he was the one who knew best how to shut up houses; this was not so very different from his activities at the Château d'Hondt when he was twenty-five: then as now the future lazily beckoned.

Alfred Austin found him a post as Rome correspondent for the London *Standard*—he had already served briefly as Italian correspondent for two London papers—and in February of 1873 he began a new life, new at least in its specific requirements and in enforced residence; but as for writing, for almost forty years—"Whether stationary, with all the comforts of my own study about me, or travelling, with probably no better study than my own bed-room; whether bothered by pecuniary complications, or with my mind utterly free from them; whether alone, or living in the midst of company, I was always at it."

Anthony could have said the same of himself, but the motives underlying the brothers' industry were dissimilar. If the younger had undergone Tom's reverses, he would have feared a complete subjugation of spirit. Tom was sixty-two and very deaf—a peculiar affliction for a journalist—but he had the courage and the zest which had helped his mother begin a career at fifty. He was peculiarly fortunate in Fanny, whom he loved without envy; but his greatest asset lay in the naturally happy disposition from which had evolved his contented philosophy of life. Not what a man had, but what he was. . . . Yet with all his complacence, he could see himself as an infinitesimal figure in the pageant of history, while Anthony was never able, except in writing, to escape wholly from the tortured consciousness of his own ego.

CHAPTER XIX

Disillusionment

1873-1875

IN THE early 1870's Anthony Trollope suffered a gradual disillusionment more painful than his adolescence, which, however darkly he regarded it, had not been devoid of hope. He had never been a happy man, although by various devices of bustle and of work he had managed an appearance of happiness which frequently deceived himself. For a generation he had been looking forward; he had been working out a pattern imagined in his youth, and, when it should be finished, he had expected satisfaction. His only notable nonperformance of its details had been his failure to be elected to Parliament. Otherwise his success was extraordinary. He was well-to-do, fond and proud of his wife, who was much attached to him and who, though not handsome, dressed with great elegance; he had two boys who, if not brilliant, were good fellows; he had a grandson; he belonged to exclusive clubs, enjoyed the friendship of gentlemen, continued to hunt, had opportunity and health to make amazing journeys.

No doubt he was tired and overworked, less healthy than he appeared to himself and others in those days, when it was taken for granted that a man so high-colored and heavy must be hearty and hale. But the vexation of his spirit could not be accounted for by the heaviness of the flesh.

The truth was that he had gained that for which he had striven, and had not found it good enough. His great object in life had been to entrench himself in the society which he considered the finest in the world. He had written his books, not primarily because he felt the necessity of revealing what he had learned of humanity, but in order to make enough money to enable him to live the kind of life he wished to live among the kind of people he admired. He was angry with the society toward which he had made such gigantic efforts, a society which was proving that it cared more for money than for either honesty or brains; though he had both, he could never make as much money as the graceless speculators who were consequently more welcome than he in aristocratic mansions. Adventurers were popular there; there a rich *parvenu* could get for nothing the recognition he himself had spent a generation earning. If rewards were to be thus unequal, he might as well have written less and written better, probed deeper into life, and told not only truth but the whole truth, as he knew it. But he was the child of the Trollopes. He had not outgrown the fears of poverty and of humiliation which had conditioned him; he did not allow himself to blame his ambition as unworthy, but his spleen rose at the mess of pottage life set before him.

Home from Australia, he took a house at 39 Montagu Square, settled as many of his five thousand volumes as would fit in his little new study behind the dining room, and put the rest in a recess in Rose's double drawing room. Then he sat down to write a passionate denunciation of the bad new times of England. *The Way We Live Now*, its title probably derived from his translation of Cicero's "It is thus we live now," was a most brilliant piece of work, of great though not inordinate length, considering the immensity of its scheme. It was a bitter, wrathful book marred by careless writing and by an awkward welding of themes which in so ample a work could have been skilfully combined; yet these defects could not spoil one of the greatest Victorian novels. Society as seen in *The Way We Live Now* was utterly corrupt; it revolved about Melmotte, the financial wizard of whom no one knew or cared to know more than that he was rich and could make others rich, too. The clubs frequented by young aristocrats were vile dens, daughters of peers sold themselves to any who had the purchase money, English gentlemen ran at the heels of the unclean speculator. Melmotte could get into Parliament, Melmotte could entertain the Royal Family and the Emperor of China.

Corruption was not confined to the upper circles; Trollope hit out fiercely at publishers and critics—all were venal, all dishonest. The roots of his wrath were a tangle of past and present. In Lady Carbury could be traced features of the mother ten years dead and sixteen years silent, so long forgotten that kindly time disguised his unfilial

use of her. Lady Carbury had run away from her husband and returned to nurse him; Anthony remembered that his own mother had
run away from his father on her fantastic voyage to America and
knew that, when she returned, she had found a broken man whom
she cared for until his death. Lady Carbury had two children, but
loved only one of them; in middle life she had taken up the writing
of trash. Anthony pronounced her ambition to be an author "ignoble,"
but her motherly love "noble and disinterested."

The virtues of the age that was past were sourly depicted in the
taciturn squire, Roger Carbury, to whom the existence of a Melmotte
was "not compatible with a wholesome state of things in general"—
who may have represented Trollope's own outlook. As always, however, his use of light and shadow in the treatment of this old-fashioned,
bigoted figure made it evident that, if the new ways were bad, the old
ones were often not much better. The tone throughout *The Way We
Live Now* was one of anger, but it was vigorous. At fifty-eight he was
surfeited neither with society nor with writing, only depressed by the
injustice of rewards.

He lived and wrote on various levels. Encouraged by the *Spectator*
critic who had just urged him "to write, if possible, colonial novels,
instead of colonial travels," he laid his major novel aside for four
weeks while he skimmed the cheerful surface of his month in the
Australian bush. The result, a Christmas novelette, *Harry Heathcote
of Gangoil,* evinced little imagination or invention but was suited to
its simple purpose. Yet the underlying motive of the story was not
unrelated to that of the larger work: in *The Way We Live Now* birth
and breeding counted for nothing, and wealth, whatever its source,
was the passport to society; in *Harry Heathcote of Gangoil,* Trollope
repeated too frequently his *credo* of caste. More than once or twice
the reader learned that the imperious young squatter must be respected
because he was an aristocrat. Trollope spoke clearly for the Empire
builders: "We are English aristocrats in new worlds, if no longer
in England, we shall rule and justly, for the good of those God placed
under us." He spoke for his class, for himself, and for his son Frederic, the big, slow fellow who had emigrated, and whom young *Harry
Heathcote* ineffectually masked. Yet there were delicate touches in

the realistic little story—the poignant suspense of those who could so easily be ruined, the free, rough language, the wistful longing for England, the sense of vast and lonely places.

Trifles nagged at Anthony while he worked on his longer book. He quarreled with Charles Reade, who had behaved badly in appropriating parts of the tortuous plot of *Ralph the Heir*, out of which he had constructed a play called *Shilly Shally*. Trollope was angry, first at the plagiarism, and then at the charge of indecency preferred by the *Morning Advertiser* against the stage production. He, who had always coveted a dramatic success, took it as peculiarly vexing that someone else should make a play out of his novel. Reade explained that Anthony had been in Australia, a place too distant for him to write for permission to make use of his novel, but said that he had intended to share with him the profits of his production. As the performance was a failure, there was little to share and Anthony refused to touch it. What made Reade's behavior excessively annoying was the fact that he had always been highly contentious in the matter of his own rights. Both men played whist at the Garrick for the next three years without speaking to each other.

Either living among the Australians had made Trollope laugh and talk louder, or his circle at the club had forgotten how noisy he was. His fits of irritation were varied by booming mirth. George Eliot thought him "wonderfully full of life and energy," but in masculine society his exuberance was unbridled. One January evening he and Billy Russell, the Irish humorist, made such an uproar that their friends threatened to call out the police. Billy Russell wept crocodile tears and moaned that Ireland was accustomed to be trampled upon, while Anthony pretended to storm at them as "conventional tyrants." In May there was discussion at the Garrick concerning the advisability of giving the members a hint as to which candidates ought to be blackballed. It was Trollope's opinion that such suggestions ought not to be made. He, who had found it difficult to enter club life, was disposed to show consideration for other aspirants.

In early June Kate Field arrived in London and the next day was a dinner guest of Rose and Anthony in Montagu Square, where they had invited Wilkie Collins to meet her, as one of those celebrities she was always eager to know. Kate was still pretty, charming and in earnest, although the subject of her enthusiasm was continually shifting. Rose and Anthony liked her extremely, and yet he could not but feel that she represented much that he heartily disliked in a woman; she did not marry, was in her mid-thirties, yet she stuck to nothing, went about lecturing, and was fast becoming "an old soldier." On July 5, Rose told him to write asking Kate to dinner; in his note of invitation he said jokingly that it was a pity she had not yet established the rights of her sex so firmly that she could dine with him at the club next week, to meet "two of the wildest of your countrymen— Joachim [sic] Miller and Mark Twain . . . and be as jolly as men!"

Anthony's interest in the fortunes of Mr. Palliser and his wife, Lady Glencora, had assumed such a personal nature that he doubted his ability to make the public share it. Thus, although the title of *The Prime Minister* referred to Plantagenet Palliser, he did not venture to make him his hero, or his wife the heroine. Unfortunately the willowy lady and virtuous gentleman to whom he gave the leading roles provided far less entertainment than the Duke and Duchess. Trollope could not conceal his own want of sympathy with Emily Wharton, whom he called "a monument of bereaved woe," but he made no comment on the awful load which her wifely obedience placed upon the shoulders of her wretched husband: "It is not my duty to have any purpose as what I do must depend on your commands." This was indeed the ultimate surrender of responsibility; yet Emily was not really submissive, because neither will nor intelligence was involved; she was merely a rubber doll.

But to the author himself, the real import of *The Prime Minister* lay in the contest between the Duke and his unruly Duchess. His aim was to serve his country; hers was to advance her husband, herself, and her children; and, as she was impetuous and there was no confidence between them, she plunged him into horrid embarrassments. In 1833, Frances Trollope had been an important guest in Tory drawing rooms; that was forty years since and long forgotten, and no one connected the ambitious Glencora with the author's mother. A critic even wrote of Glencora as "an abstraction," and Trollope had no intention of correcting him.

Yet a reader familiar with the characters of Frances and Thomas Anthony studying the parliamentary novels in the order in which Trollope wrote them—in which he wished intensely that they should be studied—could not fail to see him reshaping his parents' destiny. In *The Prime Minister* innumerable identical characteristics were cited: the Duke's smile was "cold, glittering and uncomfortable," he "knew that he was saturnine and silent," he was "too scrupulous to be practical," he was "thin-skinned and ungenial," took things "too seriously," suffered from "indiscreet fretfulness," could not, like other men, "eat, sleep, and amuse himself," and, although he was "just, unambitious, intelligent," he could not succeed because he could not keep his wife in order. Glencora was the more clever, and had the greater capacity for public life; she was a "kind-hearted, bustling, ambitious lady," but she intrigued, made friends with shabby adventurers, disobeyed her husband, and even when properly punished and repentant was "too full of vitality to be much repressed by any calamity."

In his divine wrath, the Duke charged his Duchess with vulgarity; this was retribution, indeed it briefly broke her heart. So much was made of the word, so deep was the fester from the thorn, that it may well have been an incident transcribed from life; the boy Anthony may have been horrified to hear his father call his mother vulgar. At any rate he knew the world had called her so and he believed she merited the awful charge.

Thus the shades of Frances and Thomas Anthony Trollope appeared upon a higher plane; he was more powerful than in life because of his great name and wealth (yet the wealth had come with his wife, just as Frances had supported them all after the American disaster); Glencora could have larger parties than those at Julians, but otherwise she was unaltered. Their apotheosis benefited Anthony in his aspirations as well as in the gratification of filial impulse; through them he was allied with purest aristocracy, one which would never yield to the corruptions of a Melmotte from America. Nevertheless an expectation of personal disaster trailed its dismal length through the long book; he pronounced his dolorous belief that his experiences had weakened him where they should have prepared him to endure

inevitable sorrows; that men cling to gains not because of their real
value but because the admission that they were worthless would mean
the disintegration of a spirit held together by the very act of striving.
As for the comforts of religion, whatever they were, they depended
upon the practice of it, and that required "the full energy of middle
life," which was no longer at his disposal.

Outwardly Trollope "in his successful, glowing, gusty, gesticulating
old age" was an impressive figure. Julian Hawthorne wrote with tolerant, amused respect of his "hearty, wholesome, ruddy" appearance,
his "furious white beard," and the dangerous swishing of the gold-
headed ebony cane he carried when gout troubled him. That summer
of 1874 he was in Switzerland, traveling with two ladies—presumably
Rose and Florence Bland. A ticket was lost on the return journey,
and Anthony's vigorous complaints throughout the ensuing autumn
amused the readers of the London press.

But he could be very kind, especially to social inferiors and to
young people. "It was impossible for the shyest young man to be
with him without feeling at his ease," wrote one young American, for
whom Anthony had opened the drawers of his writing desk to display
the finished manuscripts, each neatly laid away in its own drawer
like corpses in a morgue. Another acquaintance, who had been ill in
London lodgings, feelingly described how Anthony "would look in
continually, on his way to his club, for a few minutes' pleasant chat,
carrying in his hand a pheasant, or some such little delicacy as might
tempt an invalid's appetite."

In order not to surfeit his public with parliamentary novels, he
returned briefly to his earlier *genre* in the book which appeared under
the silly title *Is He Popenjoy?*, in which he introduced a delightful
dean and his equally delightful daughter. The churchman was active,
intelligent, an affectionate father, and a very worldly gentleman. The
little daughter, married to the vacillating Lord George, decided that
she could love her husband by ignoring his follies and magnifying his
merits; in her final triumph one could only regret that widowhood was
not included in her reward. The lively scenes in the country and
in London were enriched by the wicked marquis, the poor little pseudo-

heir, a flirtatious lady who hunted, a pair of impecunious lovers, a group of maiden ladies, and a speech-making German baroness.

The book was finished at sea, early in May, 1875, while Rose and Anthony were on their way to pay a second visit to Australia and to make the acquaintance of their grandchildren. No travel book would finance this journey, but the third generation was well worth the price of the voyage. Yet Anthony did not intend to lose money through idleness, and devoted only two months of his absence from England to actual rest.

He planned to complete *Is He Popenjoy?* on the voyage out, write another book on the homeward journey, and, not to waste the interval in Australia, he had contracted with the Liverpool *Mercury* to write a series of travel letters. A provincial audience would not be exacting, and the filling of two newspaper columns a week would demand neither profound thought nor overconscientiousness of execution.

The Trollopes traveled overland across Europe, visiting his brother's family on the way. Then they sailed from Brindisi, passed through the Suez Canal, which Anthony fifteen years earlier had declared could never be built, spent a fortnight in and around Ceylon, and on June 4 landed at Sydney in good time for Australian winter.

When *Is He Popenjoy?* was finished, somewhere on the high seas between Ceylon and Australia, he began his travel letters—by a disquisition on Italian politics. With his knowledge of transoceanic mail schedules, it was an easy matter to get his two columns a week to Liverpool, even though he neglected his task for months at a time. The letters had little of the freshness of personal observation; for the most part they were based on information gathered years earlier or received at second hand.

He had already contracted for a new novel with the magazine *Temple Bar* and with Chapman and Hall, his favorite English publishers, but had bargained for only £1,800, although *The Prime Minister* had brought in £2,500 and he had received £3,000 for *The Way We Live Now*, which was appearing in serial form. So many elements entered into the market that falling prices did not necessarily mean decline in popularity. He knew that he published far too often and had been long before the public, he knew that his political novels were not popular with the same class of readers as those of clerical life, but he did not ascribe his dwindling scale of prices to such causes, and worried because he was growing old. Instead of working more slowly, he flogged himself up to the rate of speed he had hitherto been able to maintain.

The stock hero and heroine of *The American Senator,* which he commenced in mid-summer, were trivial creatures; the story belonged to Arabella Trefoil and her exploits in husband hunting. Next to Arabella, interest centered on the long, lean, black-clad Elias Gotobed, whose appearance was vaguely reminiscent of Abraham Lincoln. Trollope employed him as the Observer; he was not so nearly omniscient as the same character in Henry James's and Conrad's stories, because the author's sense of decency and the Senator's good manners would not permit him to pry into secrets. But he was given an uninterrupted view of the privileged class, hunting foxes through unprivileged territory, and he saw more than a little of the subtle hunt of a woman in pursuit of a husband. The principles of the intelligent and highly honorable Senator brought him into conflict with his aristocratic host; he could not understand the power of precedent in England. But he could gauge the heart of Arabella more kindly than her creator, and piercing through the labyrinthine causes which made her what she was, observe with wonderful simplicity, "Miss Trefoil always gave me the idea of being a good type of the English aristocracy."

Trollope himself admitted that the strategy employed in Arabella's campaign and the energy with which she pursued it almost made the business appear creditable. She was thirty, penniless, daughter of detestable parents who were estranged from each other, niece to a duke whose wife treated her with appalling inhumanity; her reputation was spoiled because of previous jiltings, and she must either get a husband or go under. She was disagreeable, but not so corrupt that she could not be ashamed.

It has been authoritatively affirmed that Arabella Trefoil had grounds for a breach of promise suit against Lord Rufford, and Trollope's neglect of her interest in this legal matter probably arose from his spleen against her. Husband-hunting women were anathema to him. The chase of a fox by men was the best of sports, but the pursuit of a man by a woman was disgraceful. The dull, resourceless, selfish Lord Rufford must therefore be snatched from Arabella, and the disappointed huntress exiled to Patagonia, where, Anthony predicted sourly, but not perhaps correctly, she would make neither a good wife nor a good mother. Europe was dotted with Trollope's exiled ladies, but Arabella was the worst of them, and must travel farthest.

Back in England in the autumn of 1875, he was confronted by an accumulation of unfavorable reviews of *The Way We Live Now*. Outraged by his imputations of venality, the critics had risen in condemnation of the man who wrote like a machine. Most offensive was the *Westminster Review*, which seldom troubled to notice him, but now announced almost on the day of his homecoming: "Of Mr. Trollope's novel we feel inclined to wish that it were reviewed by his own Jones, that particular Jones who writes such slashing reviews on novels. We think that Jones might fairly point out how closely Mr. Trollope himself resembles Lady Carbury—how he too has written all sorts of books, a hack translation of Caesar, a scratch volume of hunting sketches, a boy's Christmas book of Australian adventure, all of them with no higher aim than Lady Carbury's. Mr. Trollope, like Lady Carbury, writes up to what may be called the paying point."

In bitterness of spirit Anthony accepted the challenge, and sat down to write his *Autobiography*—thus heaping with his own hand the gloomy burial mound in which he was to spend the decades following his death. Was he accused of writing up to the paying point? And why not? "I confess that my first object in taking to literature as a profession was that which is common to the barrister when he goes to the Bar, and to the baker when he sets up his oven. I wished to make an income, on which I and those belonging to me might live in comfort. . . . I am well aware that there are many who think that an author in his authorship should not regard money. They who preach this doctrine will be much offended by my theory, and by this book of mine, if my theory and my book come beneath their notice. They require the practice of a so-called virtue which is contrary to nature, and which, in my eyes, would be no virtue if it were practiced. . . .

It is a mistake to suppose that a man is a better man because he despises money. . . . Brains that are unbought will never serve the public much."

In essence the book was a piece of polemical writing—an *ex parte* appraisal "of what I, and perhaps others around me, have done in literature." He did not imagine that what he said of himself and his works would—as actually happened—be taken as the last word on the subject. The *Autobiography* would not appear until after his death. He was not averse to having a full biography written by another hand—perhaps by his own son's—and spoke vaguely of his recordings as pegs on which could "be hung those materials about my life and work which may be gathered by those who may be disposed to say something about me."

He intended to reveal little of his inner life, and yet, as it fell out, the *Autobiography* was far more important as psychology than as history. His memory was as accurate as most men's, but he wrote, as always, in haste and made no effort to verify his recollections. The book was as colorless as he could make it; it was a sad story of a neglected, unwanted little boy whose schooling had been inadequate, whose schoolmates had been cruel, who had lived wretchedly as a young man in London, and had achieved success, not because he had outstanding talents, but because he had drudged harder than anyone else. He had had no pleasure in life except from work, hunting, whist, and the society of his men friends. Once he had possessed a house at Waltham Cross and had been happy there; the house was gone.

He said so little about his wife that the reader wondered if he were ashamed of her. He forgot to mention the birth of his children until long after the proper place for them to enter the narrative. Yet, forlorn and miserable as his youth had been, it was a better time than present age; and Trollope, who had actually indulged in fleshly pleasures as little as any normal man, made a pathetic boast of joys to which he had been a stranger, in words paraphrased from his hero, Cicero. Only this, and a somewhat mawkish tribute to Kate Field— the woman who had been, "outside his own family" (Rose, two sons, two grandchildren, Florence Bland, his mother, Tom, Theo, Fanny, and Bice), his "most chosen friend"—relieved the melancholy retrospect of years which he tried to persuade himself had not been wasted.

CHAPTER XX

"I Care Only for Men and Women"

1875–1877

WHEN in 1835 unhappy Thomas Anthony Trollope died in the melancholy house at Bruges, his son Anthony was twenty years old. No doubt the boy was at first relieved, and felt the wickedness of being glad at the death of a tyrant. By degrees the understanding of his father's misery deepened, and with his compassion his sense of guilt increased. Much of the debt he saddled upon his mother; she had deserted them in Harrow Weald, she had pained his father by earning money when he could earn nothing, she had outlasted him and had forgotten him; for to the saturnine boy, her gallant cheerfulness was an insult to her husband's memory. Her subsequent notable career was another offense; it was at Thomas Anthony's cost, for she had lived and flourished when she should have been the one to die.

By degrees Anthony became his father's champion and assumed subjectively his place as the mother's rival. The novelist Frances Trollope became his unavowed enemy; he felt it incumbent on him to punish the witty Mrs. Trollope, and with her all excessively witty ladies. Nevertheless, when he thought of her as his little, brisk, home-making mother, he could be very fond of her. When he wrote novels, he suppressed clever women and glorified the little wife who made home bright for her husband and babies.

He would not admit that his mother possessed extraordinary talent, because he wished to keep her inferior to his father and incidentally to himself; he said she was healthy and industrious; her exuberance overflowed in effortless creation. Having thus set limits to her ability, he began to believe that talent was never essential to success; the chief requisite was work; he could scarcely think of himself as a creative genius and deny his mother's claims, when, alas! they two were so much alike.

The rivalry between Mrs. Trollope and her son, to which she was an unconsenting and ignorant party—although it must be confessed that she would have found a rueful amusement in it—kept him at work through the years of chagrin and disappointment; but the insistence on hurry, the confusion between speed and industry induced slovenly habits too deeply grooved to alter.

After his mother's decay had relieved him of a competitor, he spent a tranquil period in Barsetshire, where recollections of the past stimulated but did not grieve him. He had grown fond of his brother and of the little "mamma," and had only tender thoughts of his unfortunate father, whom he immortalized as Mr. Crawley. As time passed, he became increasingly interested in the relation between his parents. He was no longer angry with either father or mother, and was prepared to work out the family problem with such beautiful objectivity as to disguise from the casual reader the correspondence between the planes of history and fiction.

While writing the *Autobiography*, he spent long hours in brooding over his father's tragedy. Vainly he tried to account for the succession of disasters which had terminated in the mournful Château d'Hondt. To the practiced eye of a medical man, his father at sixty-one had looked a man of eighty; this was a peculiarly poignant memory to the son, for actually they were now the same age, abreast on the race-course, each in the sixty-second year of life. But how had fate hammered and twisted Thomas Anthony, until he, who had commenced life with noble gifts, departed, lacking a score of the years which seemed to weigh him down?

Anthony recalled "a man, finely educated, of great parts, with immense capacity for work, physically strong very much beyond the average of men, addicted to no vices, carried off by no pleasures, affectionate by nature, most anxious for the welfare of his children, born to fair fortunes. . . ."

The inexplicability of the case haunted him, and yet was not his parents' marriage the solution? For the father had been a bachelor until the age of thirty-seven, with every expectation of a life developing along a well-planned pattern; surely the disaster was attributable to the woman he had chosen. What could have made him safe from ruin even with her for a wife? For Anthony desired not only to save his father but, to a less degree, his mother. If Thomas Anthony had been grandly rich, as high in place and birth as any man in England, even Frances Milton could not have pulled him down. Anthony could make him rich and great and nobly born; he could make him Mr. Palliser, then a cabinet minister, then Duke of Omnium, at length prime minister of England.

When the *Autobiography* was in preparation, the apotheosis of Thomas Anthony as Duke of Omnium was almost complete, and it was time for Frances to die: Anthony did not intend her to triumph again in the matter of length of days: the Duke must outlast the Duchess. From his filial meditations he turned to place the crown upon the memorial arch to the late Thomas Anthony Trollope, wrecked barrister, derided scholar and forsaken husband, who had been transformed into England's mighty Duke of Omnium. Two days after finishing the *Autobiography*, Anthony was at work upon *The Duke's Children*.

A variation of the problem could not have escaped him through the years: what would have happened to the Trollope family, had his mother been taken and his father left? He would now find out what happened to the Duke's children on the death of his Duchess. The new book commenced with the husband's bewildered grief over the sudden loss of the charming, impulsive, indiscreet Glencora. He was left with three grown children, two sons and a daughter, a group similar to the Trollopes on the death of their father—Emily, who was fast dying, had scarcely seemed to live.

Added to the Duke's anxiety over the children, who were so much less his than their mother's, was his feeling of weakness; how could he go on living without her wonderful vitality? He knew that she had attached the children to herself at his expense, that she had taught them to fear his austerity; she had embarrassed him by her intrigues and her showy hospitality; she had been loudly mirthful on the subject of his services to the country, especially the project of decimal coinage which had seemed to him of paramount value. Yet he did not see how he was to exist without her, so full of life as she had been, so deeply lovable.

He managed so poorly without her that Glencora would have pitied him. He tried to be a good father, but his children had already been convinced that he was tiresome, nervous and irritable, an ascetic who thought everyone ought to do without the luxuries which were superfluous to him. He lectured his sons on their wildness and did not spare the sonorous Latin phrase; he had odious schemes, such as drawing up for their improvement "a very elaborate memorandum on the subject of amusements generally"; he was a blight upon family festivities, where "it was the Duke who made the greatest efforts to be good natured and with least success"; he quarreled irrationally with Glencora's best friend; and his tyrannical treatment of his young daughter originated in a narrow mind. In brief, he behaved as Thomas Anthony could have been expected to behave in circumstances similarly favorable. He was always on a loftier plane, because Trollope never lost his belief that high position and wealth bred better men than obscurity and poverty.

The simple plot hinged upon a last indiscretion of the dead Duchess. Anthony in his sympathy with his father judged it to be worse than indiscretion: Glencora was disloyal, because she had kept a secret from her husband, a secret which concerned him as much as it did her. In the course of the narrative, Trollope urged the flaws in Glencora's behavior, never letting his readers forget the dead woman's frailty, lack of taste, and disloyalty, but he could not efface the memory of her delicious inconsequence and the warmth of her nature.

Outside the Duke's family, the portraiture was unremarkable, although Phineas Finn had become more stodgy and self-important. Lady Mabel was a paler Lady Laura, with a mastery of telling phrase, and Frank Tregear, the impoverished gentleman who had to marry money, met with better fortune than he merited. The American, Isabel Boncassen, embodied the mistaken ideas of upper-class Englishmen as to the liberated American girl. Her pertness and her prettiness aroused both terror and admiration in the breasts of the gentlemen in the story, and the readers of the period as well as the creator of the lady were unable to gauge her mediocre quality. Trollope was never able to understand the American girl and would have been wise to leave her in the competent hands of her countrymen, Howells and James.

Anthony had come to the time of life when the days lengthen, not because there is insufficient to fill them, but because the mind and the body claim longer periods of rest. He could not use his eyes in reading more than three hours a day, nor·could he concentrate longer on what he read. He divided the time into two periods, one of which he spent upon the Latin classics, the other in reading the later Elizabethan dramatists. Both subjects possessed romantic interest, and the former was blended with wistful memories of a childhood which needed making over, and of a father who had wanted to make scholars of his boys. A writer who refuses to plot his own work often takes great pleasure in the inventions of other authors. Trollope was fascinated by the skill of the forgotten seventeenth-century dramatists and learned something from their methods, although the principal use made of his researches was the modeling of his *The Fixed Period* on *The Old Law* of Massinger, Middleton, and Rowley.

Florence Bland, his wife's niece, saved his eyes and his hand by writing to dictation, and his creative work went on at about the same speed. He could not afford to lose touch with modern politics and, for such information, leaned heavily on what he heard at the club and at dinners. Whist at the Garrick was a great comfort to him. At first he had played merely for the pleasure of sitting with congenial men, but he had attained some skill, and the cards taxed his vision less than reading and writing, so that it became his habit to spend the interval between tea and dinner "in the little room upstairs" at the whist table.

The quarrel with Charles Reade had temporarily made both men unpopular at the Garrick, as they involved others in their disputes. The principals talked at, but not to, each other; and Reade, when out of hearing, applied to Anthony such ill-selected epithets as "homunculus" and "publisher's rat." He considered that he had been insulted afresh when Mr. Blackwood requested him to change a love scene, with the excuse that Trollope, who knew all about women's hearts, was always willing to do as he was asked. At length, mutual friends effected a reconciliation, and peace reigned temporarily at the Garrick.

Anthony was appearing occasionally on public platforms, as had been his wont for the past fifteen years. Mechanics Institutes and the like provided audiences, and "novels" or "the art of reading" was his usual subject. He enjoyed provoking youthful laughter by asking his listeners whether they could read—going on to explain that many of his dearest and wisest friends could not do so. It was, he emphasized, an art which could be acquired only by practice, and not one to be put off until middle life. He continued to repeat the story of his own youth when "a relative," on this occasion remembered not as Uncle Henry but "a dear old lady," had advised him on leaving the office "to be sure to go home to tea and read a good book."

Trollope's frequent faultfinding with misguided humanitarians, from civil service reformers to American abolitionists, did not prevent him from feeling humanitarian sentiments himself in reference to matters which he was incompetent to judge. Like many liberal Englishmen in 1876, he was outraged by the Turkish atrocities in the Balkans and the pro-Turkish policy of Lord Beaconsfield's government. Thus he took part in the great meeting on the Eastern Question at St. James's Hall on December 8, 1876, at which eminent Liberals from Gladstone down vented their indignation. Trollope's speech was chiefly remarkable for his failure to observe the time limit of five to seven minutes allotted to the lesser speakers. The Duke of Westminster, the chairman, rang the bell, coughed, and finally in desperation tugged at Trollope's coat tails. Anthony turned round, exclaimed, "Please leave my coat alone!" and went on with his denunciation.

Public service of a more exacting kind was demanding much of his attention. In April, 1876, the Queen had appointed her "Trusty and well beloved Anthony Trollope, Esquire" as one of fifteen commissioners to examine into the laws regarding home, colonial, and international copyright. The commission sat intermittently for a year, taking evidence and preparing recommendations. Trollope comported himself in a businesslike manner, asking intelligent questions and not wasting time. The final report of the commission reaffirmed what had been his contention for nearly two decades—that the greatest injustice to British authors, and to American writers as well, lay in the absence of a copyright treaty between the two great English-speaking nations.

Thus passed Trollope's days: he had made some adjustments to age; he had poured a libation but offered no sacrifice. Soon he must give up hunting.

It was no longer necessary for him to write tales and articles to order, but with some grumbling he continued to grind them out for annuals and special magazine issues. "Christmas at Thompson Hall" exemplified his peculiar belief that humor was an affair of the grotesque. A prodigiously starched Englishwoman roamed at dead of night through a Paris hotel in search of mustard with which to make a plaster for her husband. Returning with the mustard she entered the wrong room and applied the plaster to someone without a claim, and he did not like it. The tale was cheerily vulgar, not the less so because, straining to be decorous, Anthony had the lady put the plaster, not upon the chest, but on the *throat* of the unfortunate stranger.

This farce was one of five short stories republished as *Why Frau Frohman Raised Her Prices*. The tale which furnished the general title was a pleasant lesson in the economics of Tyrolean innkeeping; "Alice Dugdale" celebrated the triumph of a poor but proper maiden; "The Lady of Launay" repeated the old tune of the mother who refused to sanction the marriage of her son to her impecunious companion. But "The Telegraph Girl" was the worst of a poor collection: Lucy, the heroine, was so excessively "the little brown girl" that she could risk going dirty—she had a face which "did not require to be washed every half-hour." Her virtue secured a widower with a child, as Lucy loved children—although neither she nor the reader had learned the age and sex of the encumbrance in question. Lucy's rival, frivolous, tubercular little Sophy, stood in her poor way for the joy of life, of which Anthony had once been the champion. Anthony, who had as a young man wonderfully portrayed the Irish peasant girls, now held his London workingwomen at a great distance and regarded them with tepid interest. He was at home only with great ladies or heroines from the upper middle class.

Tired of love-making, he planned a fresh incursion into the ranks of scholars. His irritation at the obscure fate of his *Caesar* demanded a brilliant success in the classical field. If he wrote an acceptable biography of a cultured Roman, he would be doing his father a service and avenging himself on the masters of Harrow who had treated him with contumely. A daily ninety minutes spent in study had prepared him to treat Cicero better than he had treated Caesar, and the subject was far more congenial.

Cicero was dear to him; if his conception of the man was not Ciceronian, it was extraordinarily lifelike. He thought of Cicero as an ideal nineteenth-century gentleman, a patron of the arts, a builder of palaces and country houses, the defender of the Old Order against the brute force of dictators. But he must have had an inkling of the discrepancy between his Cicero and the historical, when he observed that he was "so little like a Roman that he is of all Romans the most attractive."

As an historical work it was shockingly prejudiced. Professing to draw only upon sources contemporary with Cicero, he credited none but those which were favorable to his hero. With tiresome frequency, when he could neither pardon nor explain away an action, he repeated the weak, unanswerable, "Who among men has been free from such blame?" Tom shuddered at his errors and wrote, more in sorrow than in anger, "By Œschilus I know—what others could only guess—that you mean Æschylus." Anthony had not availed himself of the scholar's right to expert opinion, and had shunned particularly the counsel of his highly qualified elder brother.

But *Cicero* had the great merit of being a live book, calculated to increase a young student's interest in the times of its hero. Trollope's Cicero was an attractive figure to stand before the pleasant pathway which led up to the portrait bust within the sacred grove. The work abounded in moving references to Anthony's own religious problems. Anthony believed that men would not try to lead good lives if they had not faith in a future existence; he had not guessed the heights which mortals attain without hope of rewards or fear of punishments beyond the bounds of their own moral natures. He considered the Golden Rule as "the very pith and marrow and inside meaning of Christ's teaching," a remark which revealed no original thinking. He did not believe that God answered prayers for specific needs—

even the Bishops prayed for rain without expecting it—but it was a
good thing when one was in trouble to "hold communion with the
powers of Heaven." He called Cicero "a Christian before Christ, because he told us of the soul's immortality, and of the heaven to be
won by a life of virtue, of the duty upon us to remain here, where
God has placed us, and of the insufficiency of fame to fill the cravings
of the human heart."

Anthony seems to have pondered often upon suicide during this
later period, not with any intention of putting an end to his own life,
but with mournful speculations on his power to sustain suffering,
and anxious memories of his mother's years of imbecility. "The duty
upon us to remain here where God has placed us. . . ." His meager
and timid religious ideas afforded him cold comfort; they drifted
into melancholy thoughts upon "the insufficiency of fame to fill the
cravings of the human heart."

The parliamentary novels were finished, the great Duke was left
supreme, though doleful, and his unworthy consort had long been
dead. But the dynamic relation of father and son did not permit
Anthony to find a final settlement. In *John Caldigate*, Trollope's second
story with an Australian element, Thomas Anthony reappeared much
as he had been in life, a stern, scholarly man, an English landowner,
unsympathetic with his son's youth, harsh, but just and deeply loving.
With that son Trollope's identification was uncertain; but it was
significant that at a crisis in his late boyhood the young man sealed
with himself such a pact of regeneration as Anthony had made and
kept—and the reconciliation between John and the father suggested
wish-fulfillment.

The book was begun on February 3, 1877, but was soon laid aside
in favor of *Cicero*. It was, however, well under way when Anthony
sailed for South Africa at the end of June, and as soon as he landed
in Capetown, the completed manuscript was dispatched to his publisher. The plot was sufficiently ingenious to prove that Trollope
lacked the will, rather than the ability, to arrange events according
to artificial patterns. As he grew older, his characterization became
weaker and his devising more adroit, signs of decadence in a writer
whose interest in the individual was flagging while his cunning in-

creased. Doubtless his absorption in the schemes of the plays he studied daily, stimulated his efforts. The later novels were not well plotted throughout, but many of the episodes were arranged with great art.

John Caldigate was on the whole a virile, joyous book; the college town, the pleasant English countryside, ships on the sea, the new world with its stirring life in mining camp and provincial theatre, the mushroom morality of the colony, presented a panoramic view of Englishmen in the 1870's. The reader could see decisive, crisp movements, and hear the harsh loud voices of men as they hammered at Empire-building.

While Anthony wrote the last pages on the "Caldera," perhaps renaming his hero from the ship which bore him, he was nearing another of England's great colonies. There had been various little griefs before he sailed; he could secure only £850 for the forthcoming work on South Africa, £400 less than he had been paid for *North America* and for *Australia and New Zealand;* and there had been family opposition to his taking the journey, both because he was in his sixty-fifth year and because he might well find himself in trouble. Disturbances were expected to follow the annexation of the Transvaal, and a war with Russia was well within the bounds of possibility. He shrugged off the money loss, for he had long known that travel books paid badly and that his vogue was declining. More impatiently he freed himself from Rose's and Henry's restraint. He wanted to see South Africa; to postpone the trip was to cancel it altogether.

Capetown was reached upon a misty Sunday morning. A long delay in the customs predisposed him to dislike all he might see thereafter. "As I have as yet only been on shore twelve hours," he wrote John Blackwood, "I am not prepared to give a full and comprehensive description of the country, but it seems to be a poor, niggery, yellow-faced, half-bred sort of a place, with an ugly Dutch flavour about it." The twelve days passed in the provincial metropolis were busily employed. He stayed at the Club and grumbled as he had in America at the substantial meals, fit only for "men of heroic mould." The citizens did not take umbrage at criticisms and observed candidly that Capetown was "a beastly place." Anthony said it was not exactly dirty, it was "ragged."

There were two cathedrals, of which the Roman Catholics owned the smaller and handsomer; the public gardens were dreary; at the museum his eyes were too poor for him to appreciate the wonderful collection of butterflies and hummingbirds and those creatures large enough for him to see were in a sad state: the lion and lioness were bald, the hippo molted, and the giraffe had a broken neck. Anthony mournfully suggested oiling them.

Housed in the museum was a magnificent library graced by a first folio Shakespeare. Anthony envied its possessor and doubted Capetown's ability to appreciate such a treasure. Then, as usual, he recalled Boston. "It should always be remembered that at Boston in the United States any inhabitant of the city may take books home from the public library without any deposit and without paying anything. Among all the philanthropical marvels of public libraries that is the most marvellous." While he was refusing to look through the Capetown telescope, he recalled the disgust of Agassiz, "when I asked permission not to be shown his museum at Cambridge, Massachusetts." "In truth I do not care for the stars. I care, I think, only for men and women," he said apologetically.

He went to the Post Office, prepared as usual to give advice, bestowed it, received thanks, and went away knowing perfectly well that it would be disregarded; without doubt the public would continue to be treated as enemies of the officials and would have to go on buying their stamps, not upon government premises, but in a store across the street.

Capetowners boasted that he would find in their city plenty to eat, plenty to drink, and plenty of pretty girls. Trollope, noting their zest for life, wondered, as he had in other crude corners of the earth, if men were not quite as happy without luxuries as with them, except when doing without meant deprivation of what they had always possessed. He could not endure the thought of losing what he had.

The first stage of the journey, from Capetown to Bloemfontein and Georgetown, was made in a light cart drawn by two horses. He saw ostrich farms, and reflected on the many small landowners who went quietly to ruin, unnoticed among the prosperous few. He was grateful to those who had planted the treeless region with willows and poplars; "But the man who will plant an oak will surely feel the greenness of its foliage and the pleasantness of its shade when he is lying down down beneath the sod."

Georgetown was like a charming English village propped against the Pyrenees. One morning he left very early on a fifty-mile ride behind four mules as far as Belvidere, where the little party left the wagon at a ferry and carried their baggage three miles, Trollope taking as his share only the overcoat which he coolly managed to pass on to a mounted post boy in exchange for the latter's pony. At Knysna, another "English village," the scenery was superb but the landlady harshly independent, setting before them cabbage, mutton, and potatoes, with "And very glad you ought to be to get them."

One paid heavily for the picturesque: a week's jaunting about Georgetown cost him £30. He could never refrain from visiting caves, and traveled by fearful roads to Cango, where, in subterranean halls sixty feet long, "I was always thinking I should come upon a ghoul."

Fort Elizabeth was "built on the lines of one of those marvellous little American towns in which philanthropy and humanity seem to have worked together to prevent any rational want." But he was homesick there, although people were kind to him—not homesick for the London house or even for Barchester, but with a nostalgic longing for a youthful happiness which he had never possessed. Wandering beyond the little town, he saw a crowd of boys and girls in a green valley, playing at Kiss in the Ring, and he felt like Rip van Winkle looking on at joys forever gone.

As for British rule in South Africa, he believed it was in the main beneficent, but he disliked the cynicism which kept the humanitarian flag waving in England, while in Africa province after province was quietly gobbled. He objected to the presence of three British regiments, protesting that a colony which needed the protection of soldiery was not fit for home rule.

He was convinced that the Boers were opposed to British government. They did not want the luxuries of the English, but preferred to rule themselves according to their own social, religious, and political convictions. They were dirty, they married young and often, and were "grandly courteous." One old Boer, boasting of his family, observed to Anthony, "You won't have a new baby when you're sixty-seven years old." Anthony said he hoped not, but was disbelieved.

This Transvaal journey was arduous. During a week's trek he had his clothes off only once. Twice he would have had but half a bed, if his age had not secured him the whole while his courteous companion lay upon the floor. The butter was "evil," and though he carried his own tea, it was next to impossible to get boiling water. In Pretoria he visited the diamond fields and was shocked at the indolence "which persons can allow themselves whose occupations have diverged from the common work of the world."

Wherever he traveled he found much to annoy him, and much to amuse. At Alice people did not know the difference between hunting and shooting; they made him carry a gun "ever so many miles" and then, while a hundred Kaffirs drove the game, he was bidden to stand and told that luck would come his way. He did no such thing but, sitting down, composedly went to sleep. Charges on his excess baggage seemed exorbitant when he found that a tin box of bonnets could go at book rates for four hundred miles. Worse still, he once had to travel in company with an enormous fish, which provided, however, one of Trollope's funniest stories. When the horses which he had purchased for the Transvaal were resold, he was delighted to hear the auctioneer knowingly commend them as "bred at Orley Farm."

At King Williamstown he was waited upon by a delegation of Kaffirs, headed by "an unmitigated old savage" with a watch-key in his ear who had many complaints to make of the treatment sustained by the natives. Trollope observed that in the light of such alleged privations his interlocutor was rather grandly dressed. "Yes," admitted the chief, "we were told that we must come in and see you and therefore we put on our trousers. Very uncomfortable they are, and we wish that you and the trousers and the magistrates but above all the prisons, would go—away out of the country altogether."

Trollope's attitude toward the blacks was what it had always been —good-humored and tolerant as long as it was understood that they were congenitally inferior, incapable of freedom except under strong supervision, and unable to receive more than a surface imprint of education. His opposition to missions was compounded of prejudice resulting from his mother's droll anecdotes of Nashoba, of dislike of Evangelical methods, and of honest observation. He remarked caustically that the "sole effect of the missionary work has too often been that of saving the native from working for the white man." The only excuse for a mission station was the school, and much too often the school was nonexistent. At Lovedale he was delighted to find the pupils making furniture in the afternoon, for he believed that the natives could be improved only by manual labor for which they received wages, and by the slow process of imitation. Sorely was he vexed by the oft repeated invitation "to hear our children sing a hymn." The enthusiasm of the missionaries was "charming"; to compare it with the results obtained was "painful."

Bloemfontein, a red and white town in the midst of a grassless, treeless desert, was considered an excellent place for tubercular patients, but to reach it required a six days' journey by coach, traveling thirteen hours a day; and when the exhausted sufferer reached Bloemfontein he had to stay at a noisy, expensive hotel. Anthony pleased himself by planning a sanitarium which should not own to the name— the kitchen would be more important than the dispensary, doctors and drugs would be well hidden, and there would be novels to read and music, and a few healthy people to rid the place of gloom.

The journey was over. He worked on his book during the homeward voyage, completing it on the stormy waters of the Bay of Biscay. He apologized for hasty writing, protesting that he had been so immersed in his subject that the actual time spent was no index to the intensity of thought, but added the excuse of age, even while admitting that it was "unimportant to all save one or two." Thus ended the last great journey of Anthony Trollope, neither explorer, cosmopolitan, nor globe-trotter, but an Englishman observing purposefully the ways of the Anglo-Saxon race upon the earth, the dealings of the Mother Country with her colonies and with those lands which had cast off her rule and yet were to his mind hers still, speaking her language and giving new impetus to her culture.

CHAPTER XXI

Over the Mountain

1878-1880

ANTHONY's return from Africa in 1878 was badly timed for his inner tranquillity; the month was January, when much good sport could be expected; but at last he was unalterably resolved to give up hunting and keep only a pair of saddle-horses for London exercise. To see others enjoying what had been his greatest pleasure made him very unhappy. His retirement from the postal service had been a triumph by comparison; then, far from being put "upon the shelf," he was transferring all his energies to a field in which he was already highly successful and might, now that his time would be less divided, become preeminent. The renunciation of the sport he had lived for provided such a sense of loss as is suffered by the businessman forced to abandon what has been his chief excuse for existence. He gave away his hunters with lamentings, doled out his equipment among needy acquaintances, and wrote John Blackwood that "the abnegations forced upon us by age should be accepted gracefully."

His retirement from the postal service and then from the hunting field had cost him more than pension and amusement. His endurance of life depended on continued occupation. Leisure was not a benefit to a man who suffered intensely when he was reduced to introspection. His poor eyesight hindered study and his power of concentrating on his own characters, except when he was actively engaged in writing or dictating, had diminished with his interest in them. Fortunately a series of diversified activities in the summer of 1878 left him no time for carping anxiety.

In June his friend John Burns of the Cunard Steamship Company invited him to make one of a party of sixteen ladies and gentlemen, most of them quite young, on a cruise to Iceland, the maiden voyage of the yacht "Mastiff," designed for use in the Scotch and Irish Royal

Mail service. The land excursions would be grueling, but Anthony did not shrink from their difficulties. He was throughout the trip in excellent humor and succeeded in making himself popular with everyone in the party.

The "Mastiff" sailed on June 22, stopped at St. Kilda in the Hebrides, where the mail, consisting of one letter, was duly delivered, and went on to Thorshavn in the Faroe Islands, which was reached in the broad daylight of 10:30 P. M. on the twenty-fourth. Almost the entire population assembled to welcome the "Mastiffs," as the voyagers called themselves, and when the governor's absence was detected, a delegation of islanders hastened to rouse him from his bed. For the space of three hours, the party roamed the little settlement. Trollope, according to his custom, asked innumerable questions; what were the social habits of the islanders? their industries? politics? diseases? It appeared that there was a great deal of rheumatism, in which, as an "elderly" disease, he took an almost proprietary interest.

The next stop was at Reykjavik in Iceland, residence of the Governor and Lady Olufa Finsen. Governor Finsen could not speak English but was proficient in French. Rather than forego conversation, Anthony, who was in no sense a linguist, attempted Latin, in which they managed to exchange a few words.

The "Mastiffs" showed their appreciation of Danish hospitality by giving a dance on the yacht. Sunday morning after hymns on shipboard, they went to church and sat heroically through a service which lasted two hours and a half, under a minister who wore a great starched ruff like a dignitary in a Flemish painting. Trollope spent the succeeding hours in collecting items of interest: five newspapers were published in Iceland; literacy was general; curds, cream, milk, mutton, and fish were the staples of diet, but bread was almost unobtainable; coal was terribly dear and there was no wood—neither trees nor shrubs but only lush green grass grew in Iceland; the folk looked healthy but suffered from scurvy and sometimes—horrible to relate—from leprosy. These, his last travel notes, were as brisk and businesslike as their extensive predecessors.

As the climax of the excursion the "Mastiffs" visited the geysers. Anthony, veteran of so many laborious journeys, would never have listened to the voice of dissuasion. But he weighed 225 pounds, and the traveling had to be accomplished on ponyback, over a road which in the words of the local parson was a *via lapidosissima*. When Trollope apostrophized the guide for having assigned him "an awful brute," wailing, "O Zoega, why did you treat me so?" his unfortunate mount, if gifted like Balaam's beast, might well have retorted, "Oh, Trollope, why did you treat *me* so?" Nor was his baggage carrier much luckier, for, true to his invariable custom, Anthony's minimum would have made the ordinary traveler's maximum; his luggage consisted of several changes of linen, towels, toothbrush, soap, brush, slippers, boots, a mosquito net, a rug, a blanket, two great coats, an extra suit of clothes, a Horace, and "a big stick."

The hostess, Mrs. Burns, was exhausted and had to be left at the halfway point, but the girls were keen and reckless riders—not all Victorian ladies were pale lily flowers. The women passed the first night in a church, the men in tents; but on the return from the geysers, which disappointed Anthony as being much inferior to those of New Zealand, the entire party attempted to sleep in sanctuary, the girls within the communion rail and the men lying by twos in the aisle. There was much confusion. During the night one of the party rang the churchbell, and Trollope rose to make an eloquent plea for peace, ostensibly in behalf of the ladies.

The "Mastiff's" maiden voyage ended July 8. Trollope had enjoyed himself wonderfully. There had been plenty of chess, plenty of exercise, much laughter, the rough play which he thought of as "fun," and the admiration and liking of young people. Now that he was really becoming an old man, he had an honest, fatherly way with girls, quite at variance with the pseudo-paternalism with which in middle life he had cloaked his mingled shyness and dislike. The excursion provided him with material for an article in the *Fortnightly* and a thin volume, written for private circulation, which one of the ladies of the party illustrated with crude but characteristic picture writing.

But the summer's vacationing was not yet over, and in August Anthony visited Switzerland, where Tom and Fanny were summering on the Rigi. Warned by the family doctor to stay away from Rome in hot weather, Tom had found an ideal retreat where he had telegraph facilities and mail was delivered thrice daily; he liked the food, he liked the scenery, and the climate suited him. At night his windows were always wide open; he boasted of waking to find the bedclothes blown away, or the coverlet drifted with Alpine snow. Possibly Tom would have suffered less from head and ear difficulties had his habits been less Spartan, but the mischief, if any, had been done long since.

The brothers liked occasionally to compare their literary records, disputing in a friendly way as to which had published the more. The list of books was in Anthony's favor—47 books to Tom's 30 at this date—but Tom could point to more works of serious research, and to a vast quantity of periodical and newspaper writing which, he held, evened the scale. In the three years from 1876 to 1878 he had published nine new volumes, including three volumes of short stories, three separate studies of the Papacy and its latest incumbent, and a large German work on Italy which he had edited with Fanny's collaboration. But Fanny and he were beginning to feel that the daily correspondence to the *Standard* was labor enough for a man of sixty-eight.

Anthony wrote John Blackwood: "I have been on my legs among the hills every day for four hours, and have every day done four hours of writing. I then sleep eight hours without stirring. The other eight are divided between reading and eating, with a preponderance to the latter. It is a healthy, innocent, inexpensive life." In late summer Tom, Anthony, and Fanny went into Germany on what proved to be their final tour in each other's company. Then they separated, Tom returning to Rome, and Anthony to London.

On the day following his sixty-third birthday, Anthony commenced a long love story tentatively called *The Angel of Light*, an expression sprinkled with tiresome frequency throughout its pages. At publication the title was changed to *Ayala's Angel*; he had sought a precious name for his little heroine by which to indicate her quality. The plot was simple: Ayala searched for the lover who could satisfy her romantic yearning, while all around her other women were seeking men they might like to marry; the young men, usually with less urgency, were doing their own hunting; it was the tale of a long mating season, and at the close the marriages of five couples were managed with the urbanity of a contredanse.

The novel was remarkable for unusual beauty of style and for the finesse with which Anthony pictured the sisters' girlhood home, "The Bijou," where everyone was clever and well-bred and never talked about money and yet possessed all manner of lovely things. There was a touch of sadness, almost of envy in his design for artistic living. The talk was excellent throughout. In writing the conversations of clever men, Trollope surpassed any other Victorian novelist; his characters spoke in short sentences, avoided prolixity, did not declaim, behaved as intelligent people actually did behave. There was a slight bond between *Ayala's Angel* and *The American Senator;* justice-loving readers could rejoice to find Lord Rufford, who had treated Arabella Trefoil so scurvily, become a fat man, submissive to his wealthy wife. The shifts of middle-class poverty in the house of Ayala's "poor uncle" were described with a wry sympathy which evidenced Anthony's disgust at the "shabby-genteel."

In the large, it was a genial tale with only enough *chiaroscuro* to set off the afternoon sunset of a charming landscape. The humor, neither noisy nor vulgar, as Trollope had often conceived the nature of "fun," was refined to satire. The dealings of baffled Sir Thomas Tringle, the financier, with his daughter's sponger husband were especially amusing.

This was the last of Anthony's mellow novels. Those which came after carried the thin, sour flavor of withered, rather than of over-ripe, fruit. Not for the satisfaction of believing that Anthony Trollope died a happy man would we consent to give up such a book as *Mr. Scarborough's Family*. But we regret that it did not precede *Ayala's Angel*, over whose golden pages Anthony, like a late but less steadfast Prospero, waved his wand.

During the latter part of 1878 Anthony occupied himself for six weeks with the writing of *Cousin Henry*. In form this short novel was superior to the general run of his works, but this was due to the brevity which did not encourage wandering, and a weariness of spirit which cut short speculation; nor did the compression prevent an unfortunate and quite unnecessary change of scene. Such was the compulsive melancholy of the mood which followed the summer's activities that he selected as protagonist a whining, miserable creature in whom only a student of morbid psychology could take a lively interest. His heroine was harsh, and her ideals of duty were tainted with pride; the tedious scenes with her chosen lover hinged upon the sordid question of money; her uncle was obstinate and doleful; and no one in the story honestly loved anyone else.

Yet *Cousin Henry* was an able study of a weak nature under a mean temptation; an old man's will was hidden by a would-be heir with criminal desires but without courage to carry them boldly through. When a confession was battered out of him, he slunk back into obscurity.

A story in which it is impossible for the reader to like anyone may be magnificent, but it will not be popular. Unfortunately *Cousin Henry* was not magnificent; the problem was not on the tragic plane, the characters were mediocre, and the style, which might have atoned for both shortcomings, lacked distinction. Had *Cousin Henry* been an early work, it would have shown promise; but if the assiduous reader of the 1880's compared it with *The Macdermots of Ballycloran*, he must have realized it was high time the ring should close.

Without allowing himself a vacation, Anthony began *Marion Fay* before Christmas, but presently laid it aside in order to write a life of Thackeray for the "English Men of Letters" series, a task which occupied him from the first of February until the twenty-fifth of March, 1879. That he should undertake the work was no marvel; it was his way to accept commissions, and Anne Thackeray herself had urged this one upon him; with or without her sanction, the Life would be written, and her only advantage lay in choosing the author.

The reader of the Life learned more about its writer than of Thackeray, not because Anthony was openly egoistic but because of the strange parallels he suggested between himself and his subject. Trollope was not among the poor in spirit, though he was not above trying to persuade the world of his humility. He would seem to have pondered on the parable of the guest who was summoned from the foot of the table to a place with the rulers of the feast.

Comparisons drawn between himself and his literary contemporaries were sedulously guarded, but an occasional inadvertence gave the reader an amusing glimpse of his real opinions. His grave disapproval of Thackeray's effort to enter the diplomatic service, the severe verdict, "There never was a man less fit for the Queen's coat," was the more interesting when one remembered Anthony's own attempts to gain a seat in Parliament. It was almost as if one heard him add, *sotto voce,* "I myself made a positive success of the missions I undertook in Egypt, the West Indies, and the United States. I have been accustomed to the management of subordinates. If I was not fit for a diplomatic post, how could Thackeray imagine he would get one?"

He remarked that Thackeray made a poor editor. Trollope believed that one of his own stories had been rejected, unread. But Trollope himself could boast that he had read every contribution submitted to him as editor of *St. Paul's.*

He ascribed to Thackeray the melancholy, indolence and lack of self-confidence which were his own private burdens. Thackeray had made no secret of his suffering. There was something savagely contemptuous in Anthony's expressions of sympathy, as if he triumphed in his own victory over sloth, in his pugnacity, and in his power to conceal his wearying low spirits.

He who had shocked John Blackwood's guests by laughter at the Crown, referred primly to the allusions to royalty in Thackeray's lectures: "It is better, perhaps, that we should not deal with the personalities of princes!" He hated Thackeray's incessant harping upon snobs; was it possible that the social and political opinions of Anthony Trollope could have appeared to that flashing, mirthful spirit as tainted by snobbery? With faint disquietude he recited his own absurd list of preventives: "If you will keep your hands from picking and stealing, and your tongue from evil-speaking, lying, and slandering, you will not be a snob."

Marion Fay had been waiting many weeks for the completion of *Thackeray,* but when, in April, 1879, a clerical friend and author, Dr. Collins, offered him the use of his rectory at Lowick for the summer, Anthony could not find the courage to go on with the long novel. He amused himself by pretending that the parsonage was a boy's school, scene of a little drama played under the patronage of a rector-pedagogue, Dr. Wortle.

To populate a locality within one's physical range is an easy device both for the amateur novelist and for the weary veteran. The point of departure for Trollope's first novel had been a deserted house, visible to his bodily eyes; but he had employed it principally to give him a sense of stability and had immediately entered upon the history of its unhappy inmates. In *Dr. Wortle's School* the point of departure was the present, the reality was Lowick—whatever action went on elsewhere was obscure and, considering Mr. Peacocke's temperament, incredible. Dr. Wortle was what Anthony liked people to think him —intelligent, but scorning to be a savant, benevolent, loyal, acquisitive as far as a gentleman may be, bluff and hearty, devoted to his family, but appreciative of feminine beauty.

The plot was worth attention because of its dramatic possibilities and the unfortunate weakness with which Trollope lost them, point by point. As in *Rachel Ray*, gossip was at the roots of *Dr. Wortle's School*; Peacocke, the master, had an American wife whose past was unknown. Parents, scenting scandal, took home their boys. Rather than abandon Peacocke, Dr. Wortle determined to ruin his school.

The situation was tense; the reader felt that whatever Mrs. Peacocke had done, she was now a "good woman" and ought to be protected. Without warning, this dynamic position was abandoned, and Trollope issued a jeremiad against the Peacockes' sin in living together after discovering that the first husband was alive. Presently, relenting toward the lovers, he began to rarefy them until they became bloodless unfortunates, victims, acted upon, themselves incapable of action. By this time all tragic possibilities were eliminated, and Mrs. Peacocke had materialized as a betrayed woman lacking only the pathetic paraphernalia of the snowstorm, the shawl, and the nameless infant. But the living portrait of Dr. Wortle could ill be spared from the Trollopean gallery, and the last conversation between the boys and the reinstated master surpassed, in its simplicity and fidelity, the conclusion of *The Brothers Karamazov*.

While Anthony took his mournful ease at Lowick rectory, Tom was suffering from an excruciating attack of sciatica, his first real illness since he and Henry had played as little children around the drains of Harrow. Not until late July could the invalid be moved from Rome to a Swiss bath, where the physicians promised complete recovery in one month after he should have finished their course of treatment. But meanwhile he could not eat, walk, or lie quiet in bed, and it was clearly impossible to write. The clumsy administration of morphine scarcely relieved his pain, and Fanny, and the doctor, too, feared that with generous dosage he would become a drug addict.

At the worst of Tom's suffering Anthony came to Switzerland to condole with him. The two days he remained could not have been cheerful, for the invalid was not used to bearing pain, and Fanny had to put up with grievous lamentings from her elderly husband. Her patience and her intelligent care were exemplary, and she positively would not allow Tom to despair. Anthony wrote encomiums upon her virtue: "When I consider all the circumstances I hardly know how to reconcile so much love with so much self-control." The spectacle of the brisk, healthy and comparatively young woman lovingly nursing a tormented old man—through "four terrible months" —not only revealed her in an amiable light but suggested what Tom had meant to her in the twelve years of their marriage.

It occurred to Fanny that her husband might be better on the Rigi, and thither she took him by easy stages as soon as the course of baths was completed. In the mountains he was enough improved to make an effort to break off the drug. Hearing that the baths at Ischia in Italy might help him, he insisted on an immediate start southward; but on reaching Naples he was even more strongly advised against them. He went to bed that night a despairing invalid, and next morning awoke deliciously and inexplicably free from pain, once more Tom Trollope, although time and exercise were required before the shrunken leg was as good as its fellow.

At home again, Anthony resumed work on the long delayed *Marion Fay*. The hero of the book, which was at last completed on November 21, 1879, suggested another wish-fulfillment; Dr. Wortle had expressed the mature man Trollope would like to be, and the postal clerk who turned out a duke, represented the metamorphosis of young Anthony, the hobbledehoy. An extraordinary equalization of rank made possible the marriage of the postal clerk and the great lady; but Trollope could scarcely perform the same miracle twice in one novel, and thus the consumptive lower-class Marion Fay, loved by Lord Hampstead, had to die.

The best parts of the novel were the brief and highly suggestive scenes involving a stepmother with murderous propensities, a blackmailing clergyman, and a listless, do-nothing old aristocrat; all minor characters, but frightful in their potentialities, showing how competently Trollope could have dealt with morbid psychology had he not been deterred by the wish to please his public and by his own scruples.

When he had ground out the last pages, he felt very old and very tired. He was experiencing the difficulty, common to elderly folk, of finding the right word; but if Florence Bland, as she patiently took dictation, ventured to suggest the phrase for which he groped, he became furious with rage. On one occasion when she had incautiously tried to help him, he tore a chapter to pieces. Rose treated his bad behavior as a joke, and, falling in with her tactful implication at the breakfast table, he roared with laughter. Florence no doubt managed a pale smile.

In the early morning hours he was, like so many old people, lively and eager to be at work, but long before the day's stint was accomplished he would fag. Correspondence was a heavy burden. He courted sleep as the only relief for his uneasiness, and observed dolorously, "I am beginning to think that the more a man can sleep the better for him."

Toward the close of the previous year, he had made a will, leaving everything in trust to Rose. At her death Florence Bland was to inherit £4,000; the rest of the estate would be divided equally between Henry and Frederic. Henry was appointed literary executor.

Anthony thought a great deal about dying. Decorously gloomy, he relished writing obituaries for his friends: "Latterly misfortunes came upon him, by no means from his own fault, and they who loved him grieved to think that he was doomed to suffer"—so he wrote of Henry O'Neil, who had once painted his portrait. Charles Lever's biographer wrote to ask for his recollections, and he replied: "Charles Lever was an intimate friend of mine whom I very dearly loved, but I do not know that I can tell you any details that will serve the purpose of your book. Of all the clever men I have known, his wit was the readiest. . . . His was a kind, friendly nature, prone to cakes and ale, and resolved to make the best of life when, as you no doubt know, things were often very sad with him."

As philosophy and as prose, his death notices showed a falling-off from the dignified confidence of Bishop Grantly's end and the touching sweetness of the Warden's. Life was regarded as a penance prior to the punishment of death. When George Lewes died, Trollope wrote: "To me it has often been a marvel that he should have lived and worked, and thoroughly enjoyed his life,—as he did with a relish beyond that of most healthy men,—when I have observed the frailties of his physical nature."

And why should he be melancholy, if Lewes could be gay? To compare his state of mind with that of those less fortunate might have induced shame, had it not roused a feeling of pride because he had demanded more of life. He was half angry to recount the niggardly gifts of Heaven.

His popularity waned. He could not blame his publishers, who continued to give him his fair share of advertising. But there are unfavorable reviews which will damn a book even when the publisher supports it; and after 1875 the critical brotherhood appeared to be in league against him. In the past he had been credited with a mastery of form, an opinion less astonishing when it is recalled that the works of the great Russians—Turgenev, Goncharov, Chekhov—and the French Flaubert and Maupassant were only beginning to influence young English writers. But he had always been considered wanting in imagination; and at last even his craftsmanship was attacked: "The hand begins to falter"; he was accused of cynicism: "All the temptations of life become only so much material to the mechanical facility of long practise"; charges such as those once brought against his indifferent mother were advanced to his hurt: a "disposition to attribute to the majority of mankind an inherent vulgarity of thought." His shoddiness deserved censure, and the quality of his work was deteriorating; but to demand of him "wholesomeness" in the sense then current, and at the same time to ask that he "grasp and present the profounder secrets of human character" was to impale the goaded Anthony upon the horns of a dilemma.

In so much worry from detraction, waning popularity, and falling prices, the collected edition of "The Chronicles of Barsetshire" issued by Chapman and Hall assured him that a portion of his work was not, and would not be, forgotten. He took comfort in believing that the people of his beloved county would be long-lived folk; like baroque angels, they would support his ponderous frame into eternity and confer upon their creator a share of their immortality. Breaking his usual reticence, he wrote a preface for the new edition; he had been very happy, he said, in Barset, and was always glad to return to that imagined region. "But now, when these are all old stories,— not perhaps as yet quite forgotten by the readers of the day, and to my memory fresh as when they were written,—I have a not unnatural desire to see them together, so that my records of a little bit of England which I have myself created may be brought into one set, and that some possible future reader may be enabled to study in a complete form the CHRONICLES OF BARSETSHIRE."

CHAPTER XXII

The Passing of a Demi-Pagan

1880-1882

IN THE early summer of 1880 Anthony was advised by his doctors to try country air for his asthma, as his form of heart disease was unalarmingly called. He took a long lease on a house in Harting parish, West Sussex, where the family installed themselves during July. It was the last house that he and Rose would occupy together. There were some five acres of land—room for chickens, a cow, riding and carriage horses, and the family dogs. North End had been contrived out of two farmhouses, and possessed the charms of inconsistency; it had a square, high tower lighted by paired windows, an impressive portico, many chimneys and a variety of windows, the lower ranges opening on a green lawn. Anthony was again a country gentleman, but the scale was reduced and the vigor of the man greatly diminished since the days of settling in at Waltham Cross. He was interested in the greenhouse, pottered about with pruning shears as he thinned the shrubbery, mended breaks in his fences. On Sundays he went dutifully to church with his wife.

Before going down to Harting, Anthony had dashed off a series of feature articles for the *Pall Mall Gazette* under the general heading *London Tradesmen*. Like *Hunting Sketches* and *Clergymen of the Church of England*, they made pleasant reading but did not tax the mind. If Trollope on early morning excursions to the market districts was less at his ease than Trollope in the hunting field or the cathedral close, he was no less firmly entrenched behind the bulwark of his traditions. Stating that the plumber had been born to torment his betters, he conceded that the others, tailor, wine merchant, fishmonger, and their brethren, were worthy fellows as long as they remained in their proper stations—and deserved a gentleman's patronage, even when their wares were costlier than those for sale in large and necessarily vulgar establishments. But he did not repeat his sage advice to the young man learning to hunt, "Always shake hands with the farmer." In dealing with London tradesmen, county amenities would have no meaning.

He had lost the satisfaction formerly derived from carefully planned writing and the completion of each piece of work according to schedule. Sometimes he had two or three books under his hands at once; more often he was idle for weeks on end. He alternated the work of preparing *Cicero* for the press with the scarcely more agreeable task of writing his long deferred life of Lord Palmerston. The plan of such a work had been sketched out after Palmerston's death in 1865 but, losing interest, Anthony had put it aside until the publication of Ashley's cumbrous biography in 1879 spurred him to a fresh start. Unluckily, his early admiration for the virile statesman who had guided English policy through the troublous mid-century had not survived the interval, and *Palmerston* was one of the least enthusiastic books ever written. The style was weary and stale, suffering much by contrast with Palmerston's quoted utterance.

The record of events was frequently unintelligible. Defining his business as the explanation of the conduct and character of Lord Palmerston, the author leaped from Belgium to Spain, from Cracow to Washington, without once pausing to make clear the issues at stake or their interrelations. He shied away from controversial questions like that of Palmerston's Eastern policy with such timid excuses as, "This is simply a memoir of Lord Palmerston and does not presume to be a vindication of his policy," or, "Considerations of matters so intricate are too difficult for a little book such as this." No hint was furnished as to the appearance or manner of the most unconventional statesman of his time—an omission even more grievous in a biography than in fiction, where the reader may form his own picture without sinning against historical fact.

Only when he lingered over questions of internal politics was there a show of mastery. English government had few mysteries for a man whose perceptions were so delicate in matters of cabinet intrigue and parliamentary psychology. But *Lord Palmerston* revealed all too plainly that Anthony Trollope had never acquired a competent understanding of continental politics. A traveler and writer of travel books, he remained an insular Englishman whose early sympathies and antipathies were unmodified by reason or by observation. He might have been forgiven for calling Garibaldi a combination of King Arthur and Bombastes Furioso if under such jocosity there had been a grasp of the realities. There was not.

His work during the autumn of 1880 was the writing of a short novel with the sinister title *Kept in the Dark*. He gave his heroine a secret; a secret not only innocent, but strictly her own, yet one which she intended to share with her husband, when the diplomatic moment arrived. As with Glencora, that moment was forestalled. Her earlier lover, Sir Francis Geraldine—Trollope's perfect cad, though not a true Trollopean character—informed her husband. The original problem was of a nature to have attracted Henry James, although his subtlety of contrivance would never have allowed Sir Francis to take so directly brutal a course.

The wife's too easy forgiveness of her husband and the conventional "happy ending" which blandly skinned her wound were to be expected of Trollope; elsewhere one feels a strangeness, as of having wandered into another man's book. Yet when the story is recalled, there comes a distinct impression of Trollope's unwieldy figure and his heavy head pondering how a small matter may change the whole course of a human being, how easily any man or woman can be ruined by an error in judgment, an accident of personality; and how he, Anthony Trollope, the novelist, could please himself and his public by suspending the inevitable laws of retribution, but could expect no like mercy from the hands of his Creator.

In earlier years his ambition to be rich, to become more famous than his mother and brother, had kept him from that serene and happy state in which the novelist can enjoy his task because it gives voice, motion, and body to his own creations and makes them intelligible to other human beings. He had never attained the spiritual level at which he could work merely for the work's sake. Yet when, in December, 1880, he allowed only one day to intervene between the completion of *Kept in the Dark* and the commencement of a new novel, it was less from the old arrogant motives, less from the compulsion of long habit, than because he dreaded those reflections upon the purpose and end of life which idleness forces on the sick and old. He could not escape such thoughts, but he could deal with them more easily in fiction.

Whatever joy was left him must come from work; in life there was nothing pleasant to look forward to. Remembering the happiness autumn used to bring, he groaned because there would never be any more hunting. After winter, spring; he tried to teach himself to anticipate the thrust of crocus and Lent lily. "There is a green hill far away"; though the hymn's green hill was Golgotha, the words sounded to him like Paradise and he wrote Henry, "The expectation of green things in another garden prevents me from being sad." To such a nature the anguish of believing that death finished life was insupportable, and yet he could not grow enthusiastic over the prospect of a garden, however green. The Latin classics, which as a boy he had studied listlessly, had in the end conditioned his outlook. His thoughts of the future existence were Virgilian, but no asphodel bloomed in his meadows. Very often Anthony's lips formed the word *Melancholy*, her name appeared in his letters, and her face, wreathed with twisted tresses, peered into his troubled mind. When snow lay deep upon the lawn, he plowed his way along the avenue of firs to White Hill, and from its summit stared through the blinding mist toward an invisible country, while he thought how old and tired he was—and how insecure.

He chose for the theme of his next work that of a sour seventeenth-century comedy, *The Old Law*, in whose hasty composition Rowley, Middleton, and Massinger each had had his part. Its early popularity was probably due to its obscenity, as the few fine lines were not of a character to attract attention on the stage. Evander, duke of an unknown land in an indefinite period, revived an ancient edict: women of three-score, men who had reached four-score were to be put out of the way. With one virtuous exception, the inheritors greeted the mandate with hilarious joy. In the *dénouement* the duke announced that he had revived the law merely to test the characters of his subjects; authority rescued the old and rebuked the young with somewhat immoral leniency.

On this argument Anthony based *The Fixed Period*, placing the action in 1980, exactly a century in advance of his writing. Various scientific improvements, such as a dictaphone and a "steam-curricle," ineffectually provided the fantasy with atmosphere. At the age of sixty-seven, the aged were to be "deposited" in Necropolis, but, as in the original comedy, authority interfered to prevent the extermination of the old.

In *The Fixed Period* Trollope had designed a clumsy makeshift to carry an idea. Until he approached the Great Wall where the reality of the known ceased, he seldom indulged in errant fancies; then, as a conjuror, he was not a success, and indeed his attempts at legerdemain were only half-hearted. The significance of *The Fixed Period* does not, like the old comedy's, lie in the ghoulish behavior of possible heirs, but in the mournful question: what is an old man to do with his life?

Very often he had dealt with the problem of a woman's destiny, concealing, under a specious geniality, the brutal inadequacy of his prescription: Let her marry, have two children, and live happily ever after. In its various forms the present question touched him nearer home: Do old men block progress? Would their children gladly be rid of them? Is their apparent affection a sentimental sham? Are the old better dead? Is it not better to depart voluntarily, before the indignities of senility overtake a man? He was nearing sixty-six: how deeply he was engrossed in his own relation to the problem was shown by his decision that sixty-seven was the age suitable for leaving the world's affairs. The choice may have had an effect in hastening his own death, which occurred at the "fixed period." A friend walking with Anthony spoke of his proposal for euthanasia as a grim jest. Anthony stopped, grasped his arm, and said "It's all true.—I *mean* every word of it."

Of all this the public could know nothing. A critic in the *Saturday Review* observed with calculated ambiguity, "One thing, however, remains clear, that the author will allow of no fixed period for leaving off work and bringing a life's interest and occupation to a close." To those modern readers who with some touch of sympathy reflect upon an old man's sorrows, it is evident that when his pen freed the citizens of Brittanula from the horrors of Necropolis, he himself remained a prisoner. Silence and emptiness flowed through the stately pagan dwelling of the victim set apart to die.

When Anthony finished *The Fixed Period*, spring was still many weeks ahead. To anticipate it, he paid a flying visit to Italy in search of Roman sunshine. Rose accompanied him but, as usual, did not hamper his movements. His brother Tom, who would soon be seventy-one, had already advanced three years beyond the age for Necropolis; but Anthony found that he had recovered the use of his bad leg and was as active, cheerful and full of schemes as ever. Many years before, Tom had commiserated the old canon in his *Marietta* on the stairs he had to climb, but in his own old age he mounted the one hundred forty-one steps to his apartment in the Via Nazionale with no thought of pitying himself.

He was no longer turning out books at the old prodigious rate, but he continued to send his daily cable to the *Standard*, and was by no means ready to lay down his pen. He encouraged himself by remembering that his mother had used hers until she was seventy-six. He and Fanny had lately been publishing biographical sketches of the great Italian poets, soon to be collected in book form. An acute reader, contrasting the verbosity and overcolloquialism of Tom's essays with the finished style of his wife's, might have judged that advancing age was intensifying habitual defects.

As a newspaper correspondent of nearly ten years' experience, Thomas Adolphus had lost no opportunity to enlarge his understanding of Italian ways. With a dignity founded on self-forgetfulness and maintained by an impressive exterior, he had pushed his way into strange and forbidden places. The bizarre difference between Victor Emmanuel merely dead and Victor Emmanuel embalmed fascinated him, and the superior efficiency of the undertakers of Pius IX was a matter for record. Leo XIII, the new Pope, had once sent Fanny a special blessing as "the lady who had spoken such remarkably pure Italian." Tom, to whom air and exercise were vital, had often seen Leo as archbishop striding up the long hill of Perugia, and regretted that he should now be a prisoner in the Vatican. Anticlerical as always, Tom blamed the cardinals for the embarrassments of their superior.

Tom and Fanny were not pinched for money, and entertained a

cosmopolitan company in their spacious drawing rooms. This season their hospitality was not without a touch of self-congratulation, because people obviously came to see them instead of the charming Bice. Their bright songbird had flown. Bice had been married the summer before to an aristocratic young barrister, Charles Stuart-Wortley, who had just taken his seat in Parliament. The marriage, performed at the Paris Embassy by the chaplain of Kensington Palace, had been one to delight everyone concerned. The young couple had taken a house in the West End and settled down "to live happily ever after," in that fairy-tale phrase so natural to the Trollopes.

During his brief visit to Rome, Anthony had the good fortune to make a new friend from a former enemy when he was introduced to E. A. Freeman, the historian with whom he had once hotly contested the ethics of the hunt. Each of them readily perceived that the other was at heart a good fellow, much pleasanter in speech than in the pages of the *Fortnightly;* and since Freeman had read Anthony's novels but wisely refrained from his *Caesar* and *Cicero,* his compliments were sincere.

The historian was not robust, though he was eight years Anthony's junior, and the two were well-matched for walking expeditions. They went together into the Alban Hills, and, standing on a street of ancient Tusculum, Freeman recited passages from Macaulay's *Lays of Ancient Rome* while Anthony listened with a pleased, solemn wagging of his great beard. Nor was Anthony silent, as they strolled here and there, identifying the places mentioned in the poem, about his own hero, Cicero. Freeman was a little puzzled because Trollope rated the Roman's morality higher than his achievements in politics and literature; he actually asserted that Cicero was a Christian! Had he dropped the veil of reticence, Anthony might have blurted out still more. Was there not a deep, personal bond between his hero and himself? If Cicero was a Christian before Christ, because he lived as Christ commanded, might not Anthony Trollope also be a Christian, in spite of his doubts of theological dogma?

Anthony remained in Rome but a fortnight. On the homeward journey, on March 14, 1881, he began *Mr. Scarborough's Family,* the last of his great novels. During its composition he appeared relatively cheerful. Harting in summer was a pleasant place, with tea on the lawn on sunny afternoons, bright flowerbeds under the long windows, guests now and then to accompany him on his walks, and Henry often coming down from London. July was enlivened by a tiff with the editor of the *Graphic*, who was making difficulties over the serialization of *Marion Fay*. With virtuous indignation Anthony protested, "No writer ever made work come easier to the editor of a periodical than do I," and seemed more like himself because of the little squabble.

Trollope began *Mr. Scarborough's Family* with a seemingly ingenuous account of the events which preceded the action. His disclosures were arresting but deceptive. It was the reader's misfortune never to meet Mrs. Scarborough, the enigmatic, charming woman whose blend of compliance and lawlessness furnished the foundation of the story. One son polluted her memory; it was almost the only virtue of the other that he reverenced it; her husband cherished it secretly like precious perfume; yet she had long been dust when the action commenced, and was mentioned only at the rarest intervals.

The machinations of her husband, the chief protagonist, were astounding. Old Mr. Scarborough's intelligence was lofty, but his morals were peculiarly his own. Disliking the law, he dispensed with it, and although there was in the story another clever man who was impeccably honest and ardently loved his country's statutes, wicked Mr. Scarborough outwitted him. One of his two sons was a knave, the other an irreclaimable gambler; but the father could overlook everything except the knave's want of taste.

It was impossible not to admire Mr. Scarborough's courage. During the eight months occupied by the action, he was rapidly decomposing under the hands of the surgeons, while with amazing vivacity he fought off death and intrigued against law and order, rising above his bouts with pain until the reader loved him for his heroism and took a vicarious pride in his triumph. He died, and the book died too, save for one brief, Goya-like scene in which the gambler's creditors chased him home from his father's grave—Trollope's sullen reminder that to hoodwink the law of the land was not to stay the scourge of the avenging Furies. But, as the whips fell, the sympathy of the author

was with the son's lashed back and with the heroic, mendacious, anti-
social Mr. Scarborough. Titanlike, Trollope questioned the moral
order and writhed with pain and contempt at his own answer.

Bice's little girl was born in July, while Anthony was in the midst
of his novel and Tom and his wife were summering on the Rigi.
The first news was splendid: the baby was to be a second Bice—
Beatrice Susan Theodosia Stuart-Wortley. But three days later a tele-
gram brought word to Switzerland that the young mother had died
of childbed fever. Her death was a great grief to Tom, but his philosophy, his practiced courage, and the very verbosity with which
he talked out his trouble helped him to endure it. Not improbably
Anthony was the more affected, not because he had been immoderately
fond of his niece, but because, in this November of his life, the realization in his own family of how even the young may die induced
peculiar sadness. He did not wish to outlive Henry, nor Frederic.

More than three months passed before he could rouse himself from
the exhaustion which followed the writing of *Mr. Scarborough's Family*. The world had never seemed so wintry. Wherever he turned his
eyes he saw things gone wrong. Ireland, for which he felt a deep
affection, was in a worse state than before the famine. The Home
Rule party was practicing open terrorism from one end of the country
to the other. The peasants dared not pay their rents for fear of the
boycott. Parnell's followers were roaming the country in masked
bands, burning and slaughtering, while Mr. Gladstone in Downing
Street attempted to meet the situation with half-hearted, wholly ineffectual measures. Anthony lost faith in the Liberal party, an added
woe to an old man who held it a virtue not to change one's politics
and had been distressed at Tom's turning Conservative a dozen years
before.

He began, as old folk will, to live in the past. But it was not the
past of young Anthony Trollope. He betook himself rather to the
imaginary county of Barsetshire, indulging in memories of what had
been said and done there and recorded in the novels which had
brought him success. To recall the Irish stories was to court pain, but
the families of Barset had done well both for themselves and for
their author. He relived their garden and dinner parties, shared Mrs.

Quiverful's desperate trudge, criticized Mr. Slope's lovemaking and Mrs. Proudie's attack on Mrs. Grantly's motherly schemes; he delighted in the soundness of Mr. Crawley, and suffered with Mrs. Robarts when the bailiffs invaded the parsonage—not without a dim sense, drained of bitterness, that Mr. Crawley was his father, and that what happened in Mrs. Robarts's drawing room was very like what had occurred in his mother's at Harrow.

Meanwhile a physician ascribed his troublesome asthma to a heart condition and pronounced the word *angina*, which terrified his 'wife. Anthony blustered that he did not believe his heart was affected, but confessed despondently, "I have got to be old, and nearly worn out by the disease of age."

In weariness and flat distaste, he had finally completed *Lord Palmerston*. He attempted nothing else until late in February, 1882, when he began a short novel, *An Old Man's Love*, of which he and his secretary, Florence Bland, said so little that Henry was half surprised to find it in his father's desk, ready for the publisher. The story provided an answer to the question propounded in *The Fixed Period*, and, as its form was appropriate to Trollope, it can be read with less embarrassment than the earlier book, although at times its pervading melancholy degenerates into sickliness. What shall be given the old man? is the question, and the reply is, at any rate, uncompromising. He shall have nothing, no portion is reserved for him; he must give the girl he loves to the boy she fancies—youth to youth. Like a dead man, he must dower the bride, who is not even his widow, with house, and lands, and all his possessions. He must go, alone, on a long journey. If there is passion in the old man's love, it is the cold passion of negation; if he desires anything, it is not the young woman, but a renewal of his youth. To the young, this wistful and nostalgic little story offers sour entertainment; those who are older may have learned to smile at it.

For twenty years Anthony had been calling himself an old gentleman, and for nearly a decade the critics had been agreeing with him. He had grown accustomed to reiterated assertions that he was past his prime, that he repeated himself and strove to refurbish his palette with a barbarous mixture of colors. In the past year or two the critics had been, on the whole, more friendly. Resigning themselves to the prospect of an unending succession of Trollope novels, they greeted each new arrival with patience if without enthusiasm. Only exceptionally did a reviewer strike a harsher note, as when the *Saturday Review* commented on *Marion Fay:* "This is casting a lurid light, indeed, upon the church and her ministers; we take it as showing what a jaded fancy can have recourse to for a new sensation."

But though Trollope had subdued the critics, he could not conceal from himself that his public was gradually forsaking him. The prices paid him by his publishers afforded a reasonable index to his popularity, and their steady decline was the harder to bear because money had always been his gauge of success. In the sixties his two-volume novels had sold for £3,000 or even more, but he had been obliged to sell *Kept in the Dark* and *The Fixed Period* for £450 each. With his consent, Chapman and Hall had reduced the original price of *Ayala's Angel* from £1,500 to £1,050, a revaluation by which he forfeited as large a sum as was fetched by either of the two later stories. Still more depressing was the low valuation of £400 which *All the Year Round* set upon the serial rights of the lengthy *Mr. Scarborough's Family*.

He had frequently made the admission that "failure is the ordinary lot of man," but had hoped himself to escape the common fate. Unwilling to admit defeat while he could still put pen to paper, he roused himself to give battle. Neither he nor his mother had ever hesitated to abandon a hidebound publisher: perhaps that had been the secret of their success. There was a new firm in London, Chatto and Windus, which needed reputable authors and possessed the means of paying for established names. At their offices, in mid-September, 1882, he concluded two contracts for £600 each, the best he had secured in a dozen years. One was for publication of *Mr. Scarborough's Family* in book form; by the other he disposed of his still unfinished novel, *The Landleaguers*.

This, his last story, was like his first—a tale of Ireland, the well-beloved country where forty years earlier the hobbledehoy had become a man. *The Macdermots of Ballycloran* had been suggested by the melancholy ruins of an Irish country house and a true tale of the peasantry, but the grim inspiration of *The Landleaguers* was more immediate. On May 6, 1882, a new Chief Secretary had arrived in Dublin. Walking through the Phoenix Park with a subordinate in the early dusk, he was set upon by a ruffianly band of "Irish Invincibles." Both men were fatally stabbed. While all England held its breath in expectation of further ghastly outrages, Anthony Trollope determined to write another Irish novel, and proceeded to Ireland to examine conditions on the spot.

Love for Ireland, loyalty to England, and attachment to his friend Forster of the Garrick, for whom the blow had been designed, all summoned him to action. It seemed that he had found an answer to that tormenting question of an old man's destiny—that there was one old man who might both serve his country and do something for the harassed land where he had learned to respect himself. Departing in the teeth of family resistance, he refused to come home again until May was over, boldly asserting that the mild Irish climate was an aid to his breathing.

Back at Harting, he commenced the new novel, which his worn-out body warned would be his last. Could he finish it? His blood pressure was probably very high. He found concentration difficult and, when he tried to work the long hours of his old schedule, impossible. Although he drove himself brutally, the tale lagged. In August he said that another trip to Ireland would give him the help he needed; but when he returned he was unrefreshed. With infinite labor, forty-nine of the sixty projected chapters were put upon paper. Publication commenced in a weekly magazine, and his anxiety mounted lest the catastrophe should come before the final installments were ready. Against this possibility he furnished Henry with naked facts as to who should wed and who should be hanged, but did not invite him to complete the story. It would be hard if he who had been faithful forty years should leave the world as a defaulter.

> "Had I but time—as this fell sergeant, death,
> Is strict in his arrest—O, I could tell you—"

Alas! the tale was hardly worth the telling. The best to be said for *The Landleaguers* is that no hunting scene in Trollope's novels is finer than the day when Black Daly gave up the hunt, and that its historical aspects have interest and value. For the rest there are more blemishes than merits. In an attempt at novelty, he introduced a *prima donna* and laid bare his ignorance of music. A girl refused the man she loved and suggested that he marry her sister who loved him; thus she humiliated them both, assuming for herself a martyr's crown, worn very much awry. A young man talked a great deal about the expense of marriage. The Irish-American heroine slapped and stabbed in her determination to preserve a virginity which no one threatened.

Equally disastrous was the development of Florian, the ten-year-old son of the Protestant landlord, the first and only child to whom Anthony gave a leading role. To little Florian, Trollope entrusted a cruel secret compounded of religion, his father's ruined property, a masked man, and an oath upon a charred cross. The child, horribly frightened and confused between loyalty to his family and to the Church and his oath, was killed—shot from behind one of those barriers raised by the famine sufferers long years before. The boy talked and acted so convincingly as to leave no doubt that Trollope had narrowly observed the conduct of children, but the forlorn history was recounted without the slightest touch of sympathy. Trollope was like a bystander who witnesses an atrocity and is able to make an accurate report, but completely fails to grasp its inner meaning.

Summer was over, and Anthony shrank from the prospect of the snows and the white mists of Harting. Rose, eager to have him near Henry and the London doctor, willingly exchanged her comfortable house for a suite in Garland's Hotel, in Suffolk Street, Pall Mall. He was well enough to see his friends, to have Browning dine with him at the Garrick, and he even ventured into Somersetshire, in the latter part of October, on a visit to E. A. Freeman. On their March day together in the Alban Hills they had identified the sites of Macaulay's poem, but now in his home county the historian was determined that Anthony should recognize the topography of Barsetshire.

A neighboring bishop was summoned to a walking expedition. It was he who, stronger than Freeman, helped the unwieldy Trollope over the stiles. Anthony had detested mud ever since the days when he ran through it three miles to school, and today he grumbled at the sodden fields. To the importunities of his host he seemed to admit that Somersetshire was Barset, but insisted that Wells was *not* to be identified with Barchester. It must be Barchester, argued Freeman; there are the towers to prove it is Barchester. No, persisted Trollope; Barchester is Winchester—where I went to school. Freeman considered this inexact and unhistorical. Anthony growled that he was no debtor to Wells and had never even heard of the Wells wool-combers. Silent but stubborn, Freeman assured himself that Trollope had picked up more than one local idea, as he went to and fro in Somerset on postal service, and had forgotten where he found them.

He had thought Trollope infirm in Rome, and now the novelist was perceptibly less well. When they returned to the house, Freeman rummaged among his papers and found a compliment for Trollope's *Cicero* from a German savant, who expressed the view that the author's own busy life had enabled him to enter into the true spirit of Roman times. Anthony did not conceal his gratification.

The historian and the novelist had some talk of politics. Trollope was no longer the Liberal he had been before Mr. Gladstone attempted to solve the Irish question. But a little step seemed a long one to a man who had spent a lifetime standing on one spot, and Anthony was puzzled to find that Freeman considered his views out of date. He was not a little taken aback that his host could characterize Lord Palmerston as "the man who never failed to find some struggling people to bully and some overbearing despot to cringe to."

The visit ended, but the two saw each other once again on November 3, when they met as guests of Mr. Macmillan, the publisher. The next day, November 4, Anthony dined with Sir John Tilley, his brother-in-law. Cecelia had been dead so long that no one thought of her very often, but the friendship between the two men had commenced without her and had lasted more than forty years. Sir John's daughter acted as hostess, and the family, glad to draw closer to each other in the ring from which so many had stepped aside, laughed at Anthony's story of an altercation with a German band, and were jolly enough during dinner. But they had reached a time when, once the current joke is passed, little remains to say. In the drawing room someone suggested reading aloud. The book was one to rouse laughter, and

Anthony was laughing loudest of all when he suffered the long-threatened shock.

He had no house in London, and Garland's Hotel was not a place for a sick man, so he was carried almost immediately to a nursing home at 34 Welbeck Street. His condition was very grave, but on the fourth day he appeared better. For the next two weeks he continued to improve, and ten days after his seizure he was able to walk about the house, although his power of speech had not returned.

But on December 3, the London *Times,* which had kept the public in constant touch with the progress of his illness, contained an ominous bulletin signed not only by Dr. Murrell but by Sir William Jenner, physician in ordinary to the Queen, who had been called in consultation. Mr. Trollope had been losing strength for the last three days and his condition was less satisfactory than at the beginning of the week. The news on December 4, although even less encouraging, expressed hope of a rally. He grew a little better, then worse, and passed from unconsciousness into death at six in the afternoon of Wednesday, December 6.

The funeral, on the Friday, was at Kensal Green. Browning and Alfred Austin, the artist Millais, Chapman, the family publisher, were at the grave with the few relations able to be present. Anthony had in his time provided dignified death notices for many old friends, but his own obituary was cut short in order to make room for that of the French socialist, Louis Blanc.

CHAPTER XXIII

Aristides the Just

1882-1892

TOM, once the ugly little Saxon lad of Harrow with flaxen hair
and a mouth like a bunny's, had become a magnificent old man with
thick white locks and flowing beard, a broad lined forehead, and
prodigious brows which slanted toward the aristocratic nose of his
inheritance. His expression was less formidable than his features.
Mrs. Browning had compared his face in middle life to that of Soc-
rates; in his old age he resembled a subtle but benevolent satyr.

Tom was saddened, not dismayed, by Anthony's release. Not thinking of himself as an old man, he attributed his brother's untimely
death, at an age five years younger than his own, to overwork. He
expressed none of the pitiful triumph of the aged who pride themselves on outlasting their generation; nor did he now draw parallel or
contrast on the subject of productivity, although his own record com-
prised, in addition to a huge bulk of ephemera, fourteen novels, five
books of travel, three volumes of short stories, four books on Italian
politics, and seven historical works.

Adjusting himself to his brother's death with a facility due not to
cold-heartedness but to his philosophical habit, Tom speculated
briefly on the probable terms of the will. A few hundred pounds spared
to him from Anthony's respectable fortune—he had left an estate of
some £25,000—would not come amiss; for, though Tom felt as young
as ever, his doctor had cautioned him against the Roman summer, and
at seventy-two it was impossible not to anticipate a time when the
work of a journalist would prove too arduous. But Anthony, as it
appeared, had left him nothing, and Tom was not disappointed,
acknowledging the superior claims not only of Rose, Henry, and Frederic, but of Rose's niece, Florence Bland, who had given her youth in
Trollope's service.

Of greater interest was the question of Anthony's biography. Very probably Tom hoped he would be asked to write it; he may even have contemplated a family history which would give the ancestral setting, do justice to his mother, sketch with becoming brevity the annals of his own Florentine branch, but direct the full light of objectivity upon Anthony as civil servant and man of letters; in such a work much could be said of his brother's overt virtues, and little of his recessed faults.

The will named Henry as literary executor. When no request emanated from the nephew that his experienced uncle undertake the Life, it seemed probable that the young man, who had set himself up as a literary aspirant, intended to keep the biography in his own hands. His ability was questionable; though Henry was not dull, he was certainly not brilliant. Presently news came that a two-volume *Autobiography* was to be published directly. Apparently, no biography was even contemplated. It was a long time since Tom had been so interested in a forthcoming book.

Although Henry had been aware of the existence of the *Autobiography* for the past four years, he had not known what he was to do with it. His father had laconically assured him that he would find instructions with the manuscript. He learned that his father had made him a present of his memoirs, but it was one of those questionable gifts with which one may do only what the donor pleases; any literary hack could perform the service required of the son; he was not trusted to comment on the text, nor to add the events of the six years which had passed since its completion; he might delete portions, he might suppress the whole, he might write a preface. Thus, in effect, the present was one of money. There was something contemptuous in the restrictions, and Henry's behavior suggested that he understood them thus, for he wrote a bleak, brief preface, placed a heading at the top of each right-hand page, made cuts to the total of two printed pages, and published a book which would, if it had any effect, tarnish his father's dimming reputation. Nor did Henry ever attempt to write the biography which his father expected. The omission of such a work from the chronicles of his century would have been a great disappointment, had Anthony had prescience of it.

Tom read the *Autobiography*. As a historian, accustomed to the objective handling of personal records, he could observe the factual errors, the omissions, the perverse discrepancies. It was impossible not to be struck by evidences of haste and passion. Anthony's six weeks' employment had left streaks and stains of resentment and unbalanced emotions upon his pages. Tom was the only living being who could judge between his brother and his brother's book. Rose was not competent, for she knew only what her husband had told her of his youth; in any case, she would not have been competent. And, though Tom was the only qualified critic, he was dispassionately kind.

He realized that the book would make a poor impression; if there were no other reason, the contrast between the *Dr. Wortle* type which Anthony was popularly supposed to resemble and the embittered egoist revealed in the pages of the *Autobiography* would shock the public into dislike. But Tom was too acute an observer to suppose, as later historians have done, that the *Autobiography* would kill his brother's reputation. That was already moribund. The writing Trollopes had been at work too long and produced too much not to have wearied the reading world. In addition, Anthony was twenty years behind his own times; he belonged to the 1850's and the 1860's. In a world dominated by the new Victorians, he was already a stranger. Anthony was dead and must take his chances of a twentieth-century revival.

Fortunately the book was not all of his brother; it was merely the product of an unreconciled mood, the result probably of passing circumstances. Not that Anthony was, or could ever have been, a happy man. Tom could thank his gods for memories of early years less turbid, more rationally understood. Then, as his services were not required for his brother's Life, he set about writing his own.

In the height of the Roman summer of 1886, he resigned his post as correspondent of the *Standard*. He was already seventy-six, and though he spent the two succeeding winters in Rome, his thoughts were bent on England. As each spring came on, he went with Fanny house-hunting, at home. His friendly doctors in Italy, wishing to keep the genial, stubborn old man among them, protested that an English winter would be his death. He laughed at warnings and observed that it was high time to put an end to fifty years of exile. As he expressed it, he was like a hare returning to its form; in this implied expectation of the end there was nothing of dread, but a serene conviction that, if it were delayed, he would do many important things of which the writing of his memoirs was to be only the first.

The Tom Trollopes found, as people do, that while the houses they liked were too expensive, those they could afford were not good enough. At last, down on the coast of Devon, at Budleigh Salterton, they found a cottage which in the family phrase "could be made to do"; the example of Grandfather Milton, who had pottered about "au-mieux-ing" a century since, was followed for the last time by this last of his grandchildren. In Tom's boyhood, Devon had meant the scene of happy holidays when he and his mother visited Cousin Fanny Bent; there was sweetness in this return, perhaps a dim impression that he would find his mother waiting for him. Her immortality had made them contemporaries; she was still eighty-three, and he had grown to seventy-eight. He had loved Theo, Fanny was both wife and daughter to him, but he had known his mother longest.

Untroubled by the wind and weather of the coast, Tom and Fanny settled in the house thus reconstructed to serve "our special needs." Tom completed the first two volumes of his memoirs. Anthony had reviewed the past of his childhood only as it impinged upon the compact little mass of hurts and griefs which he thought of as himself; Tom set down old ways of life, old tricks of speech, the ancient geography of London, as these had seemed to a square little Saxon in short jacket and roundabouts; but his pictures did not center on the boy—the lad stood aside with the old man to enjoy them: he was not crowded off the canvas, but neither did he appear as a pivotal figure.

However, old faults had gained upon the good old man. If in 1887 some readers took up the earlier volumes of *What I Remember* without acquaintance with his mature works, they must have attributed the meanderings of his prolonged *causerie* to senility, whereas they were but the accentuation of his lifelong habit of telling anything of interest just when it occurred to him. There were a few inaccuracies, some of the Latin quotations were incorrect, and yet it would be difficult to mention another book of quite such genial, unpretentious charm, its dignity unimpaired by its irrelevances. To read it was to know the man.

As the long journey wore to its close, the traveler remembered best the shining hours of its commencement; Tom recalled most vividly the little lad who trotted hand in hand with Henry down the second decade of the century. Whenever he was in town, he hunted up the scenes which he and Henry had visited; it was pleasant to buy a tart at the old sign of "Pidding, Confectioner," where seventy years ago they had spent their rare pennies.

Poverty in the Trollope family had been genteel, the children had not gone hungry. His mother had thought it despicable not to give to the poor whatever was left from her table, or her servants'; some rich folk sold the scraps—a hateful custom. In his past, Tom remembered much pleasant feasting; huge breakfasts following an eight-mile tramp, stately dinners given by diplomats, candied fruits peddled on the Lido by a squat fellow in a white apron—he must, of course, be dead, poor chap—the lemonade passed like a magical elixir along the terrace of his own Villino Trollope. Poor Theodosia! He had done his best work during the last half-dozen years they spent together.

To remember Theodosia was to remember music. She had played very beautifully, and Fanny, as well as poor Bice, sang remarkably well. Educated by such women, he was not the philistine that Anthony remained, although he had for many years been deaf, and at the best had not a true ear. John Cramer, contemporary of Haydn and Weber, was his first friend among musicians; he had known Jenny Lind and heard her singing in an intimate gathering, "Let Me Wander Not Unseen." He had listened to the first performance of *Lohengrin* in Florence. Twice he had marveled at Liszt's playing, but an interval of fifty years had passed between those occasions. Liszt had died only the year before.

Tom recalled a dinner party when he had found Emerson "an exceedingly dry man," and Emerson's daughter quite a dreadful creature as she sat next to him, peevishly assuring him that four whitewashed walls did God better service than any cathedral raised by human agency. Matthew Arnold seemed to Tom a much more liberal person, with a more receptive mind than the Concord sage. But he remembered most of the literary figures of his century rather as friends who had, in his phrase, "gone over to the majority," than as celebrities; he thought more often of Landor's frantic rages and pitiful affections than of his chiseled verse; more often of the discomfiture caused by Browning's smile, the birdlike twitterings of Isa Blagden, the perverse extravagance of Rosina Bulwer, than of those performances by which the world judged them.

As was natural, Tom said little of the younger members of his own family. Bice's little daughter, the Honorable Beatrice Susan Theodosia Stuart-Wortley, was only a charming child; he could not foresee that she would marry into the illustrious Cecil family and become the mother of three children. Nothing spectacular could be hoped of Anthony's sons, although Frederic, rooted in Australia, was rearing a family of patriarchal proportions, one of whom would in the fullness of time wear the family baronetcy as Sir Frederick Farrand Trollope. Henry, Anthony's elder son, published a sorry two-volume novel, *My Own Love Story*, in the year that his uncle Tom's memoirs made their appearance. The critics observed that he had inherited the commonplace and humdrum point of view of his father, without his gilding genius. But Henry had both ability and taste, and would in time write a life of Molière of more than ephemeral value. His grandmother Trollope would have been delighted.

Although of her direct descendants little could be expected, the family could pride itself on the achievements of the sons of Frances Trollope's son-in-law, Sir John Tilley. Arthur Tilley, the eldest, was one-fourth Trollope, because his mother had been niece to Thomas Anthony. He had taken a "first" in classics in Cambridge, was a fellow of King's College, and held a University lectureship. In the twentieth century he was to become one of the world's foremost authorities on French literary history. For John Tilley's sake, Tom could be almost as gratified over the brilliant prospects of another son, young John Anthony Cecil Tilley, who was about to enter the Foreign Office and embark upon the distinguished career which culminated in the 1920's when he became his country's ambassador to Brazil and then to Tokyo.

The Trollope family habit of visiting and showing hospitality was kept up to the last. The first guest in the new cottage was Irene Jones, who had been a friend of Tom's little sisters fifty years ago, and who scolded him for writing in *What I Remember* that his parents were more interested in their children's Latinity than in their catechism. Tom was troubled; England in the 1880's was a strange place to him, and he had not intended to invoke criticism of the mother whose memory was so extraordinarily vivid. Fanny eased his mind by promising to represent her mother-in-law as a religious lady in the biography of the future.

In 1891 the Tom Trollopes went on a round of visits in the same spirit as, in 1821, the Thomas Anthony Trollopes had set out in their gig to pay their respects to their relations and enjoy the English scenery. They dined in Oxford with the once beautiful Mrs. Jeune, under whose husband Tom had taught in Birmingham; he had since become Bishop of Peterborough and Master of Pembroke. The Trollopes toured Cumberland and saw the house of Carlton Hill which he and his mother had built in the earlier days of their partnership. The trees he had planted had grown mightily through the half-century, but he was touched to find that the paper on the drawing room walls had not been changed, out of compliment to the mother who had chosen it.

He was old, deaf, and childless, and he had not much money. It suited him to quote a dolorous stanza:

> "There's many a lad I know is dead,
> And many a lass grown old;
> And as the lesson strikes my head,
> My weary heart grows cold."

But he repeated the words only because he wanted to assert his triumphant negation: "My heart is not weary, and won't grow cold." He was prepared to try a walking match with any English gentleman of similar age; he was ready to go back to Rome and climb to the top of Michelangelo's Colossus and look out upon moonlight and silvered wood, as he had done fifty years since.

He did not live to be quite his mother's age, but had the advantage of her, for his body did not, like hers, outlast his mind. She had been in this world thirty years when he came into it, and he was here thirty years after she went out of it; their life spans had covered one hundred and twelve years when he died in his Devonshire cottage, suddenly, on November 11, 1892.

Fanny's memorial to her husband was her two-volume life of his mother, of which he was the hero, and which she dedicated "to the most dear memory of Thomas Adolphus Trollope." It was not one of her best works, but even a very affectionate daughter-in-law may prove a poor chronicler of her husband's mother. Nor was it easy to write acceptably of a Georgian lady in the smug last decade of Victoria's century, and Fanny, in the interests of the family, suppressed much of the older woman's vivacity. Like other people, the Trollopes had their secrets, of which Fanny gave nothing away. She lived on until 1913, when she was in sight of eighty; but sturdy Rose outdid them all, dying in 1917 at the age of ninety-five.

When Tom died in 1892, the last of the children of Thomas Anthony and Frances Milton Trollope departed from the world they had helped to create. More than a century has passed since the father and the luckless Henry were buried in Bruges and sweet Emily was lowered to the dusts of Hadley churchyard. Cecelia, her book and her babies, have faded to a dream; Theodosia is a white flower pressed among her poems in *The Book of Beauty*. The works of Frances and of Fanny Trollope languish unread in long ranks upon forgotten shelves; a modern authority upon the history of Florence may assure you that he has never heard of Thomas Adolphus Trollope.

These departed ones are as indifferent to the world as it has grown to them. They have turned away their faces. They were a part of England, had their share in disseminating English ideals of freedom and English culture; but having done their tasks, they did not greatly care to be remembered. One only of that numerous family, standing a little apart, lifts his hand to us in antique greeting. Anthony desires us to remember him; he is still divided in heart, still seeking immortality half in our bitter world, and half in that to which he has departed.

Notes

THE FOLLOWING NOTES are intended to list all sources used in preparing the present biography, over and above the five basic works on which any study of Trollope and his family must primarily depend. It is assumed that any Trollope student will be thoroughly familiar with the contents of these five books, and no detailed references to them have been included. They are:

Anthony Trollope, *An Autobiography* (2 vols., London, 1883). The merits and shortcomings of this book have been discussed in the text, particularly in Chapter XIX.

Thomas Adolphus Trollope, *What I Remember* (3 vols., London, 1887–89). The most comprehensive and on the whole the most reliable survey of the entire family history.

Frances Eleanor Trollope, *Frances Trollope: Her Life and Literary Work from George III to Victoria* (2 vols., London, 1895). Covers much of the ground traversed by Tom, using a good deal of fresh material.

T. H. S. Escott, *Anthony Trollope: His Work, Associates, and Literary Originals* (London, 1913). Essential because of the author's personal acquaintance with Trollope, but repellent in style and thoroughly unreliable as to fact.

Michael Sadleir, *Trollope: a Commentary* (Boston, 1927). A brilliantly written book, deservedly the standard work on Trollope since its appearance. Though frequently disagreeing with it in regard to facts and interpretations, the authors have found it invaluable both as a stimulus and as a source of much otherwise unobtainable material. It should be added that, in the case of published sources used by Mr. Sadleir, the authors have invariably gone back to the originals instead of contenting themselves with the excerpts or paraphrases which he has included. In such cases the original sources, rather than Mr. Sadleir's extracts, are cited in the following notes.

Two important bibliographical works also deserve special mention:

Michael Sadleir, *Trollope: a Bibliography* (London, 1928). An admirable bibliographical study of all books by Trollope published up to the time of its appearance; used as the authority for publication dates, contracts, prices, etc.

Mary Leslie Irwin, *Anthony Trollope: a Bibliography* (New York, 1926). Lists all known publications by Trollope, including articles and reviews, together with reviews of his books and a great number of additional items of biographical or critical interest. The authors' indebtedness to this admirable compilation will be immediately apparent to anyone who examines it.

An edition of Trollope's letters is in preparation by Professor Bradford Allen Booth.

CHAPTER I

Heckfield scenery and folkways

Mary Russell Mitford, *Our Village* (London, 1832–37), *passim;* A. G. K. L'Estrange, *The Life of Mary Russell Mitford, Told by Herself in Letters to Her Friends,* II (New York, 1870), 187–88; *Victoria History of Hampshire and the Isle of Wight,* IV (London, 1911), 44–51; Richard Warner, *Collections for the History of Hampshire,* I (London, 1795?), 100.

The Milton family

On the Reverend William Milton, see Thomas F. Kirby, *Winchester Scholars: a List of the Wardens, Fellows and Scholars of Saint Mary College of Winchester, commonly called Winchester College* (London, 1888), p. 254; Joseph Foster, *Alumni Oxonienses, 1715–1886,* III (Oxford, 1888), 962. William Milton's works are listed under his name in British Museum, *Catalogue of Printed Books* (*Alphabetical*). For the genealogy of his first wife, see William Salt Archeological Society, *Collections for the History of Staffordshire,* New Series, I (London, 1898), 138. Frances Milton was the youngest daughter: *New Monthly Magazine,* LV, 416 (1839). Henry was born about 1874: London *Times,* January 18, 1850, p. 7.

Frances Milton's youth

A. G. K. L'Estrange, *The Friendships of Mary Russell Mitford as Recorded in Letters from Her Literary Correspondents* (New York, 1882), pp. 6, 172.

Henry Milton at the War Office

"Sixth Report of the Commissioners of Military Enquiry, Appointed by Act of 45 Geo. III, cap. 47" (*Parliamentary Papers*, 1808–9, No. 327), appendixes 6–8, 24.

Henry Milton's tastes and accomplishments

L'Estrange, *The Life of Mary Russell Mitford*, cited, II, 84; same, *The Friendships of Mary Russell Mitford*, cited, p. 436; Arthur Lucas, *John Lucas: Portrait Painter* (London, 1910), pp. 3, 62; his portrait was exhibited at the Royal Academy in 1830: *ibid.*, p. 109.

The Trollope and Meetkerke families

Edward Trollope, *The Family of Trollope* (Lincoln, 1875), pp. 1, 20–21; Mark N. Trollope, *A Memoir of the Family of Trollope* (London, 1897), pp. 4, 92–93; Robert Clutterbrook, *History and Antiquities of the County of Hertford*, III (London, 1827), 520–21, 576; J. E. Cussans, *History of Hertfordshire*, I, "Hundred of Odsey" (London, 1871–73), 162–70; *Annual Register*, 1806 (London, 1807), p. 533.

Thomas Anthony Trollope's education and position

Kirby, *Winchester Scholars*, cited, p. 277; Foster, *Alumni Oxonienses, 1715–1886*, cited, IV, 1441; Oxford University, *Catalogue of All Graduates, 1659–1850* (Oxford, 1851), p. 671; *Records of the Honorable Society of Lincoln's Inn: Admissions and Chapel Registers*, II (London, 1896), 26; James Whishaw, *A Synopsis of the Members of the English Bar* (London, 1835), pp. 152, 175.

Birth and baptism of the Trollope children

M. N. Trollope, *A Memoir of the Family of Trollope*, cited, p. 93; Kirby, *Winchester Scholars*, cited, pp. 304, 308.

The Merivale family

Charles Merivale, *Autobiography of Dean Merivale, with Selections from His Correspondence*, ed. J. A. Merivale (London, 1899), Chapter I.

Chapter II

GENERAL SOURCES

A. G. K. L'Estrange, *The Friendships of Mary Russell Mitford* (New York, 1882), pp. 115–23, 436; same, *The Life of Mary Russell Mitford*, II (New York, 1870), 57, 62, 64, 84.

SPECIAL SOURCES

Harrow and Winchester schools

P. H. M. Bryant, *Harrow* (London, 1936), and the literature there cited; P. M. Thornton, *Harrow School and Its Surroundings* (London, 1885); Charles Merivale, *Autobiography of Dean Merivale with Selections from His Correspondence*, ed. J. A. Merivale, (London, 1899), Chapter I. The entries and departures of the Trollope boys are briefly noted in *Harrow School Register, 1800–1911* (3d ed., London, 1911), pp. 87, 106; George Butler, *Harrow: a Selection of Lists of the School, 1770–1826* (Peterborough, 1849). Their attendance at Winchester College is noted (erroneously, in Anthony's case) in Thomas F. Kirby, *Winchester Scholars* (London, 1888), pp. 304, 308. On the general aspect of Winchester, see also [William L. Collins], *The Public Schools. . . . Notes on Their History and Traditions, by the Author of 'Etoniana'* (Edinburgh, 1867).

Guglielmo Pepe, General Lafayette, Ugo Foscolo, Frances Wright, and other social contacts

Memoirs of General Pepe, Written by Himself, III (London, 1846), 236, 270, 273; Anna W. Merivale, *Family Memorials* (Exeter, 1884), pp. 199–200, 238; A. J. G. Perkins and T. Wolfson, *Frances Wright: Free Enquirer* (New York, 1939), pp. 75–76, 178–81.

The Trollopes' visit to Paris, 1823

Washington Irving, *Journal (1823–1824)*, ed. S. T. Williams (Cambridge, 1931), pp. 41–42; Stanley T. Williams, *Life of Washington Irving*, I (New York, 1935), 258.

Thomas Anthony's law book

Thomas Anthony Trollope, *A Treatise on the Mortgages of Ships, as Affected by the Registry Acts; and on the Proper Mode of Effect-*

*ing Mortgages on Property of This Nature; and on the Liabilities
of the Mortgagee* (London: Joseph Butterworth and Son, 1823).

Mary Milton's husband, Commander Charles Clyde, R.N.
John Marshall, *Royal Naval Biography*, III, Pt. 2 (London, 1832),
402; W. R. O'Byrne, *Naval Biographical Dictionary*, I (London,
1849), 201–2; Admiralty, *Navy List*, March 20, 1853, p. 310.

The American project
The proposed status of white settlers at Nashoba is outlined by
Robert Dale Owen in *Atlantic Monthly*, XXXII (1873), 348, 448.
The opportunities in Cincinnati are glowingly described in William
Bullock, *Sketch of a Journey through the Western States of North
America . . . with a Description of the New and Flourishing City
of Cincinnati, by Messrs. B. Drake and E. D. Mansfield* (London,
1827).

CHAPTER III

GENERAL SOURCES

Frances Trollope, *The Domestic Manners of the Americans* (London, 1832) ; A. G. K. L'Estrange, *The Friendships of Mary Russell
Mitford* (New York, 1882), pp. 137–39, 158–60, 163–64.

SPECIAL SOURCES

Departure of the Trollopes from Nashoba
A. J. G. Perkins and T. Wolfson, *Frances Wright: Free Enquirer*
(New York, 1939), p. 190.

William Maclure's school at New Harmony
G. B. Lockwood, *The New Harmony Movement* (New York, 1905) ;
Perkins and Wolfson, *Frances Wright*, cited, *passim*.

The Trollopes at Cincinnati
The least prejudiced American account is that of Timothy Flint,
in *Knickerbocker*, II (October, 1833), 286–92. On the suspicious
attitude of the Cincinnatians, see Frederick Marryat, *Diary in America*, 1st Series, II (London, 1839), 152–53. The misspelling "Trol-
lop" is in *Cincinnati Directory for the Year 1829* (Cincinnati,
1829?), p. 138. A caricature purporting to represent the Trollope

family at Cincinnati appears in Clara Longworth de Chambrun, *Cincinnati: the Queen City* (New York, 1939), opp. p. 143.

Mrs. Trollope's social activities, and the "Infernal Regions"
C. T. Greve, *Centennial History of Cincinnati*, I (Chicago, 1904), 644, 919; E. D. Mansfield, *Personal Memories, Social, Political and Literary* (Cincinnati, 1879), pp. 183–84.

The Trollope bazaar
Cincinnati Directory for the Year 1829, cited, pp. 175–77; Greve, *Centennial History of Cincinnati*, cited, I, 581–82; [Thomas Hamilton], *Men and Manners in America, by the author of Cyril Thornton, etc.*, II (Edinburgh, 1833), 169–70; H. A. and K. B. Ford, *History of Cincinnati, with Illustrations and Biographical Sketches* (Cleveland, 1881), pp. 79–80; Otto Juettner, *Daniel Drake and His Followers* (Cincinnati, 1909), p. 110; Charles Cist, *Cincinnati in 1841* (Cincinnati, 1841), p. 131; *History of Cincinnati and Hamilton County, Ohio* (Cincinnati, 1894), pp. 124–25.

Anthony at Winchester and Harrow
Anthony Trollope, "Public Schools," *Fortnightly Review*, II, 477–78 (October 1, 1865); E. W. Howson and G. T. Warner, eds., *Harrow School* (London, 1898), p. 80; *Harrow School Register, 1800–1911*, 3d ed. (London, 1911), pp. 106, 134 (James Lewis).

Chapter IV

GENERAL SOURCES

A. G. K. L'Estrange, *The Friendships of Mary Russell Mitford* (New York, 1882), pp. 164–76; Frances Trollope, *Belgium and Western Germany in 1833* (London, 1834).

SPECIAL SOURCES

Opinions of "The Domestic Manners of the Americans"
Quarterly Review, XLVII (March, 1832), 39–80; *Fraser's Magazine*, V (April, 1832), 336–50; *Blackwood's Edinburgh Magazine*, XXXI (May, 1832), 829–47; *Athenaeum*, 1832, pp. 187–88, 204–6; *Edinburgh Review*, LV (July, 1832), 479–526; Harriet Mar-

tineau's opinion in Harriet Martineau, *Autobiography*, I (Boston, 1877), 240–41. Many American opinions are listed in Jane L. Mesick, *The English Traveller in America, 1785–1835* (New York, 1922; Columbia Studies in English and Comparative Literature), pp. 290–94, and by J. F. McDermott, in *Ohio State Archaeological and Historical Quarterly*, XLV (1936), 369–70.

"The Refugee in America"

Quarterly Review, XLVIII (December, 1832), 508–13; Walter J. Graham, *Tory Criticism in the Quarterly Review, 1809–53* (New York, 1921; Columbia University Studies in English and Comparative Literature), pp. 10, 52; George L. Nesbitt, *Benthamite Reviewing in the Westminster Review, 1824–36* (New York, 1934; Columbia University Studies in English and Comparative Literature), p. 155.

"The Abbess"

Published May 27, 1833, after apparently being postponed (perhaps because of its author's illness). See advertisements in *John Bull*, May 19, 26, 1833.

The Trollope finances

Mrs. Trollope's daughter-in-law states that she received £400 for an edition of *The Refugee*, but Tom told Rosina Bulwer that the combined receipts from *The Refugee* and *The Abbess* amounted to only £400: Louisa Devey, *Life of Rosina, Lady Lytton*, 2d ed. (London, 1887), p. 203. On the second Lord Northwick, see Brayley, Brewer, and Nightingale, *Topographical and Historical Description of London and Middlesex*, V (London, 1816), pp. 654–57 (Vol. X, Pt. 2 of *The Beauties of England and Wales*). The cheapness of Bruges is emphasized in Edmund Downey, *Charles Lever: His Life and His Letters*, I (London, 1906), 99.

Henry Trollope as a geologist

Geological Society of London, *Proceedings*, I (1834), 405.

Anthony's last years at Harrow School

Anthony Trollope, "Public Schools," *Fortnightly Review*, II (October 1, 1865), 482–83; F. G. B. Ponsonby, in P. M. Thornton, *Harrow School and Its Surroundings* (London, 1885), p. 250 n. The freedom with which prizes were distributed is noted by Charles

Wordsworth, *Annals of My Early Life* (London, 1891), pp. 8–34. Anthony's try for a scholarship at Trinity College, Oxford, was mentioned by him many years later to T. H. S. Escott (who confused it with Trinity College, Cambridge) and to E. A. Freeman. Freeman placed the event in 1833, a date which seems to be confirmed by the record of the successful competitor, Arthur Kensington. See Escott, pp. 70, 84; E. A. Freeman, in *Macmillan's Magazine*, XLVII (January, 1883), 236; Joseph Foster, *Alumni Oxonienses, 1715–1886*, II (Oxford, 1888), 787. Some of Anthony's cultural experiences at this period are described in his articles on "The National Gallery," *Saint James's Magazine*, September, 1861, and "Henry Taylor's Poems," *Fortnightly Review*, I (June 1, 1865), 129–46.

Chapter V

GENERAL SOURCE

Frances Trollope, *Paris and the Parisians in 1835* (London, 1835).

SPECIAL SOURCES

The English in Bruges and Brussels
Edmund Downey, *Charles Lever*, I (London, 1906), 98–101; II (London, 1906), 34, 347ff.

Anthony's appointment to the Post Office
Salaries for clerks did not ordinarily increase beyond a maximum of £260, reached in the twenty-first year of service. Edmund Yates, *Edmund Yates: His Recollections and Experiences*, I (London, 1884), 123.

The Protestant Cemetery at Bruges
The monuments of Henry and Thomas Anthony are mentioned in Mark N. Trollope, *A Memoir of the Family of Trollope* (London, 1897), pp. 93–94.

Chapter VI

GENERAL SOURCE

Frances Trollope, *Vienna and the Austrians* (London, 1838).

SPECIAL SOURCES

"Jonathan Jefferson Whitlaw"
    Athenaeum, 1836, pp. 462–63.
Mrs. Trollope's call on Miss Mitford, May 26, 1836
    A. G. K. L'Estrange, *The Life of Mary Russell Mitford*, II (New
    York, 1870), 173.
Princess Metternich on Mrs. Trollope
    Richard Metternich-Winneburg, ed., *Aus Metternich's nachgelas-
    senen Papieren*, VI (Vienna, 1883), 122.
Reverend John William ("Velvet") Cunningham
    Obituary in *Christian Observer*, November, 1861.

CHAPTER VII

GENERAL SOURCES

T. Adolphus Trollope, *A Summer in Brittany*, ed. Frances Trollope
(London, 1840) ; same, *A Summer in Western France*, ed. Frances
Trollope (London, 1841) ; Frances Trollope, *A Visit to Italy* (Lon-
don, 1842).

SPECIAL SOURCES

John Lewis Merivale
    Anna W. Merivale, *Family Memorials* (Exeter, 1884), p. 302;
    Charles Merivale, *Autobiography of Dean Merivale* (London,
    1899), p. 154, n. 3; Herman Merivale, *Bar, Stage, and Platform*
    2d ed. (London, 1902), pp. 96–99.
Mrs. Trollope's literary contacts
    [Charles G. Rosenberg], *You Have Heard of Them, by "Q"* (Lon-
    don, 1854), pp. 293–98; A. G. K. L'Estrange, *The Friendships
    of Mary Russell Mitford* (New York, 1882), p. 249; *Letters of
    Charles Dickens*, ed. Walter Dexter, I (London, 1938), 191.
John Tilley
    F. E. Baines, *Forty Years at the Post-Office: a Personal Narrative*,
    I (London, 1895), 106, 164, 174–75; Edmund Yates, *Edmund
    Yates: His Recollections and Experiences*, II (London, 1884), 200–

201; London *Times,* March 19, 1898, p. 7; "Eighth Report of the Commissioners Appointed to Inquire into the Management of the Post-Office Department" (*Parliamentary Papers,* 1837, XXXIV, Pt. 1), Pt. 1, p. 8; "Second Report from the Select Committee on Postage" (*Parliamentary Papers,* 1838, XX, Pt. 2, No. 658), appendix, p. 222.

Henry Milton as a novelist

Henry Milton wrote two novels: *Rivalry* (London, 1840) and *Lady Cecelia Farrencourt* (London, 1845).

Mrs. Trollope and Rosina Bulwer

Louisa Devey, *Life of Rosina, Lady Lytton* (London, 1887), p. 290; preface to Rosina Bulwer's *Budget of the Bubble Family* (London, 1840).

Anthony's illness in 1840

Devey, *Life of Rosina, Lady Lytton,* cited, pp. 195–204.

Mrs. Trollope and Edward Everett

Paul Revere Frothingham, *Edward Everett: Orator and Statesman* (Boston, 1925), p. 174. Horatio Greenough's very similar reaction in *Letters of Horatio Greenough,* ed. F. B. Greenough (Boston, 1887), p. 136.

Chapter VIII

Dublin society and Irish literature

W. J. Fitzpatrick, *The Life of Charles Lever* (rev. ed., London, 1884), p. 60; Stephen Gwynn, *Irish Literature and Drama in the English Language: a Short History* (London, 1936), Chapters I–VI.

Anthony's observation of the Irish character

William Lewins, *Her Majesty's Mails* (2d ed., London, 1865), pp. 276–77, 287, 299; F. E. Baines, *On the Track of the Mail-Coach* (London, 1895), p. 211; Mrs. Morgan John O'Connell, *Charles Bianconi: a Biography* (London, 1878), pp. 138–39; W. R. Le Fanu, *Seventy Years of Irish Life* (New York, 1893), pp. 204–5.

Mrs. Trollope's life in England

Mary Russell Mitford, *Letters,* ed. H. F. Chorley, Second Series, I

(London, 1872), 212, 263; A. G. K. L'Estrange, *The Friendships of Mary Russell Mitford* (New York, 1882), p. 287.

Origins of "The Macdermots of Ballycloran"

Nassau W. Senior, *Journals, Conversations and Essays Relating to Ireland*, I (London, 1868), 185–89; Katherine Thomson, *Recollections of Literary Characters and Celebrated Places*, I (London, 1854), 10–11; Aubrey De Vere, *Recollections of Aubrey De Vere* (New York, 1897), pp. 90–92; Henry Taylor, *Correspondence*, ed. Edward Dowden (London, 1888), p. 297.

Reception of "The Macdermots"

Athenaeum, May, 1847, p. 517; its publication history is in Michael Sadleir, *Trollope: a Bibliography* (London, 1928), p. 6. The unpopularity of Irish novels at this time is noted in Edmund Downey, *Charles Lever*, I (London, 1906), 256–57; L'Estrange, *The Friendships of Mary Russell Mitford*, cited, p. 343.

Chapter IX

Charles Lever on Lucca

Edmund Downey, *Charles Lever*, I (London, 1906), 303.

The Silesian journey of 1846

Frances Trollope, *Travels and Travellers: a Series of Sketches* (London, 1846), I, 3–46.

Mrs. Trollope in England, 1847

Mary Russell Mitford, *Correspondence with Charles Boner and John Ruskin*, ed. Elizabeth Lee (London, 1914), p. 75.

Theodosia Garrow

Dictionary of National Biography LVII (London), 248. The best account of her father, Joseph Garrow (1789–1857) is Stephen Wheeler, "Landor and Dante," *Times Literary Supplement*, May 27, 1920. On her mother, Theodosia Garrow, née Abrams (1766–1849), see James D. Brown and S. S. Stratton, *British Musical Biography* (Birmingham, 1897), pp. 1–2; *Grove's Dictionary of Music and Musicians* (New York, 1935), I, 7. Theodosia's relations with Lady Blessington are noted in R. R. Madden,

The Literary Life and Correspondence of the Countess of Bless-ington, II (New York, 1855), 87–88, 141–42; *The Blessington Papers: the Collection of Autograph Letters and Historical Documents formed by Alfred Morrison,* Second Series, 1882–1893 (n. p., 1895), pp. 61–62, 133–34. Her relations with Elizabeth Barrett in A. G. K. L'Estrange, *The Friendships of Mary Russell Mitford* (New York, 1882), p. 257; Mary Russell Mitford, *Letters,* ed. H. F. Chorley, Second Series, I (London, 1872), 192–93, 281–82; *Letters of Robert Browning and Elizabeth Barrett Barrett, 1845–1846,* I (New York, 1899), 156–57, 288–89. Her relations with Walter Savage Landor in Walter Savage Landor, *Letters and Other Unpublished Writings,* ed. Stephen Wheeler (London, 1897), p. 217; Walter Savage Landor, *Letters of Walter Savage Landor, Private and Public,* ed. Stephen Wheeler (London, 1899), pp. 89–90; same, *Poetical Works,* ed. Stephen Wheeler, III (Oxford, 1937), 22, 39, 49; same, *Last Days, Letters, and Conversations,* ed. H. C. Minchin (London, 1934), pp. 18–19. Poems by Theodosia appeared in *The Keepsake,* ed. the Countess of Blessington, for 1841, pp. 257–71; 1842, pp. 87–107 ("The Doom of Cheynholme"); 1843, pp. 25–26, 112–31; 1844, p. 8; 1845, pp. 212–25; 1846, pp. 27–29; 1847, pp. 179–81; *Heath's Book of Beauty,* ed. the Countess of Blessington, 1839, pp. 189–92 ("The Gazelle"), 248–49 ("On Presenting a Young Invalid with a Bunch of Early Violets"); 1840, pp. 81, 135–36; 1842, pp. 1–2; 1846, pp. 63–64; 1847, pp. 88–91 ("The Cry of Romagna"). She went to Italy about 1844: see her *Social Aspects of the Italian Revolution* (London, 1861), p. 12; *The Keepsake,* 1846, p. 29. Her relations with Niccolini in Atto Vannucci, *Ricordi della vita e delle opere di G.-B. Niccolini,* I (Florence, 1866), 339, 349–52; G. B. Niccolini, *Letter inedite: Estratto dal giornale Il Fanfani, anno II* (Florence, 1882), pp. 19–20. Her translation of Niccolini's *Arnaldo da Brescia* was published at London in 1846. Her linguistic abilities are described in *The Reader: a Review of Literature, Science, and Art,* V (April 22, 1865), 454.

"The Tuscan Athenaeum"

This publication appeared weekly from October 30, 1847 to January

22, 1848. There is a complete set in the New York Public Library.

Mrs. Trollope in Rome, 1848

Thomas C. Grattan, *Beaten Paths, and Those Who Trod Them,* II (London, 1862), 342.

Conditions in Florence, 1848

Edmund Downey, *Charles Lever,* I (London, 1906), 275–77, 283.

Tom's honeymoon journey

T. Adolphus Trollope, *Impressions of a Wanderer in Italy, Switzerland, France, and Spain* (London, 1850).

Henry Milton's illness

Arthur Lucas, *John Lucas, Portrait Painter* (London, 1910), p. 62.

Chapter X

Reviews of Anthony's books

The Kellys and the O'Kellys: *Athenaeum,* June, 1848, p. 701; *La Vendée: Athenaeum,* July, 1850, p. 708; *The Warden: Athenaeum,* January, 1855, p. 107; *Barchester Towers: Athenaeum,* May, 1857, p. 689; London *Times,* August 13, 1857; *Westminster Review,* October, 1857, p. 594.

Anthony's letters on Ireland

Examiner, 1849, pp. 532–33; 1850, pp. 201, 217, 297, 346, 377–78.

Anthony's admiration for Taylor's "Philip van Artevelde"

Anthony Trollope, "Henry Taylor's Poems," *Fortnightly Review,* I (June 1, 1865), 129–46.

Anthony's contributions to the Dublin University Magazine

Review of Merivale's *History of the Romans under the Empire,* in *Dublin University Magazine,* XXXVII (May, 1851), 611–24; XLVIII (July, 1856), 30–47; anonymous article on "The Civil Service," *ibid.,* XLVI (October, 1855), 409–26.

Anthony's Post Office work

Anthony's salary as a Surveyor's Clerk in 1849 was £150, plus an expense account of 15s. per day and 6d. per mile of travel. "Return of the Names of the Heads of Departments . . . of the Post Office, with the Salaries . . . Received by Each" (*Parliamentary Papers,* 1861, XXXV, No. 21). On the revision of the rural posts, see "Third

Report of the Post Master General, on the Post Office, 1857" (*Parliamentary Papers*, 1857, sess. 1, IV) ; *The Post Office: an Historical Summary, published by order of the Postmaster-General* (London, 1911), pp. 39–42. Anthony's claim to have invented the pillar box is questionable. Pillar and wall letter boxes were first used in 1855, but the idea of introducing them into the London area, at any rate, seems to have been Sir Rowland Hill's. "Tenth Report of the Postmaster General on the Post Office, 1864" (*Parliamentary Papers*, 1864, XXX), p. 15. The record of Anthony's appearance before the Parliamentary Committee is printed in "Report from the Select Committee on Postal Arrangements (Waterford, &c.) ; together with the Proceedings of the Committee, Minutes of Evidence, Appendix and Index" (*Parliamentary Papers*, 1854–55, XI, No. 445). His history of the Irish Post Office appears in "Third Report of the Postmaster General, on the Post Office, 1857," cited.

The Trollopes in Florence

The Villino Trollope is described in Kate Field, "English Authors in Florence," *Atlantic Monthly*, XIV (December, 1864), 663–64; Frances Power Cobbe, *Life . . . by herself*, II (Boston, 1894), 347; Lilian Whiting, *A Study of Elizabeth Barrett Browning* (Boston, 1899), pp. xvii-xviii. For the Trollopes' social life, see Elizabeth Barrett Browning, *Letters*, ed. F. G. Kenyon, I (New York, 1897), 17, 437, 476; II (New York, 1897), 177–78; Elizabeth Barrett Browning, *Letters . . . addressed to Richard Hengist Horne* (New York, 1877), pp. 168, 233; Henry James, *William Wetmore Story and his Friends*, I (Boston, 1904), 116; Walter Dexter, ed., *Mr. and Mrs. Charles Dickens* (London, 1935), p. 218. Mrs. Trollope's love of Italian landscape is mentioned in A. G. K. L'Estrange, *The Friendships of Mary Russell Mitford* (New York, 1882), pp. 300–301.

Anthony's visit to Florence, 1853

Anthony's call on Hiram Powers is recorded in Ellen L. Powers, "Recollections of my Father," *Vermonter*, XII (March, 1907), 77. On the gossiping proclivities of the Anglo-Florentines, see especially W. J. Fitzpatrick, *The Life of Charles Lever* (rev. ed., London, 1884), pp. 265–68. On the question of Bice's parentage, see

Letters of Robert Browning, Collected by Thomas J. Wise, ed. Thurman L. Hood (New Haven, 1933), pp. 69, 115, 118, 119–22, 144. In this connection it should be emphasized that the authors in no way identify themselves with the insinuations current at the time, for which no foundation whatever has been discovered.

Mrs. Trollope in London, 1855

Charles Dickens, *Letters . . . edited by His Sister-in-Law and His Eldest Daughter,* I (New York, 1881), 466; *Letters of Charles Dickens,* ed. Walter Dexter, II (London, 1938), 674.

Daniel Home and spiritualism

Elizabeth Barrett Browning, *Letters,* ed. F. G. Kenyon, cited, II, 117, 226; Elizabeth Barrett Browning, *Letters to Her Sister, 1846–1859,* ed. Leonard Huxley (London, 1929), pp. 220, 237; John Snaith Rymer, *Spirit Manifestations* (London, 1857), pp. 9–11; Daniel D. Home, *Incidents in My Life* (London, 1863), Chapters IV–V and Appendix I; Mrs. Daniel D. Home, *D. D. Home: His Life and Mission* (London, 1888), pp. 36–64; Mrs. Daniel D. Home, *The Gift of D. D. Home* (London, 1890), pp. 10–15, 97ff.; *Athenaeum* April 4, 1863, p. 460; London Dialectical Society, *Report on Spiritualism* (London, 1873), pp. 189–90, 277–78, 372. The Trollope item in Daniel D. Home, *Lights and Shadows of Spiritualism* (New York, 1877), p. 228 is certainly apocryphal. For the Trollopes' earlier interest in magnetism and mesmerism, see William James Linton, *Memories* (London, 1895), p. 169; A. G. K. L'Estrange, *The Life of Mary Russell Mitford,* II (New York, 1870), 254.

Tom's infirmities

W. J. Linton, *Memories,* cited, p. 169; Horatio Greenough, *Letters to His Brother,* ed. F. B. Greenough (Boston, 1887), p. 226.

Chapter XI

GENERAL SOURCE

Anthony Trollope, *The West Indies and the Spanish Main* (London, 1859).

SPECIAL SOURCES

Lever's opinion of Trollope
Edmund Downey, *Charles Lever*, II (London, 1906), 227, 232.

Anthony's mission in Egypt
The Post Office: an Historical Summary, published by order of the Postmaster-General (London, 1911), p. 55; Edmund Yates, *Edmund Yates: His Recollections and Experiences*, I (London, 1884), 110; "Fifth Report of the Postmaster General, on the Post Office, 1859" (*Parliamentary Papers*, 1859, sess. 1, VIII), pp. 17–18. On Nubar Bey see Alexandre Holynski, *Nubar-Pacha devant l'histoire* (Paris, n.d. [1886]).

Anthony's religious views
Anthony Trollope, *The Bertrams: a Novel* (London, 1859), *passim*.

Anthony's mission in the West Indies
Edward Bennett, *The Post Office and Its Story* (London, 1912), p. 53; F. E. Baines, *Forty Years at the Post-Office*, II (London, 1895), 158–59; "Sixth Report of the Postmaster General, on the Post Office, 1860" (*Parliamentary Papers*, 1860, XXIII), p. 28.

Anthony's travels in the United States, 1859
Anthony Trollope, *North America* (London, 1862), Chapters V, VII, XII.

Trollope and Harper & Brothers
See note to Chapter XIII. The price paid by Harper to Chapman & Hall is noted in Escott, p. 272n.

Reviews of "The West Indies"
Athenaeum, November 5, 1859, p. 591; *Saturday Review*, VIII (November 26, 1859), 643; London *Times*, January 6, 1860, p. 4; January 18, 1860, p. 12.

CHAPTER XII

Anthony and "The Cornhill"
Leonard Huxley, *The House of Smith Elder* (London, 1923), p. 97. In the spring of 1859 Anthony had been invited to contribute

to Dickens's new magazine, *All the Year Round.* R. C. Lehmann, *Charles Dickens as Editor* (New York, 1912), p. 266.

Anthony's vegetable garden

Anthony Trollope, *North America* (London, 1862), Chapter XI.

Anthony at the Post Office and his relations with Rowland Hill

F. E. Baines, *Forty Years at the Post-Office: a Personal Narrative,* I (London, 1895), 129–31, 134–35; Edward Bennett, *The Post Office and Its Story* (London, 1912), pp. 52–53; Edmund Yates, *Edmund Yates: His Recollections and Experiences,* I, (London, 1884), 89–91, 118; II (London, 1884), 223–25; "Fifth Report of the Postmaster General, on the Post Office, 1859" (*Parliamentary Papers,* 1859, sess. 1, VIII), p. 25; "Seventh Report of the Post-master General, on the Post Office, 1861" (*Parliamentary Papers,* 1861, XXXI), p. 23; "Return of the Names of the Heads of Departments . . . of the Post Office, with the Salaries . . . received by each" (*Parliamentary Papers,* 1861, XXXV, No. 21); "Report from the Select Committee on Civil Service Appointments" (*Parliamentary Papers,* 1860, IX, No. 440), pp. 122–44; "Sixth Report of Her Majesty's Civil Service Commissioners, 1861" (*Parliamentary Papers,* 1861, XIX, No. 1664), pp. 532–33.

Anthony's opinion of Thackeray

Anthony Trollope, *Thackeray* (London, 1879).

G. H. Lewes, George Eliot, and the Trollopes

J. W. Cross, *George Eliot's Life as Related in Her Letters and Journals* (new ed., Edinburgh and London, n.d.), pp. 323, 327, 333, 339; A. H. Paterson, ed., *George Eliot's Family Life and Letters* (London, 1928), pp. 91–98; Anna T. Kitchel, *George Lewes and George Eliot* (New York, 1933), pp. 204, 208, 215.

Eccentricities of Charles Reade

Yates, *Edmund Yates,* cited, II, 164; J. G. Millais, *Life and Letters of Sir John Everett Millais,* I (New York, 1899), 403–4.

Anthony's appearance and manner

Arthur Waugh, *A Hundred Years of Publishing* (London, 1930), Chapter VII; Percy Fitzgerald, *The Garrick Club* (London, 1904), p. 78; C. L. Kellogg, in *Bookman* (New York), XXXVIII (December 13, 1913), 348–49; Henrietta M. A. Ward, *Memories of Ninety Years* (New York, 1925), p. 147; Eleanor C. Smyth, *Sir Rowland Hill: the Story of a Great Reform* (London, 1907), pp. 277–78.

Anthony's method of composition

Anthony Trollope, "A Walk in a Wood," *Good Words,* XX (1879), 595–600; W. H. Pollock, in *Harper's New Monthly Magazine,* LXVI (May, 1883), 909.

The "Cornhill" dinners

Huxley, *The House of Smith Elder,* cited, p. 104; W. Partington, "Dickens, Thackeray and Yates, with an unknown 'Indiscretion' by Trollope," *Saturday Review,* CLV (March 11, 1933), 234–35.

Tom Trollope as a collector

Alfred Austin, *The Autobiography of Alfred Austin,* I (London, 1911), 166–67, 197; *Letters of Robert Browning to Miss Isa Blagden,* ed. A. J. Armstrong (Waco, Tex., 1923), pp. 157–58, 188.

Florence in 1860

Lilian Whiting, *Kate Field: a Record* (Boston, 1899), Chapter III; Kate Field, "English Authors in Florence," *Atlantic Monthly,* XIV (December, 1864), 660–71; Kate Field, "Last Days of Walter Savage Landor," *Atlantic Monthly,* XVII (1866), 385–95, 540–51, 684–705; Austin, *The Autobiography of Alfred Austin,* cited, I, 166–67; Franz Pulszky, *Meine Zeit, mein Leben,* IV (Pressburg and Leipzig, 1882), 184.

Walter Savage Landor

Kate Field, articles cited in preceding note; *Letters and other Unpublished Writings of Walter Savage Landor,* ed. Stephen Wheeler (London, 1897), p. 217.

Isa Blagden (1817?–1873)

Poems by the Late Isa Blagden, with a Memoir (London, 1873); Austin, *The Autobiography of Alfred Austin,* cited, I, 208; W. H. Griffin and H. C. Minchin, *The Life of Robert Browning* (New York, 1910), p. 171; Henry James, *William Wetmore Story and His Friends,* II (Boston, 1904), 93–97; Lilian Whiting, *The Florence of Landor* (Boston, 1905), p. 138.

"Mrs. General Talboys" and the Trollope-Thackeray correspondence

New York Times Book Review, July 13, 1941, p. 18.

Legal aspects of "Orley Farm"

Francis Newbolt, *Out of Court* (London, 1925), pp. 1–73.

Anthony's lecture on civil service

Published anonymously in *Cornhill Magazine*, III (February, 1861), 214–28, from which we quote. The original text has been published in Anthony Trollope, *Four Lectures*, ed. M. L. Parrish (London, 1938), pp. 3–26. Trollope had also lectured at a similar meeting in 1858, and Escott places the resultant difficulties in that year. Nevertheless the 1861 lecture seems to answer more closely to the one described by Anthony in the *Autobiography*, Chapter VIII. On this incident, see Escott, p. 118; Yates, *Edmund Yates*, cited, II, 229–30; London *Daily Telegraph*, January 8, 1861 (quoted in *Post Office Magazine*, III, March, 1936, 93).

CHAPTER XIII

GENERAL SOURCE

Anthony Trollope, *North America* (London, 1862).

SPECIAL SOURCES

English opinion on the Civil War

Donaldson Jordan and E. J. Pratt, *Europe and the American Civil War* (Boston, 1931).

Trollope in Boston literary circles

Horace E. Scudder, *James Russell Lowell: a Biography*, II (Boston, 1901), 82–84; Anthony Trollope, "The Genius of Nathaniel Hawthorne," *North American Review*, CXXIX (September, 1879), 207; Nathaniel Hawthorne, *Passages from the French and Italian Notebooks*, June 27, 1858; James T. Fields, *Hawthorne* (Boston, 1876), pp. 40–41.

Trollope and Longfellow

Anthony Trollope, in National Association for the Promotion of Social Science, *Transactions*, 1866 (London, 1867), p. 124; Samuel Longfellow, *Life of Henry Wadsworth Longfellow*, II (Boston, 1891), p. 424; Anthony Trollope, "Henry Wadsworth Longfellow," *North American Review*, CXXXII (April, 1881), 383–406.

Trollope and American publishers

Anthony Trollope, in *Athenaeum*, 1862, II, 306–7, 496, 529–30.

Trollope during the "Trent" crisis

Anthony Trollope, *Lord Palmerston* (London, 1882), p. 195; Frederick W. Seward, *Reminiscences of a War-Time Statesman and Diplomat, 1830–1915* (New York, 1916), p. 190.

Trollope's relations with Kate Field

The originals of Anthony Trollope's letters to Kate Field have been made available to the authors by the Boston Public Library. So much has been made of this correspondence by recent writers on Trollope that it is necessary to caution students against placing unwarranted interpretations on what Trollope actually wrote. It must also be pointed out that no complete and accurate text of the letters is now available in print. Various fragments have been transcribed, more or less accurately, by Mr. Sadleir; others are given by Mr. Zoltan Haraszti in *More Books: Being the Bulletin of the Boston Public Library*, II (July, 1927), 129–45. Trollope's comment on his own appearance is from Anthony Trollope, *The West Indies and the Spanish Main* (London, 1859), Chapter III.

Later history of the Trollope bazaar

[Thomas Hamilton], *Men and Manners in America, by the Author of Cyril Thornton, etc.*, II (Edinburgh, 1833), 169–70; Otto Juettner, *Daniel Drake and His Followers* (Cincinnati, 1909), p. 110; Charles Cist, *Cincinnati in 1841* (Cincinnati, 1841), p. 131; *History of Cincinnati and Hamilton County, Ohio* (Cincinnati, 1894), pp. 124–25; H. A. and K. B. Ford, *History of Cincinnati, Ohio, with Illustrations and Biographical Sketches* (Cleveland, 1881), p. 80; C. T. Greve, *Centennial History of Cincinnati*, I (Chicago, 1904), 552–53.

Trollope's sleighing mishap

"Miss Ophelia Gledd," in Anthony Trollope, *Lotta Schmidt, and Other Stories* (London, 1867)

CHAPTER XIV

Trollope's fashionable wife

Julian Hawthorne, *Shapes that Pass* (Boston, 1928), p. 226; *Thack-*

eray and His Daughter: the Letters and Journals of Anne Thackeray Ritchie, ed. Hester Thackeray Ritchie (New York, 1924), p. 186. Considerable sensation was caused by the publication in August, 1942 of a letter addressed by Anthony to an Irish lady, Miss Dorothea Sankey, expressing the hope that, should anything happen to his "affectionate and most excellent wife," Miss Sankey would consent to "supply her place—as soon as a proper period of decent mourning is over." The published version of the letter (New York *Times*, August 12, 1942, p. 17, col. 6) is said to be dated from Waltham Cross, March 24, 1851. Since the Trollopes were not living at Waltham Cross in 1851, we have assumed that the correct date is 1861, and have mentioned it here—though only in order to point out that the letter is obviously humorous in intention, and that no student of Trollope could take it seriously. A more trustworthy insight into Rose Trollope's personality and her relations with her husband is afforded by a good-humored letter which she herself addressed to Kate Field while in America in 1861 (now in the Kate Field Collection, Boston Public Library).

Anthony's appearance
Mabel E. Wotton, *Word Portaits of Famous Writers* (London, 1887), pp. 313–16; S. M. Ellis, *A Mid-Victorian Pepys: the Letters and Memoirs of Sir William Hardman* (London, 1923), p. 143.

Anthony's letter to Sir Rowland Hill
Postal, Telegraphic, and Telephonic Gazette, I (November 30, 1883), 274.

James Bryce on Trollope's "North America"
James Bryce, *Studies in Contemporary Biography* (London, 1903), p. 122.

Anthony's controversy with Harper & Brothers
Athenaeum, 1862, II, 306–7, 496, 529–30. His letter to Kate Field (August 23, 1862) is quoted from the original in the Kate Field Collection, Boston Public Library.

Tom's Italian decoration
Kate Field, in *Atlantic Monthly*, XIV (December, 1864), 661.

Theodosia's illness

Anthony's letter to Kate Field, August 23, 1862 (Kate Field Collection, Boston Public Library) ; *Letters of Robert Browning to Miss Isa Blagden,* ed. A. J. Armstrong (Waco, Tex., 1923), pp. 57, 64, 68, 75, 81, 83. Theodosia's contributions are printed in *Athenaeum,* 1862, II, 403, 461–62, 530–31; 1863, I, 153, 230–31, 652–53, 813–14.

Browning's opinion of Tom Trollope

Letters of Robert Browning to Miss Isa Blagden, cited, pp. 135–36, 157–58, 188.

Anthony's visit to Florence, August, 1863

Letters of Robert Browning to Miss Isa Blagden, cited, pp. 93, 95, 98; Anthony's letter to Kate Field, October 30, 1863, in *More Books: Being the Bulletin of the Boston Public Library,* II (July, 1927), 140.

Anthony and Norman Macleod

Donald Macleod, *Memoir of Norman Macleod, D.D.,* II (New York, 1876), 135–52.

Chapter XV

Anne Thackeray at Waltham House

Thackeray and His Daughter: the Letters and Journals of Anne Thackeray Ritchie, ed. Hester Thackeray Ritchie (New York, 1924), p. 137.

The "Pall Mall Gazette"

James Grant, *The Newspaper Press,* II (London, 1871), pp. 113–20; H. R. Fox Bourne, *English Newspapers,* II (London, 1887), pp. 273–74, 339–40; T. H. S. Escott, *Masters of English Journalism* (London, 1911), pp. 241–53.

Foundation of the "Fortnightly Review"

E. M. Everett, *The Party of Humanity: the Fortnightly Review and Its Founders* (Chapel Hill, N.C., 1939) ; Anthony Trollope, "George Henry Lewes," *Fortnightly Review,* XXXI (January 1, 1879), 21–22.

Anthony as defender of Christian belief
  Macmillan's Magazine, 1884, p. 47; Anna T. Kitchel, *George Lewes and George Eliot* (New York, 1933), p. 238.

Anthony's writings in the "Fortnightly Review"
  Listed in Mary Leslie Irwin, *Anthony Trollope: a Bibliography* (New York, 1926), pp. 50–51, 53.

Theodosia's last illness and death   •
  Theodosia to Kate Field, July 2, 1864 (Kate Field Collection, Boston Public Library); *Letters of Robert Browning to Miss Isa Blagden*, ed. A. Joseph Armstrong (Waco, Tex., 1923), p. 119; Isa Blagden to Kate Field, October 21, 1865 (Kate Field Collection, Boston Public Library); Alfred Austin, *The Autobiography of Alfred Austin*, I (London, 1911), 179–80. Theodosia's place of burial is noted in Lilian Whiting, *A Study of Elizabeth Barrett Browning* (Boston, 1899), p. xiv. The memorial tablet affixed to the Villino Trollope is mentioned in Atto Vannucci, *Ricordi della vita e delle opere di G.-B. Niccolini*, I (Florence, 1866), p. 339. For the gossip about her personal conduct, cf. note to Chapter X.

Anthony's visit to Florence, 1865
  Letters of Robert Browning to Miss Isa Blagden, cited, p. 121.

Tom's "History of the Commonwealth of Florence"
  More Books: Being the Bulletin of the Boston Public Library, II (July, 1927), 141–43; *Spectator*, XXXIX (March 24, 1866), 329–30.

Bice Trollope
  Letters of Robert Browning to Miss Isa Blagden, cited, pp. 65, 126, 136; *Letters of Robert Browning, Collected by Thomas J. Wise*, ed. Thurman L. Hood (New Haven, 1933), p. 164; Austin, *The Autobiography of Alfred Austin*, cited, I, 211–12; Henry Drummond Wolff, *Rambling Recollections*, I (London, 1908), 156; Frances Power Cobbe, *Italics: Brief Notes on Politics, People, and Places in Italy, in 1864* (London, 1864), p. 385; J. W. Cross, *George Eliot's Life as Related in Her Letters and Journals* (new ed., Edinburgh and London, n.d.), p. 339.

Tom as newspaper correspondent in Italy
  More Books: being the Bulletin of the Boston Public Library, II

(July, 1927), 143; *Letters of Charles Dickens*, ed. Walter Dexter, III (London, 1938), 751; London *Times, The History of the Times*, II (London, 1939), 568.

Tom's villa at Ricorboli

Austin, *The Autobiography of Alfred Austin*, cited, I, 197, 206; Morris L. Parrish, *Victorian Lady Novelists* (London, 1933), p. 27.

Tom's second marriage

Letters of Robert Browning to Miss Isa Blagden, cited, pp. 125–26; Austin, *The Autobiography of Alfred Austin*, cited, I, 193–97; *Letters of Charles Dickens*, ed. Walter Dexter, III (London, 1938), 476.

Frances Eleanor Ternan

Fanny Ternan was the daughter of Thomas L. Ternan and Frances Eleanor Ternan, née Jarman (1803–73). On her parents, see *Dictionary of National Biography*; J. M. Ireland, *Records of the New York Stage*, II (New York, 1867), p. 107; William Charles Macready, *Diaries, 1833–1851*, ed. W. Toynbee, I (New York, 1912), 111; II (New York, 1912), 313, 347f. Fanny, the eldest of their three daughters (her postscript to Tom's letter to Kate Field, March 28, 1867, in Kate Field Collection, Boston Public Library), was born in Philadelphia (*More Books*, cited, II, 144), probably in 1835. Her parents were married in September, 1834, and spent the next three years in the United States, their last appearance in Philadelphia being in May, 1835: A. H. Wilson, *History of the Philadelphia Theatre, 1835–1855* (Philadelphia, 1935), pp. 693, 708. Concerning Fanny's personality, see especially Austin, *The Autobiography of Alfred Austin*, cited, I, 209. Fanny's stage appearances at the age of nineteen or twenty are noted in Thomas Wright, *The Life of Charles Dickens* (London, 1935), p. 242n.

Dickens's relations with the Ternan family

Thomas Wright, *The Life of Charles Dickens*, cited, *passim;* Thomas Wright, *Thomas Wright of Olney: an Autobiography* (London, 1936), pp. 62–69, 236–46; *Observer*, July 7, 1935, p. 13; July 14, 1935, p. 11; *Dickensian*, December, 1935, pp. 15–21; December, 1936, pp. 1–4, 47–51. It should perhaps be pointed out that the authors refrain from taking sides in the controversy surrounding Dickens's friendship with Ellen Lawless Ternan. Their only interest has been in establishing the fact that the matter was being talked about at the time of Tom's marriage.

Anthony's lecture on copyright, 1866

National Association for the Promotion of Social Science, *Transactions*, 1866 (London, 1867), pp. 119–25.

Mrs. Oliphant on "Nina Balatka"

Margaret Oliphant, *Autobiography and Letters*, ed. H. Coghill (New York, 1899), p. 216.

Publication of "Lotta Schmidt"

Michael Sadleir, *Trollope: a Bibliography* (London, 1928), p. 288.

Anthony's history of English prose fiction

Anthony Trollope, "Novel-Reading," *Nineteenth Century*, V (January, 1879), 24–43.

Chapter XVI

Anthony on the nobility of political studies

St. Paul's, I (October, 1867), 4.

Anthony's social life

Amelia Edwards, "A Voice from the Tomb," *Literary World,* 1883, p. 93; J. G. Millais, *Life and Letters of Sir John Everett Millais,* II (New York, 1899), 415; Jane Ellen Panton, *Leaves from a Life* (London, 1908), pp. 201–3; Alfred Austin, *The Autobiography of Alfred Austin,* I (London, 1911), 166; Andrew K. H. Boyd, *Twenty-five Years of Saint Andrews,* 2d ed., I (London, 1892), 100–1; Frederic Harrison, *Studies in Early Victorian Literature* (London, 1895), p. 221; Cuthbert Bede, "Some Recollections of Mr. Anthony Trollope," *Graphic,* December 23, 1882, p. 707.

Anthony on his own literary methods

Walter Herries Pollock, in *Harper's New Monthly Magazine,* LXVI (May, 1883), 909; *Good Words,* XXV (1884), 428; Harrison. *Studies in Early Victorian Literature,* cited, p. 203; Cuthbert Bede, in *Graphic,* December 23, 1882, p. 707.

Anthony's generosity

Edmund Yates, *Edmund Yates: His Recollections and Experiences*
II (London, 1884), 229.

Tom's marital troubles

Letters of Robert Browning, Collected by Thomas J. Wise, ed. Thurman L. Hood (New Haven, 1933), pp. 69, 115, 118, 119–22, 144.

Anthony's retirement from the Post Office

Spectator, XL (November 2, 1867), 1219; London *Times*, November 2, 1867, p. 9, col. 6.

St. Paul's

Contributors are identified, and rates of payment quoted, in Michael
Sadleir, *Trollope: a Bibliography* (London, 1928), pp. 235–42,
299.

Trollope and Austin Dobson

Alban Dobson, *Austin Dobson: Some Notes* (London, 1928), pp.
78–79, 97.

Anthony's American mission, 1868

"Report from the Select Committee on Mail Contracts" (*Parliamentary Papers*, 1868–69, VI, No. 106), pp. 81, 94–95; "Postal
Conventions (England and America): Copies of the Correspondence
between the Postmaster General of the United Kingdom and the
Postmaster General of the United States, commencing 13 December
1867, relating to the Postal Conventions between the two Countries,
&c." (*Parliamentary Papers*, 1868–69, XXXIV, No. 181); Lilian
Whiting, *Kate Field: a Record* (Boston, 1899), p. 183; Anthony to
Kate Field, July 13, 1868 (Kate Field Collection, Boston Public
Library); *Letters of Charles Dickens, Edited by His Sister-in-Law
and His Eldest Daughter*, III (New York, 1881), p. 233.

Chapter XVII

Anthony's Edinburgh visit, 1868

Margaret Oliphant and Mrs. G. Porter, *Annals of a Publishing
House: William Blackwood and His Sons*, III (Edinburgh, 1898),
197–98; A. K. H. Boyd, *Twenty-five Years of Saint Andrews*, 2d
ed., I (London, 1892), 100–101.

The Beverley election, 1868

"Copy of the Minutes of Evidence taken at the Trial of the Beverley Election Petition (1869)" (*Parliamentary Papers*, 1868–69, XV, No. 90); "Election Expenses" (*Parliamentary Papers*, 1868–69, XVII, No. 424), pp. 11, 58.

Anthony's lectures, 1868–1870

Anthony Trollope, *Four Lectures*, ed. Morris L. Parrish (London, 1938); Oliphant and Porter, *Annals of a Publishing House*, cited, III, 362.

Early career of Henry Merivale Trollope

Joseph Foster, *Men-at-the-Bar* (London, 1885), p. 472; George Meredith, *Letters . . . Collected and Edited by His Son* (New York, 1912), p. 205; Arthur Waugh, *A Hundred Years of Publishing* (London, 1930), p. 94.

Anthony's controversy with E. A. Freeman

Anthony Trollope, "Mr. Freeman on the Morality of Hunting," *Fortnightly Review*, XII (December 1, 1869), 616–25; W. R. W. Stephens, *The Life and Letters of Edward A. Freeman*, I (London, 1895), 360–74.

Chapter XVIII

GENERAL SOURCE

Anthony Trollope, *Australia and New Zealand* (London, 1873).

SPECIAL SOURCES

Resemblances between "The Eustace Diamonds" and "The Moonstone"

Henry J. W. Milley, "The Eustace Diamonds and The Moonstone," *Studies in Philology*, XXXVI (October, 1939), 651–53.

"Caesar"

Margaret Oliphant and Mrs. G. Porter, *Annals of a Publishing House: William Blackwood and His Sons*, III (Edinburgh, 1898), 363–64; Herman Merivale, *Bar, Stage, and Platform: Autobiographic Memories*, 2d ed. (London, 1902), p. 96.

Anthony's letter to Kate Field
  Letter of April 15, 1870 (Kate Field Collection, Boston Public Library).

Anthony's controversies with publishers, 1870
  F. A. Mumby, *The House of Routledge* (London, 1934), p. 112.

Anthony on the Franco-Prussian War
  Alfred Austin, *The Autobiography of Alfred Austin*, II (London, 1911), 23–24.

Anthony's social life, April, 1871
  A. H. Paterson, ed., *George Eliot's Family Life and Letters* (London, 1928), p. 145; Lionel Stevenson, *Dr. Quicksilver: the Life of Charles Lever* (London, 1939), p. 290.

Anthony in New York, November 25–27, 1872
  New York *Herald*, November 25, 27, 28, 1872; Christian Bernhard Tauchnitz (firm), *Fünfzig Jahre der Verlagshandlung Christian Bernhard Tauchnitz, 1837–1887* (Leipzig, 1887), p. 149.

Tom's affairs
  Letters of Robert Browning to Miss Isa Blagden, ed. A. Joseph Armstrong (Waco, Tex., 1923), pp. 178, 180, 188; London *Times*, *The History of the Times*, II (London, 1939), 568.

CHAPTER XIX

"Harry Heathcote of Gangoil" and "The Spectator"
  Review of *Australia and New Zealand* in *Spectator*, XLVI (May 10, 1873), 607–8.

Anthony's quarrel with Charles Reade
  Charles L. Reade and Compton Reade, *Charles Reade: A Memoir*, II (London, 1887), 241–42; John Coleman, *Charles Reade as I Knew Him* (London, 1903), p. 325; Malcolm Elwin, *Charles Reade* (London, 1931), pp. 237–38.

Anthony and Kate Field, 1873
  Anthony's letter to Kate Field, July 5, 1873 (Kate Field Collection, Boston Public Library); Lilian Whiting, *Kate Field: a Record* (Boston, 1899), pp. 306, 311.

Anthony's manner

J. W. Cross, *George Eliot's Life as Related in Her Letters and Journals* (new ed., Edinburgh and London, n.d.), p. 505; G. S. Layard, *Shirley Brooks of Punch: His Life, Letters, and Diaries* (New York, 1907), pp. 526, 545, 568; Julian Hawthorne, *Shapes that Pass* (Boston, 1928), pp. 134–35, 226–27; F. W. Hirst, *Early Life and Letters of John Morley*, I (London, 1927), 63–66; "Last Reminiscences of Anthony Trollope," *Temple Bar*, LXX (January, 1884), 129; Walter Herries Pollock, "Anthony Trollope," *Harper's New Monthly Magazine*, LXVI (May, 1833), 907–12; *Blackwood's Edinburgh Magazine*, CXXXIV (November, 1883), 593.

Anthony's travels in 1874

London *Times*, September 24, 1874, p. 4, col. 5; September 28, 1874, p. 5, col. 3; November 27, 1874, p. 6, col. 6; December 10, 1874, p. 7, col. 6; *Saturday Review*, XXXVIII (September 26, 1874), 406–7.

Anthony's Australian journey of 1875

Anthony Trollope, *The Tireless Traveler: Twenty Letters to the Liverpool Mercury, 1875*, ed. Bradford Allen Booth (Berkeley and Los Angeles, 1941); review of the above by Richard P. Stebbins, in New York *Times Book Review*, February 8, 1942, p. 22; London *Times*, May 4, 1875, p. 5, col. 5.

Reviews of "The Way We Live Now"

Athenaeum, June 26, 1875, p. 851; *Spectator*, XLVIII (June 26, 1875), 825; *Saturday Review*, XL (July 17, 1875), 89; *Westminster Review*, CIII (October 1, 1875), 530.

Trollope's attitude toward a future biography

Escott, pp. vii-viii, 152; Edmund Yates, *Edmund Yates: His Recollections and Experiences*, II (London, 1884), 233.

Chapter XX

Trollope's lectures

London *Times*, November 14, 1873, p. 3; March 4, 1876, p. 11; November 29, 1876, p. 6; W. P. Frith, *My Autobiography and Reminiscences*, III (London, 1888), 386–87.

Trollope at the meeting on the Eastern Question

Eastern Question Association, *Report of Proceedings of the National Conference at St. James's Hall, London, December 8th, 1876* (London, n.d.), pp. 19–21 (copy in New York Public Library); Florence E. Hardy, *The Early Life of Thomas Hardy* (London, 1928), p. 148.

The Copyright Commission

"Copyright Commission: The Royal Commissions and the Report of the Commissioners" (*Parliamentary Papers*, 1878, XXIV).

Trollope's South African journey

Anthony Trollope, *South Africa* (London, 1878); Margaret Oliphant and Mrs. G. Porter, *Annals of a Publishing House: William Blackwood and His Sons*, III (Edinburgh, 1898), 365; London *Times*, June 18, 1877, p. 11.

CHAPTER XXI

Anthony's inertia

Letter of January, 1879, in *Blackwood's Edinburgh Magazine*, CXXXIII (February, 1883), 316–20.

Anthony's visit to Iceland, 1878

Anthony Trollope, *How the "Mastiffs" went to Iceland* (London, 1878); same, "Iceland," *Fortnightly Review*, XXX (August 1, 1878), 175–90; Mrs. Julia Blackburn, "To Iceland," *Good Words*, XX (1879), 429–32, 480–86, 559–65, 622–28.

Anthony's Swiss holiday, 1878

Margaret Oliphant and Mrs. G. Porter, *Annals of a Publishing House: William Blackwood and His Sons*, III (Edinburgh, 1898), 365–66.

Thackeray's prohibition of a biography

Thackeray and His Daughter: the Letters and Journals of Anne Thackeray Ritchie, ed. Hester Thackeray Ritchie (New York, 1924), p. 129.

Anthony at Lowick Rectory

George Leveson-Gower, *Years of Content, 1858–1886* (London, 1940), p. 70.

Anthony in Switzerland, 1879

Oliphant and Porter, *Annals of a Publishing House*, cited, III, 418.

Anthony's will

Newspaper clipping, dated 1883, in library of American Antiquarian Society, Worcester, Massachusetts.

Anthony's obituaries

Henry O'Neil: London *Times*, March 15, 1880, p. 6; Charles Lever: W. J. Fitzpatrick, *Charles Lever*, rev. ed. (London, 1884), pp. 337–38; G. H. Lewes: Anthony Trollope, "George Henry Lewes," *Fortnightly Review*, XXXI (January 1, 1879), 15–24.

Reviews of Anthony's later novels

The following reviews are quoted in the text: *The Prime Minister*, in *Spectator*, XLIX (July 22, 1876), 922–23; *The Prime Minister*, in *Saturday Review*, XLII (October 14, 1876), 481; *Is He Popenjoy?*, in *Saturday Review*, XLV (June 1, 1878), 696.

Chapter XXII

GENERAL SOURCE

Blackwood's Edinburgh Magazine, CXXXIV (November, 1883), 593–94.

SPECIAL SOURCES

The date of "Lord Palmerston"

This book evidently preoccupied Trollope over a considerable period. Sadleir states (pp. 269, 408) that it had its "origin" in 1866 and was "written" in January, 1867. The published version, however, is clearly of much later date. The principal source, Ashley's two-volume biography, was not published until 1879; and Anthony refers on pp. 1 and 34 to other books published as late as 1880, as well as referring on p. 104 to events which took place in 1882. It seems most probable that the book was completed between May and July of that year, although he may have begun work on it some time earlier. Escott states (p. 255) that he received "useful hints and help" from Sir Alexander Cockburn, who died in 1880.

"The Fixed Period"

Gamaliel Bradford, in *Nation* (New York), LXXX (June 8, 1905), 458; *Saturday Review*, LIII (April 8, 1882), 435. An edition of the marginalia in Trollope's set of the Elizabethan dramatists (now in the Folger Shakespeare Memorial Library, Washington, D.C.) is in preparation by Professor Bradford Allen Booth.

Tom's writings and life in Rome

Thomas Adolphus and Frances Eleanor Trollope, *Homes and Haunts of the Italian Poets* (London, 1881); George S. Layard, *Mrs. Lynn Linton: Her Life, Letters, and Opinions* (London, 1901), p. 193.

Bice's marriage and death

London *Times*, August 19, 1880, p. 1, col. 1; July 18, 1881, p. 1, col. 1; July 29, 1881, p. 1, col. 1; Burke's *Peerage*, sub Stuart of Wortley.

Anthony and E. A. Freeman

Freeman's recollections, in *Macmillan's Magazine*, XLVII (January, 1883), 238–40.

Decline of Anthony's popularity

Michael Sadleir, *Trollope: a Bibliography* (London, 1928), pp. 259ff.; *Saturday Review*, LIV, 64 (July 8, 1882).

Anthony's dinner with Browning

The Browning Collections: Catalogue of . . . the Property of R. W. Barrett Browning, Esq. (London, 1913), p. 63.

Anthony's last illness and death

London *Times*, November 6–9, 13–18, December 2, 5–7, 1882 (most items on p. 9); J. B. Atkins, *Life of Sir William Howard Russell*, II (London, 1911), 316–17.

CHAPTER XXIII

Tom's settlement at Budleigh Salterton

Athenaeum, November 19, 1892, p. 705.

Henry Merivale Trollope's novel

Athenaeum, May 21, 1887, p. 670; *Saturday Review*, LXIII (June

4, 1887), 808; *Spectator*, LX (July 2, 1887), 901–2; *Westminster Review*, CXXVIII (May 21, 1887), 518.

John Tilley and his sons

London *Times*, March 19, 1887, p. 7; *Who's Who* (London, annual); *Cambridge University Calendar* (Cambridge, annual).

Tom's last literary contributions

Notes and Queries, 7th series, XII, *passim*.

Tom's death

London *Times*, November 15, 1892, p. 10.

Index